THE
PIRATE
HUNTER

This Large Print Book carries the Seal of Approval of N.A.V.H.

THE
PIRATE
HUNTER

The True Story of Captain Kidd

RICHARD ZACKS

Thorndike Press • Waterville, Maine

Privateer William Dampier's map of the winds (1699).

Copyright © 2002 Richard Zacks

Published in 2002 by arrangement with Hyperion, an imprint of Buena Vista Books, Inc.

Thorndike Press Large Print Adventure Series.

The tree indicium is a trademark of Thorndike Press.

The text of this Large Print edition is unabridged.
Other aspects of the book may vary from the original edition.

Set in 16 pt. Plantin.

Printed in the United States on permanent paper.

Library of Congress Cataloging-in-Publication Data

The pirate hunter
p. cm.
ISBN 0-7862-4714-2 (lg. print : hc : alk. paper)
2002073223

To
Kristine Y. Dahl

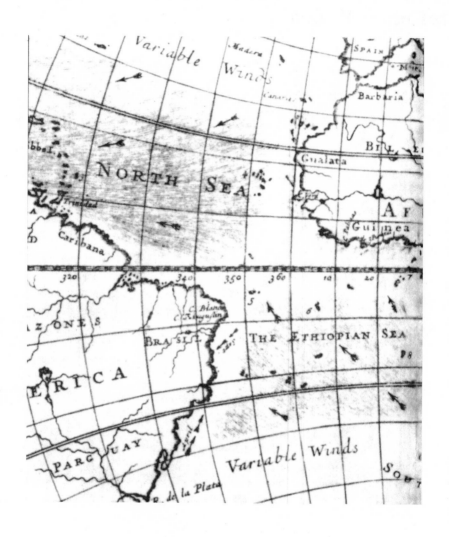

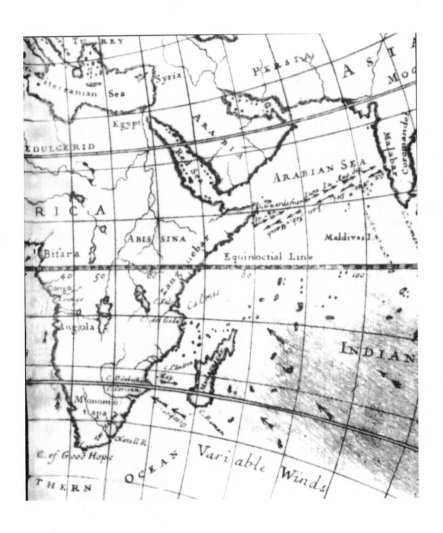

Prologue

In a cold jail cell in Boston in Massachusetts Bay Colony on November 16, 1699, a weather-beaten man with hard scarred features unbuttoned his trousers. Two men stood nearby; one wore a skullcap. The prisoner, tanned on his face and arms only, lifted his shirttail, exposing himself. Back then, men didn't wear underwear per se but rather tucked long shirts afore and behind, hammocking their genitals.

When James Gilliam lifted his penis to view, the two observers caught a whiff of the man's recent recreation. The night before, as the governor later quaintly put it in a letter to the Board of Trade, Gilliam had been "treating two young women some few miles off in the country." Colonial authorities accused him of being a member of the crew of Captain Kidd, then the most notorious pirate in the nascent British Empire, and of hiding his treasure on Gardiners Island alongside Kidd's ample horde. Two witnesses, in addition, identified Gilliam as the pirate who earlier in his career slit the throat of an English East India Company captain and stole his ship.

Despite the growing body of evidence and accusation, Gilliam absolutely denied everything, right down to his name, saying he was "Sampson Marshall," a respectable merchant. He claimed it was all a case of mistaken identity. But the witnesses added a detail that Governor Bellomont thought might hang the scoundrel. They said they had heard that Gilliam had been captured years earlier by the Moors on the coast of India and forcibly circumcised.

In the late 17th century, an era when only Jews and Moslems clipped the foreskin, this was considered an almost singularly identifying mark, as good as a zigzag scar on the cheek or a missing ear. Hence, this odd moment in American colonial jurisprudence.

The reports of the two jailhouse experts have survived and are still filed away at the Public Record Office in London.

"I Joseph Frazon of full age being of the Jewish Nation by both his Parents Declareth . . . I did search . . . Gilliam and find that he has been circumcized but not after the manner practiced by the Jewes according to the Leviticall Law, the prepuce being taken off round."

The second testimony stated: "I, John Cutler of Boston, abovesd Chyrugion, do declare, that I find that the sd Kelley alias Gilliam has been Circumcized wch he himselfe also acknowledgeth, saying that his father was a Jew and his mother was a Christian and after the Death of his father his mother intermarried with a Christian and then he was Baptized. But so far as I am able to discern I am of opinion he was Circumcized since he was grown up into years."

Gilliam's scar was an oval loop tilted from front to back, unlike any circumcision scar either expert had seen before. Apparently Gilliam had flinched at the moment of religious conversion.

Governor Bellomont, the highest ranking official in the northeast, was now convinced he had arrested the right man. He shipped Gilliam aboard the Royal Navy's HMS *Advice* to England to stand trial. The governor — who'd once commented, "I protest that I am quite tyred out taking pains for the Publick without any profit to myself" — tracked down Gilliam's gold on Gardiners Island and reluctantly shipped it also over to the Admiralty. He placed a claim for one third of the booty as Vice Admiral of the Seas.

Gilliam was locked up in London's

Newgate Prison before being carried over to Old Bailey along with twenty-three other accused pirates. In a one-day trial, the jury, with ample help from the panel of peri-wigged judges, pronounced twenty-one pirates guilty. "Ye and each of you are adjudged and sentenced to be carried back to the place from whence you came and from thence to the place of execution and there within the flood marks to be hanged by the neck till you are dead, dead, dead. And the Lord have mercy on your souls."

On Friday July 12, 1700, James Gilliam and nine others boarded carts from the stinking prison of Newgate and headed through the crowded afternoon streets of London to Execution Dock in Wapping, through Cheapside and past Tower Hill. Watching him were not just the rabble on the cobblestones but aristocrats perched in balconies. Some of the street crowd took the opportunity to bombard the prisoners with filth — eggs, dead cats, excrement — and shout such cheery invocations as: "You'll piss when you can't whistle," and "Ye be doing the sheriff's dance."

An execution in London was a day of celebration — a "day of riot and idleness" as one guidebook put it — ballasted by enough pomp and circumstance to salve the consciences of the executioners. The procession followed a mounted sheriff carrying the symbolic silver oar of the Admiralty. It stopped at the edge of the north bank of the Thames and then proceeded on foot down the stone steps. The scaffold was built upon the actual riverbed at low tide so that the English authorities — sticklers over the minutiae of jurisprudence — could state that the Admiralty performed the execution within its watery jurisdiction. Pleasure boats crowded the shore.

As Gilliam was led forward, he could hear hawkers peddling his dying confession dated the day before. And it was a pack of lies, some other man's life, but the printers didn't exactly fear a lawsuit from rogues like Gilliam. The broadsheet ended sanctimoniously: "I hope my sad Fate will be a warning to all Lude Sea Men, and notorious Pyrates whatsoever."

All ten condemned men were led upon a crudely built scaffold to the jeers of the crowd. Each man was trussed up with ropes securely lashing his elbows together behind his back. (No one was tied at the wrist because a dying man might in sheer desperation succeed in rolling his hands free.)

A noose was placed around the neck of each of the convicted pirates. Their feet were purposely not tied, to afford that well-beloved "dance upon air." The priest assigned to Newgate, Paul Lorraine, recited a prayer for salvation. Now the prisoners were encouraged to confess their sins. Some did; most didn't, but in the recollection of Paul Lorraine — as published the following day: "Beware Sham Papers!" — they all confessed, even the dour drunk Frenchmen.

Now came the crowd silence for the Psalm. Pirates whose lips had mainly mouthed bawdy ditties were primed for one final holy chorus as they stood on Execution Dock with the Tower of London looming in the distance to the west. Apparently they sang with gusto. Satirist Ned Ward noted in his *Wooden World* that a thief at the gallows will sing forth with "as pleasant a note" as a sailor calling out the markings on a plumb line as a ship enters a tricky harbor, that is, loud and clear.

The sheriff's men yanked the blocks out from under the scaffold floor. The platform toppled to the ground, but the condemned men fell only a few inches. Their ropes were purposely left short so their necks wouldn't break and they would slowly strangle to death. It was that spastic dance lasting sometimes as long as fifteen minutes that the drunken crowds savored. It was the slow empurpling of the face that delighted and the glimpsing of the ever-spreading stain upon the trousers as the last-gulped liquor exited the bladder.

Once dead, as the piemen packed up their trays, James Gilliam and the other pirates were cut down and tied to posts. Tradition dictated that three tides of Thames water must rise and fall over their heads before the execution was officially complete. Some poor sheriff's helper with a shilling or two for drink would have to sit at river's edge and guard the corpses so no souvenir-hunter would clip off a body part or a button to cadge a pint in an alehouse.

James Gilliam's water-logged body was then cut away from the slimed pole. The carpenter's boy slathered the cold corpse in hot tar and propped it in a specially built iron gibbet or cage. The caged corpse was carried by boat to Gravesend at Hope Point to hang at an unavoidable spot along the nautical corridor to London. The tar was to deter the gulls and other birds eager to peck. Nonetheless, after a few months, Gilliam became a ghastly corpse, a chunk of flesh missing here and there, an exposed cheekbone, both eyeballs gone, the penis now perhaps more than circumcised, a dread warning courtesy of the Admiralty to sailors contemplating the merry life of piracy.

At the time of Gilliam's capture, the combined power of the Royal Navy, the English East India Company, and the governments of half a dozen American colonies were all conspiring to bring Captain Kidd of New York City and Dundee, Scotland, to the same gallows in the harbor. England, on the verge of Empire, planned to show the world what it would do to a man who dared to steal in the name of the king.

Captain Kidd has gone down in history as America's most ruthless buccaneer, fabulously rich, burying treasure up and down the eastern seaboard. I, for one, ten years old reading by flashlight, pictured Kidd fierce, mustachioed, downing rums, slicing the air with his cutlass, burying boys to guard his treasure for eternity.

Washington Irving described Kidd as "somewhat of a trader, something more of a smuggler with a considerable dash of the pickaroon." Robert Louis Stevenson placed "Kidd's Anchorage" on the creased vellum map of *Treasure Island*. Edgar Allan Poe in "The Gold Bug" rummaged through Kidd's chest: "As the rays of the lantern fell within the pit, there flashed upwards from a confused heap of gold and jewels, a glow and glare that absolutely dazzled our eyes." More recently, Nelson DeMille in his best-seller, *Plum Island*, used Kidd's hideout in the climax of his ecological thriller.

But the novelists and historians and relentless treasure hunters have gotten it all wrong. Master mariner William Kidd, who lived at 56 Wall Street, was no career cut-throat, no cartoon Blackbeard, terrifying his prey by putting flaming matches in his hair. Kidd was a reputable New York sea captain empowered by a secret commission from the king of England to hunt pirates, confiscate their wealth, and divvy the spoils among his investors. The venture looked so promising in the planning stages that some of the most powerful lords of London and wealthiest merchants of America lined up to back his voyage and await the shower of gold. King William III, in exchange for his signature, took a ten percent share.

But, as is the way with these clandestine missions, the whole plot blew up in their faces. Kidd's task turned out to be far more difficult than expected: He would have to travel in a lone ship manned by a desperate crew (which included pirates), searching the vast Indian Ocean for one of the five European pirate ships then active. He would have to ignore the claims of the merchants who owned the stolen goods. And as soon as he set out toward the tip of Africa, he would find himself unwelcome, distrusted by the Royal Navy and despised by the English East India Company, who almost immediately claimed that the pirate hunter had turned pirate. The great irony is that Captain Kidd fought very hard to remain honorable, but was branded by the actions of his crew, and on his head was dumped all the piracies of the era.

When rumors of Kidd's crimes began to spread, damaging England's valuable trade with India, Kidd's backers — including King William — all raced to cover their blueblood asses and disavow any knowledge of his mission. Did anyone want to know the truth? Or was it easier to kill the New Yorker and be done with it?

The doings of this feisty American unleashed an enormous political scandal that rocked the New World and the Old, and threatened to tip the subcontinent of India to the Maharajahs. If the accusations that the king backed a "Corporation of Pirates" were proven true, it could endanger King William's perch upon the throne, and could cost Kidd's lordly backers their lives for committing treason. These happenings are *not* fiction but real-life intrigue and double cross, based on the 152-page trial record, hundreds of letters, and depositions from the likes of John Gardiner of Gardiners Island, where Kidd actually hid some of his treasure during an attempt to clear his name.

I have spent the last three years tracking down the flesh-and-blood Captain Kidd, following the paper trail through logbooks and trial transcripts at the Public Record

Office in London, and traveling in his wake to the faraway pirate paradise of St. Marie's Island off Madagascar.

As I followed Kidd, another character kept elbowing his way upon the stage: Kidd's long-forgotten nemesis, Robert Culliford. It is uncanny how the lives of these two men intertwined and how they became locked in a kind of unscripted duel across the oceans of the world.

No one has ever written in detail about Culliford; his entry in a respected nautical compendium states: "Culliford, Captain, of the *Mocha*. Little is known of him except that one day in the streets of London he recognized and denounced another pirate called Burgess."

Even that snippet, it turns out, is wrong. One morning, while sifting through a folder full of 17th century documents, I stumbled across the diary of a prisoner held eleven months aboard Culliford's pirate ship, and through it began to emerge an authentic picture of a pirate's life. Culliford didn't fly a creepy skull-&-crossbones but rather a blood-red flag that meant: "No mercy unless you surrender immediately." His surgeon was named Jon Death; he once ordered his men to haul the china dishes off a captured ship and load them into cannons to shred the sails of his next adversary.

Culliford lived the pirate life; Kidd tried to tightrope his way between piracy and respectability. One would hang in the harbor; the other would walk away with the treasure.

Mission in New York City

Chapter One

New York in the summer of 1696 was an ink spot on the tip of the map of Manhattan, a struggling seaport with a meager population of 5,000, about a fifth of them African slaves. A public whipping post stood just off the dock, and New Yorkers wanting their slaves "corrected" were expected by law to tip eighteen pence to both the town-whipper and to the bell-ringer who drew the crowds.

While London boasted 300,000 inhabitants and the architectural marvels of Christopher Wren, New York claimed only a handful of paved streets and a rundown city hall building. Hungry pigs helped the city's one sanitation man, a Mr. Vanderspiegle. "[New Yorkers] seem not very strict in keeping the Sabbath," wrote a doctor venturing south from Puritan New England. "You should see some shelling peas at their door, children playing at their usual games in the streets and ye taverns filled."

Dutch women wore scandalously short dresses extending to just below the knee, showing off their homemade blue or red stockings. Dutch girls even into their teens generally went barefoot in long white morning gowns with nothing underneath as they lugged laundry through the Land Gate at Wall Street to do their wash at a stream by Maiden Lane. Women of a different sort, often French Huguenot desmoiselles escaping the persecutions of Catholic Louis, plied their trade on Petticoat Lane just off Beaver Street. (City planners — perhaps irked by the nearness of Beaver to Petticoat — changed the lane's name to Marketfield.)

And, three hundred years ago, pirates in gaudy colorful silks with pistols in their waistcoat pockets walked the streets of New York City, and local merchants, some Dutch, some English, bargained for their goods and lined up to back their larcenous voyages. Shares were bought and sold over rum punch at Hawdon's Tavern and the King's Arms.

For a decade or so from the early 1690s on, New York edged out Carolina and Rhode Island as the pirate port of choice in the English colonies in North America. "It is certain that these villains," wrote an East

India Company official, "frequently say that they carry their unjust gains to New-York, where they are permitted egress and regress without control, spending such coin there in the usual lavish manner of such persons."

The pirates boosted the sagging local economy. New York merchants, Dutchman Frederick Flypse and Frenchman Steven Delancy, financed ships that sailed halfway around the world to sell provisions and arms to New York pirates operating out of St. Mary's Island, Madagascar. And shares in these voyages — some promising a twenty-fold return on investment — were openly traded in taverns not too far from the town wall that still stood on Wall Street.

While merchants, barkeeps, and brothel owners back then welcomed pirates and tried to lighten their coin-heavy pouches, piracy in this small English colony of New York was still officially illegal. Choicely placed gold prompted the temporary blindness of customs officials. It was all "Wink, wink." The current governor still wrote home to the Lords of Trade and Plantation that he was rooting out piracy. Governor Fletcher — a pious man who arrived at church in a coach and six — preferred his bribes to be delivered not in cash but in *objets d'art;* silversmiths thrived during his administration.

On the fourth of July, 1696, Captain Kidd in the *Adventure Galley* glided into the harbor, and greeted the people of Manhattan with a couple of shots from his cannon to announce his triumphant return home. As he had hoped, the boom of his guns stirred the merchants and the sailors out of their smoky lethargy in the taverns, away from the rent-a-pipe racks and tankards of cider, to come down to water's edge.

Captain William Kidd — a Scottish striver who often felt he never got his due in this mostly Dutch and English town — proudly guided the *Adventure Galley*, an immense warship studded with thirty-two cannon, into Manhattan harbor. Kidd, who called New York his home port, had left ten months earlier in a dinky 10-gun merchant ship, and now he was returning in this magnificent private man-of-war.

The *Adventure*'s sails were furled and men below deck leaned on long oars, called sweeps, to propel the ship forward. New Yorkers, lining the dock, were somewhat shocked to see the oars; almost no one in the 1690s — with glorious huge sails to catch the wind — put oars on a warship, but they had come to realize that Kidd always did things differently.

The captain, peacocking a bit in his waistcoat on the quarterdeck, tucked the

Adventure Galley into a neat opening amid the forest of masts of idle merchant ships. His quartermaster barked out orders; the men on deck played out the anchor cables — ropes as thick as a sailor's bicep — until the anchor hit bottom and the flukes grabbed. Small ships clustered about, and quickly learned that Captain Kidd had come here looking to line up 150 hardy men to go on a mission to hunt down pirates.

In essence, Captain Kidd had entered a pirate stronghold in search of a crew to chase pirates. Only a man with towering self-confidence (or a death wish) would dare to load his ship with former pirates or friends of pirates who, mid-voyage, with any ill luck, might find themselves shooting at cousins or neighbors.

Captain Kidd, on this summer day in 1696, was forty-two years old, in the prime of his life, physically vigorous, able to outmuscle most of his crew. His face was ruddy from decades of winds at sea.

The only surviving portrait of Kidd catches him in half profile: penetrating brown eyes arced by strong brows, a somewhat large nose. His lips seemed curled at the edge with a certain cockiness. He wears a wig, as did most successful men of his generation. (A 1703 wig tax would show that about fifty New Yorkers donned this succinct status symbol.) Kidd's choice in borrowed hair is a fairly subdued shoulder-length affair, in stark contrast to some of the "big wigs," i.e., the giant cascades of curls favored by some crotchety bald English businessmen.

Kidd was surprisingly literate in a mostly illiterate age. Sober, he showed a terse Scot's wit; with a couple of rums in him, he could turn boisterous, then argumentative or worse. Kidd was defiantly independent, a hard taskmaster, ambitious, distrustful. In this lone portrait, the artist seems to be trying to capture Kidd's temper in the clenched mouth, the slightly flared nostrils.

Captain Kidd on this July day was rowed ashore, then he walked the length of the city dock past the recently rebuilt town outhouse. The hub and meeting place for all colonial shipping back then were the town's numerous taverns offering penny-a-glass rum and wads of fresh Long Island tobacco to pack into long clay pipes. So Kidd, over the next few days and especially nights, wandered to these popular "tippling houses" to tack the ship's articles — a kind of "Help Wanted" poster — to the walls. He also sent out some of his current crew to talk up the voyage; these *Adventure Galley* men whispered that the newly appointed (but not yet arrived) governor of

New York, Lord Bellomont, was a backer of the voyage, as was Admiral Russel. These were bigwig names to impress illiterate seamen.

William Kidd, to this point, was a completely respectable individual; he was a *privateer*, not a *pirate*. (His life would later depend on the not always clear distinction between the two.)

A privateer was a kind of independent nautical mercenary, commissioned by a government to attack ships of an enemy nation in exchange for a piece of the spoils. Royal navies couldn't be everywhere, so countries in times of war turned to profit-hungry freelancers. In Elizabethan times, Drake and Raleigh had become national heroes as privateers attacking Spain. (Nearly a century after Kidd, during the Revolutionary War, the fledgling United States would commission a fleet of American privateers that captured more than 1,000 British merchant ships; while landlocked historians have dwelled on George Washington's battle plans, this economic strangulation by sea undeniably helped the colonies win their independence.)

Privateering, at its best, was a perfectly honorable profession, a unique blend of profit and patriotism. Typically, a group of investors banded together to finance a privateer mission to capture enemy ships and bring them back to port to be condemned as prizes and sold. The king might receive a tenth for granting the original privilege; the Admiralty might siphon off as much as a third for doing the paperwork and applying the stamp of legality. The investors would receive the rest and dole it out to themselves and the crew, according to a formula agreed upon before the voyage. Pirates, on the other hand, thumbed their noses at all these niceties; they weren't sanctioned by any government; they readily attacked ships of all nations and they didn't share their booty with any admirals or kings. They were shipborne thieves, the "enemies of mankind and the trading nations."

Captain Kidd, the *privateer,* in his voyage over from England in the *Adventure* had already legally captured a French fishing vessel off the banks of New Foundland with a crew of four. The conquest had resembled more a ritual at a masquerade ball than a sea battle. Kidd's warship had borne down on the fishing vessel; when close enough, it plunked a cannonball nearby; the French ship surrendered and Kidd in a few minutes had paid for his transatlantic voyage. The Vice Admiralty Court in New York sometime in July condemned the ship as worth £350, the price of a couple of Manhattan buildings. The four French sailors were shipped to Boston to be exchanged for English prisoners held in Canada.

Kidd's mission — as he'd said many times over many rums in Hawdon's and elsewhere — provided sailors with a unique *legal* opportunity to steal from pirates and from the hated French.

And yet almost no one signed up for Kidd's voyage.

No employee surveys were done at the time, but apparently it boiled down to . . . money: Kidd wasn't offering any wages, just a share of the future profits from captures. The sailors back then nicknamed this approach: "No prey, no pay." If they didn't catch a pirate ship or French vessel, they might callus their hands reefing sails for years for absolutely nothing. However, it wasn't the "No prey, no pay" that bothered them; it was the division of spoils. Kidd's Articles, his "Help Wanted" poster, specified that the 150 crewmen would split up only a *quarter* of the treasure, after expenses — that is, after they had repaid all the food, medicine, and weapons at prices set by the owners. (The weapons' charge alone was £6 or three months of typical sailor wages.) Kidd told them the split was ordained by his blueblood owners in London; he said it followed more along the lines favored by the Royal Navy that first rewarded admirals, commodores, captains, lieutenants, before finding perhaps ten percent for the crew.

The New York sailors weren't the least bit swayed. Pirates, they knew, kept 100 percent and shared with no one back at the dock; en masse, the Manhattan mates opted to ignore the appeals of Kidd.

So, despite being blessed with a brand-new warship and a potentially lucrative commission, Captain Kidd couldn't go anywhere without a crew. The man was landlocked in sweltering New York City.

In mid-July, while trying to land sailors one by one, he settled himself in at the family mansion on Pearl Street, then a posh riverfront address. He lived there with his wife, Sarah, and their very young daughter, also named Sarah.

Tax rolls reveal Captain Kidd to be among the wealthiest citizens in his affluent East Ward neighborhood; while Kidd had certainly earned some money from his merchant sailing days, he came by most of his fortune through wedlock. A half decade earlier, William had married Sarah, who — in addition to being attractive and sixteen years younger than he — also happened to be the wealthiest widow in New York City. Through her inheritance, they owned five prime swatches of Manhattan real estate, including 56 Wall

Street and 38½ acres of a tanning mill way north of the city in Niew Haarlem (located today at 73rd Street and the East River).

From his living room on Pearl Street, William Kidd had a nice view of the harbor and his idle ship. In a city already known as cramped, Kidd's three-story mansion was a double wide, at thirty-eight feet across, and also boasted an unheard of forty-eight-foot depth. Built a half century earlier by a Dutch merchant, Govert Lockermans, the house replicated the Dutch taste for six-foot stoops up to the front door (to avoid Amsterdam's rising canal waters); a high peaked gable roof (because Amsterdam's buildings were squeezed together); and the facade followed the popular pattern of red and yellow Flanders glazed bricks. A rooftop crane allowed Kidd to lift merchandise into a secure warehouse on the uppermost floor.

Inside, the furnishings were elegant: the Kidds walked on the city's first Turkey work carpet, sat in chairs from the East Indies, and dined with silver spoons and knives. (Their household inventory, however, listed only one "large flesh fork", i.e., a meat fork for cooking in the fireplace.) In the 1690s, from dukes to rag-pickers, the main course was still carried to the mouth via fingers.

31

During the day, the sound of little Sarah playing echoed through the large house; at night, twenty-six-year-old Sarah and forty-two-year-old William made love in a four-poster curtained bed, lying on cotton sheets, flat-ironed smooth by slaves. They relaxed on goose-down pillows in soft Dutch pillowcases.

Outside the cocoon of that four-poster bed, though, Kidd was still having no luck rounding up a crew.

So, with time on his hands, on July 19, 1696, Captain Kidd took a walk with the family lawyer, James Emott, over to the construction site for the city's first English house of worship, then going up on the corner of Broadway and Wall Street, to be called Trinity Church.

The English community, still outnumbered by the Dutch, for years had been complaining about saying Sunday prayers over at the Dutch Calvinist churches. The English especially quibbled about the unique olfactory experience occurring there in winter. Dutch women, in those days of semiannual bathing, routinely, to warm themselves in the unheated nave, carried with them small ornamental coal braziers and placed them under their floor-length Sunday dresses. Every so often a wisp of smoke peeped out. The aroma, it seems, provided an unintentional Protestant counterpoint to Catholic incense. Some of the rougher English-speaking citizens in New York coined the word "sooterkin" to describe "a small animal about the size of a mouse" that "Dutch women through the constant use of stoves breed under their skirts." (This flipness of New Yorkers apparently has deep roots. "No discourse [here] is thought witty unless larded with oaths and execrations," complained the Reverend Jonathan Miller in 1695.)

Kidd joined lawyer Emott, stepping over the oyster shells littered in the streets. At the building site, the two wigged gentlemen saw slaves in the July heat wearing little more than the breech-clouts of Indians as they trudged up Broadway, a rutted dirt road sometimes called Wagon Way. Babel prevailed as French and Dutch masons argued over technique. (Included in the church budget was the item that the dozen stone masons be allowed "six pennies a day to provide all of them with drink.")

Kidd was pleased by the project's progress; and this captain, who had married a wealthy Englishwoman, also very much wanted to *impress* his fellow English upper-crusters, and join their tight ruling clique. The captain dropped enough silver into vestryman Emott's collection plate to buy a family pew so he could worship near the governor and other leading citizens. (The good captain would never sit in pew number four up front.)

In addition, the meeting minutes that day, as recorded by the church founders, reveal that William Kidd lent "runner and tackle for hoisting up the stones as long as he stays here" in port.

The city at that moment in late July, as Kidd searched for crewmen, was tense with war rumors and bread shortages. Greedy merchants had exported most of the region's prized flour, leaving local bakers with little to bake. The shortage had gotten so acute that the City Council passed a law forbidding the home baking of biscuits or even cookies.

On August 2, an out-of-breath horseback rider ignored the city's "foot-tap" speed limit and galloped into Fort William on the southern tip of Manhattan. The rider delivered an "express" to Governor Fletcher that "Count Frontenac with a thousand French and two thousand Indians was overrunning the Country of the Five Nations," tribes loyal to the English, and had burned an Indian village at Oneida. The residents at Albany and Schenectady, the northern defense outposts for New York province, feared the French might attack their cities next. If those two forts fell, the Canadian force could float down the Hudson to New York City and fight their way past the crumbling wall on Wall Street.

That same day, August 2, a ship docked with the latest military intelligence from England, dated "Whitehall April 20" (in other words, a three-month-old report), that "the French were making Preparations by Shipping, and otherwise, for an attempt on some of His Majesties Plantations in America, and had put on board a considerable Quantity of Armes."

Governor Fletcher immediately issued a proclamation, hastily printed by William Bradford at his shop at the Sign of the Bible, putting the colony in a state of readiness, ordering all New Yorkers — both citizens and soldiers — to have their weapons "well-fitted" and "well-furnished with ammunition." Any person seeing three ships upon the coast was required to immediately inform the governor. The proclamation closed: "God Save the KING."

That same afternoon, Governor Fletcher rounded up part of the city's troop of soldiers to five-day march the 144 miles north (colonial figure) to Albany.

The citizens of New York City suddenly felt very vulnerable. The main English force had left the city; any coordinated attack by sea, delivering French and Indian troops, might have a fine chance against the 600 or so houses in Manhattan. The one Royal Navy ship in port, the HMS *Richmond*, was a mess, with crooked masts and some dry rot. On August 4, the City Council passed an embargo forbidding any ships from sailing out of New York harbor, effective through September 1. This locked Kidd's warship in port for a month — not officially hired, but clearly on call to protect the city.

At some point in August, a frustrated Captain Kidd made a momentous decision. At first glance, it might sound like a small point in an ongoing labor negotiation, but it goes to the heart of the man's recklessness, his damn-it-all desire to get things moving.

Captain Kidd had been ordered by his blueblood backers in London not to give the crew more than a one quarter share of the profits. Kidd decided to flip his privateering arrangement on its head. He decided to give the lion's share — three quarters of the treasure — to the crew and one quarter to the lords and other backers, such as Albany merchant Robert Livingston. He promised the men they would sign the new articles as soon as they were out to sea.

From any angle, this was a bold move, instantly tripling the projected take of each of the 100-plus men Kidd would sign up, and crippling the share of his shadowy backers in London.

Men now flocked to join up, coming from as far away as Massachusetts and Maryland. Governor Andrew Hamilton of East Jersey wrote, apologizing to Governor Fletcher, that he couldn't supply troops for the war effort, and he blamed the "large wages" available and that "several are gone aboard Captain Kidd." Fletcher pegged that at least fifty New Yorkers signed up — from an ousted former sheriff, English Smith, to an impoverished, sleep-in-his-dinghy wood-cutter Irishman named David "Darby" Mullins.

The prospects for the voyage had so changed that New York merchants were now willing to lend money to strangers from Pennsylvania in exchange for a promised piece of their share in Captain Kidd. Three day laborers came from Philadelphia: Patrick Dremer, Micijah Evans, and Samuel Kennels. Merchant Joseph Blydenbaugh provided "shoes and stockings, rum and sugar, spices, combs, knives, handkerchiefs, spoons, ropes" and expected to receive from each "one third portion of his share in money, jewels or bullion, negroes or slaves, silks." (The men carried aboard that booze and spice to supplement a sailor's diet; the other trinkets formed a small trading stock to swap with faraway islanders to supplement income.) Thomas Clark, another original vestryman at Trinity Church, a man with the smuggler's nickname of "Whisking," a longtime friend of Captain Kidd, also loaned money to the sailors.

Governor Fletcher returned from Albany on August 20 with a glowing report of his own heroic doings. "Some escaped prisoners [said] that an Indian brought tidings to Count Frontenac that I was on march from Albany with an army as numerous as the trees of the woods, which hastened his retreat."

The city was more secure with its leader Fletcher back with the troops. People in this town known for its boozing celebrated the diminished threat of war in the way they knew best. (From the earliest days, Dutch breweries had been providing a delicious alternative to Manhattan's brackish well water.) On August 24, Captain Kidd and half a dozen veteran sea dogs who had already agreed to accompany him on the voyage were sitting around drinking in the tavern of Michael Hawdon.

New York barkeeps were famous for letting sailors run up huge tabs, because they knew that in that wind-driven world, some merchant or captain would need another sailor and would come pay it off. New York merchants grew so sick of erasing bar tabs that the Common Council — mostly merchants — had passed a law that a "Public House trusting any saylor shall forfeit all . . . and shall have no benefit of law." That was in 1691, this was 1696; sailors were still running bar tabs and captains were still paying them off.

At some point in the evening, tavern-owner Hawdon struck a deal with Kidd. He called over his young apprentice serving boy, Saunders Douglas, and told him he would be sailing round the tip of Africa and hunting pirates in the Red Sea. The laughing men teased the boy about how seasick he'd get and how he'd spend freezing nights in the crow's nest, picking icicles out of his hair. The agreement signed by Kidd and Hawdon states that the master Hawdon would receive half of one share of the booty for supplying his servant. Douglas would receive nothing except the knowledge that he had chipped away a couple more years off his indenture. (Young Saunders would be among the first to die on the voyage.)

At least half a dozen cabin boys would sail on the *Adventure Galley*. In times of battle, these teenagers would act as the powder monkeys, running the obstacle course of the slippery crowded deck to carry ladles of gunpowder from the powder magazine to the gun crews.

Captain Kidd himself would be served by twelve-year-old Richard Barleycorn from Carolina. Another, Robert Lamley, age fourteen, probably the son of a Southwark prostitute, tended to the ship's cook, Abel Owens. Lamley's apprenticeship agreement, besides requiring him to faithfully serve his master day and night, keep his secrets, nor waste his goods, specified: "Taverns, inns or Ale-Houses shall not haunt, at Cards, Dice, Tables or any other unlawful game, shall not play."

The apprentice contract of William Jenkins varied from Lamley's in one handwritten addendum: "Fornication he shall committ nor Matrimony contract."

The muggy late-August weather swaddled New York. As he waited for the port embargo to lift, Captain Kidd signed up more crewmen, *quite a few of them known pirates.*

In Robert Louis Stevenson's *Treasure Island*, Long John Silver dupes Squire Trelawney into hiring a crew of pirates such as Israel Hands and others. Kidd wasn't duped; he was merely confident that he could control them.

Kidd had known John Brown for almost a decade. Brown, in his forties, had crossed the line from privateering to piracy years earlier, heading off to the Red Sea. He had made the big score but then gambled or humped it all away. Kidd signed him on.

Kidd, who had sailed the East Coast and Caribbean for years, surely knew the troublemaker reputation of gunner William Moore. When Moore was eighteen years old, he had been arrested in New York for the unthinkable act of attacking his captain, and kept in prison the uncommonly long stint of almost two years. (Usually, prisoners died before that.) Authorities in Barbados had also locked him up in the early 1690s for an unspecified charge and refused him bail because he admitted to his cellmate that he planned to "desert to the French." But Kidd apparently wanted a belligerent gunner.

Kidd's crew ran the gamut of colonial manhood and boyhood, from rough ex-pirates to pasty landsmen such as Kidd's brother-in-law, Samuel Bradley, a very wealthy young man. He had recently turned twenty-one and inherited a large estate and several pieces of Manhattan real estate. Kidd, who had only a very young daughter, felt a special fondness for Sam Bradley.

The last days of August ticked down toward Kidd's departure; the new crew carried barrel upon barrel aboard; sails were mended; ropes coiled. Looking over Kidd's shoulder throughout this process, counting pennies, was Kidd's main American backer, Robert Livingston, also Scottish, also forty-two years old. To put it bluntly, Robert Livingston was cheap. Wrote one English official: "He pinched a fortune out of the soldier's bellies." In other words, he overcharged the crown and underfed the soldiers. "Beginning as a little book-keeper," sniped Governor Fletcher, "he has screwed himself into one of the considerable estates in the province." Fletcher was using "screwed" in a gutter sense; Livingston, like Kidd, had married a very wealthy widow, one Alida Schuyler van Rensselaer.

On September 1, Kidd decided that it was time to live on board the *Adventure* to oversee final preparations. He had to leave his cushy confines on Pearl Street. Kidd's eyes recorded the walls of his home. He sat one last time in the living room chairs; he ate one last meal in the dining room; he joined his young wife in the bedroom one last time. The farewell must have been difficult because subtle clues, such as offhand comments from neighbors and friends, point to William loving Sarah very much, and Sarah returning that love. They knew that they would not see each other for at least a year and a half, if ever again.

The sails of the *Adventure Galley* were furled and the three masts, like metronomes pointing to the sky, tipped now this way, now that, as the ship felt the local current.

With departure so close, the sailors also began sleeping aboard ship. That meant that their companions would have to come visit them.

Privateers followed a Royal Navy tradition that allowed "wives" aboard in port, whether or not the woman in question was actually that particular sailor's wife. "You would have wondered to see here a man and a woman creep into a hammock, the woman's legs to the hams hanging over the sides or out of the end of it," wrote an eyewitness of a similar departure. "Another couple sleeping on a chest; others kissing and clipping, half drunk, half sober or rather half asleep."

On September 6, 1696, the entire crew of 150 men stood crowded upon the deck, which rose and fell. Trumpets blared. A magistrate, in full wig, held parchment in his hand and read aloud in a booming voice the two commissions from the Lords of the Admiralty and the king authorizing the voyage.

More than fifty smaller merchant ships with their tall masts clustered in the harbor while an English man-of-war, the HMS *Richmond*, hovered nearby.

Seagulls wheeled. The magistrate droned on. Many of the sailors were probably feeling the aftereffects of the previous night's entertainment. Joseph Palmer, a young sailor from Westchester, later said he stood upon the forecastle and didn't remember a word of what was said. The magistrate stood and read the many polysyllabic words of Kidd's commission. "Whereas we are informed that Captain Thomas Too, John Ireland, Captain Thomas Wake, Captain William Maze or Mace, and other subjects . . . of New England, New York and elsewhere in our Plantations in America . . . daily commit many great piracies upon the seas . . . to the great Hindrance and Discouragement of Trade and Navigation. . . ." The precise meaning would have probably eluded almost all of the mostly illiterate crew, but the gist of it would have sunk in. One commission entitled Kidd to attack ships of Catholic France and the other encouraged Kidd to go after pirate ships. To the sailors — mostly colonials and Dutchmen — these privateering commissions were minimally about patriotism and mostly about money. You capture the ship, you split the prize money.

Maybe some of the least hungover among them heard the words from the king: "And we do hereby charge and command all our Officers, Ministers and other loving Subjects whatsoever to be aiding and assisting you."

The gunner, William Moore, loaded several cannon with gunpowder but no balls and fired off salutes to the city of New York. The cannon at Fort William roared an equal response.

The sea of faces — white except for one Indian and one "negro," John Parcrick — feigned attention. They awaited orders to lift the heavy anchor, which weighed more than a ton. The men put bars into the capstan and to the rhythm of a shanty pushed round and round — like mules turning a millstone — to haul in the stout anchor cable.

Any "wives" remaining, any merchants out for the show, the magistrate and preacher, climbed down into small boats and canoes to return ashore.

Hours later with the anchor finally stowed, the ship headed south out to sea, accompanied by a colonial brig.

The two ships moved out past Sandy Hook, that smuggler's rendezvous in the Jersies, and out into the waves of the Atlantic. The skyline of Manhattan with its windmill and two church steeples faded into the distance.

The pair of ships headed onward; Kidd was just beginning his 3,100-mile *nonstop* voyage to Madeira, a Portuguese island, famous for its wine. The captain followed the standard southeasterly trade route of that age. From there, he planned to head around the tip of Africa to the Indies where pirates such as Captain Avery feasted on treasure-laden Moslem ships.

Four days out of port, as the seasick landsmen such as forty-two-year-old Jewish jeweler Benjamin Franks still spewed over the side, Captain Kidd fulfilled his whispered promise to the crew to let them sign new and more favorable ship's articles.

On September 10, man after man came into the captain's cabin to sign. Most merely applied an X; some had learned their initials; some tried to sign and made a mess of it.

The document has survived: "ARTICLES of Agreement . . . between Capt. William Kidd Command.er of the good ship the *Adventure Galley* on the one part and John Walker Quarter M.er to the said ships company on the other part, as followeth, vide . . ."

This contract acts like a kind of negotiated treaty between 150 men on one side and the captain on the other. On a Royal Navy ship, the captain's authority is reinforced by a troop of armed marines; on this privateer, Kidd's power comes mainly from this piece of paper (and the force of his personality and a mere handful of loyal officers).

The articles also provide a foreshadowing of life at sea aboard the *Adventure Galley* privateer.

* *Incentive Bonus:* "The man who shall first see a Saile. If she be a Prize shall receive one hundred pieces of eight."

* *Workman's Compensation:* "That if any man shall lose an Eye, Legg or Arme or the use thereof . . . shall receive . . . six hundred pieces of eight, or six able Slaves."

* *Discipline:* "That whosoever shall disobey Command shall lose his share or receive such Corporall punishment as the Cap.t and Major part of the Company shall deem fit." (*Captain Kidd could not punish his men without the consent of the majority.*)

* "That man is proved a Coward in time of Engagem.t shall lose his share."

* "That man that shall be drunk in time of Engagement before the prisoners then taken be secured, shall

lose his share." (*A drunken post-victory celebration was obviously expected.*)

* "That man that shall breed a Mutiny Riot on Board the ship or Prize taken shall lose his shares and receive such Corporall punishment as the Capt. and major part of the Company shall deem fitt." (*Again, Kidd rules by permission.*)

* "That if any man shall defraude the Capt. or Company of any Treasure, as Money, Goods, Ware, Merchandizes or any other thing whatsoever to the value of one piece of eight . . . shall lose his Share and be put on shore upon the first inhabitted Island or other place that the said ship shall touch at."

* *Sharing:* "That what money or Treasure shall be taken by the said ship and Company shall be put on board of the Man of War and there be shared immediately, and all Wares and Merchandizes when legally condemned to be legally divided amongst the ships Company according to Articles." (*Kidd reserved 40 shares for himself and the owners, with the rest to go to the crew.*)

Captain Kidd signed the document, with his signature featuring a large slashing W and a large oversized swirling K. It was with a confident hand that he agreed to give away his right to order up lashes for this uneven crew.

"When [Captain Kidd] was here, many flocked to him," Governor Fletcher later observed, "men of desperate fortunes and necessities, in expectation of getting vast treasure. He sailed from hence with 150 men . . . great part of them from this province. It is generally believed here that they will get money *per fas aut nefas* [one way or another], and that if he misses the design named in his commission he will not be able to govern such a herd of men."

As if that threat weren't enough, Kidd was faced with another more insidious problem. The ship was but a week out of the harbor when his New York partner, Robert Livingston, wrote to the Duke of Shrewsbury, secretary of state. "I am just now informed that Captain Kidd was constrained to make new conditions with his men, and to allow them the usual shares of privateers, and hath only reserved 40 shares for the ship, but this wants confirmation, the captain not having acquainted me therewith. . . . I hear he designs to make [New York] his port and to be here in 18 months' time. I am therefore of the opinion it would not be amiss if your Grace and the rest of the owners do take care that orders be sent to the Governors upon the Main and the West Indies, that if Captain Kidd on the *Adventure Galley* should come there to take care that the ship be seized, that the owners interests be secured." Not a week out of port, Robert Livingston wanted to alert the governors throughout North America to be on the lookout to seize Kidd. (Devious Livingston almost certainly knew about the change in shares; he was merely double-crossing his friend.)

So here it is: *Captain Kidd's mission is to go chase pirates — men who would rather die than surrender. He is to travel in a lone ship manned with a desperate crew, some of whom are former pirates. His ship's articles do not allow him to punish his crew, except by vote of the entire crew. As a private man of war, he will be deeply distrusted by the Royal Navy; as a commercial rival, he will be despised by the English East India Company. He is a Scot lording it over an English and Dutch crew. Once he rounds the Cape of Good Hope, he will find no welcome ports of call, except pirate ports. On the immense Indian Ocean of twenty-eight million square miles, he must find some of the five currently active European pirate ships, many of them carrying relatives and friends of his crew. And he has a one-year time limit and some of the most powerful men in the world waiting for him to return. It would be a fool's errand — except for the treasure.*

Pirate Hunter

Chapter Two

"The ship of war is the great bridge of the ocean, conveying over to all habitable places, death, pox and drunkeness; and it brings back, in return, all the foreign vices that we are strangers to in our own country."
— Ned Ward, *Wooden World*

The 152 men and boys of Captain Kidd's crew lived, as all 17th century seamen did, on top of one another, elbow to elbow, hip to hip. Space was so limited that sailors learned to walk belowdecks in a kind of perpetual Neanderthal crouch; five-foot-high ceilings were common, as were the lumpy foreheads of the landsmen.

The great irony of shipboard life is that on-deck sailors watched the sails billow in the limitless sky and scanned the waves disappearing in the vast ocean. Below deck, it was like living in a steamer trunk, a walk-in closet accommodating seventy-five.

"No man will be a sailor who has contrivance enough to get himself into a jail," observed Samuel Johnson. "For being in a ship is being in jail with the chance of being drowned . . . a man in jail has more room, better food and commonly better company."

Every available inch below deck was taken up with water-casks, barrels of salt beef, peas, beer; coils of ropes, bundles of extra canvas; a private cabin for the ship's one paying passenger might be four feet by four feet by four feet; no man could freely stretch his limbs or pace, except, of course, the lordly captain in the stern with his windows and his light.

Sleeping quarters were so cramped that the crew, divided into two "watches," dozed in shifts — with half the men catching four hours of rest while the other half worked. The starboard watch stowed their bedding on a hook to the right; the larboard cinched theirs to the left.

For landsmen, novices at this naval dormitory, the smell of that sleep chamber was gagging. Their overworked fellow sailors rarely changed their clothes or bathed; to top off the aroma of vintage sweat, toilet hygiene was rudimentary at best.

The ship's head (i.e., toilet) consisted of a plank with a hole in it, which extended forward from the bow; a sailor perched on it, rode it like a seesaw, and, while doing his business, resembled some gargoyle or perverse bowsprit; the ship's rail might provide the merest amount of privacy. A man attempting to tidy his ass risked a plunge into the sea.

Over the coming days, Captain Kidd kept the *Adventure Galley* headed southeasterly toward Madeira. The farther from port, the staler everything got . . . the butter turned rancid, the beer bitter, the biscuits became legendary for hardness; the cheese on one ship was carved into buttons. The main job of the cook, Abel Owens — who didn't know foie gras from a flintlock — was to keep giant pots of water boiling to soften the hunks of salt beef or pork or rock-hard dried salted stockfish or cod. A gallon a day of beer helped rinse away the saltiness.

For Kidd, this first leg of his five-month voyage out to the Indian Ocean — where they would hunt for the world's rich pirate ships — was supposed to be uneventful, a time to drill the crew and test the ship, to weed out the troublemakers and find out how much topsail his new rig could handle. The trip proved instead to be a series of unexpected incidents that seriously jeopardized the entire venture and ended up teaching the crew and the captain more than they wanted to know about each other.

A week out of New York, Kidd encountered a disabled English brig, heading from Barbados to England. Kidd, acting the gentleman, gave the ship a mast, rigging, and canvas, and his "kindness" as one passenger put it later, was repaid with a few barrels of flour and sugar.

Then, a couple of days later, one of the crew spotted some faint glimmer on the horizon, some incongruent breakup of the monotonous arc of vision, hinting that a sail might loom far far off. The spotter hoped for the prize reward.

The crew buzzed. What better start for a long voyage than to make a capture in the first month? Kidd ordered the helmsman to move the whipstaff so the *Adventure Galley* would follow that ship. (Readers can be forgiven for picturing the captain spinning the ship's wheel to alter the course. Wheels with their familiar spokes didn't arrive till a few decades later.) The *Adventure Galley* in the stern had a whipstaff, i.e., a giant pole on a pivot with the bottom end connected to the rudder; the helmsman by pushing the whipstaff moved the rudder through a limited arc, turning the ship. Sailors were inspired by this thick pole emerging through a slot on the deck to nickname the male organ a "whipstaff." (Ned Ward in his satiric *Wooden World* described the sailor's morning ritual: "he crawls . . . to the pissdale where he manages his whipstaff with one hand and scratches his poop with the other.")

The *Adventure Galley* laid on all possible sail and chased the unknown ship; at some point, the other crew perceived Kidd following it; the tradition for friendly ships encountering each other at sea (generally starved for news or some other captain's delicacy) would be for the lead ship to reduce sail and allow the other to join it. The ship in the distance piled on more canvas to try to escape.

This excited Kidd's crew. For three days, Kidd chased the other ship. Kidd throughout his career had proven himself an excellent mariner, never once wrecking or grounding a ship while captain; he also repeatedly steered accurate courses in that era when longitude was more guesswork than science. Kidd finally caught up. He yet again extended the spyglass and observed the ship was running up the flag of Portugal. This was not a good omen. England was now nominally at peace with Portugal, and Kidd's commission clearly forbade him from attacking any current allies of England. It didn't matter that the two countries had battled on and off for more than a century over the Indies and

Africa and South America.

Portugal was a Catholic country; Kidd's ship — with its English and Dutch crew — was firmly Protestant. Battle lines had been drawn ever since Pope Alexander VI in 1493 took a break from fornicating with nineteen-year-old Giulia Farnese and had split the entire New World into continent-sized swatches for Catholic Spain and Catholic Portugal, leaving absolutely nothing to England or any other country.

Religion in those years divided the world far more than nationality, and it's likely that Kidd's crew — in time of war with Catholic France — would have regarded Catholic Portugal as an enemy. In a contemporary account, an undereducated English sailor called the Portuguese "a nation of lying, thieving, swearing, lusty hypocrites."

Kidd bore down on the other ship. He could only hope it was a French ship masquerading as Portuguese. Kidd hailed the vessel; when it dared to ignore him, he ordered a warning shot fired across its bow.

The captain got the message and awaited a boarding party. Kidd would now find out the ship's true identity. The flag meant nothing; the nationality of the captain meant nothing; the crews consisted almost always of mongrel mixes from many nations. The single factor determining the nationality of another vessel was the ship's documents. A merchant ship would carry a "safe-conduct" or "letter of passage" from its home government, identifying the vessel and the mission, and demanding that all ships from that country and its allies *not* molest the ship. This document — often printed boilerplate with names and details handwritten in the blanks — could save or lose a ship. Merchants sometimes carried papers from several countries as owners bribed port officials to sell their nation's "safe-conduct" letters. The presenting of ship's papers over time evolved into a kind of gentleman's game, a kind of high-stakes winner-take-all moment when the captain chose which "papers" to produce to guarantee an ally. (Pirates, of course, disregarded all paperwork, and generally enjoyed burning it or tossing it overboard.)

Kidd examined the captain's papers, which appeared to him both authentic and Portuguese, detailing this merchant ship's voyage from Brazil to Madeira, both Portuguese colonies. Observing Old World politesse despite being pursued for three days, the Portuguese captain presented Kidd with a roll of Brazil tobacco and some sugar; Kidd returned the favor by ordering the steward to give the man a Cheshire cheese and a barrel of fine New York biscuit. (The steward accidentally gave the Portuguese a barrel of cut-and-dried Long Island tobacco, worth far more than bread.)

Kidd let the other ship go and some of Kidd's Papist-hating crew, especially the ones who had been pirates — John Brown, William Moore — started grumbling. The whispers began, the hard talk about taking all ships, about turning pirate. These men, at the first glimpse of a vulnerable merchant ship, were ready to cross the line into lawlessness and attack. They talked across the hammocks in the dark, voicing angry complaints, though not yet crafting any mutinous plans.

Especially galling to some of the crew, a reminder of squandered opportunity, was the fact that the two ships — the would-be predator and the spared prey — sailed in tandem to Madeira, that prosperous island of vineyards.

John Weir was a forty-year-old out of Charleston in Carolina, a lifelong colonial sailor. Weir had become part of Kidd's inner circle, drinking with the men in Hawdon's Tavern when cabin-boy Saunders was enlisted, signing the document as a witness. John Weir, a settled family man, could write his own name in a looping flowing script. (Kidd's choice for second in command, Henry Mead, was also literate, carrying twenty books aboard.) And Weir later said that at this *early* moment of the voyage, less than a month en route, he was already hearing the rumblings of the crew. Weir, "believing . . . the men had some ill design," approached Captain Kidd for permission to leave the *Adventure* at the next port. Kidd refused. He knew he needed *all* his friends onboard.

The two ships reached Madeira on October 8, and eased into Funchal, the island capital, which at the time had a population of 10,000, double that of New York City. Madeira, a map speck 400 miles off northwest Africa, thrived because of its strong full-bodied white wine that resembled a sherry. The remarkable trait of Madeira — "different from French wines and all others," noted an aficionado, Dr. Hans Sloane, "is that it keeps better in a hot Place and expos'd to the Sun, than in a cool Cellar." The wine clearly traveled very well — pop the cork, and warmth improved the robust flavor — and Kidd loaded a "pipe" of it. (Wine was then often shipped by the "pipe," a large cask holding 125 gallons.)

Madeira was a fiercely Catholic place, dominated by intolerant Jesuit wine merchants and customs officials, who denied local burial to English Protestants and who refused asylum to French Huguenots trying to escape persecution. Dark-skinned servants catered to the dark-clothed Portuguese; the high-steepled cathedral could host 800 worshipers.

Kidd stayed only one day, canceling his plans to refill his water casks. Weir's warning had sunk in, and the captain didn't want to risk anyone jumping ship in this place where a packet left fortnightly for Europe.

Kidd, a veteran trader, instead decided he would make his first extended landing at a more out-of-the-way place, so he headed southwest. After two weeks, he saw four beautiful hills, which give the island of Bona Vista its name. Soon after, on October 24, he sailed into St. Iago (now Santiago) of the Cape Verde Islands, one of those primitive places where a captain could load sea-salt for basically the labor of gathering it.

To the cabin boys, the landsmen, even to a young New Yorker like Samuel Bradley, Kidd's twenty-one-year-old brother-in-law, this place was truly exotic. While Funchal in Madeira had a European flavor with its steepled cathedral and flagstone streets, St. Iago was a rugged African island. Barren mountains — compared by one dazed traveler to Stonehenge — soared over lush valleys ripe with oranges, lemons, bananas, and coconuts. The population was predominantly *black* Catholics.

The area's reputation for sudden storms and for a strong nightly sea breeze hammering shoreward made captains prefer to anchor about a mile offshore out in the Bay of St. Iago. Buoys marked the spot. That's where Kidd parked the galley.

Kidd ordered his men to refill the water-casks at a fresh stream running into the bay. This sweaty task would take more than a week, as hundreds of casks would have to be rowed ashore in relays in the pinnace, rolled up the beach, then each filled with sixty-two gallons of water weighing 500 pounds and then hoisted back by block and tackle into the ship.

Kidd stayed at St. Iago for eight days, which gave the crew time to explore the island and the island women. These dark-skinned islanders spoke a broken Portuguese and many of the men, though half naked, liked to accessorize their outfits with a European touch, a castoff old hat with a bunch of ribbons or a slashed coat with the sleeves ripped off. They enjoyed smoking tobacco out of a hubble-bubble, made of a coconut shell.

As for the women, Dr. John Fryer and others described them as short, a bit pudgy, and lighthearted. "Their Backs and Breasts (which were large, and hanging down) [are] bare . . . to their Waists," observed Fryer, "from whence a thin Cloath in fashion of a petticoat [hangs] down to their Feet."

A French eyewitness claimed that he saw the women "carry the children upon their backs and suckle them over their shoulders."

The men of Captain Kidd's ship probably did not spend their time cataloging the uses of palm trees or recording fashion. The Reverend John Ovington, who had visited the island just before Kidd, noted: "The women were very loose in their behavior and easily led away by the sailors." The price was very cheap: a ribbon, beads, a nail. The act was often done outside in public, and thus the island became so notorious as a lewd stopover on the way to India that it inspired a proverb: "On sailing from St. Iago to India, men abandon their consciences here at Cape Verde." Many undereducated sailors — and many overeducated merchants — conveniently believed that Christian laws did not control their actions against Moslems, or any "brown skins."

After eight days, the *Adventure Galley* and its crew of 152 men and boys hoisted anchor. As they sailed away after their sexual romp, it's somehow apt that the crew's next sight on the horizon was the active volcano on the island of Fogo sending out puffs of smoke into the night sky.

The *Adventure Galley* prepared now for its longest haul at sea without touching land, at least a couple of months and possibly longer. Kidd set a course to the south, catching a ride on the trade winds, which blow "constant gentle gales" to the southwest. "The sailors make all that passage Holiday and are not forced to hand a Sail in the space of many Days," observed an eyewitness. The forecast: cloudless day after cloudless day; hot but with a breeze. The ship's bow glided forward as the full sails billowed and strained the lines.

Time to fish. The sea around these parts abounded with albacore, bonitos, porpoises, flying fish, and especially dolphins and sharks. The seamen, with little work to do, enjoyed watching the silvery dolphins streak after the flying fish, which at the last possible instant would leap airborne to elude capture. This high-stakes game of chase soon had another player. Some of Kidd's men perched at the end of the lower yardarms, dangling lines baited with rags shaped to resemble the flying fish, while others at the rail tried to harpoon the dolphins.

"As the [dolphins] leave their Element, their Beauty fades," wrote a traveler who passed this same region, "they turn quite dark and dusky at their Expiration . . . it is a lovely neat and clean fish. The Flesh of it is white and delicate, which when larded and roasted fresh, no Roman Dainties nor Eastern luxury can outvie."

Fishing for shark, on the other hand, was less about dinner and more about blood sport. Kidd's sailors baited a hook and attached it to a length of bite-proof chain, in turn tied to a thick rope. If the sailors hooked the shark, they didn't risk pulling it up by the hook but instead tried to lower a noose around the shark's tail. Once on board, the shark usually thrashed wildly and sailors learned early on to hatchet off the tail as quickly as possible, unleashing a fountain of blood from the arteries. The sailors ate shark but much preferred dolphin.

The easy sail and work-free hours ended when the *Adventure Galley* neared the equator. The trade winds petered out around 7° north latitude and didn't start again until about 2° north latitude, about 350 miles away. So pounded by an equatorial sun, many ships lingered long, thirsty weeks in these doldrums. The poet Coleridge described the sensation: "Day after day, day after day,/We stuck, nor breath nor motion;/As idle as a painted ship/Upon a painted ocean."

The sails flapped to the mast aboard the *Adventure Galley*; the sun slow-roasted the crew. But Kidd had a huge advantage over the other ships heading through the Doldrums: oars, sweeps, 100-plus healthy men. If no puff of breeze picked up, if no faint current could be found, Kidd could order his men to lean on the twenty-foot-long sweeps and muscle the galley forward. And there, five miles to this side or that, they might find fresh breezes. Kidd — judging by the overall length of his passage — made it through without too much delay.

The reward for escaping the monotony of the Doldrums was the chance for the crew to celebrate crossing the equator. Traveler after traveler in the 17th century recorded seamen's often rude *rites of passage.*

The ritual varied from ship to ship but, more often than not, it involved a chance for the crew to extort some hard liquor or money from the equator virgins, i.e., first-time crossers.

The *Adventure Galley* crew, with playful taunts, herded newcomers, including twenty-one-year-old heir Samuel Bradley and forty-six-year-old Benjamin Franks, off to one side. Then the men slung a rope through a pulley at one end of a lower yardarm. To test its strength, they tied a board to it and watched the wood splash in the sea and drag in the waves. "He, therefore, that is to be baptized, is fastened and hoisted up three times at the main yard's end, as if he were a criminal," wrote an eyewitness. "Thus, they are dipped, every one, several times into the ocean. But he that is the dipped first has the honor of being saluted with a gun."

The prospect of cooling off by swinging forty feet through the air and plunging into the water didn't thrill everyone. By buying a round of drinks, a man might spare himself. Samuel Bradley, not known for his sense of humor, no doubt bought his way out.

Now, Captain Kidd set the course to the south/southwest. While the shortest distance around the southern tip of Africa would have been to the southeast toward the coast, sailing ships rarely followed the straightest line between two points; they had to bend to the wind patterns. In the latitudes below the equator, the northwest trade winds off the coast of Africa made it tough to head southeasterly into the teeth of the wind. Ships headed southwest until they passed latitude 25° south and then started to veer east. Though roundabout, the passage was much faster.

Navigation was still an inexact *art* more than a precise *science*, a hit-or-miss proposition in which mistakes could lead to dwindling supplies of food and water and to shipwreck. Captains in Kidd's day sailed mostly by dead reckoning, plotting their courses on inaccurate charts, going from landmark to landmark along accepted trade routes. Speed was calculated by dropping a log overboard attached to a rope with evenly spaced knots. A mate flipped the twenty-eight-second hourglass. As the log rope raced out, a man counted the number of knots until the sands expired. So many knots, that's how many knots per hour the ship was traveling. A compass determined direction. Anytime he reached a landmark, the captain corrected the ship's location via known coordinates of longitude and latitude and then began the dead reckoning process anew.

Captains in the 1690s could accurately gauge latitude (i.e., north-south coordinate) so long as the clouds weren't too thick. The navigator used a device such as a backstaff to measure the angle formed by the sun and the horizon at the sun's peak. (The sun is directly overhead at noon on the equator; any variation to the north or south will yield a different angle from the horizon to the sun at its peak.)

Longitude was the killer. In this era, there was no reliable way to determine longitude (east-west coordinate) because clocks at sea weren't yet accurate enough.

(Within a decade of Captain Kidd's mission, a fleet of British Royal Navy warships — some of the most expensive and powerful vessels of that age — were patrolling the waters off the coast of England against the French in days of heavy fog. Without the sun or stars to guide them, the captains miscalculated their fleet's location. A sailor approached Admiral Cloudisley Shovell and politely informed him that, by the man's calculations, the ships were in danger. Admiral Shovell immediately ordered the man hanged for mutiny. The next day, four ships crashed into the rocks and two thousand men died.)

Throughout November, Kidd headed south/southwest through vast stretches of island-less Atlantic waters. In early December, he hit heavy fog. The logbook of a ship going through the same region at the same time described December 6 as "Extraordinary foggy misty weather; fine fresh gales; firing of guns to keep company." That is, an occasional cannon burst kept the ships within earshot. The next day: "Extraordinary foggy Weather coming and going increasing and decreasing very suddenly." Kidd meandered in and out of these tufts of fog.

On Friday December 11, at 33° 48' south latitude as the sun first glinted over the horizon, someone aboard the *Adventure Galley* spotted a sail, then another, perhaps five ships or more. In those remote waters, finding himself outnumbered five to one by an unknown adversary, Captain Kidd decided that it was best to pile on all canvas and slip-slide away. Seeing a far distant ship through a spyglass might reveal a flag, which might be a false color, a *ruse de guerre*. Kidd had the wind and the lead. Gradually all the other ships except one fell away, and it became a game of chase, of one on one. The pursuer followed the *Adventure* through the morning, through noon as each captain played the "clear moderate" winds. Kidd ordered his men to add as much sail as he dared. The other ship kept gaining. Kidd raised his long-barreled spyglass. He looked and he looked again. First mate Henry Meade, in fine beige waistcoat and wig, looked also. Both men agreed that this was an English Royal Navy ship, with about forty cannon, an even more potent force than Kidd. Kidd decided to risk a bit more sail to try to escape; the men, as word of the identity of the other ship circulated, raced to obey orders.

The odds of meeting a squadron of Royal Navy ships in the southern Atlantic during those years were incalculably small. The Lords of the Admiralty then rarely spared any ships for this duty, because of the ongoing European wars. Over time, ships of the all-powerful English East India Company were forced by necessity to become equipped with enough cannon to protect themselves.

Most of Kidd's men, who would have been thrilled to spot a cluster of pirate ships, were quite distraught to see this Royal Navy man-of-war. While the huge Union Jack flapping over the rows of gun-ports might have sparked some faint pride in Mother England, the Royal Navy meant, on a more personal level, the threat of underpaid hard labor, terrifying discipline, arrogant officers, and an excellent chance of dying in the very near future.

This was the era of the forced naval draft, the yanking of landsmen — errand boys, tailors, farmers — from their work-aday routines and hauling them off kicking and screaming to serve in the king's navy. "These were the days of press-gangs when men lay in ditches and bogs to escape the clutches of pig-tailed seamen led by cockaded officers, rounding up all whom they met," noted one observer.

Once aboard, life expectancy shrank im-mediately. The ranking physician to the Blue Squadron studying crew lists around this period found that among men who went out on a two-year voyage, and re-mained on board that same man-of-war throughout, three out of four died, mostly from scurvy, shipwreck, or battle.

A husband suddenly pressed into the

Royal Navy could send a family into a tail-spin of poverty as the Royal Navy often fell months and sometimes years behind in the payment of wages, and frequently substituted "tickets," or IOUs, that could be redeemed only at certain places at certain dates. "Lord, how some poor women do cry . . . ," wrote Admiralty official Samuel Pepys in his diary, "and [they] wept over every vessel that went off, thinking [their husbands] might be there, and looking after the ship as far as they could by moonlight."

When the Admiralty remodeled its headquarters in London around this time to befit a rising naval superpower, architect Robert Adam was hired to design a large ornate screen for the forecourt. This artful structure acted both as barricade and blinder, to shelter the lords and bureaucrats *inside* from the pitiable men pleading, sometimes on the verge of riot, *outside*.

Kidd and crew did all they could to race away, but, finally, the HMS *Tiger* overtook the *Adventure* and the captain, John Richmond, forced Kidd to lay by, i.e., to furl his sails and await the rest of the English squadron. It would now be the prerogative of Commodore Thomas Warren in the HMS *Windsor* to inspect Kidd's papers.

Meantime, the crew aboard the *Adventure Galley* had several hours to ponder life in the Royal Navy as the *Tiger* and the *Adventure* awaited Captain Warren in the *Windsor*, a fourth rate armed with seventy cannon.

As the ships bobbed with sails furled, the *Adventure* crewmen exchanged horror stories with one another about life in the Royal Navy. At least one man pleaded with Kidd not to send him over there.

As prime candidates for the draft, many of them knew that while a Royal Navy sailor's daily pound of biscuit was supposed to be "good, clean, sweet, sound, well-bolted . . . , well-baked and well-conditioned," the reality was often closer to a weevily rock that required long-term gnawing by scurvy-rotted teeth. "The bread did fetch the skin off men's mouths," ran one complaint. On Sundays and Thursdays, veterans knew the Royal Navy cook was *supposed* to serve each man one pound of pork at dinner, but they well recalled seeing pork arrive in frightening rainbow-colored hues or in servings of only "cheeks, ears, feet and other offal of the hog." The vile rations came as a result of the bribery that dogged the victualing process, and enriched many a titled lord at the top of the food chain. "The purser is the most excellent alchemist in Nature," sniped Ned Ward in *Wooden World*, "for he can transmute rotten pease and moldy oatmeal into pure gold and silver."

Looming over any stint in the Royal Navy was the ever-present cat-o'-nine-tails. (As in, on deck there was always "room enough to swing a cat.") The major offenses, such as mutiny, desertion, striking an officer, and cowardice, which carried the death penalty, required a court-martial of at least five captains. But for lesser offenses, such as swearing or thieving, the ship's captain, who served as judge and jury, had great latitude in choosing the punishment. He might be a traditionalist and opt for a dozen lashes, or he might be as quirky as the captain who sentenced a sailor caught lying "to make clean the ship's head and sides without board," that is, to be slung over the side in a rope harness to sway to the job of cleaning the plank toilet in the bow. In that era, sea captains could do almost anything to their men short of killing them without provocation.

The rest of the English warships finally arrived, accompanied by an East India merchantman, commanded by one Captain John Clark. The five ships had enough firepower to blow Captain Kidd into floating splinters. Commodore Thomas Warren, in his spotless uniform, lifted the speaking trumpet and ordered Captain Kidd to bring his papers and come aboard. Kidd

King William III (seen in cameo) granted this Letter of Marque (i.e., privateering commission) to his "well-beloved" Captain Kidd.

did not reply. Warren repeated his order. Kidd cupped his hands behind his ears as though he hadn't heard.

It is sometimes through the smallest of gestures that we learn about a man's personality. Here is Captain Kidd surrounded by Royal Navy warships, addressed by a commodore in words that, no matter how politely phrased, are clearly an order. Yet somehow Captain William Kidd had the cheekiness to pretend not to hear. It is the measure of the man's self-confidence *and* his recklessness.

Kidd, a few moments later, did agree to go on board the Royal Navy ship *Windsor* and was accompanied by Jewish jeweler Benjamin Franks and several officers. "I was on board the Commodore's ship," later testified Franks, "when he told me that Kidd's commission was firm and good and that he would not molest or hinder his proceedings for his putting his hands to his ears." Captain Clark of the East India merchant ship also saw the commission "which [Kidd] readily produced being very Authentick under the Great Seal of England."

Despite the initial contretemps, Commodore Warren graciously invited Captain Kidd to dine with him, and now Kidd and the others would learn more about the squadron they had encountered.

Ships at sea were starved for information; no doubt it took only minutes, hours at most, for the crew of the *Adventure Galley* to discover that this Royal Navy squadron was on a mission in shambles and that it desperately needed men. They also learned that Commodore Warren was mean, conniving, arrogant, and, maybe, more than a little stupid.

Warren's squadron had left England seven months earlier way back in May, under orders to join two other squadrons to act as convoy for more than 100 merchant ships. This flotilla — at first a brave sight of sails — had formed a kind of nautical wagon train through the hostile territory of French privateers.

When the West Indies convoy had peeled off, Commodore Warren shepherded the remaining fifty vessels southward, including three East India ships carrying thirty-six chests of treasure. He had expected to find himself traveling west of the Madeiras, but he had miscalculated and drifted east of them. That's when the trouble began. Commodore Warren repeatedly gave the signal for consultation with the other captains and he repeatedly chose the wrong longitude coordinates, judging himself again and again west of his true position. Far from being some abstruse mathematical problem, Warren's calculations would mean life or death from malnutrition or scurvy aboard the ships. And his men did start to die. Aboard the *Advice* frigate, a fourth-rate man-of-war, Captain Edward Acton in his log neatly recorded the names of the dead sailors. "Died Tho Grady. Died Jon Price. Died R Hinks." Next to each date in which a death occurred, he inked a small skull-&-crossbones. His log by the end of June was littered with these juvenile drawings, a simple eye-catching symbol of death, one on the verge of being widely borrowed by pirates for their flag.

Warren's troubled convoy had passed the equator on July 19. Aboard one of the East India Company ships, the *Sceptre*, Captain Phinney reduced his men to a quart of water a day, "which was but a small quantity to poor men that eat dry biscuit and salt beef boiled in salt water, and in a hot climate," wrote first mate Edward Barlow in his journal.

The captains of the East India ships found the convoy so slow — with its endless officers' feasts and debates — that these merchant ships, despite carrying treasure, snuck away, preferring to risk the open seas. (They had to *sneak away* because Commodore Warren had already reeled one East India ship back in.)

The mood aboard the commodore's flagship grew darker. Men by the twos and threes were dying daily from scurvy. "The disease brings with it a great desire to drinke, and causeth a generall swelling of all parts of the body, especially the legs and gums," wrote one 17th century doctor, "and many times teeth fall out of the jaw without paine." In later stages, a man pressing a thumb to his shinbone, the doctor observed, could easily make a half-inch indentation.

The majority of ships' doctors and captains in the 1690s knew little about preventing or curing scurvy; many still blamed it on sinfulness or lack of "land air."

Aboard Commodore Warren's flagship, the *Windsor*, the surgeon "damned the men for not dying." A lawsuit filed later against Warren stated that the men died slow, painful deaths on starvation rations, while the officers ate well, using their own private food stocks.

A cruel architectural configuration prevailed on ships back then where men lived so close together; the smell of the officers' rich food wafted over to the crew. The savory aromas tormented the starving men.

Warren had brought fourteen cows aboard the ship for his personal table, and those cows consumed great quantities of water. He had also smuggled his barber's wife aboard as washerwoman; he wanted his waistcoats immaculate. A good washerwoman needs fresh water to do her work. (Washing in salt water makes clothes stiff as a board.) "He had rather see the whole fleet parched up like touchwood, for want of water, than his washerwoman should be stinted in any way," sniped Ned Ward.

In that age of much religion and little charity, Warren, a strict disciplinarian, revealed himself a fanatical hater of swearing. (Ever since the days of Joan of Arc, who nicknamed the English "les goddams," the nation and especially its sailors have had a reputation for enthusiastic cursing.)

Warren ordered the ship's carpenter to build several wood-and-iron collars weighing *fifty* pounds each to be worn as punishment by those caught swearing. Picture the parched seaman in the tropics doing his duty in that yoke. Officers who were caught swearing were to be slapped on the hand. Warren, in his later successful defense against these many complaints, stated: "My officers [report] that they never heard less swearing on a man of war before."

This grim ship had sailed on, accompanied in August by only its three other Royal Navy vessels. The orders from London had directed it to go to the island of St. Helena in the South Atlantic to provide convoy to the East India ships returning from the Indies. The log of the *Advice* told the story: "August 30: Continue bearing away in ye Latt.d Expecting to see ye Island . . . August 31: Moderate gales. Lying by in nights for fear of missing ye Island. Died Wm Lee & Ro Trylliard."

Wrong-Way Warren could not find St. Helena. The death rate was increasing. (More than three hundred men died aboard the four ships.) The decision was made back on September 18 to head for Brazil. Even Thomas Warren couldn't miss a continent. (The Royal Navy ships had then spent a month and a half in Brazil, recuperating and loading water and beef.)

So, now, this was the convoy that Captain Kidd and the *Adventure Galley* fell in among, all mired in the early December fog of the South Atlantic. This chance meeting would harm Kidd's prospects as much as if the Royal Navy had opened fire.

With all the ships gathered, Warren called for yet another consultation. He decided that the convoy would make first for the Cape of Good Hope on Africa's southwest tip — where both Kidd's *Adventure Galley* and Captain Clark's *East India Merchant* happened to be heading.

Captain Kidd's men saw some of the crew of the *Windsor* sporting their fifty-pound collars.

The ships made good time, covering 274 miles over the next two days. Though that works out to less than 7 miles per hour (5.7 knots per hour), this was quite good for a convoy that was only as fast as its slowest ship.

Inevitably, the subject of crewmen came up. "The Commodore told Kid he had lost a great many of his men and *asked* him to spare him some," recalled Benjamin Franks, the jeweler who had lost his fortune in the Port Royal, Jamaica, earthquake. Captain John Clark of the *East India Merchant*, who took an immediate dislike to Kidd, remembered the conversation a bit differently. "Being disabled by ye loss of three hundred men, Captain Warren told Kidd he *must have* some from them." Clark said that Kidd "readily consented," and promised "thirty or more" men.

Kidd's commission entitled him to be treated with respect by the Royal Navy and he in turn asked Captain Warren to spare him a mainsail, since he had given his extra one to that disabled ship a few days out of New York harbor. Kidd offered to write a letter of credit on his blueblood owners, but by all accounts Captain Warren refused to supply him with anything but plentiful dinners and wine.

Indeed, the latest feast began on the afternoon of Friday, December 18. Course after course arrived; corks popped on bottle after bottle of liquor. Thanks to that stint in Brazil, Captain Warren's table was once again stocked, and his liquor cabinet choice. Kidd grew boisterous, "full of rodomantade and vainglory," according to Captain Clark, and late in the meal Clark said that Kidd bragged he would take a mainsail out of the first ship he met. "These and many other words in his loose discourse gave [us] great cause to suspect ye honesty of his design." Typical of captains working for the East India Company, Clark resented any other English ship daring to venture to the Indies. Such ships were called "interlopers." Although Parliament in 1694 had temporarily ended the company's monopoly, these aggressive businessmen simply ignored the ruling, and continued to harass any of these interlopers, routinely denying their fellow countrymen firewood, water, or food, sometimes even seizing cargo on trumped up charges.

The feast aboard the *Windsor* ended; Kidd must have been an entertaining drunk because he was invited to yet another feast for the next afternoon. Through the still waters, Kidd's men rowed the longboat back over to the *Adventure Galley*. Kidd staggered on the deck "very much disguised by drink," according to Franks. A calm had set in, not a puff of wind on this dark night, and Kidd slurred out the orders for the men to man the oars and row the galley away. This was a momentous decision considering the combined firepower and arrogance surrounding him. Kidd audaciously decided that his pirate-chasing mission was as important as Warren's convoy duty; he resented the fact that the East India ship contributed no men.

The log of the *Advice* records: "Dec. 19 Last night Cap.t Kidd of ye *Adventure Galley* saled from us so yt in ye Morning we Lost Sight of him faire and Clear Little

Wind and Calme."

Kidd had decamped without delivering the twenty to thirty men that Commodore Warren wanted. The crew of the *Adventure Galley*, who had witnessed the miseries aboard the Royal Navy convoy, were thrilled. Kidd had won back some of their loyalty. Jonathan Treadway, a twenty-three-year-old from Boston, confirmed there was "Great Satisfaction of our people . . . who were fearfull that some of them would have been carryd away by ye Men of Warr."

For his part, Commodore Warren was not the least bit amused to wake up groggy and spy Kidd's sail a speck on the horizon. Once again, he ordered the *Advice* and *Tiger* frigates to go out and reel in Kidd. But Kidd had a solid lead, and when he momentarily slipped out of view, he shrewdly changed his course, opting to by-pass the Cape and head straight for Madagascar.

Ten days later, on New Year's Day, the English squadron of four warships reached the Cape of Good Hope, and there soon also arrived three vessels of the East India company (*East India Merchant*, *Sidney*, and *Madras*) as well as an interloper, *Scarborough*.

Having had ten days to stew over the insult to his command and his hospitality,

Commodore Warren decided that Captain Kidd was a pirate hiding behind the king's commission, a wolf in disguise. Warren's assessment, based on no evidence, would cripple Kidd.

The Dutch, a rising power in the East Indies trade, then controlled the Cape of Good Hope, whose excellent sheltered harbor served as the refresher point on the South Africa coast for both English and Dutch ships headed to or from the Indies. (The English earlier in the century had tried and failed to establish a colony there, shipping in ten condemned convicts from Newgate, who, after a year of eating penguin, had begged to return to prison.) The Portuguese had also failed to establish a colony there, even though their explorer Bartolomeo Diaz, back in 1486, had been the first European to touch at the Cape. He had dubbed it *Cabo Tormentoso* (Cape of Storms) but the king of Portugal, in an effort at spin control, had changed the name of his property to Cabo Boa Esperanza.

Dutch port officials, as allies, routinely queried the English captains about their voyages and any war news they'd picked up. "The captains reported that after leaving Brazil, they had met a pirate, carrying 32 guns and 200 men, whose captain, Kit [Kidd], told them by commission of the King of England he had been expressly equipped to search for and destroy six English pirates in the Red Sea; but as the English themselves believed that he was also a pirate and as in conversation he had let fall that he made no difficulty about whom he captured, and after having sailed with the fleet 48 hours, he thoroughly spied out everything, he quietly skulked away during the night."

The captains also accused Kidd of using small ships such as the *Loyal Russel*, then standing in the harbor, to smuggle booty and supplies to and from the West Indies.

In an age when news traveled slowly, Warren's unfounded charges in one quick burst had reached the East India Company, an interloper, and the Dutch. Each ship would repeat the charge to any ship it encountered. In time, this gossip chain would garble Kidd into a mastermind who used a network of small ships to ferry his plunder and supplies to and from the Caribbean.

After hearing this news, the captain of the interloper, *Scarborough*, informed Dutch officials that out of fear of Kidd, he would wait for another ship to accompany him eastward toward Bengal. The *Scarborough*'s "supercargo" (i.e., trade representative onboard for the stay-at-home owners) was Allen Catchpoole, a veteran of the Indies who had been dismissed by the East India company for embezzling.

Catchpoole wrote a letter home to London: "We sail hence in company with a Dutch pinck bound to Batavia . . . we are from many hands informed that just off of this Cape here lys one Capt. Kidd, an old eminant west India privateer; he says he is going anywhere for gaine; he has 150 very stout men & a pretty frigat of 36 guns; he wants likquers & sailes & being very loath to part with any of ours, has staid us. Soo long he was on board the men of warr & shewed such an Authentick commission, that they durst not meddle with him & now [that] we are 2 ships, he will not with us."

Catchpoole sent his letter on January 15, addressing it to his backer, Thomas Bowrey, to be left at "Garrontays Coffee House in Exchange Alley" in London. He gave it to the captain of the Royal Navy's fireship, *Vulture*, to carry. The ship's log shows that the navy convoy on its return voyage north, after *finally* touching at St. Helena, reached Cadiz in June, where Captain Simons handed off Catchpoole's letter, which then reached England by the following week. So by July 1697, Captain Kidd, after having boasted in his cups and protected his men from unwanted service in the Royal Navy, was labeled a pirate in London.

From now till the end of his life, his reputation would always precede him to all places, in later years to London, to New York, to the Caribbean. And now, venturing to the East Indies, the pirate hunter would arrive dreaded as a pirate.

Pirate
Robert Culliford

Chapter Three

"[Pirates] were a unique race, born of the sea and of a brutal dream, a free people, detached from other human societies and from the future, without children and without old people, without homes and without cemeteries, without hope but not without audacity, a people for whom atrocity was a career choice and death a certitude of the day after tomorrow."

— Hubert Deschamps,
Les Pirates à Madagascar

The first requisite of living the pirate life was acquiring a pirate ship. Pirates didn't march down to the nearest shipyard and commission some flouncy frigate with hidden gunports, and silk stripes on the captain's settees. Sometimes a bunch of daring men rowed some pathetic little pirogue alongside a much bigger ship, climbed the chains, boarded it, and offered anyone aboard the chance to join up or float away in an understocked longboat. Or sometimes, they cut an underguarded ship out of a harbor, or they mutinied.

In the spring of 1696, pirate Robert Culliford was temporarily without a pirate ship, thanks to his ongoing stint in a Moghul prison.

Culliford, twenty-nine years old, from the smuggler's coast of Cornwall in England, who would one day command the biggest, richest pirate ship in the Indian Ocean, was currently cooped up in squalid accommodations at Junegadh in northeastern India. To be a Christian prisoner in a Moslem prison was a distinctly unpleasant experience.

Robert Culliford and the pirates had landed four years earlier at the port of Mangriol on the Indian coast, up to their usual pirate hijinks: bullying the local males, abusing the local females, and stealing. A woman had duped them into engaging in a target shooting contest so they would waste their ammunition. The men swigged liquor, fired off round after round, and in the end, their weapons lay spent, unloaded in an unruly pile. That night, a Mangriol boy, with a knife in his teeth, swam out to the pirate ship and cut the anchor cables, and the vessel washed ashore, jerking the pirate guards out of their drunken slumber. As the ship beached itself and tipped, the locals attacked. The pirates jumped into the water to try to push their vessel free; they hoisted out their longboats to tow it away, while trying to fight in the dark . . . with the breeze and tide conspiring against them.

In the melee, the Mangriols captured eighteen pirates, including Robert Culliford, Jon Swann, William Mason, and James Gilliam. They roughed them all up, shackled them, and carried them inland thirty miles to Junegadh, and there left them to rot in prison. Flies feasted on the human feces, piling up in the corners and pooling out in the relentless heat. The men were crowded together in misery. Month followed month until the calendar blurred. These desperate men sought any kind of recreation, consolation. It was here that Robert Culliford and Jon Swann became the best of friends. An eyewitness much later depicted Culliford as having a harem of Malagasy wives (which confirms his heterosexuality), but that same witness described Culliford as sharing home and harem with his "great consort," Jon Swann. The word "consort" was used sometimes to characterize two pirate ships sailing together, and could mean no more than the buccaneer partnership of promising to care for each other in sickness and to share booty in case of death. Alexander Exquemelin, in his *Buccaneers of America*, described this practice as a "grand and solemn custom." Or, in the case of Culliford and Swann, it could mean that these two bored men physically cemented their friendship in the stifling heat inside the walls of the Junegadh prison. (They would remain loyal to each other for years.)

In a desperate bid for freedom after half a year, that veteran rogue James Gilliam succeeded in smuggling a note to the English East India Company headquarters at Bombay:

> *I who am unknowne do lye here in a miserable prison at Junegarr do make bold to write to your Honour yt: I am an Englishm:n and taken by ye Govern/t hereof at Mangalore in ye most treacherous manner . . . I shall satisfie ye to ye full both of my comming into ye country and also of their taking me, which in this small piece of paper as you receive it is too little for it would require a great deal more.*

The tiny missive was received September 4, 1692. While the governor may not have laughed out loud, he certainly made no effort to free these English pirates. At the time, the English East India Company's efforts at expanding friendly trade relations with the Moghul Empire were bedeviled by English pirates capturing Moghul ships. Since many Moslems lumped all "hatmen," or Europeans, together willy-nilly, not bothering to sort them by country or religion, the English East India Company to its horror found itself blamed for the crimes of the pirates.

The years in prison trickled by; escape attempts failed. During this stint, James Gilliam was forcibly circumcised, and earned the oval loop that would later hang him. But it was also perhaps thanks to his circumcision, to Gilliam's "turning Turk," that the prisoners were eventually trusted to work at intervals aboard Moghul ships. Finally late in the spring of 1696, the men overpowered their guards and escaped, bursting with four years' frustration, primed to resume their piratical careers as soon as possible.

It's easy to see why they were ready to take the risk again of living the pirate's life. The alternative of honest work was bleak. Signing up on a merchant vessel often meant low wages, scant rations (to save merchants' money), and extreme hard work under an abusive captain who could mete out most any punishment short of death. One clever captain, who caught a man stealing, forced the sailor to stick his finger in a hole in a heavy wooden block, then he drove in splintered wedges and made the sailor carry the blood-splattered block around for two hours.

So much misinformation has been scribbled over the centuries about pirates, so many movies made, from Errol Flynn as Captain Blood to the various Captain Hooks in *Peter Pan*, that it might be helpful, in one quick blast, to sweep away some of the common misconceptions.

Pirates rarely sailed under the black flag with skull & crossbones, and certainly not in the 17th century. They generally opted for a *ruse de guerre*, and used a flag of some country likely to lull the intended prey into sidling closer. If that failed, pirates in this era hoisted a simple Bloody Red Flag (Jolie Rouge), the succinct notice to the merchant vessel that any attempt at fighting free would result in death for every single person aboard.

Pirates rarely buried treasure but drank it up or spent it on whores. If they didn't bury it, then that standard, the treasure map, didn't exist either. Edgar Allan Poe and his "Gold Bug" notwithstanding, not a single authentic treasure map has ever been preserved. As for walking the plank, most pirate victims rarely made such a ceremonious exit.

The captains of pirate ships were not autocrats but commanded with the voted permission of their crew, and pirate captains, in any case, commanded only during chase and battle. All other major decisions, such as where to sail to look for prey or what punishments should be meted out, were voted on. The pirate ship circa 1700 ranked among the most democratic institutions in a world that still mostly honored the Divine Right of Kings.

All food and liquor was to be shared equally, a mind-boggling concept for sailors long used to watching officers dine and guzzle for hours on end. Treasure too was divvied up on an almost equal basis, with perhaps a double share for the captain and quartermaster. Historians might niggle, but some of the concepts of "Liberty, Equality, Fraternity" that blossomed almost a century later in the American and French revolutions, were practiced aboard pirate ships. Also, a healthy disrespect for authority spurred many of their actions.

And in this disrespect, some of the myths about pirates turn out to be accurate. Pirates cursed a lot and often wore wild, outrageous clothes. On shore, for instance, in Boston in 1691, shoemaker William Smith was overheard saying to his wife, "God damn you!," "the Devil rot you!," and "Pox take you." For this he was sentenced to two hours in the stocks. When William Snelgrave was captured by pirates off the coast of Africa, he was astounded by the "execrable oaths and blasphemies [which] shocked me to such a degree that in Hell itself I thought there could not be worse." One pirate captain, in his cups, vowed: "If we swing our grappling hooks onto the clouds and attack Heaven itself, I'd aim my first shot at God."

As for clothes, in most countries sumptuary laws still regulated what the poor could wear, forbidding the non-property owners from donning luxury items such as fur collars or wigs or silks. Where laws didn't dictate drab clothes for the poor, custom discouraged anyone not wealthy from ostentatious dressing. Pirates, on the other hand, damned the whole business and outfitted themselves in whatever insane mélange of stolen finery they fancied. Prisoners observed pirates teetering ashore in ill-fitting silver-buckled pumps or cinched into tight waistcoats with gold buttons. Sailors, who often had to mend sails, were generally adept at needlework; so, while merchantmen might turn a scrap of canvas into tarred trousers, pirates would take the richest striped silk of the East Indies to fashion their wardrobe. One favorite accessory was a bright-colored sash draped over one shoulder, with loops to carry two or three pistols. (Gunpowder at sea was so unreliable that extra weapons were a must, and reloading could take a half minute of extreme vulnerability.)

It is of course hard to generalize about hundreds of pirate ships that preyed on merchants from the waning days of Caribbean privateering in the 1680s to the mass hangings of the 1720s, but from perusing trial testimony and eyewitness accounts by prisoners, certain facts about their lives come into focus.

Pirates were mostly young, foul-mouthed men on stolen ships on a constant search for liquor, money, and women. More often than not, they terrified undermanned merchant ships into surrender without having to fight. Since few of them ever returned home with their stolen loot, pirates knew they were choosing a lifestyle — "A merry life and a short one," boasted Bartholomew Roberts — rather than a shot at accumulating a nest egg. Few pirates were married, and some crews even forbade married men. "Their lives were a continual alternation between idleness and extreme toil, riotous debauchery and great privation, prolonged monotony and days of great excitement and adventure," wrote John Biddulph in *Pirates of Malabar*. "At one moment, they were revelling in unlimited rum, and gambling for handfuls of gold and diamonds; at another, half starving for food and reduced to a pint of water a day under a tropical sun."

Drunk, cursing, hungry, horny. And violent. Pirates — these cursing young men in their crazy clothes, brandishing swords and pistols — expected immediate surrender and were deeply offended by being forced to fight.

When pirates prevailed, they tortured their victims to reveal where any scrap of treasure might be concealed. (Some merchants swallowed jewels — pirates off the China Sea forced captives to take purgatives.) A simple hoisting and drubbing was most common, but some pirate captains delighted in offbeat torture. "Sweating," to take one example, neatly combined sadism and amusement. The fiddler struck up a tune and the pirates poked the victim with forks and daggers to keep him dancing and dancing until he confessed or collapsed.

And pirates often raped the female prisoners. The Admiralty clerks who took depositions from rogues under arrest wrote phrases such as the women were "barbarously used" or "outraged," but the simple fact was "rape." A member of Bartholomew Roberts's crew was being led to the gallows in Cape Coast Castle off West Africa. David "Lord" Symson recognized a woman's face in the crowd, one

Elizabeth Trengrove, a passenger on a ship they had captured. "I have lain with that bitch three times," bragged the unrepentant pirate, "and now she has come to see me hanged."

Robert Culliford, James Gilliam, and the rest of the escapees straggled into Bombay in March of 1696. The men, after four long years of filth and starvation and humiliation, wore rags, which allowed them to blend into this overcrowded island city ceded to England as a dowry by the king of Portugal. At this time, the English East India Company maintained its main headquarters here, castle home to the general overseeing the various company factories (or outposts) throughout the East Indies. Bombay was a natural place for Englishmen to look for work, and it's not as though illiterate sailors had to produce a résumé; callused hands and sailor jargon sufficed.

Culliford, affable, the first among them to find work, managed to sign on as gunner's mate aboard the *Josiah* ketch, a locally built ship, carrying "country trade" for East India Company officials. "Country trade" meant local commerce, not traffic back to Europe; tight-fisted East India Company officials in London repeatedly tried to forbid their reps in India from profiting via this sideline. Culliford tried to get Jon Swann signed aboard, but he failed.

Before sailing off, Robert Culliford planted the seed of a far-fetched plan, a daydream perhaps, with his dozen prison pals. They should try to steal some ship and meet up in Achin, gateway port to the Spice Islands, on the northern tip of Sumatra, and from there sail to China. Culliford was already inching his way toward command, pitching this bold enterprise to the penniless men.

The *Josiah*, with a crew of twenty, sailed from Bombay, heading south and then east round the tip of India, to load cargo at Madras, a thriving port pounded by the hard surf on the Cormandel Coast. The Grand Moghul had granted permission to various European trading companies to set up their outposts in specified spots in India. The English East India Company here had taken a defunct seaside village and over two decades transformed it into a lucrative cloth-dyeing center, and renamed it Fort St. George.

The *Josiah*, with Culliford aboard, sailed in looking to load cloth from the warehouses of the wealthy merchants. Among the merchants jockeying to traffic with the *Josiah* was a wealthy man by the name of Elihu Yale, who was somewhat disgraced. Yale, born in Connecticut, shrewd and

successful, as governor of Madras, had overseen the explosive growth in trade, but Yale's personal fortune had grown too rapidly for the company bigwigs in London, who determined that Yale was profiteering at company expense; he was ousted and by 1696 had become something of a nuisance to the company. (Years later, Yale buffed up the family name when he agreed to endow a tiny property-less college, as would-be rival to Harvard, by sending a shipment of East India goods.)

Unrelenting heat that June cooked the harbor; even the usually steady sea breezes provided little relief. The captain of the *Josiah* ketch, a man not named in the records, took sick and went ashore to recuperate. His illness delayed the ship's departure, leaving Culliford in town for a few days.

Little is known of the early life of Robert Culliford; he was born in 1666 in East Looe, Cornwall, a region notorious for smuggling and wrecking. Locals would mimic a lighthouse lantern far inland and trick ships into crashing on the rocks; they'd then row out and scavenge the floating cargo. He was bred to the sea. We know he was athletic (from the hardships he survived), was cunning (from the men he duped), a bit amoral (from the decisions he made), and courageous (from the battles he refused to leave). He was also surprisingly literate for a seaman. (He could read and write, and signed in a bold confident hand.) He was a carouser, a passionate man. We know he could be a charismatic leader (from the size of the crews he later attracted). But at this moment in June 1696, Culliford, fresh out of Moghul prison, was a mere gunner's mate on this dinky ship anchored in Madras.

Culliford went ashore to have a drink in "White Town," a small walled city about 400 yards by 150 yards, with two churches and a hospital, an area dominated by the St. George Fort in the center, and housing 500 or so Europeans. Nearby "Black Town," walled on two sides, hosted the several thousand Hindus, Moslems, and converted Catholics who lived there to participate in the town's cloth-weaving and -dyeing operations. The sailors were drinking; Robert Culliford and James Croft, armorer on the *Fleet* frigate also in port, were throwing back arrack, and downing fresh beer. Culliford told his drunken buddy Croft that he'd give him a tour of the *Josiah*, and the two men rowed out.

On the night of June 11, 1696, timing the tide, Robert Culliford cut the anchor cable on the *Josiah* ketch, causing the vessel to drift out to sea. Culliford in whispered orders directed the men to unfurl the sails. The ketch picked its way amid the silhouettes of anchored ships and headed out to sea, with twenty-two men aboard: four English, three indeterminate Euros, and eighteen lascars who would be forced to do all the hard work. ("Lascars" was a vague term for Indian sailors.)

The next morning the council in Madras rushed out "express" letters by quickest available vessels to all the other English factories that a ship had been stolen, carrying English East India Company orders and the King's Colours.

Once Culliford guided the *Josiah* out of Madras Road, the pirates were much safer. The next great challenge for men who wanted to go a-pirating, after securing the ship, was to find a place to get enough food and water to continue their search for riches, booze, and sexual companions. They needed an outlaw port, far from the reach of the East India Company.

Culliford set the course to head a few points south of due west for the 800-mile journey to the Nicobar Islands near Sumatra. At this time of year, the steady monsoon winds would make for an easy sail. Relying on the potent breezes at their back, the pirates now had little fear of encountering a ship coming toward them; all they had to do was make sure not to overtake anyone or be caught from behind.

It was a fast sail and, depending on how much booze was aboard, quite pleasant. Captain Culliford by day ordered all sheets to the wind, checked the latitude at noon, tweaked the rudder, and then waited till he bumped into the Nicobars. In less than a week, averaging more than 100 miles a day, the ship reached the islands.

The Nicobars are a long cluster of islands, ranging from rocky uninhabited flyspecks to a handful of larger fertile oases. Parrots and monkeys abound, but no horses or cows; no European or Asiatic country deemed this odd primitive place worth conquering. The pirates anchored their ship offshore and came by jolly boat to the land. They were greeted by men with tails.

Reports from earlier travelers such as Marco Polo and Sir John Mandeville had stated that tailed men lived on some of the islands in the East Indies. Most of these accounts had been dismissed as medieval mysticism or misinformation. However, when Elizabethan adventurer James Lancaster, whose voyages helped found the East India Company, touched on the Nicobars in 1602, his ship's journal records that the island priest "had upon his head a pair of horns turning backward" and the other natives showed "their faces painted green black and yellow . . . and behind them, upon their buttocks, a tail hanging down, very much like the manner as in some painted clothes we paint the devil in our country."

This tail, painted or fleshy, spurred a round of bawdy musings. French revolutionary Mirabeau later summed it up: "The [travelers] brought back word of these tailed men, who by an extension of the coccyx bear actual tails of seven, eight and ten inches, which are sensitive and as far as mobility able to do all the movements demonstrated by the trunk of an elephant." Mirabeau wondered what Catholic theologians would rule about "an easy-going Islander" enjoying sexual intercourse with one woman in front of him and one behind him. Would the actions of the tail count for fornication? Or did that require emission?

The pirates came ashore for food; the islanders, besides hog and fowl, specialized in a fresh-cooked, salted dried yam, called by a Scottish sea captain "the best I ever tasted." One account, relayed by an East India Company factor, said they came ashore "to murder and plunder." This is of course possible, but since only six armed Europeans came ashore with fourteen unhappy lascar forced laborers, it seems much more likely that they would barter, especially since it turns out many of these pirates returned regularly to the Nicobars.

Culliford left two men aboard to guard the ship: James Croft, the armorer from the *Fleet* frigate, and a lascar. (An armorer is the man aboard a ship of war that maintains the small arms, such as pistols.) For Culliford, this time ashore might have been his first real celebration after almost four years of captivity. The native bonfire roasted the whole hog and Culliford, awash in wine, could restore his appetite for female company. While the handful of pirates partied ashore into the darkness, James Croft, much soberer than many a 17th century judge, cut the ship's cable and steered out to sea. He later told East India Company officials that he had never intended to turn pirate and that Robert

Culliford had gotten him drunk and "trapanned" him aboard the *Josiah*.

Croft, with no crew or navigational skills, pointed the vessel in the direction he imagined to be Achin, a bustling port 200 miles away on the tip of Sumatra.

So Culliford, who was briefly captain of a stolen ship, now found himself abandoned upon an island full of green-faced men with tails a-wagging, who could easily surround his handful of men. The pirates, many of them veterans of the Indies, would certainly have heard the rumors about cannibal feasts. It was said that the nearby Andaman islanders were cannibals and that Nicobar islanders each year had to furnish five fresh human victims, by way of tribute, to their fierce neighbors to the north. Lacking a giant stewpot, the Andaman islanders prefered to smoke the human meat, slow-roasting it over a leafy fire, or so the story went. Robert Culliford and the other five Europeans eyed their small stock of ammunition. The pirates' cannon and kegs of gunpowder were long gone, as was their getaway ship; nothing remained in the harbor but dugout canoes.

On the very same night — June 18, 1696 — that Culliford lost the *Josiah*, at least nine of Culliford's former prison mates, including Jon Swann and James Gilliam, cruised just south of the Nicobars, aboard one of the English East India Company's finest ships, *Mocha Frigate*. This vast 350-ton, 36-gun ship was heading to China, at that moment passing through the Great Channel that separates the Nicobars and Achin on the tip of Sumatra. For fear of running on shore, Captain Leonard Edgecombe gave the order for the ship to lay by under the mainsail, that is, with its bow pointed into the wind and just one sail, the ship's largest, unfurled.

The *Mocha Frigate* was a deeply unhappy ship. Morale was low, with the captain routinely flogging the men for trivial offenses. Edgecombe was stubborn, sadistic, and unusually unbalanced, even when judged by the lax 17th century standards for a captain's behavior. We know some of the details of Edgecombe's actions because of an odd feud he had had on the voyage out from London to Bombay.

Captain Edgecombe had been convinced that his surgeon, John Leckie, was trying to poison him. He forbade Leckie and his servants from entering the cook's station, and ordered the cook to be alert that "they threw not any of [surgeon's] powders among my victuals."

John Leckie — an experienced surgeon with more than a decade's training in the Royal Navy before joining the English East

India Company — was outraged. So, at great risk to his career, he later brought charges against the captain.

Leckie said Edgecombe, after accusing him of stealing from the surgeon's chest, had beaten him with a cutlass, and had beaten his two servants.

When Edgecombe slashed Leckie a second time with his cutlass, Leckie had the temerity to strike a blow at the captain in self-defense. This was unthinkable in that era of infallible captains. Edgecombe had ordered Leckie tied up, and then — without any trial or court-martial of any sort — had decreed the worst punishment short of hanging. Leckie was to be keel-hauled, i.e., dragged by ropes *under* the full length of the barnacle-encrusted hull of the ship. (The man would likely drown or at least be shredded.) However, the ship's officers had refused to obey the order.

Leckie also charged that Edgecombe's high-handedness extended beyond the crew, that the captain had kidnapped some islanders whose only crime was to live near a place suspected of harboring pirates; Edgecombe had uncovered no evidence that these particular men and women of Johanna island had done anything wrong.

When *Mocha Frigate* had arrived in Bombay, Leckie presented his complaint to Sir John Gayer, general and commander in chief, the highest ranking English East India Company official. Gayer, a son of a merchant, was a veteran sea captain who had risen through the ranks.

Upon due deliberation, Sir John sided with Captain Edgecombe. He decided to ignore the feud as a personal matter and had supported the kidnapping of islanders. "Considering he did this to prevent enemy pirates doing further mischief in those seas . . . we [do] not think to turn him out as Mr. Leckie required." (Gayer, however, did allow the angry Scot, Leckie, to leave the ship.) Gayer then entrusted Edgecombe with an important trading mission to China.

When the *Mocha Frigate* docked in Bombay, almost a third of the eighty-man crew had jumped ship. Captain Edgecombe, desperate for replacements, had signed up nine new men, wizened, hard men, but clearly veteran sailors. James Gilliam, using the alias Sampson Marshall, had spoken for the escaped pirates, concocting a tale. They tied a few obscure knots and got the job. The captain had also needed a new surgeon, and the only available man he could find in Bombay had been Jonathan Death.

The ship was making good time and now, three weeks out of Bombay Harbor, on June 18, in the middle of the night about four o'clock, the shout of "Fire" shattered the quiet, ripping over the hum of the rat lines, awakening the hammocked sleepers below deck. The cry of "Fire" echoed quickly from man to man throughout the ship; cabin boys and officers alike scrambled in the near dark. Footsteps could be heard everywhere; bodies bumped into one another. Almost nothing strikes more fear aboard wooden ships than the threat of fire. "I immediately ran out to see what was the matter," later recounted the steward, twenty-six-year-old Thomas Vaughn of Worcester, England, "and was told that the ship was taken."

In the confusion, Vaughn stumbled into Captain Edgecombe's cabin boy. "[He] was crying, saith the captain was killed and thrown overboard into the sea, which made me more afraid," recalled Vaughn. Pirate James Gilliam had snuck into the captain's cabin and slit the sleeping man's throat from ear to ear.

As Mr. Negus, the chief mate, told it in a hasty diary he kept: "A number of Desperate and Bloody minded men between 3 & 4 this morning arose in armes, secured ye gunroom, killed ye captain in his bed, forced me and others from ye quarter deck with flourished pistols in their hands and dreadful oaths in their mouths swearing the death of all who shall oppose them."

Mr. Negus said he was weighing his chances of sneaking into steerage and on to the gunroom when a shot rang out. Negus judged by the heavy sound that it was a blunderbuss. He heard the carpenter cry out that he was wounded. Negus then made his way toward the forecastle, whispering to any officers to follow him, but the mutineers caught sight of them and blocked off the forecastle and trained their weapons on them until daylight.

Negus called out to "sev:ll of those hellish assossiates," asking what would be done to them. They promised not to harm a hair of his head if he would come aft. Negus, along with several other officers, reluctantly agreed and were put in a circle and guarded.

As dawn broke, the pirates were now in complete possession of the ship. They offered to let anyone join them for "that merry life and short."

However, twenty-six men and boys, almost half of those on board, asked to leave the ship. Some of the mutineers decided they'd rather *kill* the principal officers; they put it to a vote, but the majority voted to let them live. That evening, the mutineers lowered the pinnace, and allowed eighteen men and boys to depart, mostly officers and their servants, but also one Jacob Fig, the trumpeter.

"There were severall more desirous to leave ye ship wth us and am confident [they were] reall therein namely Jon Death, chirugeon, . . . all four Carpenters crue, John Brand cooper, Isaac Coleman foremast man, & ffrances Dyer cooks mate. To all outward appearance can say no less of Ralph Stout, our Designed Pilott for ye Streights of Malacca."

Pirates often forced skilled men to remain aboard. The reason Negus specified "am confident [they were] reall therein" because sometimes crewmen who *wanted* to join the pirates were canny enough to have the pirates include them on a list of names of those forcibly detained. That bit of play-acting might save their lives, if the pirate ship later got caught.

The mutineers were fairly considerate of the men they cast off in the boat. They supplied them with fourteen or fifteen fathoms of rope, a small anchor, oars, a mast and single sail, some bread, and a leaky "lamp can" of water. Unlike Captain Bligh in that more famous mutiny, these castaways were set adrift within sight of land, only four leagues from a little island called Poola, and not far from Achin.

The men and boys in the little craft labored hard against the wind and current all night to make the short distance to Poola, but failed. They woke up on Friday to discover themselves two full leagues farther from Poola than the night before. They struggled with oars and sail the entire day through ten o'clock that night with no progress; they were on a kind of perverse exercise machine, rowing in place and getting hungrier and more tired every hour.

The wind kicked up and swells almost entombed the overloaded boat. The spray fouled their drinking water. They rigged a rug into a foresail to try to steer toward land that one of them thought was Golden Mountain, off in the distance. They fell asleep, huddling together, bedraggled.

They woke up Saturday to find they had drifted into a sheltered bay on the mainland of Sumatra, where they were able to land, replenishing their water, and buying rice and fish.

Revived, they tried again to row toward Achin, rather than risk unarmed land travel, but the strong current forced them to come ashore, tie the boat up, and abandon it. They bargained four Malays down to two pieces of eight to escort them to Achin. They arrived Sunday afternoon, where they were welcomed by the small English community led by East India Company Chief, Mr. Soames, and by Captain Goslin and a merchant, Mr. Edward Fleetwood. The exhausted men vowed to "remember" the date as one when they

114

were saved from the danger of the seas and from pirates.

When these castoffs from the *Mocha* arrived in Achin, there riding in the harbor was the *Josiah* ketch, stolen back from Culliford and steered there by luck, by Croft the armorer. "It pleased God to deliver them here — not one aboard understanding navigation," later wrote a pious East India Company official, who added hopefully: "The pirates are left upon the Nicobars where doubtless the natives will punish them."

Achin, in a river estuary on the tip of Sumatra (modern-day Indonesia), was famed as a midway port for trade and travel between India and China. The region was well known for its high quality gold found by panning the streams of Golden Mountain, and for its ivory culled from the hordes of local elephants, bred not only for their tusks but also to entertain tourists. Scottish sea captain Alexander Hamilton witnessed one highly trained elephant that with its trunk could pick out a single gold coin from a pile of coins tossed into a puddle. The town boasted crueler entertainments, such as public punishment: a man convicted of stealing placed his wrist on an upturned ax blade and the executioner pounded down a heavy wooden mallet to cut off the hand.

Once the survivors of the *Mocha* recuperated a bit, they were introduced to James Croft, who was something of a hero in the small English community in Achin, for rescuing the ketch. Over dinner, he told his tale to the men from the *Mocha* and also to another guest, George Wallis, captain of a small country-built ship, *Elizabeth*, which was to carry cargo to Bengal. Nine of the eighteen who had survived the two-day pinnace ride decided to head north with Wallis to Bengal on Sunday, June 28, 1696.

They hatched a plan to capture Culliford. Captain Wallis and the others decided that they would call at the nearby Nicobars and pay a surprise visit to Culliford and his would-be pirates. If the natives hadn't eaten them, Wallis was certain that the East India Company would pay a nice reward for the rogues. And, the *Mocha* officers were eager to punish pirates.

The plan was simple: Croft would help guide them to sail into the island harbor, and there they would pretend to be a defenseless merchant ship in need of wood and water. They would lure Culliford aboard.

Four days later, the *Elizabeth* sailed from Achin to the Nicobar island identified by Croft. Palm trees framed the deserted beach. Within half an hour of the *Elizabeth*'s arrival, three men paddled over in a dugout canoe; they were Robert Culliford, master; Raynes, quartermaster; and Crags, the boatswain, all formerly of the *Josiah* ketch. Culliford, in the canoe, spun out a tale of woe, of shipwreck off the coast and floating to shore on spars; he told of the angry tailed men and he requested permission to come on board. Captain Wallis, straight-faced, invited the trio aboard; the three men climbed into the *Elizabeth*. Culliford was still recalling the brutal storm that had wrecked his ship when out sprung from below deck the seven men from the *Mocha*, all heavily armed; the pirates drew their swords and attempted to fight their way free to jump overboard. An officer fired his pistol and caught Crags in the chest. The eight men fought close enough to Culliford and Raynes to tackle and subdue them.

Wallis ordered the pair of pirates tied up and stowed. Delivered from the tailed natives, Culliford was now bound below deck, to be handed over to the mercy of the English East India Company. Although by law the Company did not yet have jurisdiction to hold Vice Admiralty courts and hang pirates, it could lock the accused up in a foul dark pestilential cell pending trial or deportation, and wait for disease to rid the world of the rogues or it could order them whipped for some lesser offense.

The *Elizabeth* headed north on the 1,000-mile journey to Bengal, carrying its miserable pirate cargo. The winds picked up and a chill suddenly hung in the air. A storm hit hard, and Captain Wallis decided to seek shelter in the river-mouth harbor at Mergui in Siam. The wind and rains must have been especially brutal for him to choose this harbor because over the past decade, *since the massacre,* Mergui had not welcomed Englishmen. (Elihu Yale, back when he was a Company governor, had tried in 1687 to crack down on an interloper, one Samuel White, operating out of Mergui; the Siamese, outraged over a battle between two English forces in their harbor, had attacked and killed more than thirty Englishmen carousing in town.)

The men aboard the *Elizabeth* warily settled in to wait out the storm and contrary winds. The next day, they noticed the sail of a large ship arriving. It bore the unmistakable cut of an English East India Company ship.

Through the spyglass, Captain Wallis perceived none other than the *Mocha Frigate,* flying the St. George of England. The *Mocha,* manned by its pirate crew of about thirty-five men, sailed to the edge of the harbor and dropped anchor by one of the islands there guarding the entrance. The crew sent a boat ashore to ask permission of the Mergui governor to remain in the harbor. It must have been especially galling to the seven men aboard the *Elizabeth*, cast off from the *Mocha*, to see their old ship. The governor at Mergui welcomed the *Mocha* and allowed the ship to remain and stock up on provisions. And the pirate crew, knowing they'd be in port at least a week, visited the local brothels. There they discovered that, according to local custom, the Siamese expected that foreigners, instead of paying for a half hour with a prostitute, would select and marry a temporary wife for a longer period of time. The women were usually passionate, obedient, and faithful, according to one appreciative sea captain.

With the winds against them, the *Elizabeth* was stuck in port. As soon as Captain Wallis confirmed that the new arrival was the *Mocha*, he alerted the local Siam authorities that this vessel was a pirate ship, stolen from the East India Company. He proposed that with the help of local soldiers and shore cannon, they could surprise the pirates and recapture the ship. Wallis was certain the East India Company would reward the rulers of Mergui.

The local officials, weighing profit and loss, and recalling the boorishness of the

English back in 1687, decided to let the feuding English work out their own problems. The *Mocha* could stay, unmolested. But the Siam governor neglected to relay his decision to Captain Wallis, who, along with the former officers of the *Mocha*, kept waiting for a response, all the while plotting a plan of attack, salivating at the prospect of sailing to India triumphant aboard the *Mocha* bearing Culliford and the other pirates in chains.

While Wallis waited, someone, perhaps one of the local tradesmen in one of the harbor boats selling oranges or ivory statuettes, informed someone aboard the *Mocha* that the little merchant ship, *Elizabeth*, was holding two pirate prisoners.

The *Mocha* immediately demanded the prisoners. The *Elizabeth* refused. A standoff ensued.

This became almost a press-gang parody, where instead of the British Royal Navy bullying a merchant ship to hand over seamen, the pirate ship was doing the bullying. The *Mocha* could easily blow the *Elizabeth* to splinters, but Culliford would die and the Siamese — with their neutrality disrespected — might attack. The standoff dragged on for days; the pirates with their temporary wives could wait.

Finally, Captain Wallis, anxious to leave, decided on a plan. On a moonlit night, he sailed the *Elizabeth* toward the entrance of the harbor and as it was gliding forward, put the two bound pirate prisoners in a local boat to be brought ashore. Wallis sent along a message begging the governor to arrest the men for piracy. He hoped Culliford and Raynes — fearful of arrest — would make enough noise that the pirates would spend their manpower rescuing the rowboat while the nimbler *Elizabeth* could escape.

The plan worked. As soon as the pirates heard Culliford and Raynes raising hell while being taken ashore, the *Mocha*'s long boat, packed with rowers, raced to pick them up. The pirates left aboard decided not to cut their cables to chase swift *Elizabeth* in the dark.

Culliford and Raynes were untied and hoisted aboard like heroes. Hugs and drinks. A celebration. This was the reunion of Jon Swann and James Gilliam with Robert Culliford, who had plotted a pirate rendezvous back in May in Bombay.

The crew had already elected Ralph Stout to be captain since he knew the waters. The pirates the next day voted to rename the *Mocha*; they eschewed the usual frivolous *Bachelor's Delight* or *Fancy* for the bolder name *Resolution*. And the crew voted Robert Culliford to be quartermaster, second in command to the captain, and the man who directly controlled the crew.

The newly renamed *Resolution* remained in the harbor for a while, partying, spending the honorable Company's money. During the bacchanal, two pirates stole off with almost 4,000 pieces of eight, but were captured ashore by the governor. The pirates of the *Mocha/Resolution* demanded the thieves and the silver be returned. Siamese officials refused.

When the pirates left a few days later, they captured one of the ships belonging to the king of Siam and took out fourteen bales of paintings. They politely sent a note ashore stating that the paintings seemed worth the 4,000 pieces of eight stolen from them and they viewed the matter as closed.

An East India Company roundup of reports from India around this time summarizes the events: "These villains having begun with the murder of the commander and the seizing of one of your Honour's ships will doubtless go on in making a prey of any ship they can meet with and master. . . . And the mischief falls heavier on the English than on any other European nation, because the pirate ships pass under the name and colours of the English and it is known there are many English aboard them. So that whereas the English nation

122

has been generally respected in all parts of India, they will now lie under the character of pirates and robbers, and our soldiers in garrison and our seamen in country and Europe ships will be allured by the pirates' success to run to them as several stragglers have already done."

Another note added ominously: "God preserve innocent men from their villainous and bloody hands."

Off the coast of Siam, Robert Culliford was quartermaster, on track to be captain, of the biggest pirate ship attacking merchants in the Indian Ocean.

William Kidd, privateer, was well along on his commission to hunt down pirates in the Indian Ocean. The two men's ships were almost equally armed with more than thirty cannon; Kidd had a bigger crew and oars to beat the calms.

What very few people knew at the time was that the paths of Captain Kidd and Captain Culliford had crossed before.

Chapter Four

In February 1689, Robert Culliford, twenty-two years old, and William Kidd, thirty-five years old, both rootless, living from voyage to voyage, turned up at Isle à Vache, joining the stampede of Caribbean riffraff, men who prefered the rough adventurous life to any steady work. The two men arrived separately at Isle à Vache — a land speck off Hispaniola conveniently located halfway between the English rogues of Jamaica and French rogues of Tortuga — which was rapidly becoming the new staging ground for privateers. They mixed with other men, all armed with pistol and cutlass, who were ambling in and out of the island's ramshackle taverns and whorehouses.

Word was out that the *Sainte Rose*, a rickety French privateer ship, was gathering a crew, and Kidd and Culliford signed aboard. The final tally of X's and signatures revealed 110 Frenchmen and 7 English and 1 Scot.

Culliford and Kidd and the half dozen others from Britain would have preferred to sail with men of their own nation, but they had little choice. England, unfortunately for these mercenaries, was at peace, and was actually clamping down on illegal privateering. Captain Henry Morgan, the notorious buccaneer who had relentlessly attacked the Spaniards and been rewarded with a knighthood, had recently died in Port Royal, Jamaica, a bloated old man, rum-drunk, his body swathed in magic clay by a local witch doctor.

However, thanks to the endless cycle of European alliances and betrayals, France stood at war with Holland, and Kidd and Culliford opted to take their opportunities for violence and plunder wherever they could. So, the *Sainte Rose*, armed with a flimsy commission from the French mayor of Isle à Vache, set out to prey on the Dutch merchants. The voyage was shaping up as a typical mission for a privately owned armed vessel in that era: a bunch of rowdies out for gain, lacking a lawyer's precision over the fine points of maritime law. Sometimes the dice fell on a legal capture; sometimes they didn't. Rum flowed; blood flowed; home governments bellowed far away.

The crew of *Sainte Rose*, mostly Huguenots, welcomed Kidd and Culliford, and the rest of these Protestants from Britain. Religion often trumped nationality, and these Frenchmen stood closer in allegiance to English Protestants than to French Catholics, who had persecuted them out of their homes. Before embarking, the crew loaded aboard some of the famed smoked beef of Isle à Vache, literally, "Cow Island." (The word "buccaneer" comes from the hunters-later-turned-pirates who slaughtered wild cattle, then smoked the meat on trestles, called "boucans." Pirates were early barbecue men.)

Within weeks, the *Sainte Rose* found a Dutch merchant ship and hauled off the cargo, carrying it north to sell to the pious traders of New England. The crew, replenished, headed south, loading up on fine New York biscuit; they moored in New York harbor and held a council on where to go. This privateer life could be dazzlingly spontaneous. The crew voted to seek their fortune in the Red Sea or the South Sea (Pacific). They would go toward Africa and then let the winds decide: southeast or southwest from there. Too many navies prowled the Caribbean; they wanted fresh waters, fresh victims. The *Sainte Rose* was inching toward piracy. None of the men aboard seemed too upset.

William Kidd, longtime veteran of the

Caribbean and the Atlantic, was eager to explore the other oceans. He was bred to the sea, early. Kidd was born on January 22, 1654, in Cromwell-ravaged Dundee, Scotland, a once thriving port, bullied to poverty by England; his sea-captain father died when he was five, and the Kidd family, formerly prosperous, slogged through very lean years, his mother constrained to take a widow's meager dole from the Local Seafarer's Society. The Scots, as a nation, were hard-pressed in those years, and the fatherless boy ran off to sea some time after his mother remarried. He bounced around in anonymous freedom for three decades from ship to port to ship mostly in the Caribbean, well beneath the scrutiny of government record-keepers — maybe he did some buccaneering with Morgan — before turning up on this French privateer.

The *Sainte Rose*, with Kidd and Culliford aboard, sailed across the Atlantic; the trade winds did most of the work; Kidd and Culliford probably learned to curse in French beyond the usual *merde*. This small overcrowded vessel approached Bonavista in the Cape Verde Islands and ran smack into seven ships. A perilous half hour of jockeying ensued until the lead ship hauled up a French flag. The *Sainte Rose* had stumbled into a French privateer fleet commanded by the notorious Admiral Jean DuCasse in his 44-gun flagship, *Le Hasardeux*.

Kidd now had the opportunity to meet — and observe close-up — the famed DuCasse, who would become a kind of Captain Morgan for the French, a respectable captain who could whistle up a thousand privateers to fight the king's battles, a man who would later become governor. Kidd also heard the story of DuCasse's bravery: the Gascon captain was running slaves off the coast of Africa when a giant Dutch man-of-war appeared out of the mist athwart DuCasse's tiny ship. Instead of fleeing, DuCasse threw the grappling hooks and boarded with twenty men; they set fires in four corners of the Dutch behemoth and forced the butter boxes overboard or below deck, then spiked shut the hatches. His ship, thinking all was lost, had sailed away; he signaled for it to return, which it did very nervously. DuCasse, hero, later sailed the Dutch prize into La Rochelle.

Now DuCasse, tall, thin, a touch dandified, commanded this privateer mission, whose backers included the king of France. Their goal was to take Dutch Surinam — a rich hub for slaves and sugar — and repay Louis 300 slaves for his paperwork, that is, his permission. The crew of *Sainte Rose*

voted to join DuCasse's little fleet. Plans be damned; Surinam sounded promising.

At the time, England, France, and Holland were squabbling over the carcass of New Spain, gnawing an island here and there. Stakes were high. These Caribbean islands turned out to be the lynchpins of empire. (Barbados alone would export more to England in 1715 than *all* the North American mainland colonies combined.) Bridgetown, Barbados, already dwarfed Manhattan. The fortune of the first Englishman to die a millionaire, William Beckford, came mainly from West Indies trade and sugar plantation on Jamaica.

Within days, the eight-ship French fleet encountered a Spanish vessel from Havana; they chased down the ship and, as they closed in, fired a warning shot across the bow. The Spaniards, far outnumbered, lay by. The French privateer captains held a conference aboard *Le Hasardeux*. Kidd and Culliford later heard all the details, learning about a *finesse capture*, about tightroping the line between piracy and privateering.

Any of the French ships had the firepower to take the Spaniard, but the niggling problem remained that technically France and Spain were at peace. One French captain claimed he had heard a rumor that Spain had joined the Dutch but DuCasse dismissed this as wishful thinking. Here was this rich prize, what could they do?

The council decided that the *Sainte Rose* — which DuCasse said held no valid commission — would make the capture, and then the rest of them would *quietly* share the plunder.

Captain Fantin, backed by the likes of Kidd and Culliford, boarded the Spanish vessel, locked up the crew, and hoisted out the cargo. The French ships divvied up 50,000 pounds of tobacco, 2,500 leather hides, tons of dyewood from Campeche, and 4,000 pieces of eight.

The men of the *Sainte Rose* — in addition to their share of the cargo — decided they preferred this new, more heavily armed vessel, and voted to move en masse over to the freshly caulked Spanish prize, a fast sailer with sixteen guns.

Prospects were now looking up for Kidd and shipmate Culliford aboard a fine Spanish ship with a rowdy 120-man crew as they sailed in a squadron along with hardy DuCasse to attack Surinam (Dutch Guiana), a place with at least 50 sugar plantations and 1,500 slaves. Forty-year-old DuCasse ached for a big victory to prove himself to his important backers and to the king.

In the predawn darkness, DuCasse eased his vessels near the mouth of the harbor of Paramaibo, Surinam, ready to pounce at daylight. At the sun's first rays, perfectly positioned, his little fleet was stunned to discover seven armed Dutch ships sitting in the harbor, including a 50-gun man-of-war. The Hollander crews scrambled out of hammocks to man the guns while harbor batteries pounded the French. DuCasse had banked on a slave revolt, which never happened; instead, slaves fought alongside Dutch soldiers, and eighty-four Jewish settlers even joined the fight. The French were routed; to salve their wounds, the French fleet (with Kidd and Culliford on the Spanish prize) sailed along the coast to attack little Berbiche at the narrow mouth of the river. Again they were trounced, when fort musket fire proved surprisingly deadly. To save face, the huge French force extorted a small ransom of 125 barrels of sugar from the Dutch to leave the harbor; even that piddling prize had to be returned later when the *Sainte Rose* beached itself in a later mission nearby.

Kidd and Culliford were aboard this reeling French fleet near Barbados when the stunning news hit on July 9, 1688: England three weeks earlier had declared war on France. King William III — a hump-nosed, blunt-speaking Protestant zealot imported from Holland — bore a lifelong hatred for Catholic France. War had been inevitable.

The declaration of war was sweet music to DuCasse's ears, adding a dozen ripe *English* islands to his list of Dutch targets. Culliford and Kidd and the half dozen English crewmen, however, found themselves in an awkward position, but the French privateers pegged them as the kind of mercenaries who wouldn't do anything stupid for king or country. The French, it turned out, miscalculated.

DuCasse rendezvoused with other French ships near Martinique and found himself outranked, forced to take orders from the *Governeur-Generale* of the French West Indies, Comte de Blenac. The comte decided to attack St. Christopher's (St. Kitts), which was wealthy and then *jointly* owned by the French and English.

The idea of the French and English sharing anything, let alone a small island, sounds like a bad joke; to make the arrangement even stranger, this oasis of sugar and tobacco plantations was divided into quarters, with north and south swatches to the English, and east and west to the French. While the English could travel a rutted mountain path between their zones, the French had to either walk along the English coastline or sail to their settlements. On July 17, a French fleet of twenty-two ships, including DuCasse and the Spanish prize with Kidd and Culliford, glided menacingly by; the Irish Catholics — the white menials in the English Caribbean — revolted over to the French. The French and Irish looted and burned the houses of the English who retreated en masse to Fort Charles, a large squat sturdy fortress on the coast with timber walls reinforced by heavy earthenworks.

The Irish — many originally prisoners of war deported by Cromwell — had shown their true loyalties. "We have an enemy in our bowels," complained Governor Codrington.

On July 19 in the tropical torpor, the French fleet unleashed a heavy naval bombardment of Fort Charles, which held about 1,000 English women and children, and 450 fighting men. A later English dispatch disparagingly noted that a dozen French ships fired 970 rounds at the fort "and killed a turkey, a dog and three horses." The next day's mortar fire did little damage as well. Comte de Blenac decided to employ a classic siege strategy, which would require lots of manual labor. Over the next two weeks, the French dug a deep trench on the inland side of the fort to fully isolate it; they also labored to raise an earthenwork circumvallation, so that protected cannon could be moved closer and closer. DuCasse, disgusted by the slow efforts, tried to convince the comte to mount cannon on a steep hill overlooking the fort. The comte refused to assign any men, but DuCasse took a few of the privateers to drag six cannon up the steep slope; once there, the English were at the mercy of a rain of ten-pound balls.

At the end of July, Comte de Blenac launched his massive land attack, featuring the *Sainte Rose* privateers, eager to come ashore to pillage and eat the Englishmen's beef and perhaps abuse his women and slaves. Blenac ordered 110 of the privateer crew of 130 to join the French forces; he left 20 men, including the Englishmen, on board to guard the ship. The fall of St. Christopher's to the French appeared imminent. The privateers, cutlasses glinting in the bright sun, rowed ashore and marched down the beach.

The twenty men left to guard the ship passed the time the way most sailors did with leisure: boozing, dicing, sharpening their knives, smoking pipes. The smell of gunpowder hung in the heavy air of the harbor; the sun roasted the metal cannon. The hours passed. Robert Culliford and William Kidd stood whispering in the tropical heat on the deck of the French privateer in the harbor of Basseterre, St. Christopher's. The gentle lapping of the waves was pierced by the far-off pop-pop of gunfire. Kidd and Culliford listened to the singsong patois of the bored Frenchmen, chatting, joking.

Kidd, the senior man at age thirty-five, then orchestrated the attack. He waited until the tide was clearly going out; he scanned the shore to make sure no troops were returning. He noticed one Frenchman going to perch himself on the head. Kidd gave the signal. The eight men quietly drew their daggers and crept forward. Kidd assigned a French throat to each Englishman. If their attempt to steal the ship failed, they would all be killed. If the Frenchmen succeeded in ringing the alarm bell or firing the cannon, their chances of escape would be slim. The twitter of French ceased; the deadly slash-and-wrestle among twenty men began.

Culliford slit a throat; the rest hacked away as best they could. They tossed the Gallic dozen overboard, both dead and alive. The eight men from Britain chopped the thick anchor cables, unfurled the sails, and headed across the Narrows to the nearby island of Nevis. The ship moved achingly slowly.

Wrote Colonel Codrington, commander in chief of English forces in the Caribbean: "They set upon the [French] killing some and wounding others, soon overcame them without the loss of one Englishman and brought the ship hither. [It] is now fitting for their Maj:ties Service; the Captain's name is William Kid, which ship with my two sloops, is all the strength we can make at sea and is very inconsiderable in comparison w. their ffleet [of 22 ships]."

The eight men received a hero's welcome in war-torn Nevis, probably the first hero's welcome of their lives. Kidd especially enjoyed it, and he also enjoyed being ushered into the governor's office for a drink. Now Kidd was "Captain Kidd" for the first time, commanding his own 16-gun ship that he could take privateering against the French. Colonel Codrington added four guns to the vessel and they renamed it *Blessed William*, ostensibly after the new king, but with perhaps a wink to Kidd himself.

The situation in the Caribbean was growing desperate for the English; St. Christopher's fell on August 5; the English troops had not been paid for six years, and, according to an eyewitness, arrived "almost naked" on Nevis. The French devastated the English sections of St. Christopher's, as Comte de Blenac hauled off boatloads of portable plunder and gave his blessing to an orgy of destruction. They burned the houses of all the English, except those willing to convert to Catholicism: only three families took the offer. During the weeklong mayhem, 2,000 farm animals went unfed, and died. DuCasse, with eight warships at his disposal, wanted immediately to attack Antigua, Nevis, Montserrat, but Comte de Blenac hesitated, concentrating instead on returning to safe Martinique to auction his loot.

The English citizens, who never expected the French to waffle, braced for the next attack. They frantically awaited the reinforcements from England of soldiers, ships, and ammunition, promised for that summer. (They would not arrive until almost a year later.) On Montserrat, the Irish outnumbered the English 800 to 300, an uneasy situation for the English. Anguilla fell and the French propped up an Irishman as puppet governor.

Captain Kidd and his cadre of men

would now play a small but key role in continuing the war effort until the Royal Navy arrived. Word spread that the *Blessed William*, an English privateer ship, was fitting out, and rogues of all sorts drifted in and signed up. To later generations this might represent a forgotten chapter in a forgotten war, but at the time, these battles, in which Kidd fought, seemed hugely important. Ran one English report to the Crown: "The preservation of the English interest in America now depends wholly on the success of arms, and the French are masters of the sea, exceeding us both in ships and number of men ashore."

Tired of waiting for help from London, Colonel Codrington hired Captain Kidd to sail on September 26 from Antigua to Barbados (315 miles) — along with Codrington's own two sloops — to try to get troops and ammunition from that island located farther away from the current front lines of battle. He also encouraged Kidd to try to pick up some stray Frenchmen to ferret out the enemy's plans.

Codrington, one of the wealthiest planters in the Caribbean, owned huge sugar plantations on Barbados; the Crown had also granted to his family in 1685 the entire island of Barbuda to use in an ambitious plan to breed slaves, much like a horse stud-farm.

More than a month later, Kidd had not returned and Codrington dipped his quill to write a report stating he was "apprehensive of their ill success" just as the *Blessed William* reached Antigua. Kidd, with Culliford in his crew, returned triumphant, one bright spot in a bleak war. They had surprised a French brigantine and two French sloops, loading water at the island of Dominique, a place "inhabited only by Indians." Kidd aimed his cannon at the vessels, and the Frenchmen scatttered into the woods. Kidd hauled back the three prizes; the auction money was shared out among captain and crew.

Kidd also helped land some unexpected reinforcements. He got word to Captain Hewetson, a privateer commanding a 40-gun, 150-man ship, who had convoyed a merchantman toward Bermuda, to sheer off to Nevis to see whether Codrington wanted to commission him. The wealthy planter was thrilled to hire him. (French war reports call Hewetson a *"scélérat cruel"* ("vicious rogue") and a *"soudard"* ("old mercenary/ruffian").

During a frenetic Christmas, Colonel Codrington tried to light on some plan to scare the French into not attacking. He chose Mariegalante, a small French island in the Windward group off Guadeloupe. While Jamaica and Barbados anchored the

139

English Caribbean colonies, and Martinique and Sainte Domingue provided the backbone of the French, there were far too many other islands for the limited resources of both powers to defend. The war devolved into a game of cat and mouse, as a marauding force tried to select an enemy island at a moment of weak defense, when no home fleet cruised nearby. The French picked off Anguilla and St. Christopher's; now the English targeted Mariegalante, a ten-mile wide disc of sugar plantations, first discovered in 1493 by Columbus and named after his ship *Maria Galanda*; beset by droughts, it hovered like a moon in the orbit of bigger French Guadeloupe.

At the war's outbreak, a couple of French Huguenots had fled Mariegalante, defecting over to the English; they now offered to help Codrington. On the day after Christmas, in a cozy tavern on Antigua, Codrington discussed final orders with Captains Hewetson and Kidd, in a conversation punctuated by rum punches. (Recipe: "Rum, Water, Lime-Juice, Egg yolk, Sugar with a little nutmeg scrap'd on top.") Codrington placed Colonel Hewetson in charge of the attacking force, which would include Hewetson aboard the 40-gun *Lion*, Captain Kidd on the 20-gun *Blessed William*, one Captain Perry in the 10-gun *Speedwell*, and Codrington's two troop-carrying sloops, *Barbuda* and *Hope*.

The mission for the captains and men was clear: wreak havoc on Mariegalante and collect your pay wherever you can. This was: "No prey, no pay"; Codrington in time of war was legally transforming this 1,000-person French colony of 61 square miles into a giant treasure chest, a scavenger's paradise.

In that era when military salaries were often delayed, the practice of allowing soldiers to plunder and sailors to pillage at sea was commonplace. "It is lawful for all . . . seamen," stated a proclamation of 1664, "to take . . . as pillage without further . . . accompt to be given . . . all such goods and merchandize as shall be found by them . . . upon or above the gun deck of the [prize] ship." Looting was a perq of war.

Governor Codrington, however, knowing full well how plunder might lead to rape and torture, especially among the ne'er-do-well crews of Kidd and Hewetson, also ordered that the Articles of War, both military and naval, be read aboard each ship.

On December 27, the 540 sailors and landsmen, dressed in whatever old clothes they chose, lined up on the decks of the five ships; they carried their own weapons. Aboard the *Blessed William*, the drummer played a brief roll, then Captain Kidd read aloud from the solemn Articles of War. Death by hanging for treason, cowardice, mutiny. It was a harrowing list. And for some of these men, these harsh, strict words delivered an unpleasant flashback to their days in the Royal Navy.

The five ships sailed out of Falmouth Harbor on Saturday, December 28, tacking out into the Atlantic for the 100-mile zigzag journey to Mariegalante; they gathered at sea on Sunday night; the men sharpened their cutlasses and cleaned their pistols. Kidd helped Hewetson gauge where to lay by, so that a predawn sail on Monday, December 30 would land them exactly at sunrise at a beach four miles from the island's main town of Grand Bourg. Kidd pegged it right and the ships, sails furled, clustered just off the deserted beach. They lowered pinnaces, loaded them with men, and ferried 440 soldiers ashore. Hewetson led the land force along the coast road to Grand Bourg. The few French troops quickly mustered to fight skirmishes, lay ambushes — all to buy time for their citizens to flee. Kidd, meanwhile, directed the little fleet in a scissors movement into the harbor. He pounded the town.

The two English forces overwhelmed the French; the townspeople rushed to gather what they could carry off of family heirlooms and jewels, then raced along little paths into the woods, leaving Grand Bourg at the mercy of the invaders. With the sun setting, Hewetson let the privateers spend the night looting the abandoned homes, searching for hidden valuables, drinking the Frenchmen's wine. These seamen slept in beds still redolent from the French families. Young Culliford was elbow-deep in petticoats. Kidd, for his part, easily captured two merchant ships in the harbor, newly arrived from France.

The next day, the English found a couple of slaggard Frenchmen who had tried to hide instead of run. After threatening unspeakable pain, they found out from them that the French governor and citizens, along with their slaves, were hiding in a little enclave about twelve miles away. No cannon protected it; no provisions were stocked there.

Colonel Hewetson dispatched a letter to the governor demanding surrender; the governor replied that he would answer by twelve noon tomorrow.

Hewetson knew the Frenchman was stalling, especially when on the following day no answer arrived. Kidd came ashore and he, Hewetson, and the other officers debated what to do. They decided that it was too risky to march the men over narrow paths so far from the ships, especially since the French might have sent a pirogue off to Martinique to get help.

They ordered the men to carry the choicest goods near the shore onto the ships, and destroy everything else. Most of the 400 men turned into a moving company, spending the next four days toting valuables from the homes to the dockside, there to be ferried to *Blessed William* and *Lion*, hoisting the loot aboard by runner and tackle. The rest of the men fanned out, scavenging the manor houses of sugar plantations, then setting fire to fifty sugar works, torching cane fields and the sugar in giant cakes. The smell of burnt sugar filled the air. The men who had been cow hunters on Isle à Vache and Hispaniola volunteered to slaughter the livestock. They slit the throat of terrified beast after terrified beast until some of these privateers were literally drenched in blood. The men killed 2,000 horses and cows because there wasn't enough time to take them, nor enough cargo space to transport them home. For four days, the attacking force gorged on fresh beef, roasted in the abandoned kitchens of the French.

"Tho' we have not done ourselves the benefit that a greater force would have enabled us to do," reported Colonel Codrington, "yet we have sufficiently mischiefed our Enemies and in some measure revenged the Injuries done us at St. Xtophers."

The English had three men killed and eighteen wounded, while the French lost as many as twenty men, with dozens more wounded.

By January 5, Kidd, Culliford, and the others started the return voyage to Antigua; Hewetson had plunked half his crew aboard one of the captured French ships; the prize crew, drunk on French wine, fell to leeward. This was the constant problem of Caribbean sailing — where stupendously steady breezes (outside of hurricane season) blew from east to west. If you missed your latitude mark, you had to tack your way back. The delay of Hewetson's prize crew seemed a small worry at the time. Kidd and Culliford and hundreds of others in Antigua counted their legal booty and celebrated.

A sloop came suddenly into Falmouth Harbor. A man raced to the governor's mansion with bad news. An English regiment of 600 men from Barbados under Sir Timothy Thornhill, after a successful attack upon tiny St. Bart's, had attempted to capture St. Martin's and was now trapped by Admiral DuCasse.

The St. Bart's campaign, which had lulled Thornhill by its ease, had been a study in the "gentlemanly art of warfare";

Thornhill had routed the French and demanded surrender; when the governor had balked at the terms, Thornhill started burning houses, threatening that after three days he would extend no quarter to anyone; two days later the French governor surrendered; that night Thornhill treated the governor and the local friar to a fine meal. "The major-general [Thornhill] so well warmed the Friar with good Madera wine," wrote an eyewitness, "that he spoke Latin so fluently upon transubstantiation that he confounded himself." Thornhill sent all plunder and French males over ten years of age to England's Nevis while he shipped the women and children to French St. Christopher's. Sir Timothy also kindly allowed the French governor to keep some of his negroes, horses, arms, and apparel, and send them to St. Christopher's as well.

Thornhill expected to repeat his success on St. Martin's — a plum possession boasting natural salt-ponds and sugar — but he came in for a rude shock. Wily Captain DuCasse of the 40-gun *Le Hasardeux*, at the head of fleet of three warships, a brigantine, and a sloop, trapped Sir Timothy's force of 600 men. DuCasse's arrival forced Sir Timothy's flotilla of small transport ships to scatter. DuCasse lobbed cannonballs at the English troops while the local French forces rallied and retook the main fort at Marigot, pinning down Sir Timothy. The next day, smelling victory, DuCasse the privateer flew "Bloody Colors," the blood-red flag that meant no quarter unless immediate surrender. The English, after sending off a boat for help, tried to stall for time.

Colonel Codrington instantly dispatched Hewetson in the *Lion*, with only half his crew to St. Martin's, as well as Kidd in the *Blessed William* and one of the governor's own sloops, for a total of 380 men. The English aimed to make the sail in a day and arrive at dawn to surprise the French ships packed in the harbor. Kidd ordered all sail, as did Hewetson, and they played every trick of wind but found themselves about a league from St. Martin's as the sun glinted over the horizon. DuCasse's lookouts were alert, and the French squadron slipped anchor and sailed out to meet the English. The French had almost double the firepower and better sailing ships and more seasoned crews.

The arriving English, however, at first, had the wind; both sides lined their ships up for a traditional line of battle. Both sides would pass each other, like targets in an arcade game, and fire. (It was surprisingly hard to sink a wooden ship, unless several shots hit the side as it crested above the waterline; cannonballs were aimed to rake the sails, fell the masts, and land where the shower of splinters would porcupine the crew.)

"DuCasse gave us his broadside smartly before we fired a gun," recounted an unidentified "gentleman" aboard Colonel Hewetson's ship. The English, when at closer range, returned cannon fire. Sharpshooters on both vessels tried to pick off opposing crewmen as the rows of ships glided by each other. DuCasse in *Le Hasardeux* with 250 men and 40 guns led the French line; Hewetson with 75 men and 40 guns in the undermanned *Lion* guided the English. All the ships passed one another in this strange ritual, decks nearly empty, men below feverishly loading and reloading cannon. The ships tacked, re-formed the line, and this time the French vessels, being faster sailers, gained the wind. For agonizing minutes as they passed, the two sides bombarded each other, shredding sails and rigging. The only Englishman hurt was a sharpshooter who, as he was raising his gun, took a musket ball in the thumb. The English then called a council of the captains. Hewetson was ill, so more responsibility fell on Kidd. Since the English had less firepower and because their third ship, the sloop, was miserably slow and unarmed, Kidd decided to try to board the French. This was the bold choice, the privateer choice. The English tacked way wide to try for the wind, but failed to out-angle the French; for the third time the ships passed in a line taking shots at one another, with the French upwind. The French landed a couple of prime shots into the *Lion*'s side, and several more into sails and rigging.

The English tried a fourth time to gain the wind, and this time they succeeded; Culliford and others readied the grappling hooks. They hung pistols in their sashes. But at the last instant, the French bore away south toward St. Christopher's, and did not engage. The English ships rushed to shore to rescue Sir Timothy and his 600; the French land forces tried to pin the major down in a skirmish, but he managed to start loading some of his men onto boats; then DuCasse appeared again on the horizon, adding to his fleet yet another ship, a giant Guineaman, i.e., a slaver, with thirty-plus guns.

Now, the French completely having the wind on their return, sailed down on the English, who barely had time to scurry out of the cul-de-sac harbor. The English saw the French heading straight for them as though to board, so the English decided to lay by and prepare for the hand-to-hand attack. Kidd's rough men of the Caribbean much preferred hand-to-hand to the tactical, detached, aim-and-fire, count-the-wounded approach of a line-of-battle.

The moment of confrontation approached: six French ships to three under-manned English. DuCasse vs. Hewetson and Kidd. Culliford on deck, cutlass in hand, pistol in sash.

We have an account by DuCasse of what happened next. "I proposed to the governor to board their flagship . . . he praised my conduct and my bravery . . . but at the first mention of the word *'abordage'* [boarding], a flock of fifty miserable citizens became petrified and we judged because of this *'de ne pas jouer si gros jeux'* [not to throw such big dice, i.e., not to take such a risk]."

The two sides fired broadsides again and the French, now on the landside, pounded Sir Timothy, who was forced to scamper into the woods. Night was falling, and Kidd and Hewetson and Perry conferred again in a Council of War and decided to spend the night in a broad tack to be absolutely assured of gaining the wind advantage at dawn. At midnight, the sleepless sailors tacked the ship.

In the morning, as the sun peeked over the waves, the English bore down on the French. Once again the French veered off. Once again DuCasse had wanted to attack but the general had refused.

The English quickly loaded up Sir Timothy's men without a single casualty and escaped. The ships had rescued the key English land force in the Caribbean. Colonel Hewetson later recalled the attack on Mariegalante and on St. Martin's. "[Kidd] was with me in two engagements against the French, and fought as well as any man I ever saw."

The ships returned to Antigua. The citizens threw a banquet for Hewetson and Kidd. They toasted them with "English Lemonade," a tasty mixture of Canary Island wine, sugar, lemon juice, cinnamon, nutmeg, clove, and a bit of amber essence.

The captains banqueted and received some rewards in silver, but for Kidd's crewmen, the rescue of Sir Timothy shaped up as a pretty empty affair: they had tasted a traditional line-of-battle fight that served them up as target practice for the enemy with little chance for plunder for themselves; they received the thanks of Sir Timothy but no cash.

Kidd's privateer men were restless; in whispers in a tavern, they proposed to him that they all go off pirating, attacking Spanish and French ships and towns. That fine ship, the *Blessed William*, they said, was being squandered in patriotic folderol. Kidd refused.

A week later on the night of February 2,

when Kidd was ashore, his crew, led by Robert Culliford, William Mason, and Samuel Burgess, stole the *Blessed William* out of Falmouth Harbor, Antigua, and away from Captain Kidd, who was left high and dry. On board was Kidd's £2,000 in booty, as well as an ample supply of arms and ammunition. Codrington complained that the loss could not have come at a worse time. "Most of the crew were formerly pirates," he said, "and I presume liked their old trade better than any that they were likely to have here."

As many as eighty men went off aboard that stolen ship; among them was veteran John Brown (whom Kidd later allowed to sign aboard the *Adventure Galley*). When later asked why they had run off with the *Blessed William*, Brown replied: "We were disoblidged by Captain Kidd's ill behaviour to us." (At least that's what the polite clerk wrote down.) Blunt Hewetson had a different take about what the men perceived as ill behavior. "His men wanted to go a-pirateering and he refused and his men seized upon the ship."

Clearly, thirty-six-year-old Kidd and twenty-three-year-old Culliford were at the crossroads of their lives. Culliford chose piracy; Kidd chose respectability. Their paths would cross again: the pirate and the pirate hunter.

Chapter Five

"New Spain for pirates was a prey offered by Divine Providence, they lived to pillage it."

— Hubert Deschamps

Governor Codrington expected the pirates to head north to the smugglers' haven of St. Thomas, a Danish island. Instead, Robert Culliford and the mutineers in the *Blessed William* headed south toward the Spanish Main. William Mason now commanded the stolen ship, while Samuel Burgess was quartermaster. And Robert Culliford was that promising young thief of whom everyone expected great things, clearly the captain's favorite. The crew's plan was to steal enough money or food to victual the ship for a pirate voyage to the Red Sea. So the men, hungry for plunder, went to the piggy bank known as New Spain, knowing well the

153

fading hidalgos couldn't protect their far-flung empire.

From a small, single-decked Spanish coasting vessel, the men provided themselves with fish, fowl, Indian corn, and forty pieces of eight. They let the vessel go. After this hors d'oeuvre, the pirates sailed northeasterly where they took a Spanish barcalonga, "out of which they took 400 pieces of eight and several boxes of sweetmeats worth about £30, and eight black men" as well as piles of clothing. (Pirates, it appears from numerous depositions, loved to steal clothes and often made their victims strip naked.)

As for the "eight black men," while pirates sometimes allowed *already* freed slaves to serve as equal crewmembers, most pirates were not Great Emancipators. A slave — worth ten ounces of gold — was simply too valuable a commodity to free cavalierly. Culliford and the others treated these eight bondmen of African descent as booty, chattel to be sold.

They didn't fire a single shot in taking these ships; they merely raised their swords in the sun and screamed bloody oaths to scare their outnumbered prey into submission.

Now, the pirates, in the grand tradition of the buccaneers who raided the Spanish Main, decided to terrorize a *land* target next, a small Spanish island lying sixty leagues from Barbados. Just south of the main harbor, they anchored and sent their armed men ashore in boats, surprising the town, corralling dozens of men, women, and children. The pirates — Robert Culliford, William Mason, Samuel Burgess — demanded a ransom to return the hostages and depart; when their demands weren't met quickly enough, they started burning houses to accelerate the negotiations. The local Spaniards handed over more than 100 sacks of cacao nuts and sweets, worth 2,000 pieces of eight.

The pirates now needed a place to sell their stolen cargo, so they headed to New York City, home port for several of the crew, including quartermaster Samuel Burgess.

Reaching New York in May, they had no difficulty finding merchants to buy their stolen goods. They sold the eight black men for the slightly off market price of £20 each, generating a sum that would buy the pirates 72 gallons of rum.

Culliford later mentioned that they sold everything except the clothes, which they shared equally. So they must have sauntered along Wall Street wearing some Spaniard's silk finery, a frilly shirt and a sash; these habitually barefoot men teetered on ill-fitting silver-buckled pumps to impress the barmaids.

When the pirates in the *Blessed William* hit New York harbor, they found a city in deep turmoil. The Catholic governor had fled when Dutch William had assumed the throne of England in late 1688. Now a bullying merchant of German extraction, Jacob Leisler, with no love for the town's richest English citizens, had taken over in the name of Protestant cause and King William. (Whether Leisler's claims to power — a vaguely addressed letter received from the Crown, powers granted by a hand-picked council — were legitimate would be argued in courts for almost a decade after his death.)

Jacob Leisler, believing God on his side, welcomed the pirate ship.

A lawyer, Thomas Newton, charged that Leisler had hired the "pirate from the West Indies" (i.e., *Blessed William*) ostensibly to defend New York City, but really so that he could escape on the ship whenever a legitimate governor arrived. "He has put all the merchants' stores on board the pirate without giving them so much as a receipt."

The pirates, blessed with the acting governor's approval, swaggered through the narrow streets. Petticoats flapped on Petticoat Lane. Pirates bought liquor at any of the 100-plus private Dutch homes, which doubled as informal taverns.

Jacob Leisler granted a privateer's commission to Captain Mason in the *Blessed William* (this ship stolen by French privateers from the Spanish, then stolen by English patriots from the French, then stolen by pirates from the English). He authorized Mason to sail with two other ships to attack the French along the Atlantic seaboard north of Massachusetts. A shrewd merchant, Leisler also invested in the venture.

In the crisp late-spring weather of May, Culliford stood on deck of the *Blessed William* as it sailed north out of New York, along the safer Long Island Sound, then out around Cape Cod and on up the coast toward Port Royal (modern-day "Annapolis Royal"). A fleet from Boston had conquered this long-standing French settlement about a month earlier, extracting a modest ransom from the citizens. The conquered town with a valid paid ransom receipt was supposed to be safe, but the New York attackers conveniently claimed that Port Royal had broken the ransom agreement by changing commanders.

The *Blessed William* and two other privateers sailed into Port Royal and the several hundred men plundered first, then laid waste to the place in the tradition of Henry Morgan's burning of Panama City. "Leisler's man of war made desolation there," wrote one Boston merchant. Unlike Governor Codrington in the Caribbean, Leisler had not demanded that the Articles of War be read aloud on board, so the sailors ran amok, raping, burning, and hacking their way from house to house, looking for hidden jewels. Their orgy of violence received added fuel when the men captured a huge supply of French wine and brandy. The privateers loaded up as much booty as they could carry.

The little flotilla, after this jolly sack, sailed north, arriving on August 1 at Ile de Perce. They surprised at anchor two ships just in from France: *L'Esperance* frigate and pink *St. Pierre*. The privateers cornered the vessels, forcing the frightened crew to scatter ashore, and then they trashed the harbor, smashing eighty small fishing sloops as well as the equipment for drying the season's catch. The men grabbed an extra sail and loaded in as much fish as they could carry, then spoiled the rest, urinating, defecating on piles of fish, destroying a season's hard labor. They gutted the fishing village. After setting fires, they departed, carrying off both ships.

The privateers renamed the *L'Esperance*, which was hauling twenty tons of salt and 150 Kentell fish, the *Horne Frigate* and gave the command to twenty-four-year-old Robert Culliford. He was "Captain Culliford" for the first time.

This bully fleet, cruising southward, captured more French ships, bringing their capture card to eight, some of them dinky flyboats. Captain Mason convinced the men to take the plunder from Port Royal — the wine, brandy, and furs — the heart of their profits, and load it onto two captured ketches, which Mason then sent back to New York. A likely reason for sending this booty away early, under-protected, was that the men were drinking up all the profits, pirate-style, nicking off the necks of bottles and filling hatfuls from the brandy barrels.

This New York privateer flotilla decided to stop in Boston in mid-August on their way south, before weathering the Cape. It was there that they learned that three French privateers, who had been ransacking Martha's Vineyard, had stumbled onto their two booty-filled ketches off the eastern tip of Long Island and recaptured them for the French.

This disaster prompted these pirate-patriots to drink away their disappointment in the taverns of Boston; their curses rang too loud in the old Puritan port town; their bawdy songs hit a sour note.

"A number of tradesmen one day did combine,

With a rum-ti-dum, tum-ti dum
    terro,
To the best of their skill, to make
    something divine,
    With a row-de dow, row-de dow
    derro.
The first was a Carpenter, he
    thought it fit,
    With a rum-ti-dum, tum-ti dum
    terro,
With a bonny broad axe to give it a
    slit,
    With a row-de dow, row-de dow
    derro.
Then in came a Furrier, so bold
    and so stout,
    With a rum-ti-dum, tum-ti dum
    terro,
And he with a bear-skin did fur it
    about,
    With a row-de dow, row-de dow
    derro.
The fishmonger next. . . ."

Court records from August 1691 are lost, but Culliford and others probably took a turn in the stocks for blasphemy or drunkenness, harangued by the good citizens. "The Gouvernour of Boston and some of the chiefest in town," complained Captain Mason, "have apprehended my men going about their lawfull occasiones and detaines [them] in prison."

After a long week, the pirates escaped the Puritans.

The fleet sailed back to New York, where a Vice Admiralty Court, commissioned by Governor Leisler, condemned five of the six French ships as legitimate prizes of war.

In a smoky dockside tavern, New York merchants, at auction, bid £2,000 for ships and cargo — mostly salt, fish, and a few hundred animal skins. After deducting expenses of food, gunpowder, etc., the captains computed the individual shares, which turned out to be quite disappointing. The divvying turned ugly. Several men complained they were not given a full share; one captain countered by claiming some didn't deserve any payoff. Louis DuBois "was a good man on shore but no seaman [and] . . . his gone [gun] was not fitt for service"; Pieter Cavellier "sayde he would redder be shott as to remaine aboard"; as for Cornelis Gelderse, "his gune was stopt wth a bullet about halfe way . . . and did severall times misfire."

These pirates who had come up from the Caribbean on Kidd's old ship were frustrated, eager to leave New York for warmer waters, juicier prey. Enough of this low-reward government work, they were ready to hit the Indian Ocean.

Mason and Culliford and the others decided to ditch the *Blessed William* and shift over to the remaining French prize, *L'Union* of La Rochelle. They spent October and November in New York preparing this fine 200-ton vessel, scraping the hull, adding cannon, and stocking up on liquor and biscuit. They renamed the ship *Jacob*, in honor of the acting governor, who now granted them a new privateering commission.

With a crew of about eighty-five, the *Jacob* left New York in early December of 1690, sailing north through Hell Gate, via Long Island Sound to Rhode Island. The captain was again William Mason, the crew's quartermaster, Samuel Burgess, and this time, the captain's quartermaster was Robert Culliford. In Rhode Island, veteran sea dog James Gilliam joined the crew. Just after Christmas, the *Jacob* headed out into the Atlantic, and promptly turned pirate, voting to take ships of *all* nations.

Within a week, they captured a Dutch vessel, then a Portuguese one. That promising lad Culliford, trained in the Caribbean, was now on his way to becoming the captain of the most lethal pirate ship in the Indies.

Chapter Six

After Captain Kidd's *Blessed William* had been stolen out from under him in Falmouth Harbor, Antigua, in February of 1690, Kidd had suddenly found himself stranded, both shipless and jobless. He decided to stay in the Caribbean, and Governor Codrington soon hired him to command some of the English privateer ships fighting the ongoing war against France. Kidd performed such yeoman battle service for the governor that Codrington late in 1690 rewarded him by giving him a 16-gun captured French ship; they renamed it *Antigua*.

Kidd heard rumors that his *Blessed William* was in New York, working for Governor Leisler, with pirates like Culliford openly walking the streets. So, now that he had his own ship once again (and the Royal Navy had finally arrived to handle Caribbean defense for the English), Kidd opted to head north to New York City; he reached port in February 1691, missing Culliford by about two months.

Within days of stepping ashore, Captain Kidd was galled to hear stories of the *Blessed William* mutineers squandering his money on whores and drinks. Kidd quickly learned that Leisler had welcomed his mutinous former crew, even giving them privateering commissions. Kidd was furious with Leisler; his chance for revenge against the acting governor would come surprisingly soon, since the turmoil surrounding New York's government was bubbling to a head.

The newly appointed governor, Richard Sloughter, who had gotten blown off course to Bermuda, was finally on his way to the city, and in fact his support troops had already arrived. Their leader, Colonel Ingoldsby, had for the past two months been demanding that Leisler step down.

Leisler's policies were splitting the city like an ax. He rewarded his Dutch working-class supporters by swearing in a carpenter as sheriff and a bricklayer as marshall; when certain wealthy merchants refused his four percent war tax, he jailed some of them, humiliated others. "Colonel Bayard was carried round the fort walls in a chair [in chains] to terrify the people," wrote a lawyer, "and all for no other crime but speaking words against Leisler which he declares to be high treason." These class-conscious Englishmen complained to London, straining their vocabulary to vilify him. "That incorrigeable brutish coxcomb Leisler is here," wrote one, "our despott backt by the insipid mobile. . . . out of hell certainly never was such a pack of ignorant, scandalous, false, malitious, impudent, impertinent rascals herded together."

Leisler kept refusing to hand over power to Colonel Ingoldsby. So New York — this eighth of a square mile maze of narrow streets bounded by a teetering wall — became a city occupied by two opposing forces, both claiming to represent the English government. It was pathetic and ludicrous, like playground bullies at a standoff. Leisler's forces were holed up inside Fort William while English troops, representing the new governor, were quartered in the rundown City Hall and in private homes.

The tension between the two parties, divisively nicknamed Black and White, was tearing the city, undermining defense against French invasion.

On the night of March 15, 1691, the English soldiers, under Colonel Ingoldsby, circled the fort, trying to taunt Leisler's men into action. Leisler's rabble-rouser son-in-law, Jacob Milbourne, issued declarations in *Dutch* that the English troops were secretly working with Catholic sympathizers to overthrow the Protestant king and queen. Leisler's men opened fire from the fort's blockhouse, killing "Josiah Browne an old soldier and one negro" and wounding seventeen others. Leisler was also accused of firing forge-heated bullets from the cannon to set parts of the city on fire.

At the time, only one powerful armed vessel stood in the harbor, and that was Captain Kidd's *Antigua*. A cadre of wealthy merchants approached Kidd to join them in overthrowing Leisler and clearing the way for the legally appointed royal governor.

Kidd — eager for respectable employment by some of the most powerful men in colonial America — agreed. The government in exile (i.e., the rich merchants) provided him with 200 pounds of gunpowder. He already had the cannonballs. Their plan called for Kidd to bombard the blockhouse lying just outside the fort.

New York weather can be very unpredictable in late March. A storm kicked up. Fat drops of rain turned into wet snow, blanketing the city in slush. Kidd and his chilled crew positioned the *Antigua* in the harbor, its cannon aimed at the blockhouse. The storm grew, seesawing the ship, and Kidd, ever pragmatic, decided not to risk firing, with private homes so near the target. He waited, a menacing presence, snowflakes on his black gun barrels. While the storm still raged, Leisler gave orders from the fort to surrender the outlying blockhouse rather than confront Kidd.

Governor Sloughter finally arrived two days later on March 19, 1691. Even now, opposing winds prevented his ship, HMS *Archangel*, from sailing into New York harbor, but Kidd went downwind a ways and then personally ferried the new governor ashore, rowing him in his pinnace.

Sloughter read his commision and demanded three times that the fort surrender. Leisler, stalling, sent messengers; the new governor arrested the messengers. William Kidd, irritated by the lack of respect shown the new governor, cursed at and roughed up one of the messengers. (Kidd's dark roots sometimes showed through.) The English troops, under Ingoldsby, massed in front of the fort. The new governor ordered Kidd to sail around the tip of Manhattan island and train his guns upon the backside of the fort. With Kidd at his back, Leisler finally agreed to surrender.

To the small English community, Captain Kidd was a war hero, although he never had to fire his cannon. His star was burnished when Leisler complained about him, calling him a "blasphemous privateer."

Leisler's enemies had dreamed of this moment for months. Leisler told a Dutch minister "that he was spit in the face, and that he was robbed of his wig, sword and sash, and of a portion of his clothes which were torn from him, and that they abused him as raging Furies, putting irons on his legs and throwing him into a dark hole underground full of stench and filth." They had relocated Leisler from the governor's mansion to the fort's privy.

The populist tyrant's overthrow set off a dizzying round of celebrations among the wealthy English merchants. In mansions along the river, the anti-Leislers toasted their victory and plotted retribution. The well-to-do English, unlike their frugal Dutch neighbors, were known for ostentatious outfits, and they slipped into silken waistcoats with jeweled buttons, full wigs, lace cuffs. Each outdid the other to impress the new governor, trying to serve up delicacies in war-torn New York. Servants cinched the merchants' wives into narrow-waisted, floor-length, bright-colored dresses of silks and satins; any of the women up on the latest fashion trends in London wore a padded bustle, which plumped out the backside of their many-petticoated dresses; in front, a slight décolletage was de rigueur.

At one of these parties in 1691, Captain Kidd, the gruff thirty-seven-year-old Scottish sea captain, met Sarah Bradley Cox Oort, beautiful, twenty-one, the city's most eligible widow. Anyone marrying her would instantly become one of the most wealthy and powerful men in the city. She had already buried two husbands. Kidd, a man exuding physical strength and no shortage of self-confidence, charmed her.

Sarah, born in England around 1670, was the daughter of Colonel Samuel Bradley Sr., a slightly potted and impoverished retired officer who lived with his teenage daughter and two young sons, Henry and Samuel Jr., in New York City. (There's no mention anywhere of a mother still alive.)

Back in 1685, choosing from among all the young marriageable women in the city, William Cox — a very wealthy flour merchant, an elderly man with properties all over town — had selected fifteen-year-old Sarah Bradley. One can't help assuming that she was very attractive. This was clearly an arranged marriage, but what's strange about it is that it's as though Cox married the whole family. In his will, which Cox made out on July 15, 1689, he made some bequests, then left half his goods to Sarah and the other half to her young brother Samuel. He left the main house on

Pearl Street to Sarah and his current home on Wall Street to Samuel; he left 38½ acres on Saw Mill Creek in New Haarlem (modern day 73rd-74th Streets and the East River) to her younger brother Henry Bradley. He also forgave Sarah's dad, the colonel, loans over the years of hefty amounts of spending money. Cox's will implies that he and Sarah would not be having any children — since it makes no mention of *their* offspring — while it clearly spells out bonuses to be given to her brother Samuel for having a son and naming him Cox Bradley.

Husbands then often died of smallpox, or gunshot; William Cox died in a rather unusual way while people laughed. "Mr. Cox to shew his fine cloaths undertooke to go to Amboy [in East Jersey] to proclaime the King," wrote one catty letter-writer. Cox stumbled climbing out of a local canoe that was ferrying him out to a larger boat off Staten Island. "He slipt downe betwixt the canoe and the boate the water not being above his chinn, but very muddy, stuck fast in and striving to get out, bobbing his head under receaved too much water in." The writer couldn't help but point out: "There is a good rich widow left."

What the letter-writer didn't know, what no one knew at that moment, was that the government at the time in New York province, under Jacob Leisler, would tie up Cox's estate for years. Tantalus-like, Sarah Bradley and family could live in Cox's fine houses, but they could not touch any of his money or goods, thanks to Leisler's minions. (Ironically, Leisler was Sarah Bradley Cox's neighbor, a three-foot-wide alley separating the two homes.)

Auditors pegged the Cox wealth, which could magically transform the Bradley family, at an astounding £1,900 at a time when most people in rural England earned less than £10 a year. And that sum didn't include half a dozen real estate properties. Cox's immense inventory lists everything from 548 gallons of rum to 273 half barrels of flour, 21 yards of red cotton, horses, "one Negro man by name 'Titus' (£30), one Negro woman by name 'Moll' (£25), one gray horse and one bay (£11)," 75 small personal debts owed him, partial shares in voyages, a purse of wampum. Just hearing the list read must have been infuriating for Sarah. Her father, the colonel, was too cracked to fight in the courts; Sarah's brothers were both minors.

So she did what any young woman in that era would have done: she found another husband. Unfortunately, she picked a Dutch merchant named John Oort, who had telltale signs of being a gold-digger. At *his* sudden death the following year, just before Kidd arrived in town, Oort was deeply in debt to several merchants and he also owed three different widows £6 each, a sum that would keep a person in fine clothes but not launch any business ventures. And Oort, in his brief marriage to the heiress, had completely failed in his legal battles on Sarah's behalf. (The executors of Cox's estate, Leisler cronies, had demanded a £5,000 bond from Oort, which he couldn't provide.)

So now, in 1691, across the room at one of these demise-of-Leisler gatherings stood Captain Kidd. Under the candle and whale-oil light, Kidd cut a fine figure: tall, well-dressed, animated, one of the heroes of the hour. His glib wit was laced with the hint of a Scottish accent. His boisterousness rose drink by drink.

Over the next two months, Kidd laid siege to the pretty widow. A favorite courtship walk at the time was out through the land gate on Wall Street to Lover's Lane, a stone's throw from Maiden Lane. A perfect afternoon excursion for the couple would be to take a carriage ride out Wagon Way, as Broadway was still sometimes called, to visit her father on the Bradley property at Saw Mill Creek (modern day 73rd Street). They could walk amid the "pastures, water, marches, underwoods, trees, etc."

described on the deed. On the way home, they could stop at Clapp's pleasure garden, where the menu featured: "An Excellent Soupe — Beanes and bacon — roasted Lamb and Sallad — young peas — roasted chicken, and desserts: curds & Creame, or Cherries, or a dish of mulberries & Currants."

Kidd's prospects for being accepted by Sarah improved when she saw how the new governor and the Council treated him; they sent a recommendation to the Assembly to reward Kidd. He later received the biggest bounty of any of the volunteer participants, £150, enough to buy a nice toft of land and home in Manhattan.

And that respect even filtered down to saving him from abuse by the Royal Navy, no mean feat. On March 24, a few days after Leisler's capture, when the captain of Royal Navy ship HMS *Archangel* pressed away some of Captain Kidd's best sailors, the City Council immediately ordered the men restored to Kidd.

And, financially, Kidd was in far better straits than her last husband; Kidd owned his own privateer ship.

Now that he was in their inner circle, the cunning English merchants also found a way to give Kidd a bonus for his war work, one that would cost them nothing and that was — to them — attractively vindictive.

The merchants encouraged Captain Kidd on March 27 to file a Prize Court claim against a French ship that his old crew Mason and Culliford had captured half a year earlier in Canada, a vessel that had been auctioned to one of Leisler's cronies for £500. The logic ran that since Leisler was not a legal governor, then his Vice-Admiralty Court was not legal either, therefore its decisions should be vacated, including this Prize sale, allowing others to put in a claim. (Call it cosmic justice: it *was* indeed Kidd's former ship, *Blessed William*, that had made the capture.) Kidd received another £250.

As Kidd was finding acceptance and monetary rewards in New York, his love affair and courtship of Sarah moved quickly. No stack of letters exists by which to measure their love — Kidd was a most reluctant letter-writer and Sarah was illiterate, being barely able to scratch out an awkward "SK" for legal documents. But there are strong clues. From his later actions — deeply trying to avoid being branded a pirate in front of her, sending her his last gold coin — it is clear that William Kidd passionately loved Sarah. And Sarah seems to have returned the love; she remained steadfast to William during his troubles.

When she agreed to marry him, they did

not know that their wedding day would be soaked in blood.

The wealthy merchants wanted revenge upon Leisler, and so did Sarah Bradley Cox Oort, whose inheritance had been waylaid by his government's mishandling. A hastily convened Grand Jury of upstanding citizens, who just happened to be Leisler's enemies, brought back indictments for murder and treason against five men, including Jacob Leisler and his pamphleteer son-in-law, Jacob Milbourne. They charged them all with murder, stemming from that moment when Leisler follower Abraham Gouverneur had shot and killed the English soldier Josiah Brown on Stone Street, with a pistol ball, plowing a one-inch-wide, ten-inch-deep hole into Brown's chest. In addition, they also laid against them the graver charge of treason, accusing the five of levying war against the Crown "at the instigation of the devil . . . [acting as] false Traitours, Rebells and Enemyes of our said Lord and Lady the King and Queen."

Captain Kidd now had a front-row seat to observe what happens when two men refuse to plead in an English court. Both Leisler and Milbourne, instead of pleading guilty or not guilty, demanded instead to wait to find out whether the king and Parliament recognized Leisler as lawfully empowered governor. That seal of approval, which would take months to travel across the Atlantic, would clearly invalidate any treason charge, but the judge, Joseph Dudley, denied their request for delay.

Kidd watched as the new attorney general, Thomas Newton, in a packed courtroom argued that, under English law, no plea equals a guilty plea, or as he put it, "he that will not put himself upon the Enquest *de bono et male* shall have the same judgem.t as if they were found guilty by a verdict of 12 men." (The following year, Newton acted as king's counsel for the Salem witch trials; the court there took a different tack when faced with the same problem; court officers tried to "press" a plea out of eighty-two-year-old accused witch, Giles Correy, until, at 300 pounds, they crushed the old man to death.)

In this case, the two main defendants, Leisler and Milbourne, were warned at least four times about the dire consequences of not pleading. Kidd saw what happened, and would remember the hard lesson.

Judge Joseph Dudley passed sentence for treason against Leisler and Milbourne on April 17: "that they be Carryed to the place from Whence they came and from thence to the place of Execucion that there they shall be severall[y] hanged by the

Neck, and being Alive their bodies be Cutt Downe to the Earth that their Bowells be taken out, and they being Alive burnt before their faces, that their heads shall be struck off and their Bodys Cutt in four parts and which shall be Desposed of as their Maj:ties Shall Assigne."

Governor Sloughter told friends and informed fellow governors that he would prefer to wait to hear back from England before carrying out the sentence. Almost daily, however, the anti-Leislers pleaded with Sloughter to sign the death warrants. He kept refusing, until, so the gossipy story runs, he was drunk at a party at Nicholas Bayard's house, possibly Captain Kidd's engagement party, and that "the wives of the principal men threw themselves at the feet of the governor, begging him for the love of God to have compassion on them and the country" by agreeing to execute Leisler and Milbourne. He finally consented.

A Dutch minister, who despised Leisler, delivered the news to the prison just as the twenty or so prisoners were sitting down to dinner: "I have good news for you," said Domine Selyns, and he paused. "Not all of you will die." And then he turned to Leisler and Milbourne and smilingly informed them they would die in two days.

The governor allowed the execution, but he nixed some of the more grisly aspects of the sentence: the pair would *only* be hanged and beheaded. He denied a petition for mercy with 1,800 signatures on it, an enormous number in a city of 4,000 free citizens.

The partisans quickly constructed a gallows from wood that Leisler had set aside to shore up the walls of the fort. Bayard and his friends kept up an almost nonstop party, with Bayard flying a victory flag at his house.

The small English community had more to celebrate than just the demise of Leisler, because Sarah and William had chosen the day of the scheduled execution to get married. The briefest of municipal records states: "A lycense of marriage granted unto Captain William Kidd of New York, Gent., of the one part, and Sarah Oort, the widow of John Oort, late of New York, merchant, deceased, the 16th of May, 1691." (The key word is "Gent."; although the New World was much laxer than the old in bestowing the title, it was still a sign of status to be referred to in official records as "Gentleman," as opposed to, say, "mariner" or "sailor.")

So, by way of entertainment, by way of celebration, Captain Kidd and Sarah attended the hanging and beheading of the two convicted traitors. More than a thousand people turned out on that damp spring Saturday afternoon near the fort.

The sheriff escorted Leisler and Milbourne up on the ladders; nooses were placed around their necks. Leisler forgave everyone and said he had tried hard to raise a Christian family. The executioner tied a kerchief around his head. "I hope these my Eyes shall see our Lord Jesus Christ in Heaven," he said. "I am ready. I am ready."

But Leisler had to wait a moment for the last words of his son-in-law, Jacob Milbourne, who forgave his judges, but chose one man to curse. He singled out Albany merchant Robert Livingston, who had started plotting against Leisler when his cozy government contracts were canceled. Milbourne pointed at him with his chin. "You have caused the King that I must die," shouted Milbourne, "but before God's tribunal I will implead you for the same." Then he turned to his father-in-law. "We are thoroughly wet with rain, but in a little while we shall be rained through with the Holy Spirit."

The executioner yanked the ladders out from under each man; they dropped a foot and started the gangly dance. Fights broke out in the crowd; Dutchmen surged toward Livingston. Afterward, the executioner cut down the hanged bodies; a hooded axman beheaded them. Blood oozed and trickled down the wooden chopping block in the rain. The men's torsos and heads were quickly buried in unconsecrated ground.

So began the married life of William and Sarah. That night, they consummated their marriage in Sarah's grand four-poster by the river. William Kidd, whose father had died when he was five, whose life had been a struggle, was snuggled in bed with his young, wealthy wife. That night or the night after or some night after that, they in the throes of their passion conceived a daughter.

But the French didn't let Kidd linger in the marriage bed, nor did the English governor. On Kidd's fifth day of married life, an Indian named Sheeps reached New York City with reports that a French privateer had ransacked Block Island, off the eastern tip of Long Island. "I ran out of my wigwam," he told city officials. "I saw people crying, heard guns . . . The French staved all the canoes and boats." Two merchants also reported that the same French privateer, Captain Montauban in *La Machine*, had taken their vessel and that the Frenchman had kidnapped a Rhode Island pilot, so it was likely he intended to remain in these waters.

Governor Sloughter hired Kidd to protect the region, sending him out on May 25 in the *Antigua*, along with a Captain

Walkington. (Walkington was commanding the *Horne Frigate*, the French prize ship captured by Culliford in Canada and later sold.) Kidd, rushing out of port, had time to drum up only forty men, barely enough to work a few cannon.

And Kidd and Walkington did drive the privateer off the coast of Long Island. They then rounded Cape Cod, and when they reached Boston, the governor of Massachusetts Bay wanted to hire the New York privateers to go after another French ship of war, which had grabbed three fat merchant vessels on their way into Boston.

Kidd was already commissioned by New York to chase French ships, so he really didn't need this second commission from Massachusetts, unless it provided him with something of value: either crewmen (hard for Kidd to find in New York City after he had helped kill off a popular leader) or cash or provisions in wartime. The Puritan governor made a rather tight-fisted proposal to the swaggering Scot newlywed from New York.

Governor Bradstreet offered to let Kidd sign aboard forty Massachusetts citizens, "not taking any children or servants without their parents' or masters' consent," and he informed Kidd that he would have to hand over a list of all his local recruits and must deliver back every one of them within fifteen days. Bradstreet also said that, upon the ship's return, he would reimburse Kidd for food expenses, but not if they captured any prizes. He offered the captains £20 each.

Kidd, the newly minted New Yorker, countered. (We get glimpses of the captain's shrewdness.) To paraphrase Kidd: None of that asking permission to take boys or on return forcing local Massachusetts men back onshore. And none of that pennies payment . . . the Frenchman could be hundreds of miles away. Kidd was a businessman first, patriot second. He also showed a certain succintness of expression, traditionally attributed to Scotsmen.

Kidd counteroffered: "To have forty men with their arms, provisions and ammunition. Secondly, all the men that shall be wounded, which have been put in by the country, shall be put on shore, and the country to take care of them. And if so fortunate as to take a pirate and her prizes, then to bring them into Boston. Thirdly: for myself to have £100 in money; thirty pounds hereof to be paid down, the rest upon my return to Boston; and if we bring in the said ship and her prizes, then the same to be divided amongst *our* men. Fourthly, the provisions put on board must be ten barrels of pork and beef, ten barrels of flour, two hogsheads of peas and one barrel of gunpowder for the great guns. Fifthly, I will cruise on the coast for ten days' time; and if I see that he is gone off the coast, that I cannot hear of him, I will then at my return take care to set what men on shore that I have had and are *willing* to leave me or the ship."

It was a clever proposal; the Massachusetts governor immediately rejected it. A week later, Governor Bradstreet, still clearly annoyed, dashed off a letter to the new governor of New York complaining that the two New York captains had ignored this chance for a good prize and patriotic duty, and, what's worse, had carried off runaway servants and slaves for their crews. This encounter tarred Kidd in the eyes of many New Englanders. When reports came in a month later that a New York privateer had sacked Great Island off Cape Cod, Captain Kidd was the first name mentioned and repeated in false rumors across New England. (Later, it was confirmed that the pirate was someone else entirely, a Captain Tew.)

What was it about Kidd — his swagger? his vitality? his contrariness? his immense competence? — that brought so many false accusations upon his head?

The Great Island report was rubbish; Kidd had by that time sailed north to Canada. There he captured the *Saint Jean* and returned to New York City in late summer of 1691 with a prize that was valued at £577. He showed a tidy profit for his three-month cruise.

Perhaps it was the birth of his daughter, or maybe it was deliciousness of domestic life with twenty-something Sarah, but in any case, Kidd around this time agreed to settle down and become a merchant captain. The next half decade would be the calmest of Kidd's life. Now that he ranked among the wealthiest New Yorkers, Kidd turned himself away from warrior privateering and toward commerce, carrying cargo to and from the Caribbean. Before Governor Sloughter traveled north to negotiate with the Indians at Albany, he wrote a letter to Kidd's former patron, Governor Codrington in the Leeward Islands. "I have commanded Capt Kidd for their Matys Especial service here," wrote Sloughter, "but hope in a few months he may be with you *if his wife will let him.*"

That phrase "if his wife will let him" is playful and surprising in an otherwise serious letter about Indian affairs and short provisions. It implies that Sarah is strong-willed and wants William around and also that this military man loves her enough — at a chauvinist time in history when a husband could legally beat his wife — to listen to her. Codrington probably chuckled thinking of that hard-to-command Scot privateer as a newlywed.

For the next few years, Kidd worked with his lawyer, James Emott, to clear up Sarah and Samuel's estate problems. Sarah received her inheritance (valued at £600) and Kidd did the right thing, paying off the heavy debts of her ne'er-do-well second husband, John Oort. Plenty of money left, at least £400, plus Kidd's £300 or so, plus the properties, confirmed their family's prosperity. Sarah's youngest brother, Henry, died, so she and brother Samuel jointly inherited another 38½ acres up island.

During these extended months in Manhattan, a special relationship began to develop between Captain Kidd and Samuel. Kidd, then in his late thirties, who had lost contact with his own family in Scotland, began to shepherd young Samuel, then in his late teens. When the boy was nineteen in 1693, he wanted to set himself up as a merchant, but his inheritance was still two years off. So Kidd loaned him a huge stake interest-free to invest. Before leaving port, Samuel made out his will, as collateral for the loan. But the document meant more than a mere provision for paying back the loan; it is testament to the bond between the two. "Whereas my loving brother-in-law, Captain William Kidd, hath been very careful of me, and hath likewise for my encouragement, now in my minority, at my desire and request, advanced and paid unto me ye sum of £140, current money of New York, which I now employ in trade and merchandize. In consideration of his so great love unto me, as well as in recompense and full satisfaction of ye said sum of money, I do give and bequeath unto my said loving brother-in-law Captain William Kidd": his half share of two family houses, and his vacant lot on King Street. Samuel also left "one third" of the rest of his estate to the captain.

Kidd, a man who had been constantly at sea for decades, stayed now in port long enough to perform civic duties; he cemented his status as an upstanding New Yorker by serving as foreman on a Grand Jury in 1694. One of the cases he heard reveals quite a bit about New York smugglers and, more particularly, about the moral character of Kidd's future business partner, Robert Livingston.

The facts in brief: A New York sea captain, Cornelius Jacobs, while a prisoner of war in French Hispaniola, was told by Admiral DuCasse, now governor of the region, that he would be well-rewarded if he could deliver a cargo ship full of supplies. Jacobs returned to New York, and searched for a merchant greedy enough to be willing to trade with the enemy during time of war. He found Robert Livingston, and the pair agreed to ship off 403 half barrels of flour, 75 firkins of butter, 12 boxes of candles, 8 barrels of tar, 2 hogshead of bread, and 10 barrels of pork. Captain Jacobs sailing in the *Orange* told New York port officials he was heading for Jamaica, but instead went to Port au Paix in the French colony. There he traded his goods at a handsome rate and returned home with £1,500 of cargo, mostly fine linens.

Captain Jacobs later claimed that a storm had forced him into Port au Paix, where Governor DuCasse, after first confiscating vessel and goods, returned the vessel and one quarter of the goods. (An English customs official, after hearing the story, noted sarcastically: "A warme Charity in such an Enemie!")

While the *Orange* stood in New York harbor, customs officers performed a thorough search, and found hidden in the ceiling a crumpled piece of paper torn in three parts. It was a letter of recommendation from Governor DuCasse endorsing Captain Jacobs to a merchant on St. Thomas. "*Un honnête homme, nommé* Capt Jacob . . ." (An honest man named Captain Jacob.) The "honest" is a bit of Gallic wit.

A customs official, Chidley Brooks, charged that the man masterminding the scheme was Robert Livingston. "[Livingston] is one that wants not craft or Assiduity to carry on his designes, & put a fair Gloss upon the foulest Actions where his interest is concerned," wrote Brooks. "Tis certaine the provisions carried into the French by this Briggantine did in great Measure enable Mons. Ducass to invade Jamaica this last summer."

The invasion in question occured in June 1694, when DuCasse led a force of 22 vessels with 1,500 men, attacking, burning, and destroying English settlements, and carrying off 1,300 slaves. An English governor claimed the French encouraged some slaves to rape their former owners' wives and daughters.

The case of "Chidley Brooke etc. v. Barq *Orange* Cornelius Jacobs" came before Kidd's Grand Jury in October 1694. This case appeared quite promising for the prosecution, but it swiftly crumbled when all the sailors suddenly developed amnesia and refused to testify against their captain or investor, Livingston. The Grand Jury had no choice. Kidd, the foreman, returned his panel's decision of *"Sur proditiore ignoramus,"* which meant that unless new information were brought forward immediately, the defendant was free to go.

★ ★ ★

Captain Kidd continued to live the life of a merchant sea captain. He made a run south to the Caribbean, touched at Antigua, and returned north to Boston, where in January 1695, as the influential man he was, he chatted with Lieutenant Governor William Stoughton, giving him war news from the Caribbean. The fight against the French was entering its sixth year, with no end in sight. Once he returned to Manhattan, Kidd spent night after night ashore in the family mansion, the house bought by Sarah's first husband, William Cox. Together he and Sarah walked the narrow streets, picking their way through the Land Gate and out into the countryside. He watched his daughter grow out of baby clothes. But there must have been a certain restlessness in Kidd, a craving for adventure, for open-ended voyages, for battle. Kidd was respectable now; it wouldn't do for him to just sail off to the Caribbean, or to attack the French willy-nilly.

He decided that, for his next career move, he wanted to become the captain of a ship in the Royal Navy. Kidd's naivete is staggering — only matched by his gall, perhaps. The path to a captain's post in His Majesty's Navy was an arduous and serpentine one, up through the ranks from midshipman to mate to lieutenant to captain. The son of a titled aristocrat, preferably one who could afford to purchase "interest" at court, might rise faster, skipping steps. But William Kidd, the son of a dead Scottish sea captain, who could not turn to a single Navy officer to recommend him? That he would be made captain of even the HMS *Codpiece*, a worm-ridden sixth rate in perpetual drydock, was ludicrous.

Nonetheless, Kidd turned for a letter of recommendation to fellow Scot, attorney general of New York, James Graham. The letter, which encapsulates Kidd's career to date, reveals the unctuousness required back then when approaching a high-ranking official, such as William Blathwayt, Secretary of War.

I humbly presume to . . . recommend this bearer Cap|tn Wm Kid to your honors favor. He is a gentleman that has done his Maj|ty signall service in the takeing of S|t Christophers Station and some other islands in the west Indies, was also assisting to Coll Ingoldsby & Coll Sloughter in quelling the disorders that happened here on their arrival for which service he was notticed by our Assembly. He

*hath likewise taken a prize upon
the banks of N. Foundland and
since that time [1692–1695] applyed
himself to private trafficque. He is
now bound with his Brigantine for
London, with design to enter into
his Majltys service if he can have
any encouragement. I know him to
be very hearty and zealous for the
government and is a gentleman
that has served long in the fleet &
been in many Engagements & of
unquestioned Courage & Conduct
in sea affairs. He is a stranger at
home [i.e. London] which gives
birth to the presumption of earnestly recommending him to yor
Honors favor, in the procuring him
a Command of one of his Matlys
ships of warr. He hath large experience and doubt not but will do
signall service. He has been very
prudent and successfull in his conduct here and doubt not but his
fame has reached yor parts and
whatever favor or countenanse yor
Honor shows him I doo assure yor
Honor he will be very gratefull,
being a person of good ability
amongst us here. I hope yor Honor
will pardon this boldness & impute
it only to the true affaction I bear to*

yor Honor in truth which shall ever be maintained by

May it please yor Honor, yor Honors most faithfull and most dutyfull servant, Ja: Graham. N.yorke May 29th 1695.

Graham folded the sheet and, at the spot where the pages overlapped, applied a dab of hot wax, into which he pressed his seal ring. He and Kidd no doubt drank a toast while the wax cooled. Captain Kidd carried the letter with him; he had decided to waste no time in pursuing his goal; he was sailing almost immediately with his brother-in-law, Sam Bradley, for London.

Job Hunting in London, 1695

Chapter Seven

London had risen from the ashes of the Great Fire, reclaiming its place among the cosmopolitan capitals of the world. Visitor after visitor remarked about the hectic vitality of the streets of London, the sheer noise from peddlers shouting their wares, from boys rattling drums outside alehouses, from the Thames roaring through the narrow gaps between the twenty pontoons supporting London Bridge. Adding to the noise off the Thames was a phenomenal water wheel on the north end of the bridge, pumping thousands of gallons of water daily throughout the city, obsessed with fire prevention. Despite this remarkable pumping system, Londoners generally refused to drink the stuff; for man, woman, and *child,* the basic liquid of life was beer. "Small beer is what everyone drinks when thirsty, and costs only a penny the pot," observed a French visitor.

London in 1695, despite a rising merchant class, was a city deeply divided along class lines, especially when sessions of Parliament drew the nation's wealthiest to town for politics and pleasure. Chairmen toted aristocrats through the narrow streets, forcing passersby to the walls. Carriages roared past beggars in rags, hands out. An enormous portion of the population struggled by on annual incomes that were less than the price of an aristocrat's wig.

Captain Kidd sailed past the corpses hanging at Tilbury Fort, under the menacing battery of cannon, and on up the Thames. He guided the *Antigua*, carrying a couple hundred bales of cloth, along the twenty-five-mile river stretch toward London, passing elegant Greenwich where Queen Mary hoped someday to build a hospital for broken down old sailors; then, Kidd was forced to wait on line.

Despite starting to rival Amsterdam as the world's busiest port, London was still hamstrung by antiquated customs facilities and dwarfish docks only five hundred yards long. Sometimes, more than 1,000 tall-masted ships stood, becalmed, waiting to pay import duties and off-load goods to bonded warehouses. Daniel Defoe found a bright side to this bottleneck: the spectacular view of a seemingly endless parade of masts and sails bracketing each side of the Thames.

Instead of lingering aboard the *Antigua*, Kidd delegated the tedious inching forward in the line to an underling, and he along with Samuel came ashore in late July. Kidd and Samuel Bradley stayed in Wapping with distant relatives of the Bradley family: a Mrs. Sarah Hawkins, and her husband, Matthew, a butcher. The Hawkinses greeted the pair warmly. (Husband and especially wife would become close friends of Kidd, and care for him during an illness later in life.)

Wapping was no tony address; it was London's terra firma for the nautical caste; sailors during their brief shore stay bunked in this warren of rumble-down buildings. Often, a parish church reveals a district's relative wealth. The meanest church in all London was St. John's Wapping (built in 1617), according to William Maitland's *History and Survey of London* (1760). He said the church "tower might be taken for a lengthened chimney"; a gloomy brick box with low windows, cross-hatched by thick bars.

Kidd's mission in London was to sell his bales of cargo and, more important, try to land a captain's post in the Royal Navy. Kidd promptly sought out the office of Secretary of War Blathwayt to deliver his letter from James Graham, only to discover that Blathwayt was summering in Amsterdam with homesick King William. Maybe the crowd in the minister's waiting room opened his eyes to the bleakness of his prospects.

So now, forced to await a response from Amsterdam, Kidd had time on his hands, as did twenty-one-year-old Samuel.

Their own neighborhood, Wapping, provided little more than dark taverns, with sailors eating herring and headcheese. One observer described the packs of sailors wandering the streets "in search of land debaucheries" as "such wild, staring, uncouth animals, that a litter of squab rhinocerouses, dressed up in human apparel, could not have made a more ungainly appearance." Near Wapping stood notorious Ratcliffe Highway, a wide thoroughfare of streetwalkers and whorehouses. *"So, mind those buxom lasses, / In their flying colours gay / Or soon they'll clear your lockers, / In Ratcliffe Highway."*

The travel guides to London at the time featured the usual churches (St. Paul's) and palaces (Whitehall) but they especially recommended that tourists go to the Bear Garden to see that uniquely English sport in which ferocious little dogs nipped and harassed chained bulls and bears to *death*.

The architectural marvel then on everyone's must-see list was Christopher Wren's astounding-for-its-simplicity 205-foot free-standing stone pillar, a memorial to the Great Fire of 1666. "Here, by Permission of Heaven, Hell broke loose against this Protestant City," the inscription read, "by the malice of the Hearts of the Cruel Papists, and by the hand of their Agent, Hubert, who upon the Ruins of this Place, confessd and declared the Fact, for which he was hanged, viz. in this Place began that terrible Fire . . . erected 1671." (French historians, on the other hand, would say that Thomas Farryner, a baker on nearby Pudding Lane, was the more likely culprit.)

Some guidebooks also recommended an odd diversion: Go to Royal Bethlem Hospital (better known as "Bedlam"), which housed the insane. For a penny or two to the guards, visitors were permitted unguided tours of this human zoo. "Tis a very undecent, inhumane thing," complained an eyewitness, "to make . . . a show of those unhappy [patients] by exposing them, and naked too perhaps of either sex to the idle curiosity of every vain boy, petulant wench or drunken companion." One guidebook noted that a French visitor said he was forced to pay to exit as well.

Another offbeat stop was the Royal Menagerie in the Tower at "Term Time," when the exotic animals gave birth; or Bridewell, to watch convicted prostitutes work twelve-hour days, pulling hempen threads to make rope.

In early August 1695, Captain Kidd found himself stalled in London, still deluding himself with the ever-receding hope that the secretary of war would deliver him a plum job; he was a colonial merchant captain lost in the big city, when a chance meeting changed his life. Sometimes a man's fate depends not on his courage or character, but simply on what street corner he turns at what exact moment.

In the heavy August heat, Kidd was walking down a street — its name is lost — in London when he bumped into two New York acquaintances: merchant Phillip French and Captain Giles Shelley. The colonials greeted one another warmly, shared news, then the two men mentioned that they were seeing Albany merchant Robert Livingston that Sunday for a boat ride out to the village of Chelsea; they invited Kidd to join them.

If the odds of this meeting in the metropolis were slim, it bordered on the miraculous that Robert Livingston was in London at all, *alive,* considering the horrific transatlantic voyage he had just survived.

Livingston and his son, John, had left

New York harbor in the *Charity* under Captain Lancaster Syms eight months earlier, back in December 1694. The first day out of port they ran into a heavy storm, which lasted three weeks, ripping the foresail, mizzen sail, mizzen topsail, spiritsail, until finally around Christmas the main course itself shredded. During a bit of calm, the crew repaired the sails and the ship looked able to proceed again, but on January 3 at daybreak the heaviest storm hit, yanking the rudder off the ship, and blasting a hole near the bow. The crew frantically shoved blankets and bedding into the gap, but the sea soon sucked out the makeshift stopper, forcing them to man two pumps round the clock to keep the ship afloat. Now as the *Charity* drifted, rudderless, lost, the wind snapped the topmast so that it flopped in a tangle of ratlines. Only twenty gallons of drinkable water remained for the twenty-five people aboard. Livingston had to stand special guard to prevent the crew from stealing his personal stash of food, which he chose not to share. At each new adversity, Livingston, writing in his diary, thanked God for his mercy in sparing their lives. He read devoutly in *The Practice of Godliness*. Livingston, whose father was a renowned Scottish preacher who had fled to Amsterdam, was appalled by the godless, cursing crew, but noted approvingly that after the rudder broke off, they attended his twice-daily prayer sessions.

The captain tried to steer the vessel, which was veering south out of the shipping lanes, by means of two long strands of cable drifting after the ship, but this method failed. By then they'd been forced to cut down to a pint of water a day, and everyone was growing weak from dehydration.

Rain brought some relief in the form of two barrels of fresh water, but the wind that came with it pointed them farther to the southwest instead of west. Livingston advised the men to prepare for death. In his private diary, which he kept in Dutch, he made a dramatic vow. "If God delivers me from this tribulation and puts me and my son safely ashore, I promise upon my return to my family to give 100 pieces of eight to the church at Albany and, if we salvage anything from this ship, to use all that I have therein for purposes of Christian charity and to satisfy those whom I may in any way have cheated." (Even close to death, his vow is tight-fisted and full of *caveats,* such as "if we salvage.")

As the days stretched out, the ship became divided: officers and passengers versus the crew. Rumors spread that the captain planned to escape in the longboat at the first sight of land; mutineers had to be shouted down. On February 3, "mountain high" waves flooded the ship, putting it on the verge of sinking. The crew and passengers couldn't pump out the water fast enough, so the captain decided they would have to throw most of the cargo overboard to lighten the ship. The crew spent an entire day casting out 6,000 pounds of ginger as well as some bundles of fine beavers and peltries, bear skins, elk, chamois. Sailors started dying: Jacob Snyder "from exposure and being eaten by vermin," thrown overboard without a ceremony. Livingston, delirious, claimed a wicked sailor named Haman was trying to blow up the captain.

Fourteen weeks out: nine crewmen remained, along with the captain and first mate and six passengers. "I read and reflected with sadness how many Sundays I had spent godlessly and idly. O how much I would not give now to hear a good sermon!" On April 25, a sailor spied land, which turned out to be Cabo da Roca, Portugal. On July 18, Livingston reached Falmouth, England; at Exeter he boarded a coach for London, where he met a Mr. William Carter, who promised to introduce him to the newly appointed governor for New England, Lord Bellomont.

Livingston knew the roads around

London weren't safe, so he sent his goods along by courier and traveled lightly. At Hounslow Heath near London, highwaymen stopped the carriage and he heard the familiar "Stand and deliver." Livingston was carrying only thirteen shillings, just enough to avoid a gun butt to the head. At four in the afternoon on July 25, the coach rolled to a stop at Saracen's Head Tavern on Friday Street in London, and Robert Livingston and son alighted exactly 225 days after they left New York City.

So, now in early August, Livingston, along with New Yorkers Kidd, French, and Shelley, planned to spend a day in the country; they boarded a pleasure boat for the ride out to Chelsea. The August sun burned off the damp, a perfect day for an outing. Despite the heat, all four men wore wigs, broadcasting their success in life.

Giles Shelley was thirty-three years old, tall, broad-shouldered, and pockmarked, the youngest of the group, an experienced captain often working for French Huguenot New York merchant Stephen DeLancey. Phillip French was a successful merchant, who a decade later would become mayor of New York City. Robert Livingston had come to London mainly to try to recover the huge sum of £4,000 that he claimed the government owed him from his loans for troop victualing and from Indian affairs work. The accounts, which spanned back almost a decade, were endlessly muddled by "discounted tallies," "8% interest," claims, and counterclaims. A decision by the Lords of Trade could seal Livingston's financial fate, either guaranteeing his ascent into the coterie of the wealthiest men in North America or tumbling him back into the pack of moderately successful merchants.

Kidd had met Livingston in New York — and once sold him a piece of Manhattan property — but the two men were not close friends.

The four New Yorkers walked in the leafy park in Chelsea, drank, and talked. As far as they dared, the three men pricked Kidd's bubble of commanding a Royal Navy man-of-war. Shelley and French spoke of voyages to trade with the European pirates on Madagascar. And Kidd, to amuse the others, showed off some of his knowledge of pirates, of their secret harbors — some of it picked up firsthand in his youth and the rest of it from cabin scuttlebutt over recent years.

And Livingston, silent, began to hatch a plan.

The day before, Livingston had met with the Earl of Bellomont at the lord's Dover Street mansion. Bellomont had mentioned that the king had a passion to wipe out the pirates operating out of the American colonies. That night, when the men returned downriver, Livingston took Kidd home with him to his lodgings by the Exchange. Livingston encouraged Kidd to tell him more about the various pirates.

It was that night that Livingston, the spider, began to hatch a scheme of spectacular deviousness, one that would eventually backfire into the faces of half a dozen of the most powerful men in London and New York, and deeply imperil Kidd.

A couple days after spending Sunday afternoon and evening with Captain Kidd, Robert Livingston paid another visit to Lord Bellomont on Dover Street. Livingston then proposed that Bellomont approach the king about outfitting Captain Kidd in a Royal Navy ship to attack pirates. He told Bellomont that Kidd was "a bold and honest man" and the fittest captain in America to hound pirates. Bellomont was quite receptive to the idea.

Livingston, unlike Captain Kidd, could gain entrance to personal meetings with lords such as Bellomont because, besides his wealth, Livingston could trace his family line back to 1124, earls of Linlithgow, Scotland. (A Livingston ancestor had served as maid of honor to a Scottish princess marrying a French king.) The forty-one-year-old Livingston stood there in his finest, his long coat, a silk ruffled collar, lace sleeves and cuffs, silver-buckled shoes. He had donned a long curled wig that followed la mode in rising to twin peaks astride a center part. Livingston told Bellomont's servant to announce him as "Colonel" Livingston, which would have amused the merchants back in Albany. (In an age when most gentlemen carried weapons, Livingston rarely wore a sword.)

Bellomont was a tall, gout-ridden, sixty-year-old Irish aristocrat with a quick mind and a desperate shortage of cash. This staunch Protestant (only third generation in Ireland) had been an early supporter of Dutch William, and the Irish Parliament, to punish his loyalty to a Protestant king, had taken away his titles and estate. Now in 1695, increasingly embittered, Bellomont had landed the appointment as governor of Massachusetts Bay; he was hoping to add New York and New Hampshire so that the three posts would bring him £1,800 a year and restore his fortune.

In personal relationships, Bellomont was either a fanatical friend or enemy. This man, raised as heir to a baronetcy in Ireland, seemed genuinely outraged at how often he found himself scrounging for money. His gout exacerbated his frustration. Despite his financial woes, he still had connections to the most powerful men in England.

Bellomont approached the king about outfitting Kidd in the Royal Navy but was told that the Admiralty could spare no ships or seamen due to the ongoing war with France. Livingston then encouraged Bellomont to look for "persons of consideration" to join in with them as partners to launch Kidd as a privateer, so that they all could profit and do a good deed for England, ridding the seas of pirates.

Bellomont began to approach his lordly friends.

It was at this time that Robert Livingston and the noblemen involved became extremely secretive about their project. Livingston, who kept mountains of receipts and records throughout his life, abruptly ceased writing in his diary starting August 11. He summarized August 12 to October 3 in one entry: "I have been continually employed at Whitehall to obtain my money . . . to my great expense and trouble . . . The other matter of Kidd has also given me much trouble and at last, this evening being Thursday [Oct. 3], I discussed the matter with two great personages and satisfied them. They take the Earl of R. into partnership and they are now 4 in number and the business is to proceed. I hope that by this means my affairs may have a happy ending."

Even in this, his private Dutch diary, he was being cryptic: citing someone as "Earl of R." Livingston was lowering the curtain on his doings because he knew how explosive it all was.

While privateering was perfectly legal, this cadre of investors was covertly planning to try to gain extremely lucrative (and possibly illegal) privileges that had never before been granted to a privateer partnership. They wanted the right to be able to keep any captured pirate ships and not have to carry them before any Admiralty court to be declared as lawful prizes; and they also wanted to be entitled to keep all stolen goods found on board pirate ships without having to submit any accounts to the king or anyone else. Basically, they were hoping for a glorious license to take stolen goods from thieves, without the headache of having to return anything to the original owners.

Given the shadiness of the plan, the four lordly backers — not surprisingly — decided to remain hidden from public view.

Finally, by October 3, after a surprisingly hard time, Bellomont and Livingston had lined up four investors to help come up with the £6,000 needed to build and outfit the ship. Who were these men who secretly backed Kidd? whose names would never appear on any contracts? They were four of the most powerful men in England, Whig lords who occupied plum jobs in the government. These men had risen by being among the earliest and staunchest supporters of William on his way from Dutch Prince to king of England. In brief:

★ Charles Talbot, born in 1660, was the *twelfth* Earl of Shrewsbury, and was among the seven noblemen to attach his cipher to a letter inviting William of Orange to England in June 1688; in August of that year he along with Edward Russell (future Lord Orford) traveled to Holland. Mortgaging some family estates, Shrewsbury placed the enormous sum of £12,000 in an Amsterdam bank for the prince's use. In 1694, he reluctantly accepted the post of Secretary of State, and in 1695, he was among the elite Lord Justices appointed to rule in the king's absence on the continent from May to October.

★ The Earl of Romney, Henry Sidney, often touted as the handsomest man at court, honed his talent for intrigue in the bedrooms of aristocratic women, such as the

Duchess of York, and personally delivered secret documents to William in Amsterdam. He spent much of his time avoiding his illegitimate children. King William showered him with rewards, such as 50,000 acres of confiscated estates in Ireland, worth £17,000 a year.

* Lord John Somers was an extremely intelligent Oxford-trained lawyer, born of landed gentry, who rose to become attorney-general, a speaker of the House of Lords, and, later, Lord Chancellor. At the time of Kidd's stay in London, Somers was Keeper of the Great Seal and member of the Privy Council, and was said to be Dutch William's second most favorite Englishman. Shrewd, he worked during 1695 with Sir Isaac Newton, then master of the mint, to solve the problem of coin clipping.

* Admiral Edward Russell, a younger son of the Duke of Bedford, went off to sea and rose through the ranks until he abruptly quit the Navy and started plotting the crown for William of Orange. Accompanying the prince during his triumphal march through England in 1688, Russell was

rewarded soon after, becoming treasurer of the Navy, then Admiral of the Blue Squadron. When Kidd arrived, Russell was First Lord of the Admiralty, on his way home from the Mediterranean.

In sum, these were four unspeakably important men, operating at the heart of the English empire, well-beloved of the king himself, people whom one didn't muck with lightly.

Livingston was thrilled to have backers of this quality in place, supplying four fifths of the £6,000 seed money, while he agreed that he and Kidd would supply the final fifth in exchange for a fifth of the investor profits. He told Kidd the good news, but Kidd was starting to have second thoughts. After two months of dealings with Robert Livingston, Kidd's head was spinning, and he wondered whether Livingston had *really* lined up any of these shadowy backers.

So Livingston carried Kidd — they arrived by chair — to the mansions of the Duke of Shrewsbury, Lord Justice Somers, and Earl of Romney "for my satisfaction that these great men were concerned in the Expedition," Kidd later wrote. "He discoursed them but would not suffer me to see or speak with any of them." Livingston had brought Kidd there to these ornate

London homes, but had then compelled the Dundee-born sea captain to cool his heels with the fart-catchers, i.e., the footmen, in the waiting room. Kidd was swayed, but perhaps also insulted. When the captain returned with pirate treasure, he expected that these lords would greet him more warmly.

On October 10, 1695, Lord Bellomont, on the one part, and Kidd and Livingston, on the other, signed the first contract for the privateer mission.

"Whereas the said Captain Kidd is desirous to obtain a Commission as Captain of a private Man of War. . . ." The articles of agreement basically called for a ship to be built to the liking of Captain Kidd, it required the crew to be hired on a "No purchase, no pay" basis and the men's share should not exceed a quarter of the take. The earl was protected from Kidd dragging his heels by a clause that stated that Kidd must return by March 25, 1697. Confident Kidd successfully lobbied for a deal sweetener that stated that if Kidd brought in more than £100,000 in treasure for the partners, he would receive the new ship as a reward. The investors knew that if Kidd captured just two rich pirate ships, they were looking at a tenfold return on their investment.

Kidd, Livingston, and Bellomont each

dipped quill in inkpot and scratched out his signature and affixed his seal in wax imprinted by his seal ring.

Much of the foregoing was boilerplate for a privateer, but what was unusual about the contract was Clause 2: The earl agreed to procure a grant from the king for all "Merchandizes, Goods, Treasure and other Things, as shall be taken from the said Pirates." Also, Clause 10 stated that while enemy prize ships should go through Admiralty court, the pirate goods should be delivered directly to Lord Bellomont in Boston, with no account to be given to the Crown.

This is the start of the shenanigans: Lord Bellomont and his lordly backers clearly planned on getting a grant from the king to claim the pirate goods, no questions asked, and divide them up in a way that would make it almost impossible for the original owners to reclaim their cargo. What if the pirate goods were stolen hours earlier from an East India Company ship, or from the Grand Moghul? This was a nicety the lords preferred to overlook. They wanted a glorious license to steal from thieves.

The next legal instrument that Kidd and Livingston, the commoners in this venture, signed was actually far more terrifying than the initial contract, whose burden rested more on Bellomont. William Kidd, who, after a lifetime of privateer struggle, had finally married into a Manhattan fortune, signed a Performance Bond for £20,000. Basically, if Kidd failed to fulfill his end of the bargain as captain, he would be ruined, and worse, he could be forced to spend the rest of his life in debtor's prison, possibly joined by his wife and family. Only a reckless or extremely confident man would sign that bond, to be held by a lord and governor. So why did Kidd sign? The simplest explanation? Kidd had absolutely *no intention of failing to fulfill his mission.* Livingston too signed a performance bond, his for £10,000, a sum that would deeply dent, if not wipe out, his burgeoning fortune. Why would Livingston sign? He was riding high: the Lords of Trade had just approved most of his enormous claim for payment of £4,000. And no one had ever bested him in a contract dispute.

During the rest of October, Kidd sketched out plans for his dream warship; in order to raise the £600 share that he had agreed to pay, Kidd sold his ship, *Antigua,* which was far too puny to use on this ambitious pirate chase.

While he waited for the backers to deliver their money, he heard the news at Lloyd's coffeehouse that French privateers had captured three more English East India ships; over at Jonathan's where stock was traded, East India Company shares plummeted from 76 to 54.

A scant couple weeks after signing the contract, Kidd began to oversee the building of his new ship; traveling downriver to Royal Yard at Deptford, he consulted with the shipbuilders. For a man who had commanded only mid-sized ships stolen from the French, this must have been a remarkable moment. And Kidd had great confidence in his vision of how the ship should be designed. Defying the current shipbuilding wisdom, Kidd chose a galley — which, in addition to three tall sailing masts, would have banks of long oars along each side. He firmly believed that he could domineer his privateer crew to work the so-called "sweeps," an exhausting task usually relegated to slaves or prisoners. He wanted the rowing option so he could slip close to becalmed pirate ships and blast them into submission.

On November 13 to celebrate the king's birthday, Lord Romney, one of Kidd's backers, orchestrated England's biggest fireworks display ever, somehow re-creating a famous English victory. The king honored Romney by watching from Romney's balcony.

Around this time, Admiral Russell returned triumphant with the fleet after capturing twenty-three enemy prizes, without a single ship lost, receiving a huge hero's welcome. These were the titans with whom Kidd had blithely gone into partnership.

Thanks to lordly influence, Kidd's project moved to the head of the queue at Castle Shipyard at Deptford, where his 287-ton warship was built in a stunning five weeks, leaving drydock December 4. (He would learn later that workmen had perhaps raced *too fast* on the caulking of the planks of the double-hull.) This formidable beast boasted thirty-four cannon, and was christened the *Adventure*.

Kidd now struggled to line up a crew and load provisions; they put aboard 36 barrels of gunpowder, more than 1,000 cannonballs, and 100 pistols and muskets.

Bellomont, for his part, fulfilled his promise to get commissions. On December 10, 1695, the Lords of the Admiralty granted a privateering commission to the *Adventure Galley* under Kidd to attack the king's enemies; Kidd, however, in this time of war, was to be allowed only seventy seamen, half of them to be landsmen. (The Royal Navy, always desperate for sailors, was reluctant to allow a privateer the chance to steal away men.)

On January 26, 1696, Kidd, again thanks to Bellomont's politicking, received another commission, this one not from the Admiralty but from the king himself, to attack pirates, bring them to trial; the king also required all his officers and subjects to aid Kidd in his mission. And the document contained an ominous warning to Kidd: "And we do hereby jointly charge and command you . . . That you do not, in any manner, offend or molest any of our Friends or Allies, their Ships or Subjects."

Though Kidd was never granted the honor of meeting the king, he was finally allowed to emerge from the footmen's anteroom and meet a couple of his lordly backers, but not through Robert Livingston. Kidd's old commander from the West Indies, Colonel Thomas Hewetson, took Kidd twice to visit Admiral Russell and once to see Lord Romney. Kidd apparently felt the meeting with the sea veteran Russell went well, because several times later he turned to Russell for help.

Kidd moved along gearing up, signing crew, buying extra sail, rope, anchors, but he had to do it all *on credit.* The lords were quite slow in ponying up their shares of the investment money; account books reveal that Kidd was forced to borrow £700 at twenty-five percent interest to buy biscuit, beer, and peas. The *Adventure Galley* could not leave London until that loan and other bills, such as the huge one to the ship-builder, were paid off. The *Adventure* was stymied.

In early February, as rumors of a French invasion started swirling in London, Robert Livingston engineered a deal for him and Captain Kidd to sell off part of their shares. They were perhaps worried that the whole project might crumble, especially since Bellomont was having a very hard time coming up with his portion. They decided to get a little money out now while they could. Gamblers call it "hedging your bet."

Livingston struck a deal with an unsavory merchant named Richard Blackham. (Blackham a half year later would be indicted for bribery, and a decade later, by then Sir Richard, would be found guilty of "treason for melting down the coin of England and making foreign coin of it.") Kidd and Livingston each sold one third of their ten percent shares (of the profits) to Blackham for £198 each. Kidd was still in deep; he had just extracted a little ready money to tide him over.

The lords were *still* delaying payment when on February 19 they received advance warning of an event that could scuttle the entire mission. Spies informed Admiral Russell that the French were planning to invade from Dunkirk and Calais. Did the patriotic lords order Kidd to help mount the national defense? No, they commanded him to prepare to sail away quickly before the harbor closed or his crew got press-ganged from him.

On February 20, with this new crisis, the lords had to deliver their monies immediately or risk disaster. But Bellomont was broke as usual; he found himself forced to beg help from a very prosperous London merchant, Edmund Harrison (soon to be Sir Edmund), who eventually put up all of Bellomont's share and half of Shrewsbury's. "When [Harrison] saw that I had not time nor could not easily otherwise raise it, he then gave me a terrible hard Presbyterian grip."

Harrison slivered Bellomont's share, even though it was Bellomont who had brought in the other investors.

The next day, February 21, word leaked out that Admiral Russell was headed to the Downs to ready the English fleet to attack. The pretender, James II, was gathering troops at Calais. On February 23, the Admiralty placed an embargo on all outbound *merchant* ships and gave orders for the captains to deliver one third of their crews to the Royal Navy. For now, a private man-of-war such as the *Adventure* could still leave.

Captain Kidd immediately readied the *Adventure Galley* for departure. On February 25, Lord Bellomont gave Kidd his final written orders, directing him to write frequent progress reports to Edmund Harrison. "I pray God grant you good Success."

Kidd spent his last night in London at the dockside taverns. The city was jittery. The latest war order forbade all Catholics "except merchant strangers and settled householders" from venturing within ten miles of London.

After months of being jerked around with promises from Livingston and Bellomont, Kidd was finally about to depart aboard his fine ship, which dwarfed almost all of the thousand merchant ships around. Never shy, on his last night in London, Kidd downed rums with the Royal Navy captains at dockside taverns and bragged that his commission directly from the king entitled him not to have to dip his flag to *any* other ship. A Royal Navy surveyor, Jeremiah Dummer, said the captain of the king's yacht, *Katherine*, overheard Kidd and told his men to be sure that Kidd showed them the proper respect.

A yacht, however royal, stands puny next to a 290-ton warship. Nonetheless, a yacht carrying the King's Jack requires some flag-dipping by law.

Kidd gave the order, and his men put shoulder to the capstan and raised the anchor. Hours later, Kidd's mighty galley set sail down the Thames; Kidd walked the quarterdeck. The ship passed Cuckold's Point, a sharp turn in the river, clearly marked on 17th century city maps, around which London could no longer be seen. (Sailors joked that out-of-sight wives could now play.)

Kidd and his crew aboard the *Adventure* passed Greenwich, and there they encountered the king's yacht, *Katherine*. Kidd was in a hurry to beat the rumored expansion of the war embargo; he decided not to dip flag or furl his topsails to show respect. The *Katherine* fired a warning shot demanding deference; instead, Kidd in the galley, having both wind and current, glided on downriver. "Kidd's men in the tops turned up and clapped their backsides in derision," said Jeremiah Dummer. Kidd's sailors mooned *Katherine*. While Kidd didn't order his men to drop their trousers, his signature cockiness must have been infectious.

The next day, Kidd reached the buoy at the Nore, naval staging waters off the mouth of the Thames. Here, Kidd, attempting to make all speed and believing his privateering commission quite powerful, glided past Royal Navy ships, again without dipping flag or pulling canvas. Captain Stewart in HMS *Duchess* fired a shot across the bow of the *Adventure Galley*. Kidd was in a forest of Royal Navy warships; he furled sail and waited. The *Duchess*'s pinnace was dropped overboard; Captain Stewart boarded the *Adventure*. Kidd showed him his royal commission, and expected to be allowed to carry on. Instead, Captain Stewart told him he would choose from among Kidd's men which ones to draft into the Navy. Kidd warned the officer that his mission was backed by the Lord Admiral himself, but Stewart scoffed. The captain pressed thirty of Kidd's most experienced seamen. Kidd was left with five sailors and thirty-five landsmen, making it impossible for him to sail the giant ship out into a war zone.

Kidd's bold mission had lasted all of three days.

Now Kidd would need some help to try to restore his crew, so he tried to locate Admiral Russell, who was at that moment a bit busy fending off a French invasion. Kidd eventually learned that the admiral's headquarters were at Sittingbourne on the north coast of Kent, but Kidd had a hard time gaining access to the naval commander. His notes from anterooms apparently went unanswered. So, Kidd, this captain who fancied himself on a mission for the king, backed by lords, was once again mingling with the fart-catchers. A week went by, then another.

Kidd finally reached Admiral Russell,

who issued an order dated March 20 to Captain Stewart to return Kidd's men. Though Captain Stewart eventually returned the *same number* of sailors that he had taken, he chose not to return the same men, and instead Stewart saddled Kidd with his own rotten eggs and landsmen. One troublemaker sailor of Kidd's, however, whom Stewart willingly returned, was Joseph Palmer of Westchester. The war by now was in full swing and the Admiralty had issued an embargo, effectively sealing the coast; Kidd was forced to sail back to London to wait it out.

Ten days later, on April 1, 1696, Admiral Cloudisley Shovell pounded and burned Calais. Finally private ships were again permitted to leave England; Kidd unmoored and advanced downriver; he dropped off his Thames pilot at the Downs on April 10 and by April 23 he was leaving Plymouth on the southeast coast.

Captain Kidd was finally heading out into the open Atlantic in command of a powerful private warship. He was blessed with a chance to make a fortune for himself and his backers . . . if he could find any pirates.

Chapter Eight

Kidd headed to New York, as you'll recall, and had signed on a crew. Now, mid-journey, he was rounding the Cape of Good Hope and was already branded a pirate for doing nothing more than protecting his men from Commodore Warren's press gang. The date was February 1697, and Captain Kidd still hadn't seen a pirate or a French ship.

Kidd's strategy now was a logical one: go to the shipping lanes where pirates steal and go to the secluded harbors where they sell their stolen goods. To catch a thief, one must first find a thief, or at least get to the general vicinity for finding thieves.

Next stop: Madagascar.

Nowadays, Madagascar is famous for its unique animals such as lemurs and zebu; in Captain Kidd's time, this enormous island off the African coast was primarily known as the *new* outlaw refuge for pirates. As opportunities dried up in the Carib-

223

bean, a new generation of pirates, cutting-edge rogues, abandoned Port Royal, Jamaica, and Tortuga to experiment with setting up criminal havens on Madagascar, especially at St. Augustine's Bay on the southwest and St. Mary's Island on the northeast. These two hangouts were hardly a secret: Manhattan merchants skirted Navigation Acts to send ships halfway around the world to cater to this rogue clientele . . . because the profits were dizzying. One captain reported buying a gallon of rum in Manhattan for two shillings and selling it in Madagascar for sixty. The captain added that besides liquor, the pirates also eagerly overpaid for pistols, gunpowder, ship's gear, needles, knives, and other hard-to-find items, even combs. Manhattan was grooming the ne'er-do-wells of the Indian Ocean.

Word of mouth, from sailor to sailor, inflated the pirates' prowess. Part of Captain Warren's mission — besides convoying ships to and from St. Helena — was to gather intelligence on pirate activity. Expensive decisions would be made based on his reconnaissance. He gullibly relayed the inflated claims of one New York captain, Sam Burgess, that 1,500 European pirates were operating in the Indian Ocean, sailing out of a staunchly fortified base on the island of St. Mary's, with forty or fifty

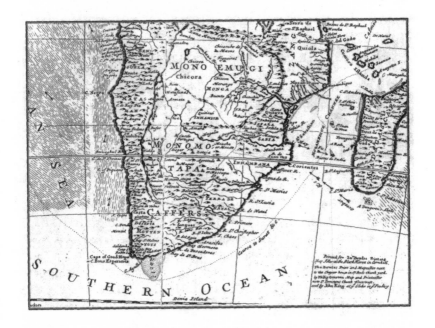

cannon installed. The pirates, Warren was told, could muster a fleet of seventeen ships, including seven large ones armed with more than twenty-four cannon.

After a couple of decades of retelling, the pirate community on Madagascar would mushroom into a well-populated utopia, called "Libertalia," where all money was stored in common, no hedges separated property, and no one owned slaves.

Unfortunately for Kidd, when he arrived at St. Augustine's Bay on January 28, 1697, he found *no* pirate ships there at all, utopian or otherwise. His detour around the Cape of Good Hope to leave Captain Warren had forced him to stay at sea an extra six weeks; many of his men were weak from the first signs of scurvy. And the *Adventure Galley*, only one year old, wasn't wearing well; its hasty construction led to leaks, and the crew was exhausted from pumping out the relentless seawater. The weakest of the men were ferried ashore first at nearby Tulear, with jeweler Benjamin Franks among them. "The first care was to send the sick men ashore," wrote Dr. John Fryer of a similar landing. "It is incredible to relate how strangely they revived in so short a time, by feeding on Oranges and Fresh Limes, and the very smell of the Earth."

The first European to step foot on Madagascar was Portuguese explorer Fernando Soares, who came ashore in 1506 and called the island Sao Laurencia. He was surprised to find that the natives resembled Polynesians, with straight hair and café-au-lait complexions, rather than the Africans across the Mozambique Channel. For the next couple of centuries, the Portuguese, French, and English all tried — and failed — to set up permanent trading outposts. Englishman Walter Hammond in the 1640s thought he had found paradise, calling the friendly natives "the happiest people in the world." Nonetheless, Hammond's settlement on St. Augustine's Bay soon sputtered. Running out of the natives' favorite colored beads shortened the lifespan of several colonists.

Without a central government in the 16th and 17th centuries, Madagascar — the world's fourth largest island — remained a hodgepodge of petty kingdoms. "They have innumerable little princes among them who are continually making war upon one another," wrote Captain Charles Johnson, who learned about the island while studying pirates in the early 1700s. "Their prisoners are their slaves, and they either sell them or put them to death, as they please. When our pirates first settled amongst them, their alliance was much courted by these princes, so they sometimes joined one, sometimes another but wheresoever they sided, they were sure to be victorious, for the Negroes here had no firearms, nor did they understand their use; so that at length these pirates became so terrible to the Negroes, that if two or three of them were only seen on one side, when they were going to engage, the opposite side would fly without striking a blow."

For Kidd's men, the reality of Tulear was probably a flea-bitten, mudbake ramble of huts where anyone with a couple of coins or some trading gewgaws could eat well and find a sexual partner. Traveler after traveler to Madagascar during this time period described the eager promiscuity of the women. "A woman gives herself to anyone she pleases," ran a Malagasy saying. In general, tales of native women racing to embrace strangers are always to be taken with a grain of salt. Marco Polo once described a region in Tibet where, to prevent girls from being inexperienced and *virginal* on their wedding night, fathers offered their daughters to travelers. "This is a good region for young men age 18 to 24," concluded Polo. The existence of that locale — despite much subsequent searching — has never been confirmed. Polo's is a classic traveler's tale. On the other hand, there *are* promiscuous regions on the globe. British sailors on the first European ship into Tahiti in the mid-1700s discovered that native women would have sex in exchange for a single nail. What happened there is matter-of-factly recounted in the journals of two of the ship's officers. "The boatswain informed me that most of the hammock nails was drawn and two-thirds of the men obliged to lie on the deck for want of nails to hang their hammocks," wrote George Robertson. One sailor almost killed another for giving a girl a seven-inch spike, which made his two-inch nail worthless.

It is likely some kind of similar trade occured in Madagascar, where many tribes practiced very open marriage and an open attitude to receiving gifts for sex. French anthropologist Alfred Grandidier, writing in 1890, said there existed a sex-to-all-strangers tradition in some parts of southern Madagascar. "The tenets of Malagasy hospitality hold that the village chiefs and paterfamilias should put at the disposition of travellers the most beautiful girls of the region." Grandidier also noted in the 1890s one could see many light-skinned Malagasies around Tulear in southwestern Madagascar "in this region where all the women vie for the honor of temporary marriage with sailors, as is still the case when a European ship anchors here today."

The *Adventure Galley* waited in Tulear harbor, ready to pounce on any pirate ships. The crewmen regained their strength, eating fresh zebu beef; the carpenter tried to patch the ship's leaks, but warned Kidd that the galley would have to be overhauled soon.

Tulear was a prime spot to lay in ambush. A few years earlier, three treasure-laden pirate ships had staggered in there after a storm, under a patchwork quilt of *pure silk* sails. Although Kidd's choice was sound, two weeks passed without a ship arriving. The temporary wives accumulated lots of trinkets. Finally a sail appeared at daybreak and seemed to be heading straight for the *Adventure Galley*. Anticipation mounted . . . for all of a millisecond, because it turned out to be one puny merchant ship, single-masted, packing only four guns and a crew of perhaps fifteen.

The crew of the *Loyal Russell* hallooed the *Adventure Galley* and told them that the ship's owner was deathly ill and they had no surgeon on board. Captain Kidd immediately ordered that the owner be carried over to the *Adventure* and made comfortable in Kidd's own cabin; he ordered Dr. Bradinham to sober up and tend to the man.

The *Loyal Russell*, a trading sloop from Barbados just out of the Cape of Good Hope, claimed to be on a slaving mission, but its cargo of gunpowder, guns, and rum seemed more likely intended for sale to pirates.

The sick man lingered for a few days; crewmen and officers were constantly in Kidd's cabin, which inevitably led to chats. It was then that Kidd learned for the first time that Captain Warren in the Cape of Good Hope had been telling everyone that Kidd was a pirate.

Under Dr. Bradinham's care, the patient soon died. A quarrel erupted almost immediately between the ship's master and the supercargo (owner's rep). Kidd for days tried to make peace between them but failed, and, exasperated, ordered the merchant vessel to steer clear.

A few days later, in late February, Kidd decided to give up waiting for pirates on Madagascar and he sailed for Johanna, an island in the nearby Comoros chain, a known stopover for East India Company ships. He wanted to find a safe place to careen and repair his ship, but instead he stumbled into a hornet's nest.

Kidd followed the shipping lanes north, still hoping for pirates, but true to his rotten luck, he ran smack into a wicked storm.

Waves pounded the seams of the galley, straining the carpenter's recent repairs. Seawater spilled down the tilting decks. For days, all Kidd and the crew could do was tie up every stitch of canvas and ride out the storm. Always an excellent seaman, Kidd survived the weeklong misery and near the end of March found himself a half day's sail from Johanna.

The morning lookout spotted a sail (possibly two) also heading toward Johanna. A far-off sail could mean fortune or disaster. Was this the pirate ship that would make their voyage?

Kidd was upwind of the other vessel and, as usual aggressive, ordered as much sail as he thought the masts could handle, and headed directly for the other ship. That vessel veered *toward* Kidd.

The crew aboard the *Adventure* was puzzled to see a strange ship eager to meet its course. Who would be fearless enough to do this? A French privateer? A pirate? English Royal Navy?

Captain Brown aboard the *Scarborough*, an interloper, thought that the *Adventure Galley* was one of the three East India Company ships he had been separated from in the storm off Mozambique. (Ironically, it was the *Scarborough* that had lingered in the Cape of Good Hope to avoid Kidd; aboard was Allen Catchpoole, whose letter would tar Kidd in London.)

Kidd piled on the sails, and the gap between the two ships lessened. At sea, it is impossible to know for certain the nature of the other ship: A pirate ship was merely a stolen merchant vessel . . . a brown-skinned crew meant nothing other than a brown-skinned crew — the ship could still be French or pirate. Pirates didn't fly a convenient Jolly Roger to trumpet bad intentions. A flag meant nothing . . . decoys were a completely accepted *ruse de guerre*.

As the *Adventure Galley* closed in on the other ship, Kidd could tell only that this was a stout ship armed with thirty-plus guns and a crew of about a hundred.

At that moment, Captain Brown, squinting through his spyglass, realized his mistake: the heavily armed vessel closing in on him was *not* one of the three East India merchant ships he had been traveling with before the storm hit. Captain Brown now tacked hard and piled all possible sail to double back to the southwest; he figured the East India ships must be behind him. Complicating matters, the *Loyal Russell* had stumbled onto the group and was giving chase as well, making Kidd and the little sloop look — from Captain Brown's point of view — like a pair of pirates.

Kidd closed hard on the *Scarborough*, but before he could catch up, yet another ship came into view.

Captain Brown carefully eyed the vessel and realized this time he had indeed found a familiar East India Company ship. The *Scarborough* raced to get within protective range of the *Sidney*, a 40-gun behemoth with a crew of 133.

Now, with the *Scarborough* and *Sidney* in tandem, Kidd was clearly overmatched. He had the wind but little else. Up to this point, none of the three ships had shown their colors. Now, just before noon, the sun beating down, Captain Gifford on the *Sidney* ran up English colors: the East India Company's distinct flag of red-and-white stripes with a St. George cross, as well as his red pennant, announcing his superiority among this little group of ships. Kidd was not happy to see that red pennant streaming in the breeze, a clear symbol that the Company claimed rank over him, and that it expected him to show deference by lowering his topsails. As the boats glided in the water, Kidd did nothing. This was not the response that Captain Gifford of the *Sidney* desired. Captain Gifford fired a shot "across Kidd's forefoot", i.e., in front of the ship. Kidd responded by hoisting his English colors and King's Jack and pennant, and then lowered a boat and sent an officer over to the *Sidney*, "who told us his ship was called the *Adventure Galley* Capt Kidd commander hav:g a commission to take all pyrates and rovers in these seas." Kidd's contention from day one of his voyage was that he — with his commission directly from the king — outranked East India Company merchant ships, and he expected Captain Gifford to strike his red pennant. Gifford refused.

Despite this squabble over rank, the four ships sailed together toward the mountains of Johanna the following day, weathering the point and entering Johanna Road. That encounter, while not exactly warm and fuzzy, was typical of strange ships meeting at sea. That Kidd bore down hard on the *Scarborough* was a hostile act but in keeping with his mission to seek out pirates. Once it became clear that he was dealing with two English merchant ships, he backed off.

As for the flags, the respect for rank, stubborn Kidd in the harbor once again demanded that Gifford strike his pennant. Gifford, an East India captain used to being cock of the walk, wasn't amused at all, and threatened to board Kidd.

The next day, during this mildly tense standoff, two more East India Company ships arrived, including Captain Clark, who had met Kidd with Commodore Warren back in December. Kidd wisely forgot about the pennant and invited all the captains to have dinner on board his ship, but they declined. They even sent him an insulting note, speculating about the "honesty" of his mission.

Once Clark entered Johanna whispering that Kidd was a pirate, any hope of cordiality vanished. Kidd informed the captains that he was headed to St. Mary's Island to look for pirates, but Clark, in a later letter, stated that Kidd's men told his sailors that they had come to Johanna expecting to find a lone East India ship, ripe for the plucking. Clark didn't hesitate to pin the crew's daydreams, perhaps mentioned over palm wine in tropical Johanna, onto the captain himself.

Clark — a Company loyalist who never liked Kidd — was deftly picking up the smear campaign where Commodore Warren had left off. In Clark's report, he also embellished the pennant-striking incident to include Kidd firing at Gifford, a fact not included in Gifford's own logbook.

Kidd clearly felt Johanna Road wasn't big enough for all of them, but he wouldn't be bullied out of port; he stayed long enough to gather firewood and especially water before heading to nearby Mohelia. English sailors claimed the waters of Johanna boasted an enduring freshness that would outlast any other eaux, except Thames water. But it was odd stuff. "For though it stinck like Puddle-water when opened first," wrote Dr. Fryer, "and have a scum on it like Oil (which Coopers affirm they are as cautious to strike with their Adze on the Cask for fear of taking fire, as of Brandy itself) yet let it stand unbunged on the Deck twenty-four hours, it recovers its goodness and is the only water they rely on in an East India voyage."

Johanna, mostly because of its sheltered harbor, was considered the most hospitable of the four main Comoros islands, "a plentiful island in Cattle, Goats, Fowls and Fish, with good Lemons and Oranges." Around this time, the East India Company ships, wanting to avoid pirate-friendly Madagascar, would often restock here on the voyage north to India. "Plenty of provisions and fruits all very cheap," wrote Edward Barlow, who happily noted many locals preferred to receive old clothes or bits of iron over coins.

The islands of Comoros were predominantly Moslem, originally settled by Arab traders, but the people didn't exhibit the fanatical anti-Christian attitude of many Moslems in that time period. And since the city of Johanna had been built up briefly by the Portuguese, it was a bit "civilized-looking" though tumbledown. Arabic was spoken and one observer noted that the women did most of the manual labor, waiting on their husbands and beginning their meals after the men finished eating.

Captain Kidd, after but three days in port, sailed out on April 4, 1697; Kidd once again tried to ditch the merchant *Loyal Russell* — four guns, fourteen crewmen — but the logs of the East India ships note that the pilot fish followed the shark the next day, April 5. Kidd headed the scant ten leagues to Mohelia, also lush, but less populated, less civilized. Here he could find cheaper provisions and he could also repair his ship.

These two African islands of Mohelia and Johanna shared so much in common: Both were paradise-like tropical refuges; both had a dark-skinned population of mixed African-Malagasy heritage; both were Moslem. And yet they were bitter enemies, and had been so for decades, if not centuries. Fortunately for the islanders, their weapons were primitive, barely lethal; their epic war almost ritualistic. "Multitudes indeed could not well be mowed down by their Martial Weapons," wrote the Reverend John Ovington, who visited Johanna in 1690. "[They used] neither Sword nor Spear, only Hand-stones taken up in the Streets, and thrown at their Enemies."

The Mohelia men who greeted Kidd's first pinnace ashore wore white cloth wrapped around their waists and small, colorful knit skullcaps on their heads. When they smiled, they revealed mouths full of blood-red teeth. With all the talk of cannibals that seamen like to spin, it must have been unsettling to see those red stains extend around the lips and chin like some man-eaters fresh from the orgy. (The islanders chewed betel nut for its narcotic effect, *and* for its attractive ornamental red dye.)

Captain Kidd found a deserted sandy shore to careen the *Adventure Galley*, which desperately needed an overhaul both for the leaks and general maintenance. Any ship traveling in tropical waters needed to have its hull cleaned and patched every half year or so, and Kidd had been at sea for eleven months. Barnacles built up, slowing the ship, and sea worms bored holes; seams between planks gradually opened up as the wind and waves contorted the vessel. Obviously, he wanted a fast, leak-free ship to chase down pirates.

Careening a ship was a strikingly laborious and tedious job. There was never a convenient dry dock to sail into, pull the sluice gate, and commence easy work on the ship's bottom. The *Adventure Galley*, rated at 287 tons, would have to be sailed ashore, then flopped onto its side, like some beached whale.

As Kidd was getting started, he noticed his unwanted pal, the *Loyal Russell*, had followed him, so Kidd put it to work.

The first order of business was to offload as many of the heavy items as practicable and to lash down whatever was to be left on the ship. The *Adventure Galley* had thirty-six cannon; we don't know the exact size of each, but, given the pattern of the time, some of them must have been at least sixteen-pounders (i.e., capable of shooting a sixteen-pound iron ball), and these cannon would weigh about 2,000 pounds each.

Usually the gravest danger during careening was the threat of attack while the ship was immobile and defenseless, like a turtle on its back. Kidd lessened that risk by mounting cannon on the *Loyal Russell*, his guard ship. Kidd probably also took some other cannon and mounted them in strategic spots along the shore. Barrels upon barrels of salt meat and water would be hoisted out of the hold. Cannonballs, gunpowder, and ballast were lugged ashore.

Some of the foretopmen, so nimble at scurrying up the ratlines, climbed the tall trees by the shore and found strong limbs on which to place pulleys, probably the same ones used to hoist stones for Trinity Church in Manhattan. The men then slung ropes through the pulleys so they could haul the 125-foot-long ship over on its side.

When the ship was flipped, Kidd and his carpenter discovered that the bottom was even worse than expected: it was severely worm-eaten. (Ravenous, wood-boring sea worms thrive in these southern waters.) The plank was a relatively meager 2½ inches thick, with no lead sheathing over the bottom. All along the hull, the men pounded hammers onto scraping irons to sheer off the encrustations. They opened seams to pack in oakum fibers reinforced by tar to seal the joints. Day after day they worked in the heat, doing the best they could, but the ship's leakiness would be a constant worry for the rest of the voyage, requiring relentless manning of pumps.

By night, there wasn't much recreation on the island for the exhausted men. Mohelia was Moslem — wives and daughters were strictly sequestered — and wine was prohibited. The sailors could join the locals in chewing slivered betel nut; once the narcotic kicked in, the sport became the aiming of spittle gobs at the hole in the floor. "It cheers and heats their spirits even almost to . . . Intoxication," wrote an English priest.

Day followed day of backbreaking labor; and then the men began to die.

More than 100 of the 150 men fell sick from some kind of tropical disease; it was the job of the surgeon, twenty-six-year-old Robert Bradinham of London, to take care of them. In the 1690s, doctors mainly turned to bloodletting, enemas, laxatives, and sudorifics (sweats), the basic concept being to rid the body of evil humors. Bradinham's surgeon's chest — one of the most valuable items on board any ship — was loaded with all kinds of powders, enhanced in the sailors' minds by high-sounding Latin names. "Surgeons and doctors of physic in ships are many times very careless of a poor man in his sickness," noted longtime sailor Edward Barlow, "feeling his pulses when he is half dead, . . . then giving him some of their medicines upon the point of a knife, which doeth as much good to him as a blow upon the pate [head] with a stick."

Bradinham's ability to cure might have been diminished by his appreciation for medicinal wine. (Captain Kidd later said that Bradinham spent months at a time drunk below deck, and Bradinham himself once admitted being a daily customer at a dram shack on Madagascar.) The surgeon was one of the only officers on board besides the captain, captain's steward, etc., who had access to wine and rum; when sawing off limbs, the surgeon needed to administer a "spoonful of cordial" by way of the only anesthetic.

Bradinham's numerous patients lay in the shade, feverish or freezing, shaking, weak, cracked lips calling for the doctor. This sudden disease was later described by one of the patients as a "bloody flux," apparently, a virulent dysentery. Suffering from extremely unpleasant diarrhea, some of the men grew too weak to move from their own mess. Bradinham's assistant, surgeon's mate Armand Viola, a twenty-two-year-old from New York, fell sick too, so he couldn't help. Kidd's brother-in-law, Samuel Bradley, also fell ill and barely recovered.

In all, about forty men died within a week. So Kidd's manpower dropped from 150 to 110, which would make it impossible to man all his cannon in time of battle.

The survivors had to finish the job of careening. It took five long weeks of opening the seams and wedging in tar-laced oakum fibers; the carpenter tried to patch the extensive worm damage. Then the ship had to be flipped onto the other side and the work started anew. Every so often the men took a break to dig a grave and say a hurried prayer over victims such as veteran sea officer Henry Meade. The body of young Saunders Douglas, who had carried pots of ale and bottles of wine at Hawdon's Tavern in New York City, was laid to rest in the fertile soil of Mohelia, half a world away from his home.

At some point, while so many of the crew lay ill, the pinnace from Captain Clark's *East India Merchant* hove into view carrying a bunch of deserters: "four English men, an English boy, two ffrench men and a Black." Kidd welcomed them, inviting them to sign aboard. One of the Englishmen, Nicholas Churchill of Dorsetshire, later said he left Clark because of "hard usage." The "Black" was Ventura Rosair, age sixty from Ceylon, whom Kidd took on as his personal cook. The two Frenchmen were pirates who had already made some scores in the Red Sea. (When Clark later learned where his stolen boat had gone, this further infuriated him against Kidd.)

Captain Kidd, watching his crew die daily, was not too picky about adding fresh manpower. Kidd, however, did repeatedly refuse to let any of the crew of the tiny sloop *Loyal Russell* jump ship, which would have disabled that vessel. Nonetheless, when boatswain Hugh Parrott got into a fistfight with his *Loyal Russell* captain, Kidd did allow him to come over. Judging by his later windy depositions, he richly deserved the nickname of Parrot. The incentive to join Kidd was obvious. Instead of working for a monthly wage paid at completion of voyage, the men could dream of a share in a big score.

His ship seaworthy again, Kidd anchored alongside the *Loyal Russell* and the crew shifted the guns back aboard the *Adventure Galley*. Once again, Kidd ordered the *Loyal Russell* not to follow him. (This time, it did not, and soon after, it crashed upon some rocks about nine leagues off the coast of Madagascar. The ship was lost, but the dozen crewmen rowed ashore and survived, and later turned pirate, sharing in a rich capture off Surat.)

The *Adventure Galley* sailed back to Johanna for a load of provisions. To add to Kidd's headaches, he was apparently almost out of ready money and his credit —

not anchored to the English East India Company — wasn't accepted in these parts. Kidd tried to buy provisions with a letter of credit on the king of England, but was refused. Instead, he borrowed some money from the two French pirates and bought the foodstuffs he needed.

The decks were now cleared, so to speak, for Captain Kidd. With his galley seaworthy again, his supplies restocked, his 100-plus man crew seasoned and regaining health, he was finally ready to fulfill his mission. He had survived disease, storm, Royal Navy interference, East India Company slander; he was now ready to hunt for pirates and enemy French.

So, in early May, Kidd set his course north toward the Red Sea, where he knew some of the world's richest ships would straggle back in late summer from Arabia to India, ships full of wealthy Moslem pilgrims returning from their once-in-a-lifetime *hajj* to Mecca, full of Indian merchants carrying back enormous profits from selling to those devout tourists. For the European pirates lurking in the East Indies, this "Red Sea trade" was the big score: what the Spanish treasure *flota* meant to an earlier generation of Caribbean buccaneers. These ships carried silver, gold, and jewels — portable internationally acceptable wealth — and not the usual merchant hold full of linens or coffee that would have to be transported and back-alley trafficked at deep discount. Sailors then used the slang term "rich as a Jeddah ship" to signify something unbelievably valuable.

The two former French pirates Kidd had picked up promised that they could guide him to where the pirates usually struck near the Red Sea.

Captain Kidd's motives for choosing to head to the Red Sea would later be called into question. Was he going there to hunt for pirates? Or did he just want to attack a rich Moslem ship?

Kidd, who was not the kind of leader to go blathering to underlings, clearly told two members of his inner circle — jeweler Franks and brother-in-law Bradley — that

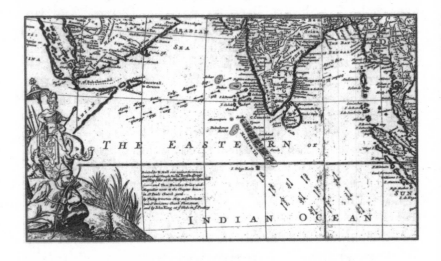

he planned to attack pirates.

This was Kidd's intention, but some of the *Adventure Galley* crewmen, who had logged nine long months without pay or capture, were whispering that they planned to attack a fat Moslem prize; the mutinous whispers and grumblings were starting again.

As Kidd's divided ship headed northward to the Red Sea, unbeknownst to Captain Kidd, the English East India Company was sending three heavily armed ships to the same exact region, to protect the Moslem fleet.

Two of the three East India Company ships soon ran into difficulties at sea, and had to turn back. So, the Company mission, to act as convoy and protect the Red Sea pilgrim fleet from pirates, wound up falling upon the third ship, the *Sceptre*, which had just arrived in Bombay from London. And on April 10, 1697, the East India Company, thanks to permission from the Crown, was pleased to commission the *Sceptre* as a pirate-hunting privateer, hoping that booty would flow into company coffers.

That meant that two licensed English pirate hunters — one backed by the bully company of the Indies, the other by a shadowy consortium of London lords — would trawl the same waters of the Red

Sea. In those days, the Company almost never welcomed another English ship into its backyard. The *Sceptre* would no doubt treat the *Adventure* as a rival bounty hunter, or worse.

But first they both had to get there. The *Sceptre* lay in Bombay, rushing ashore its thirty-one chests of treasure, clocks, cloth, and other goods from London, in early April. The *Adventure Galley* finished loading in Johanna in early May. Both ships stood about 2,000 miles from the Red Sea port of Mocha (in modern-day Yemen). Seasonal trade winds would help the *Adventure* and hurt the *Sceptre*.

The Company's stakes ran very high, since the Grand Moghul of India had once again threatened to cut off all English trade if European pirates captured any more Moslem pilgrim ships.

The Moghul, Aurangzeb, whose empire stretched from Persia to Bengal, had suspended trade in 1689 and 1695; he was still furious about Captain Avery's capture two years earlier of the *Gunsway*, during which, rumor had it, Captain Avery himself had raped the Moghul's niece. The Company's representatives had yelled themselves blue — English pirates do not work for the English East India Company — but to no avail, and finally the Company had agreed, along with the French and Dutch, to convoy the pilgrim fleet from the Red Sea to India, as a kind of preventive medicine. If the convoy failed and English pirates struck hard enough, the English could be London-bound, their rich commerce quashed before it could blossom into the Raj.

The Company's *Sceptre*, a 36-gun Indiaman under Captain Phinney, on April 13 picked its way through the crowded harbor of Bombay to start its important mission.

Around May 10, the *Adventure Galley* sailed north using the northeast monsoon winds up through "Ethiopian seas," little-charted by European navigators, and so plagued with unmarked rocks and unknown islands. The race between the bounty hunters was on.

The *Sceptre*'s navigation shaped up as much tougher than Kidd's because the East India Company ship needed to travel due west from India at a time of year when the seasonal winds were already blowing hard in the opposite direction. Captain Phinney would have to zigzag far to the south.

Phinney was a hard, decisive, fat, foul-tempered man. On the voyage out, he had bought from some rogues in a canoe a pretty native boy who was clearly kidnapped, the captain hard-bargaining to pay twenty-five shillings, less than one fifth the going rate for slave boys; another time, when Phinney saw a cluster of pirate pirogues hauling a captured ketch into a cove, he ordered his men to take the 150 yards of fishing nets nearby as instant punishment to villagers *presumably* harboring those pirates. (This East India Company employee stood instant judge and jury.)

Phinney set the course south-southwest for a full month, eventually reaching six degrees *below* the equator before tacking to catch steady winds and head up off the African coast.

Because of his long detour, he ended up following the same route north that Kidd would follow, but the *Sceptre*, thanks to his one-month head start, still had the lead (although neither side realized that he was in a race). The *Sceptre* stood at least 400 miles north of the *Adventure Galley*.

On board the *Sceptre* was a remarkable first mate, Edward Barlow, a watercolorist who kept a detailed sea journal, recounting this voyage as well as his life at sea.

"So hauling up as near the wind as we possibly could, the next day we had the sight of the mainland [modern-day Somalia]. . . . The country seemed very desolate and barren and high land, and not a tree or bush to be seen, the ground very smooth and even although high, and seeming dry and burnt up with the heat of the sun."

On May 21, the *Sceptre* spied the steepest cliff so far, and rounded the easternmost point, called "Cape Guardefoi," i.e., "Keep the Faith."

The *Sceptre*, six weeks at sea, was starting to run low on water. Winds powered the ship; water fueled the men. A man can survive only a couple of days without water before becoming delirious, but can last weeks without food. A sailor at full ration drank about a gallon of water a day (once the beer ran out), which weighs eight pounds a gallon. So each man needed 240 pounds of water a month. A ship with 150 men carried 36,000 pounds of water for a month of drinking (not cooking or washing). A ship was a thirsty beast and water holes — in that desert of salt water — were sometimes far apart. Wood and especially water were the two items — bulky and consumed daily — that sent ships risking their way to unknown shores.

Captain Phinney, caught in a calm just around the Cape, debated whether to send men ashore for water. "The next day came from the shore two canoes, having five men in them in a naked and poor condition; they came aboard to beg any old clouts [i.e., nails] or what they could get. We could not understand their language, but by what signs they could make; we made signs to know whether there was any fresh water to be got near the shore. They made signs to us that there was, pointing to the place, and that they had sheep and other things. But the country was unknown to us and we did not go to see what they had, being in great haste of our way."

Captain Phinney set his men on short water rations, chose not to risk going ashore, continuing to head west-northwest. Fighting the winds, it took him almost a month to travel 300 miles to chalky Prelock Island near the mouth of the Red Sea.

By this time, Kidd, closing the gap in this undeclared race, passed Cape Guardefoi and he, unlike Phinney, decided to risk going ashore. He sent his pinnace to load some water but the local people there, leery of strangers, refused to allow it. The next morning, Captain Kidd ordered two boats ashore, with forty armed men aboard. The men probably fired shots and raised hell because most of the locals fled and the crew filled up water casks and brought off what they wanted: apparently a few cows and sheep, some corn, dates, and chickpeas. To ensure a safe exit, the crew took a handful of hostages, two of whom were later ransomed for a pair of cows and three sheep. By the standards of the age, it was merciful that a fully armed European ship, which was denied water, succeeded in filling its casks without killing anyone.

Aboard the *Sceptre*, Edward Barlow got a sudden career break, which would pit him directly against Kidd.

Captain Phinney grabbed Barlow's hand and touched it to his forehead, and told him that he wasn't feeling well. Phinney ate little at the noonday meal and complained, despite the great heat of Arabia in the early summer, that he was unable to sweat. The ship's doctor gave Phinney a "sweat," i.e., sudorific medicine, and Phinney lay down on his bed, under covers, to sweat out his illness.

Around seven in the evening, Captain Phinney, with a gush of black blood out of his mouth and ears, suddenly died. The carpenter made him a coffin — an ordinary seaman would have been sewn up in canvas — and Phinney was laid inside with iron bullets and coals for ballast. After prayers, the coffin was cast into the sea, with twenty blasts as funeral knell.

Barlow became captain, determined at age fifty-five to finally shake his tag within the company for being "too timid" to command a ship. Three days later, the *Sceptre* reached Aden on the Arabian coast, a mere forty leagues from the mouth of the Red Sea. Barlow now tried every trick to cover his final westward stretch to the Red Sea, but contrary winds and a strong current actually took him twenty leagues farther from his destination. Barlow decided to try to head south again to Ethiopia, to try to make progress that way, but found himself back again at Prelock Island. Barlow, trying to gain a point or two into the wind, split a set of sails.

Captain Kidd, not far behind in his unusual galley ship, had the advantage of being able to row into the wind and was gaining ground.

Then Barlow caught a break: he lucked into one solid day of unusual wind from the south and was able to make his way to the "Bab-el-Mandeb" islands at the entrance to the Red Sea. "We passed through the middle of them, having no less than fifteen fathom water on a moonshiny night."

Around two o'clock on June 17, Barlow caught sight through the spyglass of Mocha Road, the deep-enough-water harbor outside of town of Mocha where ships anchored. He stopped four miles short of Mocha Road, because he worried that ships might open fire on him, mistaking him for a disguised pirate. His East India Company orders were to send a pinnace ahead into Mocha to announce himself. The summer before, pirate captains Shivers and Hore had captured two ships south of

Mocha near the Babs traveling under English colors, merchant ships carrying goods for the high-ranking local Indian trade reps working for the East India Company. The pirates had hauled the two ships into the harbor of Aden along the southern coast of Arabia that August, demanding ransom. The governor refused to allow any monies to be paid, protesting that other merchants would shun his port for making deals with pirates. Pirates, Shivers, and Hore, burned first the *Callicut Merchant*. The captain of the other ship, limping John Sawbridge, was already known as a bad-luck captain (a career-threatening stigma) since Arab pirates years earlier had chained him to the mast during an attack and a wood shard from a French cannonball had sliced deep into his leg. Now Sawbridge, facing the loss of yet another ship, ranted and cursed at Shivers and Hore to mend their ways and spare his ship. "They ordered him to hold his Tongue," recounted a local sea captain, "but he continuing his Discourse they took a Sail-needle and Twine and sewed his Lips together, and so kept him several Hours with his Hands tied behind him." When no ransom came, the pirates burned Sawbridge's ship with prize horses still aboard and the people of Aden saw English flags sink into the harbor waters. Sawbridge, though allowed ashore in a small boat, died a few days later.

Alert to the anger of local Arabs against English pirates, Captain Barlow sent his boat ashore at Mocha to make sure no one mistook him, but despite his East India Company flag and despite having a Moorish merchant speak for him, the townspeople still refused to trust him. They persisted in believing that Barlow might be a pirate who had captured an East India ship and was trying to decoy. They immediately sent word overland to Jiddah, port for Mecca, to hold the pilgrim fleet until they could verify Barlow's identity.

By this point in late June, Captain Kidd had reached the same waters near the mouth of the Red Sea, but his Frenchmen aboard warned him that no Arab port would ever trust him since he was a heavily armed ship not associated with any of the major trading companies of the region. Kidd therefore was forced to hover, to hide in the searing heat, with no friendly contacts in the region, and wait for pirates.

Mocha was then the trading hub for a new luxury drink sweeping the Old World: coffee. The first coffeehouse was opened in London in 1652 by Pasqua Rossie, a servant of a Turkey merchant. (Tea would remain an expensive novelty *digestif* through the 1720s before growing later in the century into the number one export of the East India Company.)

Apparently, right from the get-go, some customers bought a single cup in a coffeehouse and lingered over it for hours, while others, looking for good conversation, didn't even buy anything. The *Dictionary of the Vulgar Tongue* stated that a friendly prostitute sometimes "made a coffee house of her [private parts]," i.e., she allowed a man to go in and out without spending any money.

Arab merchants shipped sack after sack of coffee beans via camel mainly from inland Bait-il-Fakih, called "Beetlefuckee" by the English. By 1717, 4,000 tons of coffee passed annually through Mocha.

Barlow, after being paraded through the streets by a scrum of screaming beggar boys, reached the house of the Turkish governor of Mocha and presented his letter from the East India Company. The governor — a thin pockmarked man in a turban — served him two "dishes" of coffee, examined his papers, and accepted that he was not a pirate, had him sprinkled with Persian rose water as he exited. Barlow rented a house, settling in to wait for the Moslem pilgrim fleet to come down from Jiddah, and made plans to share convoy duties with two Dutch ships that had arrived there before him.

Within a week, word reached Barlow, via harbor gossip, that a "pirate" was hovering near the mouth of the Red Sea.

Mocha was hot and exceptionally dry — the locals said it rained only two or three days a year. Water was carried on ass-back from twenty miles away and "cost as much as small beer." Biblical clouds of locusts descended twice while Barlow was there. "[They] go in swarms darkening the sky . . . and seemed like when it snows hard in England, with your great flakes of snow in the sky. And wherever they light and settle they eat up all the leaves and green herbs presently. They are something above two inches long with a great head and a devouring mouth, with four large wings."

And sometime during Barlow's stay from June 18 to August 11, probably sometime around August 1, Captain Kidd daringly slipped into town, or at least into Mocha Road.

The *Adventure Galley*, with Kidd displaying as fine seamanship as Barlow, had somehow arrived just west of the Bab-el-Mandeb islands at the narrow mouth of the Red Sea, about fifty miles south of Mocha. Pirates, years earlier, had tried to dig a well on one of the islands there, with much labor, pounding fifteen fathoms through hard rock down, but never found drinkable water.

So Kidd, in the searing late July heat off Arabia, with dwindling water supplies, waited at the Babs for the Moslem pilgrim fleet. A mood of anticipation gripped the ship. Below deck, a clique of would-be pirates were whispering loud enough for Jonathan Treadway, a twenty-four-year-old sailor from New England, to hear some say they were intent on "taking as many of the [pilgrim] fleet as they could."

So day after day passed, but there were no ships to be seen. Empty water casks marked the passage of time. Kidd decided to send his pinnace to Mocha to try to learn the plans of the pilgrim fleet. He worried that he might have missed them in the night.

Twice Kidd's boats rowed upwind among the ships in Mocha Road, and twice they learned nothing. His men didn't speak Arabic, and it would have seemed extremely suspicious for a strange boat to ask about the pilgrim fleet. Maybe all they did was row close enough to use a spyglass. The third time, around August 1, Captain Kidd went himself in the pinnace, taking along quartermaster John Walker. Kidd brazenly might have passed himself off as a sailor on one of the three European convoy ships in port. In any case, Kidd talked to some people and came back with the juicy knowledge that seventeen ships would be soon coming down the Red Sea.

Captain Kidd stationed two men on one of the Bab islands. Their orders: when they spotted the pilgrim fleet, they were to wave the "Jack," i.e., the King's Jack or Privateering Jack. Flags back then were often huge (twelve feet by twenty-one feet) and could be seen far away. This signal system would give Kidd time to prepare the sails and row to the exact spot desired. (The lookouts could row back to the *Adventure*.)

The men bided their time on the *Adventure Galley*, with little to do in the searing heat but daydream about fresh beer and treasure. As more casks grew hollow, Kidd had to cut the water ration. Long summer day followed long summer day. Roasting in the cross-tree, a foretopman stood in constant watch toward the lookouts on the island. Two weeks passed, then on a Saturday in late afternoon, he spotted the men waving the King's Jack. The crew, pushing their capstan bars round and round, hoisted the 2,000-pound anchor from the 15-fathom depth. Kidd ordered the decks cleared; he set the sails just so.

The pilgrim fleet of seventeen sails passed through the Babs in the evening. One huge merchantman belonging to the Grand Moghul himself carried more than 700 passengers: men, women, and children. The sheer size of the ships almost guaranteed that dozens of chests of money and jewels were stowed on board.

Kidd cagily kept the *Adventure* just out of view.

On Sunday morning, at daybreak, a lookout quickly roused Captain Edward Barlow and pointed to a gap in the straggled-out pilgrim fleet, which he had been sent to protect. Barlow could see in that opening, out of gunshot, a strange ship. "He showed no colours but came jogging on with his courses hauled up, under two topsails, having more sails furled that usually ships carry, namely a mizzen topgallantsail and a spritsail topgallantsail." Barlow was showing off that his acute observation through the glass had revealed that this unknown ship was in abnormal readiness to pounce or race away. "She showed no colours but had only a broad red pennant out without an cross on it." The red pennant was *not* a no-mercy pirate flag, but rather this long narrow strip of red signified a ship claiming superiority; it was used by the commodore in a Royal Navy or merely the lead merchant ship in a group. Kidd was once again claiming superiority.

Aboard the *Adventure Galley*, as the sun peeped over the corner of Arabia, the crew perceived the captain had positioned the ship well, sneaking in among the fleet. The wind was dying down, which suited the galley, and Kidd advanced closer to the lead cluster of ships.

Barlow, on the 40-gun *Sceptre,* immediately, with no hesitation, decided that this unidentified ship was a pirate and that he would lay low until it drifted within range. Barlow ordered some of his men and boys to go about routine duties on deck while directing all others go below to ready the guns to be rolled out. "Seeing the pirate as near as he intended to come, being almost abreast of us, we presently hoisted our colours and let fly two or three guns at him well-shotted, and presently got both our boats ahead having very little wind, towing towards him."

Kidd was shocked to see an English flag hoisted, then to find the ship shooting at him, plunking cannonballs into the nearby sea. And now, amid the calm waters, he saw them using two longboats to tow their giant ship toward him. Dutchman Nicholas Alderson said he heard Kidd say that it was an "English man of war . . . convoy to the fleet" and "that there was no good to be done." Kidd scanned the horizon and saw far off in the other direction Dutch colors. Kidd did not fire back.

When the wind died down even further, Kidd found himself closest to a fat Moorish ship, which Barlow later noted had a great deal of money aboard. The Moorish ship, alerted by Barlow's fire, also took aim at Kidd, as did several other Moorish ships. Cannonballs splashed around him. Some caught his rigging.

This time, Kidd fired at least five shots back, catching the Moor in the sail and hull above the waterline.

Now the slow-motion chase was on in earnest. Barlow's men in their two long-boats were desperately trying to lug their 400-ton behemoth into range to do damage. Barlow admitted in his journal that Kidd never once fired back at him, never aimed at his ship flying English colors. As Barlow brought his forty guns closer, Kidd had a decision: retaliate or quit the scene.

Kidd ordered the men to the oars. Just then a breeze sprang up and the *Adventure Galley* sailed out from among the fleet. "We fired at him as long as he was anything near and judged did hit him with some of our shot," wrote Barlow. But Kidd, in command of a faster ship, sped away to just out of range, and then Kidd waited there, as though daring Barlow to come closer.

Barlow, as fast as he was able, once again approached almost within gunshot of Kidd, but at the last moment, the *Adventure Galley* sailed away again, though not piling on full sail. Apparently, Kidd did not want to stray too far from the fleet but the *Sceptre* kept driving him away. The pattern continued. The *Adventure Galley*, freshly careened, a much faster sailer, opened up a gap between the ships, then Kidd furled the lower sails and waited; the *Sceptre* continued to pursue. Finally at sunset Kidd sailed away for good. Barlow laid by, since he was five leagues from the fleet, and waited for the seventeen pilgrim ships.

Barlow later wrote that the Moorish ships were carrying great quantities of money and that the "pirate" could have plundered the headmost ships and escaped, which would have caused the East India Company untold grief back in Surat and elsewhere.

"The Moors ships seemed very thankful for being secured at that time from the pirate." Barlow would not learn the name of the supposed pirate until a month later.

While Kidd's actions might seem suspicious, they are perfectly consistent with a man trying to catch pirate ships *after* they had plundered the Moslem fleet. His unusual commission granted him the right to steal from thieves with no need to restore the stolen goods to the owners. He was like a bounty hunter lingering outside Tiffany's to steal from the diamond thieves and then thumb his nose at Tiffany's. Kidd's job was sanctioned by five of the most powerful men in England including the king; the *not* restoring the goods was made easier by thousands of miles of ocean, language barriers, communication at ten knots per hour, smoldering religious hatreds.

For the men on the *Adventure Galley*, who had weathered eleven months without any plunder, being forced to flee the pilgrim fleet spelled disaster, a bucket of sand on the fire of their hopes.

At one o'clock in waters off the southern coast of Arabia, in the midday August torpor, the sails furled, the ship drifting, Captain Kidd assembled the entire crew on the deck of the galley. About 120 men and boys gathered.

William Kidd was clearly captain, but captain of a privateering mission (or a pirate ship, for that matter) was quite different from captain of a merchant ship or a Royal Navy ship.

Three hundred years later, it's difficult for a contemporary reader to understand the nature of Kidd's authority over his men. Christopher Codrington, commander in chief of the English armed forces in the group of Leeward Islands, once complained that trying to command militia and ships from the various islands such as Barbados and Antigua, was as difficult as being a privateer captain, leading *with the permission* of his crew. "All his authority is precarious," wrote Codrington, "and his motives dependent on a multitude of uncertain humours."

Kidd offered the crew two choices: linger near the *hajj* fleet or head for the highlands of St. John (modern-day Daman) on the coast of India. The crew voted for the highlands of St. John. That locale, then obscure to many cartographers and mariners in Europe, was quite well-known to the sailors aboard the *Adventure Galley*. At "Cape St. John" or "highlands of St. John," Captain Avery had made his big score taking the *Gunsway*.

Was Kidd at this point chasing pirates or rich pilgrim ships? Kidd — laconic Scot — did not reveal his intentions to the crew, according to forty-five-year-old Dutchman Nicholas Alderson, but many in the crew, however, stated their desires quite clearly to one another: they wanted a fat Moslem pilgrim ship straggling from the fleet.

The crew piled on sail, the monsoon winds pushed the *Adventure Galley* eastward. The crew — their recent disappointments sinking in — grew more dissatisfied. Water rations were shortened to about a quart a day, brutal for a man eating salt beef and trimming sails in the 100-degree heat.

On the fifth day, the complaints grew so

loud that the crew pushed the quarter-master to go complain to the captain, to set up a parley, i.e., a mass meeting followed by a vote. Aboard a privateer, little protects the captain from the crew . . . except mutual self-interest and the simple fact that most of the weapons are locked away.

We know only snippets from the meeting. Some men made arguments for continuing to head east to St. John, others for heading north to the nearest coast to look for water. These half-naked, tanned, angry, thirsty men stared up at the captain and quartermaster on the quarterdeck. A vote was called. The men chose St. John, greed over thirst.

To add to his growing predicament, Kidd, new to these waters of the Arabian Sea, accidentally shot sixty leagues or so south of the mark.

Three parched days later on Saturday August 28, the watch spied a sail. Kidd piled on all canvas to bear down upon the ship. Now the typical dog-sniffing ritual at sea. As Kidd neared, he could see the other ship was a "grab" of about a hundred tons, i.e., a two-masted, square-sailed vessel used in the Indian coastal trade. About noon, closing in, Kidd expected the other ship to slow; when it didn't, he fired across the other vessel's forefoot. Responding with the appropriate deference, the ship lowered her topsails and hoisted her colors, in this case, *English* colors, making it yet another ship that Kidd couldn't legally attack. Kidd, using the voice trumpet, demanded that the master come aboard the *Adventure Galley*. A boat was lowered from the other ship and Captain Thomas Parker, an Englishman, was rowed over and lifted into the *Adventure*. Captain Kidd and Captain Parker went below deck into Kidd's cabin and closed the door.

Since leaving Johanna harbor in the southern hemisphere back in April, this was Kidd's first opportunity to gather any information about other ships, pirates, weather, war news, the East India Company. This Parker spoke English and did not work directly for the English East India Company. Kidd and Parker talked and talked, the minutes flowing by.

In the meantime, Captain Kidd sent his men over to inspect the other ship and they asked what cargoes were aboard: some coffee, pepper, and food for the crew. The ship was the *Mary*, heading from Aden to Bombay, the dozen-man crew, all "Moors," i.e., dark-skinned natives of India, the passengers were five Portuguese monks from Bombay and a Portuguese translator, the pilot a Moor. The ship was owned by the

Girderdas Rupgee, the local Bombay broker for the English East India Company.

The ornery men from the *Adventure Galley*, making themselves more than welcome, ate and drank what they could find handy, and then they brought the Moor pilot back with them. They took nothing from the other ship.

And minutes flowed into hours and Kidd stayed below, behind closed doors talking to Captain Parker. Then some of the men from the *Adventure Galley*, including some of the former pirates, led by John Walker, quartermaster, and accompanied by gunner, William Moore, piled into the *Adventure Galley*'s boat and rowed over and boarded *Mary*.

They ransacked the ship looking for anything of value: They took five bales of coffee, a sixty-pound sack of pepper, plumb lines, myrrh, navigation instruments, some clothes, and the Moor crew's rice. They also grabbed two blunderbusses and six muskets, weapons they might use to mutiny against Captain Kidd.

The former pirates tortured some of the dark-skinned men to find out where any valuables were hidden. They took two of the Moorish officers, and tying their arms behind them, hoisted them up and beat them with "naked swords." The technique is to slap hard with the flat side so that any flinch could cause the prisoner to be nipped by the blade. Terror — that is, fear of being cut — sometimes outstrips the actual pain. Several crew members aboard the *Adventure Galley* said they heard the men's screams echoing across the gulf between the ships. Even jeweler Benjamin Franks, sick with fever, said he heard a "great noise." (To avoid collision, the ships were bobbing a safe distance apart.)

At least two Moors were cut.

Either Kidd didn't hear it, ensconced in his cabin, which is quite likely, or he chose to ignore it. There's a good chance that Captain Parker and the Portuguese monks aboard a Moslem ship had a hefty supply of spirits left. And Kidd had probably shared more than a few glasses with Parker.

The *Adventure Galley* men returned in the longboats with their booty, and Captain Kidd, when he realized what had happened, was furious. He called them a "parcel of rogues." And he made them *return* much of the stuff. The testimony of the five Portuguese monks has been ignored for three centuries, although it still exists in the records of the India Office at the British Library [IOR #6444]. "Deposition of ffras: D: Rosaro, Dom Gonsolvis . . . Christians Inhabitants of this Island

Bombay and Passengers Aboard ye *Mary* Brigantine." The monks under oath stated: "Two Compasses, six Musquets & four Bales of Coffee they returned again."

What self-respecting pirate would actually go to the trouble of returning stolen goods? Kidd clearly was trying to prevent his crew from committing piracy, as well as from arming themselves.

In another deposition, routinely missed, Jonathan Treadway, of Boston in New England, stated: "The said grab, having but a small Provision of water, Captain Kidd would not take any of it from them."

After a day of drinking with the man, Captain Kidd, who had never traveled down the coast of India, decided to take Captain Parker along as his pilot; he also took a Portuguese linguist, fluent in English and several local Indian dialects. Kidd's mission was on the verge of disaster; Kidd simply didn't plan on failing. By adding these two veterans of the region, he would dramatically boost his chances. The *Mary*, in no danger, stood fifty easy leagues off the coast, with favorable winds.

Several witnesses said that the "linguister" was taken by force but as for the captain, he returned to the *Mary* and calmly gathered his belongings.

At nine o'clock that night, the two ships parted. The *Adventure Galley*, confident under Parker's navigational advice, set sail, despite the darkness. By morning the monks aboard the *Mary* said they could not see the *Adventure Galley*. The Moor pilot, using his compass, easily guided the *Mary* two days later into the port of Bombay; the monks immediately complained to Portuguese authorities about Captain Kidd's "piracy."

Meantime, Kidd in the galley headed a bit southerly, and five days later, on September 3, reached Carawar, one of the smaller outposts of the English East India Company on the west coast of India. A foul mood pervaded the ship. Some of the crew were frustrated that Kidd wasn't more of a pirate; others were worried that he would soon become one.

The English Company headquarters, at Carawar, as elsewhere in the Indies, was basically a fortress/warehouse, overseen by a handful of Christian whites operating in a sea of brown-skinned Moslems and Hindus. No matter how many cannon or firearms they possessed, the English were at the ultimate mercy of the masses surrounding them.

Kidd, depending on advice from Thomas Parker, sailed into Carawar, and avoided the wreck in the north channel and the submerged pyramidal rock in the south channel.

Kidd desperately needed water as well as wood. Morale was so bad that Kidd hand-picked the most loyal men to oversee the watering mission. One crewman later estimated that all but thirty of the crew wanted out. Kidd wasn't finding pirates or French; the men were galley slaves to this Scottish taskmaster.

Kidd himself went ashore and met with the East India Company agents, Thomas Pattle and John Harvey. The two company men rushed a note dated September 9 to Sir John Gayer at Bombay headquarters. "These are all express to acquaint your Excellency of 3rd instant [September] came into ye cove Captain Kidd in ye *Adventure Galley*. He has on board 140 well men and 36 guns. He sayeth he hath been at Mohilla, Madagascar, etc. other places to look for pyrates but yet hath not met with any and now is come to this coast for ye same purpose; we understand he hath been at Moco [Mocha]. He says he thought to meet with pyrates there but we are inclined to believe had it not been for ye convoy ships he would have made no scruple of taking 2 or 3 Suratt men. He makes many protestations that he will not injure anyone but those he has a commission from King of England. But notwithstanding his fair pretences, we much doubt his designes are as honest as they should be. He talks of cruising off Comerine [southern tip of India] expecting to meet them — they haunted the place last year. He is now wooding and watering in which we do not think it prudent to molest him for fear it should aggravate him to mischief."

Thanks to the gossip chain leading from Commodore Warren of the Royal Navy to Captain Clark of the *East India Merchant*, Kidd upon arrival was greeted with even deeper suspicion than usually accorded an interloper.

Carawar acted as a key hub in the company's coastal pepper trade, but from a European visitor's point of view, especially a European captain or wealthy merchant, the town was best known for two recreations: hunting and dancing girls. Alexander Hamilton noted at Carawar there thrived the "good old custom of treating Strangers that come from Europe with pretty black female Dancers, who are very active in their Dancing, and free in their Conversation where shame is quite out of Fashion." The English company bred hunting dogs to impress clients.

The jeweler Benjamin Franks, who had been "mortal sick" and who had always planned to set up business in India, repeatedly asked Captain Kidd for permission to go ashore at Carawar. Kidd kept refusing.

Franks offered to give Kidd a beaver hat and Kidd agreed. Big mistake.

The ship's pinnace rowed Franks ashore and all nine men immediately deserted. Of them, Benjamin Franks, forty-four, and Jonathan Treadway, twenty-four, sought asylum at the East India Company head-quarters. Treadway, who certainly needed an excuse for jumping ship, said he "had been trapanned to be a pyrate instead of a privateer."

Although the company officials had fin-ished their note to Bombay, they grabbed it back and scribbled a postscript: "Since we wrote is come to the factory 2 of Kidd's men who informes us they have taken an English vessell off of Bombay and they have got the commander aboard a prisoner, they took out of her 100 pieces of gold, some rice and raysons, their going to Mocha was with full intent to take ye Suratt ships had not ye convoy prevented them, that they intend to take Abdul Ghaffur's ship in the cove and watch for her as she goes out."

These two deserters were preaching to the choir; the East India officials were thrilled to have their worst fears about Kidd confirmed.

This was devastating news (especially in the Company's slanted retelling): that a captain carrying a commission from the king of England had turned pirate. Franks and Treadway were suddenly star witnesses, to be ferried to Bombay headquarters. (Neither man would get to enjoy India, both were kept as prisoners, then shipped back in January aboard the *Charles II* to England to testify in person before the Board of Trade.)

Reports would now be circulated to all East India Company outposts saying eyewitnesses labelled Kidd a pirate. Wanting to gather as much information on Kidd as possible, hoping perhaps to free Captain Parker, the two Company agents sent a couple of men to spy on Kidd. They picked two veteran sea dogs: Charles Perrin and William Mason. Both had worked as captains on and off for the East India Company.

Perrin and Mason were rowed out to the *Adventure Galley* and hailed the ship with smiling faces. Captain Kidd instantly recognized Mason as one of the men who had helped steal his *Blessed William* in the Caribbean a decade earlier. Kidd showed both captains his commission with King William's hooked nose and curly wig authenticating the beautifully printed document. Kidd, however, didn't allow Mason and Perrin to wander around his ship; they never did catch sight of Thomas Parker. They whispered questions to the crew to find out where Kidd was headed: some said Gulf of Persia, others Cape Cormorin.

Mason, a former pirate with no love for Kidd, reported: "Kidd carries a very different command from what other pirates used to do; [Kidd's] commission having heretofore procured respect and awe . . . this being added to his own strength — being a very lusty man, fighting with his own men on any little occasion, often calling for his pistols and threatening anyone that durst speak of anything contrary to his mind to knock out their brains — [this] causes them to dread him. [They] are very desirous to put off their yoke."

Captain Mason said the crew begged him to help them overthrow Kidd and take command of the ship but that he "honestly" refused. Mason was burnishing his own star at Kidd's expense.

Captain Mason's words were relayed to Sir John Gayer in Bombay who put them into the monthly news roundup that would circulate around the company factories and on to London.

Sir John was apparently unaware that his informant had helped steal Kidd's ship almost a decade earlier because Kidd had *refused* to turn pirate.

This big world of 1697, growing constantly bigger by exploration and trade, was sometimes, especially at sea, a very small world of a handful of men whose ambitions collided.

Resilient Kidd, though wracked by gossip, was still determined to fulfill his mission.

Chapter Nine

Kidd stayed in Carawar for a week, but he denied shore leave to everyone except a trusted handful of men. At one point, awakened at midnight, he caught eight men, including Westchester native Joseph Palmer, trying to steal the *Adventure Galley*'s pinnace and sneak ashore.

Did Kidd order a dozen stripes on the bare back for each? No, Kidd wasn't able to punish them since his privateer articles required him to have all punishment voted through by the majority of the crew.

This was one disgruntled ship and Kidd was ruling by the sheer force of his personality.

Kidd had long missed his March 25, 1697, deadline for returning, but he expected it to be forgotten when he sailed home with treasure. However, a new deadline loomed: an East India Company report estimated in mid-September that the *Ad-*

venture's food supplies would last only about a month.

After ten days total in port at Carawar, he was still trying to take his fill of wood and water, when someone tipped him off about a dire development. Three of his crewmen, he was told, had escaped and hitched a ride to Goa where they informed the Portuguese authorities that the *Adventure Galley* — which they described as the "pirate ship" that had harassed Portuguese monks on the *Mary* — was now a sitting duck in confines of Carawar harbor.

The Portuguese quickly fitted out two men-of-war and headed down the coast to bottle him in and pound him to submission. The Portuguese in the Indies were a faded empire, high on Catholic dignity, low on actual might. When Pope Alexander VI had so kindly divided the "undiscovered" world in half in 1493, the Portuguese portion included all of Africa and territories to the East. Throughout the 1500s and well into the 1600s, Portugal had dominated the East Indies, but the rise of the English, French, and Dutch, operating as lean trading companies, combined with turmoil at home, pitched them headlong from their dominance. (A further mark of decline came when the crown of Portugal gave the island of Bombay as a dowry portion to Charles II when he married their Katharine in 1662, and the Portuguese church refused for years to turn over the city.)

So, now this upstart *Adventure Galley* provided the Portuguese with a perfect opportunity to hammer an English pirate, and humiliate Protestant England. "It is believed that all Englishmen are pirates who sell in Bombay all that they steal at sea," wrote the Viceroy of Goa to the King of Portugal. "If our frigates meet them at sea they produce the [English East India] company's papers and we can do nothing with them; but when they come across our merchantmen they rob them and the company then excuses it by saying those ships are pirates."

On September 13, once informed of the Portuguese threat, Kidd instantly ordered the crew to weigh anchor — the men putting their backs into turning the capstan. Unless a captain opted to cut the ship's thick anchor cable, leaving a buoy to mark the spot for later retrieval of the 2,000-pound brake, a ship's departure was a slow affair, a matter of several hours. Kidd chose not to cut the cable but to weigh anchor; he harangued the men to be quick, to sing the anchor chantey *vivace*.

That evening, with Captain Parker shouting advice from below deck, Kidd eased the *Adventure Galley* safely along the north side of the river mouth and then tried to head south, but he was a prisoner of the variable winds. This period marks one of the two seasons (September/October and March/April) of the year off the Malabar Coast of India when the winds are unpredictable, during the shift from the six months of eastward monsoons to six months of westward monsoons. The watches passed an uneventful night under a dome of stars.

As the sun's first ray glinted in the east, Kidd was appalled to discover two large Portuguese vessels almost within gunshot of him. The largest Portuguese ship was a towering man-of-war, bristling with forty-four guns, a cross-laden tribute to some saint or virgin, and its sister ship packed twenty guns. All the guns were rolled out. With the light changeable winds, the two Portuguese ships were soon bobbing toward Kidd.

Now Kidd could put his men to the oars and try to make a getaway. Instead, he gambled and allowed the Portuguese ships to get close.

An officer aboard the larger Portuguese ship raised the voice trumpet and hailed the *Adventure Galley*. The Portuguese captain wanted to make certain that he was confronting the correct "pirate" ship and not some Frenchman or East Indiaman.

"Where are you from?" came the question, probably in the hybrid Lingua Franca of sea travel. Kidd, not tipping his hand, answered politely that he was "from London." And the Portuguese identified itself as sailing "from Goa." This oh so civil exchange ended quickly. As Kidd recalled: "the ships parted wishing each other a good voyage."

The wind picked up and Kidd headed south, and the two Portuguese ships dogged his path during the day. Just the sight of the far-off crosses on the sails threatened the Protestant crewmen. Kidd was the faster sailer and opened up a gap, but that night the Portuguese were willing to pile on more sail along a coast which their nation had been sailing for two centuries.

At daybreak, the two Portuguese ships were once again within range. The larger ship without any warning or request for surrender, opened fire six great guns, scoring direct hits to the *Adventure* above the water line, the flying splinters wounding four of Kidd's men. Shards sliced tanned skin. Kidd returned the fire briefly. Seeing sixty-four guns ready to blast him to kindling and seeing that the giant man-of-war was maneuvering to board him, Kidd ran.

Piling sail upon sail, playing every game

to catch every puff of power, he worked the *Adventure Galley*. It was now a deadly game of chase. The oddest feature of this kind of naval warfare is that ships back then could not fire heavy balls forward over the ship's head, due to design problems with recoil, etc. So while the pursuer might twit his adversary with light chase guns, he was certainly not going to inflict mass carnage or sink him.

Kidd raced; the Portuguese followed. The gap widened. The 44-gun man of war could not keep up, and over the hours it fell far behind. The smaller 20-gun ship could sail at just about the speed of Kidd. Around noon in the bright waters off the Malabar Coast, famous for its pepper, Kidd suddenly tacked.

It was a crucial moment. Kidd's helmsman had pushed the whipstaff hard a lee while the men pulled at the crosstrees. Would these light winds catch or would the sails flutter limp, hanging the ship in irons? If the maneuver failed, the Portuguese could swoop down on Kidd. If the move succeeded, he would be upwind and could control the fight.

It must have been a sickening sensation for the Portuguese captain when he realized he had been tricked into a one-on-one engagement and Kidd was upwind of him, with almost twice the firepower.

Kidd pounded the other ship, at some point dismasting her. The winds died so Kidd did not have to fear the 44-gun commodore's arrival. In this calm, the enemies were stuck in an endless battle, like boxers during a round with no end. Kidd, with his thirty-six guns, raked the smaller ship. Kidd had a huge advantage because he could use his oars to maneuver the *Adventure Galley* into position. Like all captains back then, he "aimed" the ship since his main cannon had no sideways swivel.

The fight lasted seven hours. The Portuguese landed a few blows — Kidd had eleven men wounded, but the Portuguese got by far the worst of it. As the East India Company official, Thomas Pattle, heard it: "When [two ships] came near, ye Portuguese valiantly fired into him as fast as they were able but Kidd's hardy rogues soon gave them enough and mauled them miserably. The small ship was very much damaged with abundance of men wounded and killed."

Samuel Bradley lay below deck, still sick from Mohelia. The men told him that they wanted to board and plunder the Portuguese ship but that Captain Kidd would not let them. When the winds sprang up again, Kidd could see the 44-gun flagship approach; Kidd sailed off to the south.

Kidd, never the modest man, later commented: "I believe no Portuguese will ever attack the King's Colours again, in that part of the world especially."

The jolts of the Portuguese cannonballs, though, had reopened some of the leaks on the *Adventure Galley*; Kidd now needed a safe harbor to do some repairs. He sailed southwest toward islands off the coast of India.

Any sliver of doubt in the minds of East India Company officials about whether Kidd was a pirate was gone. Company reports now bristle with his misdeeds.

"Kidd had been at the Laccadive Islands ravishing & murdering men, women and children and acted all ye villainies possible." So wrote Sir Jonathan Gayer, *from Bombay.*

Barlow in his journal placed "Kidd the pirate" at another island group one hundred miles further south, the Maldives. "Having careened his ship, he had taken their boats and broken them in pieces for firewood, and forced their people to work for him for nothing, and had ravished some of their women; in requital whereof the black islanders had killed one of his men; and to revenge his death the pirates had killed several of the islanders, and had made much trouble amongst them, taking what they pleased away."

Kidd's atrocities seemed to multiply by

the number of retellings; truth grows more elusive as he becomes the catchall pirate bogeyman.

Based on later testimony from men *un*sympathetic to Kidd, it's clear that Kidd's actions were not as sinister as Company reports painted them.

Kidd, unwelcome on the Indian Coast thanks to the Company, sent his men ashore to get water on some strange island, inhabited by dark-skinned people speaking an incomprehensible language. The sailors took the pinnace full of empty barrels to fill them up. The cooper, i.e., barrel-maker, was a key member of the mission: repairing, plugging, etc. The natives helped with the watering.

At some point, an argument broke out — possibly over a woman. (Remember the men have not had shore leave for half a year.) And a local man slit the throat of Kidd's cooper, killing him. The shore party scrambled back to the galley and Kidd himself led a squadron of men ashore to capture the culprit. One local man, apparently identified as the killer, was tied to a tree and put to death. A later report said that Kidd ordered the people who had helped fill water casks to tie white flags onto their huts and that he ordered his men to burn the rest. Rough justice? Passover ritual? (Was this harsher than when

Captain Phinney of the East India Company took the 150-yard fishing net in the vicinity of pirate activity or when Captain Leonard Edgecombe plucked men, women, and children off Johanna island to discourage the local people from welcoming pirates?)

In any case, Kidd later denied ordering any huts burned.

Kidd sailed back along the coast of India. He had been at sea for a full year from New York and had not run into a single French or pirate ship. Kidd raised a French flag hoping to decoy some monsieur into range. No such luck. And after his disaster with the islanders, Kidd was still low on water.

He decided to sail into Callicut Road, fading but still a major pepper depot on the Malabar Coast. He was determined to water at a civilized place where he would be welcomed. But half a world away from London or New York, the English East India Company factories controlled the only English outposts in the region. Kidd arrived in Callicut harbor, promptly raised English colors, and sent a boat ashore requesting permission from the English factory to gather wood and water. The chief there, Thomas Penning, refused him.

So, Kidd, hoping to buff up his reputation, sent Penning a polite note (Kidd never wrote a single letter home during his three-year voyage; so for terse Kidd, this is book length):

"I cant but admire that the People is so fearfull to come near us, for I have used all possible meanes to let them understand that I am an English man [i.e., English ship] and a ffriend, not offering to molest any of their Cannoes, so thought it convenient to write this, that you may understand whom I am, which I hope may end all suspicion. I came from England about 15 months agone, with the King's Commission to take all Pyrates in these seas, and from Carwar came about a month agone, so do believe you have heard whom I am before this. And all that I come for here is wood and water, which if you will be pleased to order me, shall honestly satisfy for the same, or anything that they'll bring off, which is all from him who will be very ready to serve you in what lyeth in my Power." — Wm. Kidd

Callicut was famed in history as the city upon stilts that jutted far out to sea; Hindu temples once boasted marble pillars compared to the Roman Pantheon; centuries later, on that spot, the Portuguese built a castle that seemed to rise directly out of the white-capped waves. All of that splendor was toppled by storm and attack, and now lay buried in the harbor, a risk to ships come to lade sacks of peppercorns, kegs of palm-tree oil, bundles of sandal-wood. The Portuguese relocated to Goa, leaving a tumbledown church; the French were sizing up land to build their own trading spot, but at that moment the English had the only European outpost there.

Thomas Penning wanted nothing to do with Kidd, distrusted him, and continued to refuse him wood and water. Anchored near Kidd in the harbor was the *Thankful*, an English ship owned by factor Penning, mainly for private coastal trade; the captain was none other than Charles Perrin, who had boarded Kidd a month earlier in Carawar. No doubt, Perrin had painted an ugly picture of Kidd to factor Penning. Kidd sent armed men in two boats to board the *Thankful* to force the issue.

Kidd then commandeered Captain Perrin into carrying a message into port to Penning: "You deserve to have your ship burnt for refusing me wood and water." Kidd added that he would make Penning's rudeness known at Whitehall when he arrived in England. The tense standoff continued. Would Kidd burn an English ship? Would the English outpost open fire with shore batteries?

On the horizon appeared a sail heading into port. Kidd focused the cylindrical barrels of his spyglass and could tell that this

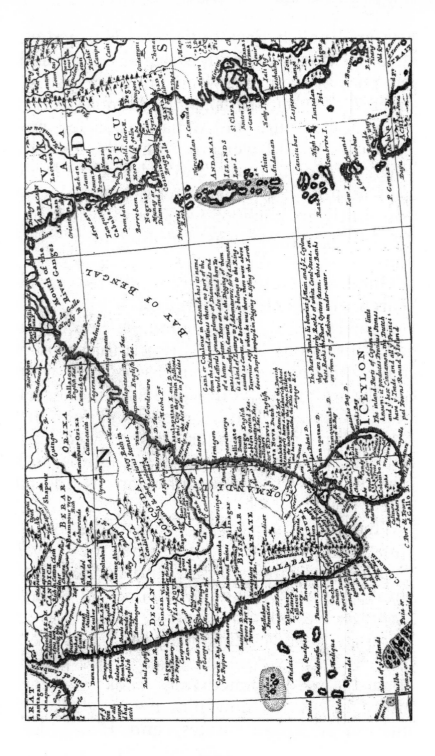

291

was an English East Indiaman. He made a snap decision; he quickly weighed anchor and left port, without his wood or water on October 7. (He left the *Thankful* unmolested.)

Kidd, cocksure and defiant, was fed up. No ports would welcome him; the Dutch, English, Portuguese, and Moors had all shot at him. He was running out of food, constantly in need of wood and water for his 140 men, and was traveling in a leaky ship.

Once again, he ventured out to sea in search of French and pirates.

A week or so later, someone spotted a sail; this could be the capture that would make the voyage prosper. Every sail, with its glint of white, offered that glimmer of hope. Captain Kidd bore down on the other ship. The smaller ship showed due deference, raising its colors, English, and lowering its topsails, allowing Kidd to catch up.

The *Adventure Galley* hailed the other ship, which turned out to be the *Loyal Captain*, an English East India Company ship sailing from the Madeiras to Surat. Captain Howe stepped lively and ordered his men to lower the boat; he was rowed over to the *Adventure Galley* and lifted aboard. Kidd immediately took Captain Howe below to show him his king's commission to chase pirates, and Howe displayed all due deference. Howe was quite charming, bringing over several fine bottles of Madeira. In addition to the wine, Howe said he gave Kidd several "pishcashes," an Indian word for tribute, the first-fruits paid to an important person. He was the first captain in a long while to show Kidd any respect, and the two men settled in for a long chat. Howe flattered Kidd, and Kidd in turn treated Howe "civilly."

What Captain Kidd didn't know was that Captain Howe was play-acting. A couple months earlier at Johanna, Howe had run into Captain Gifford of the East India Company, who had warned him about Kidd, giving him the company line about the pirate hunter turning pirate. Howe informed Kidd he was carrying only sugar, and Kidd, in gentlemanly fashion, accepted his word for it. The two men lingered over a fine afternoon meal no doubt provided by Howe, since his supplies were more plentiful. All was amicable.

Kidd's crew, meanwhile, chatted up the sailors who had rowed the captain over. Among them was a Dutch *mustiz,* i.e., a mixed-race fellow, half Dutch, half Indian. And this man, perhaps unloved by both races, told some Dutchmen in Kidd's crew that traveling aboard the *Loyal Captain* were some Greek and Armenian merchants who had an "abundance of silver and diamonds."

The whispers of treasure intoxicated Kidd's crew. These men had been living for months on what sailors then called a "dog's portion," i.e., a lick and a sniff, and they were hungry for something more substantial.

William Moore, Kidd's gunner, started the ruckus. He acted as ringleader, this troublemaker who had survived stints in New York and Barbados prisons.

Moore was able to lay his hands on eight or nine muskets, which he distributed to his cohorts. Men scurried about looking for other weapons. *Diamonds, jewels.* They tiptoed barefoot; they shushed each other. One reached for the rope to lower the boat, then a man loyal to Kidd confronted the stealthy men.

He started yelling at them; he was attacked. Captain Kidd heard a noise and came on deck. William Moore wasted no time. "You ruin us because you will not consent to take Captain Hoar's [Howe's] ship," said Moore. And one of the Dutchmen in Kidd's crew chimed in that he had a trick to share: "I will put Captain Kidd in a way to take this ship and come off fairly [i.e., without committing a crime]." Kidd cut him off, telling him to shut up.

The crew stood there on the deck; all the

men had knives, some had guns. Moore started a palaver, that is, he called a meeting of the crew; the 100-plus men on the rocking deck of the *Adventure Galley* discussed in hard sailor slang and burbles of French and Dutch whether to take the *Loyal Captain*. The crew put it to a vote and two thirds voted in favor of plundering this English ship.

We do not know what Kidd said during the palaver; it would have fit his Scottish terseness to wait till the men were done.

So, here he is with no marines to back him, with more than two thirds against him. He stood up to them; he told them: "No, I will not take her." He refused to attack an English East India ship, even after the inhospitable way that he had been repeatedly treated by the company factors. Kidd said that the weapons belonged to the *Adventure Galley* and that he had no commission other than to take pirates and enemy ships.

At that point, Moore beckoned the men to go right now, to grab the pinnace of the *Adventure Galley* and board the other ship, which had a small merchant crew. And some of the men moved to the rail.

Kidd was furious. "If you desert my ship," he said in loud, clear tones, "you shall never come aboard again, and I will force you into Bombay, and I will carry you before some of the council there." His tone was iron. He later said he used all the arguments and menaces he could muster. The mood of the mob balanced on the fulcrum of Kidd's personality.

The men backed down, grumbling.

Some captains would have packed Captain Howe off and sailed their ship away, or encouraged Captain Howe to sail away. But Kidd was a very hard, in-your-face kind of commander, especially when he thought himself in the right. He allowed the two ships to rock side by side that night, and in the morning dismissed the *Loyal Captain*. As Howe set sail, many of Kidd's crew leaned over the rail and yelled insults and threats at him.

The best cure — maybe the only cure — for the hostility between captain and crew was a fat prize, a deep-laden treasure ship.

For ten days the galley cruised in the shipping lanes off the Malabar coast and then a man spotted a sail. Kidd gave chase, closing the gap between them, continuing on even by moonlight. The following day, a calm hit, locking both ships in place about a league apart.

The captains eyed each other through the spyglass. The other ship raised Dutch colors, and Kidd responded by ordering up English colors. The *Adventure Galley*'s uncanny streak of bad luck remained intact.

The men aboard the galley immediately began grumbling again, with William Moore once again the ringleader. This time no palaver, no official vote, took place, but it was clear to Kidd that the men wanted to raid that Dutch ship. "She is our friend," Kidd told the crew, meaning that Holland was England's ally.

Since the galley was an oared ship, this calm provided the perfect battle advantage; the *Adventure Galley* could row into position and fire broadsides into the Dutch ship until she surrendered. Kidd refused.

The crew was still making signs of plotting, sharpening weapons, checking the pinnace. The *Adventure*'s cook, Abel Owens, said he heard Kidd confront the would-be mutineers and say: "You that will take the Dutchman, you are the strongest, you may do what you please. If you will take her, you may take her; but if you go from aboard, you shall never come aboard again." It was the second time in less than two weeks that he had felt compelled to make that threat.

Moore was sitting on the deck with a grinding stone, sharpening a heavy iron chisel. He goaded the men to take the other ship.

Now, this was clearly mutinous behavior, but Captain Kidd under the privateer articles he had signed with his crew wasn't able to punish Moore. "That man that shall breed a Mutiny Ryot on Board the ship or Prize," according to Article 12, "shall lose his shares and receive such Corporall punishment as the Capt. *and major part of the Company shall deem fitt.*" Kidd would need a majority vote to inflict any welts on the back of the popular Moore.

Moore told the men clustered about him that he knew how the captain could *legally* take the Dutch ship. Kidd moved along the deck and confronted Moore. As Kidd recalled the incident, Moore explained that his plan was to invite the Dutch captain and crew aboard, tie them up and go plunder the Dutch ship, then refuse to let them go until they signed a paper saying that the *Adventure Galley* did not molest their vessel. "This is Judas-like, I dare not do such a thing," Kidd replied.

"We may do it, we are beggars already," Moore answered back.

Kidd: "Why! May we take this ship because we are poor?!"

Then Kidd paced the deck. As he passed Moore, he heard the gunner mutter, "You have brought us to ruin." Kidd stared straight at him. "We are desolate," said the gunner.

Kidd snapped, words streaming from him. "Have I *brought* you to ruin? I have not *brought* you to ruin. I have not done an ill thing to ruin you. You are a *dog* to give me those words."

Kidd took up an iron-hooped wooden bucket that lay nearby and, in a fury, swung it by the handle and caught Moore flush in the temple. Moore was knocked to the deck, the chisel spilling from his hand.

He lay there not moving, then slowly stirring. Mutinous comrades raced to him, yelling for the surgeon. Bradinham was forced to put down his glass and come on deck. The men carried Moore down to the gunroom, and at least one sailor said he heard Moore say: "Farewell, farewell, Captain Kidd has given me my last." At which, Captain Kidd, looming above, grumbled: "Damn him, he is a villain." The ship's surgeon later stated that the "wound was small but the skull was fractured."

Moore died the next day. He was sewn up in canvas with some ballast, the white sack addressed with a brief prayer and heaved overboard.

The *Adventure Galley* seethed with discord. As evidenced by the vote to take the English ship *Loyal Captain*, more than two thirds of the crew wanted to turn pirate. Only about a dozen men, including Kidd's brother-in-law, Samuel Bradley, and Carolina merchant John Weir, preferred to stick to the original mission of *chasing* pirates.

Kidd was the flesh-and-blood buffer against the pirate faction.

Besides the risk of having his throat slit in his sleep, Kidd had other worries, almost as pressing. He still desperately needed food and drink for the crew. Men, already mutinous, were on half rations; water was short. Liquor — except for some in the doctor's chest — was long gone. He hoped reports of his good deed in saving Captain Howe would by then have circulated among East India Company factors, earning him a welcome and an opportunity to buy provisions. So, after much deliberation, Kidd decided to venture into another outpost of the Company, this time into Tellicherry, another well-fortified pepper port on the Malabar Coast. The English factory boasted a high-walled compound, with a battery of cannon. A handful of cozy English punch-houses along the esplanade made the long slow lading of heavy pepper sacks much more tolerable.

Kidd's luck ran true. A few days *before* Kidd reached Tellicherry, the *Sceptre* had sailed in under Captain Barlow (Red Sea skirmish), and Barlow was carrying factor Thomas Penning (Callicut harbor tiff). To add to the negative word-of-mouth, also in port was the *East India Merchant*, under Captain John Clark (Warren escape, Johanna flag duel), who had arrived from

Bombay and was very ill.

At seven in the morning on November 3, Captain Clark died in his cabin and was buried on shore that afternoon. Less than half a year earlier he had unjustly tarred Kidd; now his corpse would feed worms on the Malabar Coast.

Kidd arrived in Tellicherry Road that same afternoon, flying English colors. Barlow reported that Kidd lay almost within gunshot of Clark's ship and stayed there for a quarter of an hour. Chief factor Penning, ashore at the time, was furious that the *East India Merchant* — captain or no captain — didn't open fire. Penning ordered the cannon at the English factory to shoot at the *Adventure Galley*, no questions asked. The factory was located some distance away from the shipping road and the cannonballs splashed well short of Kidd. In what was probably a *jeu d'esprit* by an exasperated man, Kidd hoisted French colors and fired a parting shot, also well short of its mark, back toward the fortress. And then Kidd sailed south. As he left the harbor, a cabin boy jumped overboard and swam ashore, and soon told a slightly jumbled tale: Kidd had shot his quartermaster and mutiny was afoot.

Still very short on rations, Kidd lingered for two long weeks off southern India without encountering any other ships. The parched men bickered. About eight miles off the coast, just north of Callicut, stands a notorious landmark called Sacrifice Rock. Legend had it that Indian pirates, in a frenzy of small cruisers from the town of Cottica, had captured a large Portuguese vessel and one by one sacrificed all the Portuguese upon the rock. A pinkish tint, it was said, showed blood not yet washed away despite decades of pounding surf.

As Kidd passed just south of Sacrifice Rock on November 18, 1697, someone spied a sail. The galley hoisted French colors and followed. The hoisting of false colors was extremely commonplace at the time. (The Dutch had once put *half its fleet* under Portuguese colors to trick the Portuguese into a major blunder off Ceylon in 1658.)

Kidd, flying the white flag of royal France, piled on all sail and followed for nine hours through the night, the watch desperately trying to follow the ghostly clouds of another ship's sails in the moonscape. At dawn, as the galley finally overtook its quarry, the other ship hoisted both French and Moorish colors. However, the smallish merchant ship still made no effort to slow down, so Kidd fired two shots across its bow. The vessel's sails were furled.

Captain Kidd ordered a Monsieur LeRoy

to hail the other ship in French. Pierre LeRoy had joined the galley back in Johanna, and was one of the "French pirates with gold" whom Kidd had allowed aboard, and from whom Kidd had borrowed money. The ship, now rocking alongside the *Adventure*, was a 150-ton ketch; the crew lowered its boat and sent it over to the *Adventure*.

The captain, Dutchman Mitch Dekkar, a veteran sea dog, climbed over the side and descended below deck into the captain's cabin with Monsieur LeRoy. The story, which some members of the crew enjoyed telling afterward, was that LeRoy sat at the captain's table and handled the formalities with Dekkar. LeRoy politely asked in French to see Dekkar's papers. And that Dekkar carried a stack of passes from various governments and that when he realized he was dealing with a French ship, he handed over a French pass. At that moment, Kidd emerged from the shadows and exclaimed: "By God, I have got you! You are a free prize to England!"

In Captain Kidd's version of the events, he said LeRoy hailed the ship but that he personally dealt with the Dutchman and that Dekkar handed him a French pass. Kidd wondered whether the man gave that French pass by accident or on purpose. In any case, Kidd said that Dekkar "swore sacrament [that] she was a prize and would not return again aboard the Moors ship." Kidd is clearly implying that Dekkar wanted to jump ship.

Kidd held the French pass in his hands. From his Caribbean days aboard French privateer ships and from his high level of literacy, Kidd was able to puzzle out and understand the *passeport*. The ornately handwritten document was graced at the top with the flowing curlicue of "De Par Le Roy" ("By order of the King") and in the lower left corner bore the seal of French East India Company, emblazoned with the royal fleur-de-lis.

The document began: "Nous, Jean-Baptiste Martin, directeur-general de la royalle compagnie de France des Indies Orientales, a tous ceux qui ces presentes lettres verront, salut . . ." ("We, Jean-Baptiste Martin, director-general of the Royal Company of France of the East Indies, to all who will see these present letters, greetings. . . .")

It states that Vameldas Narendas, a merchant of Baroche, intends to send his 150-ton ship, the *Rouparelle*, from the port of Baroche to the Malabar Coast, Brugal, and Bassora. The French head of their East India grants the passport and begs their allies to honor it, and not to inflict any hindrance. The document was executed at

Surat, the date left blank and signed simply: "Martin."

Word of the French pass spread quickly from the captain's cabin; some of Kidd's men immediately crossed over to the prize, manned by a crew of two dozen or so. They easily subdued the smaller ship.

Kidd called his men back on deck and explained the situation: the *Rouparelle* was an Indian-owned ship, carrying Dutch cargo, and it had presented a French passport. Samuel Bradley, still ill below deck, said he was told that Kidd tried "to persuade the men to restore the Moorish ship to its owners."

Not surprisingly, the crew overwhelmingly voted to keep the ship as a legitimate capture. And, by the maritime laws of the age, this capture was indeed legal.

After fourteen months of no pay, the men finally had something to show . . . but not that much. The cargo was paltry: two chests of opium, a dozen bales of cotton, two horses, and fifty inexpensive quilts, and the family possessions of an unfortunate Dutch official. Governor van Duyn was moving his household from Carawar to Ceylon. The three Dutchmen aboard all wanted to switch over to the *Adventure*. Kidd soon after appointed Mitch Dekkar, who liked to be known as "Skipper Mitch," as his new master, to replace Henry

Meade, who had died. (Maybe Kidd thought an outsider could better control this crew.)

A handful of Moors also came over to the galley, and were put to work manning the relentless pumps, since the ship was leaking again. Kidd allowed the other twenty Moors aboard and the ship's owners to take their ship's boat and row the two leagues into Callicut. Kidd was making no effort to conceal his actions.

It was a tradition among privateers (and pirates) to rename captured ships. Some men voted for the derisive name of the *Maiden*, since it was *Adventure*'s first capture. ("Sign of the Maidenhead" hung over many taverns.) But the rest of the crew outvoted them to dub the *Rouparelle* the *November*, as in the month of capture. Kidd now needed a crew for this prize ship, and he apparently tried to offload some of the worst troublemakers. We know tippling surgeon Robert Bradinham went aboard, as did Westchester man Joseph Palmer.

Kidd sailed south to the smuggler's port of Kalliquilon and sold the goods for about £150, a pittance, but thankfully enough to buy provisions to keep the men from starving. The crew loaded sack after sack of rice into the hold.

The next two months, Kidd cruised off

the Malabar Coast with his usual luck. He met no French merchant ships and no pirate ships. It is significant to note that absolutely no one — no matter how hostile to Kidd — claimed that the captain through these first sixteen months of his voyage encountered a single pirate ship or ever shirked the chance to attack one.

Finally wising up, Kidd avoided East India Company factories and he traded with local vessels. Two men who turned Crown evidence against him claimed Kidd roughed up nine or ten native vessels, but there's no confirmation elsewhere, and the English East India Company, which extensively documented Kidd's actions, made no mention of it. Also Kidd returned to the port of Kalliquilon several times, where he certainly would not have been welcome if he was robbing ships every time there.

The *Adventure Galley* and the *Rouparelle/November* cruised, sometimes together, sometimes drifting as far as five leagues apart. Kidd often sent the *Rouparelle/November* off to the shore to get water for both crews.

All the while, Moslem merchant ships sailed along this same busy coast, as did ships belonging to the English, French, Dutch, Portuguese. Many of these voyages involved participation by several different nations all at once.

One typical trading mission around this time was that of the *Quedagh Merchant*. A group of Armenian merchants, operating out of Surat in northeastern India, had banded together in April 1696 to hire this 350-ton ship, *Quedagh Merchant*, owned by an Indian named Coirgi. Helping to broker the deal was a local representative of the English East India Company, named Augun Peree Callender, who was free-lancing to supplement his income. The pilot was Captain John Wright, with two Dutchmen as first mates and a French gunner; the ninety-odd crewmen were all Indians.

This multinational venture kept getting delayed, but eventually the crew loaded the tons of cottons aboard in Surat and headed around the tip of India, reaching Bengal in late 1697. The *Quedagh Merchant*'s group of 30 Armenian merchants sold their cottons for an excellent price and filled the ship in Bengal with 1,200 bales of muslins and other cloths, 1,400 bags of brown sugar, 84 bales of raw silk, 80 chests of opium and some iron, saltpeter, and miscellaneous smaller goods and valuables. The merchants applied to François Martin, the chief of French East India Company, for a passport, which he granted. (If they also applied to the Dutch or English for passports, no records have survived.)

Then the heavily laden ship lumbered uneventfully south along the Coromandel Coast and the tip of India.

On January 30, 1698, someone aboard the *Adventure Galley* about twenty-five leagues off Cochin spied the sails of the *Quedagh Merchant.* The man hoped it would be a prize so he could reap the reward of 100 pieces of eight.

Kidd ordered the *Adventure Galley* to hoist French colors and follow hard. After four hours, about ten leagues off Cochin, Captain Kidd caught up with the other vessel. At the time, all Kidd knew was that

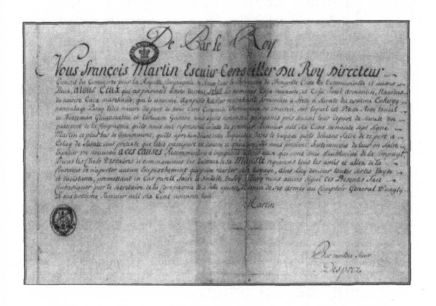

The French East India Company issued this "passport" (i.e., letter of safe passage) to the Quedah Merchant *for its upcoming voyage.*

other ship was big, about 400 tons, carrying 18 cannon, showing Armenian colors. Kidd commanded the master of the other ship to come aboard. All was still relatively amicable.

An old Frenchman, hoisted into the ship's boat, came over to the *Adventure Galley*. When the Frenchman stepped aboard, Kidd said he gave the orders to hoist English colors, which was done. The Frenchman looked up at the flag, presented his French pass, and said, "Here is a good Prize." Kidd examined the pass, which was duly authentic, with the French East India seal, and signed simply, "Martin." Kidd, for his part, showed the Frenchman his commission from the Admiralty to take French ships.

If the politeness of the exchange seems baffling, you have to realize that Kidd had thirty-six guns and a hundred very irritable crewmen, overmatching the eighteen guns and ninety docile lascars of the *Quedagh Merchant*. More to the point, the Frenchman wasn't really the captain; he was merely a hired hand, with little real stake in the cargo. Kidd drank a dram or two with the old fellow.

The *Adventure* had snagged a fat prize.

The Armenian merchants on board, as soon as they found out that their Frenchman had surrendered the ship, went berserk, screaming and crying and yelling at their huddled crew to fight. It so happened that Kidd was cruising alone at that moment and Kidd, for his part, decided to wait for the *Rouparelle/November* to rejoin him before making any further decisions. (Privateer protocol forbade prize crews from losing out on any booty or missing any important votes, after they had agreed to go aboard a captured vessel.)

While Kidd and crew waited for the *Rouparelle/November*, it gave them a chance to inspect the rich cargo of the enormous *Quedagh*: bales of silk, muslin, calico, opium. Moslem historians set the ship's value at 400,000 rupees, or about £50,000; that would mark at absolute minimum a doubling of investment for the backers of the *Adventure Galley*.

In the captain's cabin of the *Quedagh*, Kidd found a sturdy wooden chest, strapped with iron, double-padlocked. Before opening it, he cleared the room, deciding to inspect it right away before the troublemakers aboard the *Rouparelle* returned. So, all alone, he used a chisel and hammer to break the locks.

Kidd lifted the lid; inside were little pouches. He picked several up and poured out the contents: rubies, emeralds, diamonds, and gold nuggets. Kidd raised up a silver jewel box and opened the top; inside were four diamonds set in gold lockets and one very large diamond set in a gold ring. By the oil light, he burrowed in the chest: a bag of silver rings and precious stones, a bag of unpolished gems, two pieces of crystal, two carnelian rings, a bezoar stone, two small agates, two amethysts, as well as a sack of silver buttons, and a silver lamp that weighed almost two pounds. Kidd scattered the dazzling pile of jewels on the table and sifted through them. He then gathered up all the items and locked them back into the chest. It's likely Kidd showed the jewels to no one.

Now, at some point, while the men of the galley were still celebrating, perhaps as long as five days (says Kidd) or as short as one day (say Kidd's accusers), the Frenchman admitted to Kidd that he was not the captain. Somewhere below deck on the *Quedagh Merchant* was located an Englishman named John Wright, nominally in command. He was identified on the ship's French pass as "pilot Rette." He told Kidd that he owned a tavern in Surat and was just along for the ride. More important, he revealed to Kidd that an agent for the *English East India Company* was brokering the shipping.

Kidd immediately realized the implications of English interests being involved in the *Quedagh*. "The taking of this ship will make a great noise in England," he warned members of the crew. Around this time, the *Rouparelle/November* finally caught up to the *Adventure* and all accounts agree that Kidd called a council, proposing to the crew that they vote on whether to sell the ship back to the Armenians.

An apprentice, sixteen-year-old William Jenkins, says Kidd offered to sell it back for as little as a single piece of eight. And, to bolster his argument, he asked the crew: "Where will you take this ship? And where will you take the cargo?" The hysterical Armenian merchants were "shouting and wringing their hands." One of them, Cogi Baba, offered 20,000 rupees (£2,200) to buy back ship and cargo, basically about 1/20th of the real value.

Not surprisingly, the crew voted to turn down the offer, and said they would carry the vessel to St. Mary's Island, Madagascar, the pirate haven.

Now Kidd could fight his men as he did when they voted to take that English ship *Loyal Captain*. But this time, Kidd knew that this was technically a legal capture, so he chose to accept the legitimate vote of his privateer crew. He read the French pass over and over; he looked at the embossed fleur-de-lis. Besides being legal, this capture might salvage Kidd's voyage. Kidd made arrangements to head south. Before the embattled captain did anything, though, he found a safe storage place in the lining of his waistcoat for his two most valuable possessions: the two French passes that justified his actions.

What Kidd didn't know, when weighing his options, was that hundreds of bales below deck belonged to a nobleman, close to the Grand Moghul himself.

The celebrating *Adventure* crew prepared the boats of the *Quedagh Merchant* to take the captured vessel's crew ashore. Kidd allowed pilot John Wright to retrieve his goods (and possibly some extra) off the *Quedagh Merchant*; Kidd also bought from the Englishman, for a farthing or more, a navigational pendulum clock. (He would carry it all the way back to Boston.) This amicableness of the men from Britain stank in the nostrils of the Armenian merchants, who were *not* allowed to salvage *any* of their goods. They also said that Wright refused to fight because he told them that Kidd showed him a valid commission from the king of England.

Kidd ordered the boats of the *Quedagh Merchant* to take the ninety crewmen ashore and he allowed Thomas Parker, the captain who left that Portuguese vessel *Mary* five months earlier, to go ashore now as well. (Neither Parker nor Wright ever testified against him.) Kidd knew he wouldn't be needing any more navigational tips; he was preparing to leave India. He had decided to head home.

So he steered his three-ship fleet southeast to Cochin and Kalliquilon to sell the opium and other goods for rupees and gold. By contract, Kidd was not supposed to break cargo before returning to England or America, but this was the real world: the pragmatic captain needed to buy food to feed 100-plus men for at least six months; he also knew he needed to give the disgruntled men some wages, to have any hope of convincing them to ferry the two prize ships one third of the way around the world.

In Kalliquilon harbor, boat after boat came out to Kidd to trade. As the ships bobbed at sea, Kidd's men tied ropes around each bale, which might weigh 300 pounds, and pulled hard to hoist it out of the hold and carry it around to lower it to an awaiting vessel. This time Kidd was not bartering a couple of horses and some cotton; he had a large valuable cargo, and he easily found buyers, few questions asked.

He sold 132 chests of opium and 122 bales of silk, generating almost £10,000 in bar gold and gold nugget, a fat sum, but really merely a taste of the *Quedagh's* wealth.

And Kidd was still hopeful for more captures. While trading in Kalliquilon harbor, he accosted an incoming ship that appeared European. The captain, once he was rowed over to the galley, identified himself as Portuguese bound from Bengal to Goa, with a lascar crew of seventy. While they were talking, the crew of the *Rouparelle/November* and the *Adventure Galley* started to hassle the other ship. Kidd did little to stop them. Maybe he felt it was retribution for the damage the Portuguese had caused him. It would be like cocksure Kidd to appoint himself judge.

The sailors snatched from the Portuguese galliot two small chests of opium and at least four small bales of silk, as well as dozens of bags of rice. Night fell.

From Kidd's perspective, after all the heartache, his fortunes had at long last improved dramatically. He now commanded three ships, could feed his men, and was carrying a valuable prize cargo that would pay off his investors.

At daybreak, Kidd awoke to see four large ships heading toward him. He could see through his glass that the two frontrunners were immense English East India merchantmen, about a league away, and the two trailing vessels appeared Dutch.

Kidd didn't know it, but the two captains of East India Company ships had received a tip about his whereabouts peddling stolen goods, and they had decided to try to surprise him. The Dutch, heading in the same direction, tagged along. The English East Indiamen had hoped to reach the harbor mouth by dawn but fell just short, by an hour.

Kidd ordered his men instantly to the capstans. He hated to sacrifice anchors, so he started hoisting them, staying as long as he dared, checking the spyglass. The early-morning breezes still favored him, but he saw the cannon-studded ships tacking closer; he could wait no longer. He gave orders to cut the remaining anchors.

Kidd needed to escape the harbor, but he wasn't going anywhere without his prizes. The men hurled tow ropes between the ships. The men's livelihood hung on this slow-motion getaway. He barked orders to unfurl sail. The *Rouparelle/November* lurched forward towing the Portuguese vessel; and the *Adventure Galley* caught the breeze with the *Quedagh Merchant* in tow.

As the vessels were creaking underway, Kidd yelled to his prize captains: if separated, the ships should all meet in St. Mary's Island, Madagascar, and he would give the men their shares of the gold.

With the sun lifting off the Indian countryside, the two East Indiamen were desperate to seal off the harbor, but they were large, lumbering beasts, better for mule-hauling pepper than dancing across the waves. Kidd and *Quedagh* easily escaped the harbor at Kalliquilon. But the *Rouparelle* looked trapped; the prize crew quickly realized that they were not up to towing the Portuguese vessel, and chopped the braided cord with an axe. The *Rouparelle*, too, escaped the harbor's throat while cannonballs from East Indiamen splashed harmlessly nearby.

Captain Hide in the East India's slow *Dorrill* realized he couldn't catch up, so he stayed behind with the Portuguese galliot in the harbor. The other East Indiaman tried to give chase, but clearly lost ground with each moment, and soon gave up. However, the Company captains were buoyed that the Dutch, faster sailers and farther out to sea, had the perfect angle to close on Kidd. The undermanned *Quedagh Merchant* poked along; as did the *Rouparelle*, with its ne'er-do-well crew struggling to set the correct sails. The Dutch looked poised for the kill. Kidd watched through the spyglass. Would the Dutch do everything to increase their speed? Would they pile on top royals? Would they lighten their water load?

Instead, the Dutch, without even a token pursuit, tacked into port. "I have no orders to meddle with pirates, unless a Dutch ship is attacked first," Captain Jan Coin informed Captain Hide, who later wrote: "The [Dutch] could have taken all but Kidd and hee could not have escaped without difficulty." Sir Thomas Gayer of Bombay added bitterly in his report for London: "The Dutch do seem glad of the scandal we lye under for pyracy."

So, thanks to the Dutch, Kidd had escaped. All three of his ships were far apart; each had angled to baffle pursuers. Night would separate them further, especially since the captains of the other two ships made no effort to return to Kidd.

The *Adventure Galley* was carrying at least £10,000 in gold aboard. Kidd hoped it would be enough to lure his ornery crews to carry the other two ships the 2,500-mile journey to St. Mary's, Madagascar.

Kidd's ship was once again leaking badly. The seams on the hull had started to open up. The vessel was literally falling apart, and Kidd had ordered the men to "woold her round with cables," that is, wrap the ship in very thick ropes to hold her together. Kidd said he feared she would sink, and he had to keep eight men pumping her out hard every hour. Someone's job was to flip the half-hourglass twice and announce to the next shift of pumpers to make their way below. Fortunately for Kidd, when they had cut and run from Kalliquilon, seven Moors had still been aboard. These brown-skinned men were forced to do the bulk of the pumping.

For the *Adventure Galley*, it was a race against exhaustion and the seasonal changing direction of the monsoon winds. Several men complained about the captain's "hard usage." This must have been an incredibly bruising stint, but if Captain Kidd lightens up, not plying every sail to every puff of air, maybe he doesn't make it.

The *Adventure Galley*, traveling alone, limped into St. Mary's Island and hovered just off the coast. Inside the harbor stood one large ship with more than thirty guns. Kidd thought he could see a handful of men rowing ashore and scuttling into the woods. A canoe of Malagasy natives came out to Kidd and he asked what ship was anchored in the harbor. He was told it was a pirate by the name of "Colliver" or "Cullifer" or "Culliford." Another man remembered "Captain Robert Culliford."

Kidd had finally found a pirate.

Pirate Captain Culliford

Chapter Ten

Robert Culliford had been living the pirate life . . . ever since his rescue off that merchant ship in the harbor of Mergui in Siam. The crew had immediately voted him to be quartermaster of their pirate ship, *Resolution*, formerly the *Mocha Frigate*, darling of the English East India Company.

The *Mocha* was an enormously potent ship: thirty-four mounted cannon and twelve mortars, including a saucy pair in the bow. Some lower-tier cannon could throw a sixteen-pound ball. Culliford talked the men into sailing from Siam to the Nicobars, where he hoped to rescue those few hardies who had stolen the *Josiah* with him and also to pick up some lascar crew. When the *Mocha Frigate* arrived, the pirates and lascars were gone; they had probably hitched a ride on a passing ship; some of the crew assumed that they had been eaten by the Andaman islanders.

While they didn't find Culliford's comrades, the *Mocha Frigate* did run into a ship full of "tough old pirates," called the *Charming Mary*. (It turns out "old" means many of the crew were in their early forties, actuarially ancient for a sailor of that time period.) Despite operating over thousands of miles of ocean, the world of pirates in the East Indies could be surprisingly small. Not only did they visit the same handful of outlaw harbors (Nicobars, St. Mary's) and trawl the same shipping lanes (Bab-el-Mandeb, Straits of Sumatra) but they often hailed from the same American colonies. Cousins who barely hallooed in the streets of Manhattan hugged in the tropics.

Most of the crew of this *Charming Mary* had sailed out of New York in 1695 with Captain Thomas Tew (a pirate identified on Kidd's commission) in an ill-fated cruise aboard the *Amity* — seventy tons, eight guns, and a crew of sixty. Tew joined Captain Avery's pirate flotilla, but the ship was a bad sailer and kept lagging behind. When Captain Avery caught up off the highlands of St. John with the *Gunsway* — one of the richest captures ever — the *Amity* was not in sight, and hence its crew wasn't eligible for shares. When they did arrive, they reaped the bitter fruit of watching each of 180 pirates aboard three other ships share out about £1,000 per man. Soon after, the captain, Thomas Tew, was blown in half by a cannonball and *Amity*, with thirty surviving crewmen full of ill will, struggled into St. Mary's Island, off Madagascar. They wanted a better, faster, stronger ship. Adam Baldridge, the resident trader for Frederick Phillips of New York, tipped them off that the *Charming Mary*, 200 tons, 16 guns, with a restless crew of 80, had headed south to Port Dauphin to trade for slaves and rice. So, the *Amity*, sailing into the harbor at night, surprised the *Charming Mary* at anchor and took the ship. Actually, they were surprisingly civil about it: they exchanged ships, and allowed any crewmen to join them.

Despite the name of their adopted ship, *Charming Mary*, this was one argumentative bunch of pirates. They had elected John Ireland as their captain on the *Amity* after Tew died; when they got the new ship, they voted in Phillip Bobbington; by the time they reached the Nicobars, Joseph Skinner would be captain. Instead of marooning the ousted leaders, they kept them aboard, which couldn't have brought much amity to Mary.

The crews of the *Charming Mary* and *Mocha/Resolution* decided to consort together; *two* pirate ships make a lone merchant vessel far more likely to surrender. Most pirates, despite their bloodthirsty reputation, generally preferred not to risk spilling their own blood.

The pair of pirate ships headed for the southern tip of India. The fall of that year was uneventful: only one capture, a small Moorish ship carrying mostly rice. Their lives packed more boredom and waiting than riotous debauch.

Their captain, Ralph Stout, had never been a pirate before, and he mainly concerned himself with the business of navigation, while Robert Culliford, holding the titles of quartermaster and first mate, handled almost everything else.

The pirates hovered on the edge of the shipping lanes looking for unescorted ships; men strained their eyes looking in every direction, hoping for the prize-spotter's bonus. Meanwhile, they continued that endless quest for wood and water, for places that would serve pirates, no questions asked. The rigors of running a large ship were no less on the *Mocha Frigate* now that it was a pirate vessel, but the tone was more easygoing camaraderie than harsh discipline. The pirate captain served by permission of his crew; whipping was almost unthinkable.

A pirate ship was dirtier. Aboard a Royal Navy man-of-war, the crew holystoned the deck, that is, scrubbed it with sand and Bible-sized stones, every morning; pirates skipped that routine. A pirate could concentrate on the important things: sharpening his cutlass and knife, cleaning his pistols, practicing running out the cannon, teasing the turtles, daydreaming about tipple-houses and dark-haired doxies.

The pirate dream girl of the 1690s looks so different from today's model, circa 2002, that it bears pointing out. While individual preferences, of course, varied from dreamer to dreamer, the desired type as featured in novels such as *Moll Flanders* and erotic engravings of the time period, were not skinny girls, but women full in the hips, thighs, and buttocks, with firm abundant flesh and medium to smallish, half-cantaloupe breasts. (Large breasts — highly impractical before the invention of the brassiere around 1915 — suited peasant wet nurses.)

Aboard a pirate ship, there was plenty of music; one set of pirate articles speaks of giving the fiddler a day off, which implies the tunes flew for the most of the week. The musicians acted like a kind of human jukebox, with the scoundrels hollering out requests. They danced on deck, told tall tales, sang dirty songs.

There is a bonny handsome Girl,

that lives beneath "The Sun";
A wench that's kind and willing
    too, and ready for a run:
She'l walk with you from place to
place, where e're you please to
    go,
She'l kiss and play, both night
and
    day, for a trick that I do know.

Some pirate ships banned gambling; some didn't. Dice games were popular, but so were the knife fights accompanying them.

The daydream spell aboard the *Mocha* finally ended in January 1697 when someone spotted a fleck on the horizon in the evening. Culliford consulted Stout and they decided to hoist English colors as a decoy while the *Charming Mary* put up a Moslem standard, and they headed for the other ship, which was cantering under light sail along the shore. The stratagem worked, as the other ship's captain, William Willock, mistook the pair for a couple of ships that he had noticed making ready to depart Bengal just as he was leaving. Willock felt secure and lay by for the night.

At daybreak, he realized his mistake when the pirate ships bore down on him and aligned themselves, one on each side. The rogues in their fearsome motley yelled across the waves, demanding with sarcastic politeness, intermixed with curses, that he come aboard. When Willock hesitated, each of the pirate ships lowered a boat, and dropped in twenty armed men to speed up his decision-making. They captured *Satisfaction* without firing a shot.

This taking of a small merchant vessel carrying a few hundred bags of sugar from Bengal would be of little importance except for the fact that Captain William Willock was taken prisoner and later wrote a 5,000-word memoir of his eleven months held captive aboard Robert Culliford's pirate ship.

Pirate prisoners have left few authentic accounts — most of them brief or crafted much later with the dubious help of a professional writer. William Willock, merchant sea captain, stepped ashore and immediately wrote up his unvarnished narrative. A scribe painstakingly made a copy, which was shipped overland to London and eventually filed with other "Plantations General" material, where it remained, almost untouched, for three centuries.

A pirate ship was a messy democracy, and while the three ships sailed to get provisions, Captain Willock, a Scot and veteran sailor, overheard the Culliford-led debate over the fate of his 150-ton *Satisfaction*.

"There was a great disputing among

them what they should doo with the ship," recorded Willock. "Says one, 'If wee lett this fellow goo, he descryes us and sends the Dutch ffleet from Cochin upon us.' In fine, they concluded to sink her and keep us Prisoners till they went off the coast and as soone as wee came in sight of the Cape, they took all the Provisions both Rice and Water and about 200 Baggs of Sugar out of her with all her rigging, sailes, anchors and cables."

A small unarmed ship wouldn't help them in any fight; better to bury the evidence. So without wasting any gunpowder, they instructed the pirate carpenter to cut a hole in the side below the waterline.

Captain William Willock watched as *Satisfaction*, stripped to its sticks, its deck strewn with spilled sugar and the rubble of ransacking, slowly sank into the waters off the southern tip of India. The flagless mast dipped last below the surface. Sinking the ship was burying the evidence, making the crime fade.

"Then the [pirates] went into the shoar and anchored about 5 leagues to the Northward of Cape Comorin, where the natives brought them off water, Goats and ffowles in abundance, which they paid a considerable rate for."

Willock was precise in locating the place that welcomed the pirates. He expected that someday some authorities — Dutch, Moghul, or English — would want to pay the villagers a visit. Pirates, when they weren't plundering a village, were notorious for *over*paying, which infuriated tight-fisted merchants. "Those sparks are generous, getting it easily themselves," wrote William Penn.

On February 7, in the evening, the pirates, glutted on goat, jittery from fistfuls of sugar, saw from their sheltered inlet three large ships pass, heading toward the Cape. Culliford wanted to follow immediately but Stout thought it too risky, since at that time of day the sea breezes were blowing hard toward the nearby lee shore.

The pirates were forced to wait for the land breeze to kick in at night. They weighed anchors by lantern light, turning the capstan, singing dirty chanteys in the darkness. They set off south in pursuit.

Willock said at dawn the pirates sent their keenest-eyed man to the top masthead: one of the ships was almost out of sight, but the other two he pegged to be about two miles away, and to be Portuguese. Culliford decided to put out French colors. The French and Portuguese, both being Catholic nations, were generally sympathetic to each other at this time. "The Portuguez seeing that tooke them to be ffrench ships," wrote Willock, "and stayed for them till they came almost within shott of them."

The trusting Portuguese captain finally put a spyglass to his eye and perceived the deception.

"Then they [Portuguese] began to make the best of their way from them. The small pirat sailed the best and with a small breez came up with them and fired her broadsides in with a volley or two of small armes which portuguez ships answered as well as they could."

The captain of the bigger Portuguese ship opted to try to fire broadsides while making his getaway; unfortunately for him, he miscalculated the wind and the cannon's recoil spun the ship until he had the bow pointing cockeyed into the wind. "The *Mocha* came up with her and called her to strike. They said they would not; the *Mocha* fired her forechase gunns into her quarter which rackt her fore and aft."

The *Mocha Frigate* was that rare vessel in the Indian Ocean that had potent forechase guns, i.e., strong mortar that could shoot from the bow of the ship as the *Mocha* angled in from behind. The Portuguese, with their cannon along the sides of the ship, was a sitting duck unless they could turn their ship to fire broadsides.

"Then the [Portuguese] struck their topsailes & called out for Quarter. All this while, the other [merchant ship] was making a running fight and by chance gott the start and put into the shoar, the other [pirate] after her but lost her in the night. Next morning I could see her lying close by the shoar, near Quiloan and much vext were the Pirats that they had lost her."

Quiloan was a Dutch outpost, with a garrison of about thirty, in territory captured decades earlier from the Portuguese. The guns of the fort protected anyone running from a pirate. The men of the *Mocha/Resolution* and *Charming Mary* fell to the bird in hand, with Culliford leading the way.

"To plundering they went of this they had taken wch was a ship about 300 tunns from Macao in China very richly laden. They took out of that ship which I could see a 100 pound weight of Gold, 2,300 pieces of silk, besides of Bread, Porke and all sorts of Provision and sweetmeats [candy]. A great quantity above 50 bales & chests of coarse silks and gause [silk] they hove overboard."

For some of these men, former merchant sailors who had been drubbed while loading goods, it was wicked fun to toss cargo overboard, to watch it splash in the sea. The joys of plunder were enhanced by the merchants' misery and by hefty gulps of the Portuguese captain's finest liquors, in turn fueling an even more passionate hunt for treasure. While most loot was stored in locked chests in the captain's cabin, the pirates always wondered if any might be tucked elsewhere, in a rafter, in a blanket roll.

"[The pirates were] most terribly punishing their Prisoners to make them confesse if they had noo more Gold in their ship, to the value of a button," wrote Willock. "One of the Padres they hoysted up with his hands tyed behind him and with a cutlass cut some part of his beard off."

The beard trim does not seem especially cruel unless it was a blindfolded pirate whirling on the pitching deck with a razor-sharp cutlass. (Willock, in his messy script, might have written "yeard/yard," sailor slang for penis, but the copyist didn't recognize the word.)

Culliford, Gilliam, and Stout continued their drunken party for days; they dressed up in the fine clothes captured. They swaggered in pumps and slept in piles of stolen silk. Culliford enjoyed exquisite Madeira. They singled out one Portuguese after another.

Pirate tortures often involved hoisting and beating or cutting; a naked man hoisted with his arms trussed behind him was extremely vulnerable. The pasty bellies of the Portuguese merchant friars jiggled in the sunlight, as their weight threatened to yank their arms out of their sockets. For ballast for the skinny ones, a couple of bags of sugar worked nicely.

(Back in the harsh 1690s, torture — not just by pirates — was almost commonplace since the judiciaries of most European countries, including France and Spain, accepted it as the primary, and perfectly legal, means of eliciting a confession.)

The pirates — excellent knot-tiers — sometimes suspended prisoners by their thumbs, ankles, or . . . genitals. Thin whipcord, instead of braided rope, increased the pain. Fiddler, strike up a tune.

"A few dayes after[ward], God Almighty was pleased to show a Judgement on him that did it [i.e., tortured the priest]. In three dayes all his flesh turned to corruption soo that he dyed gnashing his teeth but could not speake." Captain Willock, a Scotch Presbyterian, was impressed.

"They were about four days in robbing of this ship. Some was for burning of her. Then says they, 'What can we do with all the Prisoners?' Some cried, 'Burn them in her.' But at last they saw another sail so they sent this ship away, and sent all my lascars in her, which was about the 14th or 15th ffeb.ry."

After the four-day plunder, Culliford enjoyed the pleasant task of dividing the booty into a hundred shares; each man scooped up about a pound of gold and twenty-five pieces of silk.

The pirates took two more ships in the shipping lanes in the next week. The larger one was called the *Aurangzib*, after the Grand Moghul. After a brief battle, they plundered from it 100 bags of rice and an anchor and sent it on its way; they kept the smaller one, the *Advice* pink, a merchant ship from Bengal. (A pink is a smallish vessel, with a narrow stern, about a fifty-foot keel and seventy-five-ton burden.) These pirates, who generally preferred a hit and run approach, had stayed in a relatively small area for two weeks.

"Now they were bound off the Coast for feare of the Dutch ffleet and they must go for Maldivas, there to clean their ships. The Pink they tooke in a tow & carryed with them promising me that as soone as they had carreen'd their ship that they would send mee away in that Pink. About the 6 of March they fell in with the Maldevas [Maldives] in 6½ North Latttitude."

The Maldives — where Kidd was falsely accused of rape and plunder — are an island group, a close-clustered spray of sandy unfertile islands that extend in a long swath from 7° to 1° north latitude off the tip of India. Europeans, rather than learn a pile of unpronounceable names, identify the islands — except for one, King's Island — by their latitude. Like the whale to the Eskimo, so was the coconut palm to these islanders, who used it to make everything from clothes to boats to cooking oil. They eked out a living selling dried Bonetta fish to passing ships. (The fish — like mackerel or small tuna — is caught, deboned, wrapped in coconut leaves, and baked under the sands by the heat of the sun.)

"[The pirates] stood in among the Islands and anchored, then went ashoar a-Robbing & burnt several Villages. Some were for staying to clean their shipps, others for going to the Kings Island."

The pirates captured a local boat, who mistook them for a couple of merchants, and they forced the pilot — under threat of severe pain — to navigate them through the tricky shoals to King's Island. "When they came there, they saluted the place with some Guns."

Firing salutes to other ships upon entering harbors bears a long European tradition, but you have to wonder what the local island king, in a colorful cloth wrap, made of the "boom, boom, boom," whether he knew it was in his honor or whether he thought it was to scare him.

Then a little accident occurred. "One of [the cannon], being shotted, carryed the shot ashoar into the Towne."

Honorary salutes were supposed to involve a small pile of gunpowder, a boom, a puff of smoke, *not* a cannonball. The pirate gunner was either drunk or a screw-up.

Imagine the flotilla of three ships coming into the palm-lined harbor and the pirates waving and looking friendly, then a cannonball comes whistling toward the huts.

"They went ashoar with their boat and carryed a Present for the King to the value of £100 sterling. The Present was accepted but they could have noo admittance to the King nor to the Commerce."

That gift was a very expensive bauble for the Maldives, but it failed, post-cannonball.

"They weighed from thence & went about 4 leagues to 2 other Islands & sent their boats out which brought them Oyl which was the principle thing they wanted for cleaning their ships. There they lay about 6 weeks before they were ready to saile again."

The "cleaning" in question involved no tidying up or mopping the decks; the pirates "careened" their ships, hoisting them over, scraping off the barnacles for smooth speed to swoop down on victims; they massaged in oil to seal the wood. Ashore they gambled, and searched for willing (and unwilling) women.

"Then there arose a great difference between the shipps companyes so that they parted. Most of the men came onboard the *Mocha*, & the small ship sailed with 40 men. Then there was on board the *Mocha* 65 besides blacks." Culliford, first mate, was apparently charismatic enough to lure whomever he wanted onto the larger ship. Now Willock expected that he would be set free.

"When they were ready to sail there was a vote whether I should be lett goo in the Pink," wrote Willock. "The vote carryed [that] I should not goo, so they sett the Pink on fire with most of her Lading, being Sugar and bale Goods."

At the end of April, they sailed, "bound for Quiloan there to take in Arrack."

The word "arrack" over the centuries has evolved to encompass various types of intoxicating liquor, imbibed in Asian countries from Turkey to Mongolia. In southern India at that time, arrack was made from fermenting the sap of the date palm tree or "toddy palm." The pirates were so desperate for liquor, they were going to go to the Dutch port and actually *pay* for it.

The *Mocha*'s rogues, all liquored up, then cruised for about two weeks with no luck off the west coast of India, until a storm dragged them to the Laccadive Islands.

The pirates, knowing the seasonal winds, abandoned any hope of sailing *west* to meet the Moslem pilgrim fleet and instead returned to the familiar Nicobars. "They sent their boats out a plundering the Island which brought in 2 days abt 300 fowls & 8 or 10 hoggs wch was not two day Provision for them."

Freshly killed meat and poultry could not be preserved without elaborate drying or salting methods. These pirates, who had subsisted mainly on rice and dried fish, were now feasting. Doing some third-grade math reveals that the sixty-five pirates averaged about two birds each a day and a few slices of pork.

On May 20, 1697, they sailed toward Achin, spotted a plump Portuguese vessel, and after a five-day chase — thanks to that extra dollop of speed from the clean hulls — caught it. They humiliated a fidalgo on board who was appointed to become the next general at Macao, and fell to looting.

But the pirates would now pay a price for being lazy in the Nicobars, where they loaded only a month's supply of fresh water. (Heat and democracy apparently had dulled the work ethic.)

So, while most of the crew was still plundering the Portuguese ship, Captain Ralph

Stout with ten armed men and four lascar oarsmen went six leagues ashore in the ship's pinnace to Sumatra to scout for a watering place.

They saw a deserted Malay boat and were preparing to steal it, when the Malays jumped out of the bushes and ambushed them, attacking them with spears and knives. Ralph Stout was killed, along with six others. Three escaped, pummeling the four lascars to row.

"They made Robt Colliver Captain, the same which ran away with the Ketch from Madras. He had formerly acted as mate."

Robert Culliford, of East Looe, Cornwall, was thirty years old. Almost precisely one year earlier he had stolen the small *Josiah* ketch, now he was captain of the 36-gun *Mocha Frigate*. What was it about him? Why had he been elected over the circumcised rogue Gilliam, over any of the *Charming Mary*'s past leaders?

Culliford was daring without a death wish, a man with larcenous plans, a surprisingly good bottle companion; witty, athletic, clearly devious but trustworthy to his mates. Combine all that with the ability to read and write, which impressed his brutish colleagues, and he was one tough candidate to beat.

The winds were blowing east and the men wanted to head to China. And the captured William Willock, the diarist, suddenly became more pivotal to their plans.

"Then I was importuned every day, sometimes [with] fair promises, sometimes with threats, to take upon me to carry them through the Streights. For now their Pilott was killed, which was Ralph Stout, who made them believe great matters was to be found on the Coast of China. I, by God's helpe, rebuked them, tho' many times [they had] their Pistolls to my breast telling me that if I would not, they would maroun me for my lifetime."

For days in early July, Captain Culliford and the crew threatened Willock; the staunch Scot refused to bend; then they spotted a sail in the predawn gloom. As they neared it, Culliford through the spyglass recognized it was an English East India Company ship, a fat prize, but also a heavily armed one, with about thirty cannon to their thirty-six. The vessel was trying to weather Diamond Point off Sumatra and follow the shipping lanes into the straits, but contrary winds were stymying it.

What the pirates didn't know was that this East Indiaman, the *Dorrill* under Captain Hyde, was carrying a fortune in gold and silver to finance a trading voyage to China.

The ships moved close to each other;

Captain Hyde got a troubling first impression of Culliford. "After having been forced to ride fifteen days off Diamond Point, I spied a saile to windward, bearing down upon me. [It] came up under my quarter and gave a Levitt [i.e., a flourish] with the Musick of trumpets, oboes and drum, [then] dropt astern without hailing or anything of parley."

It's not every day at seven in the morning that a ship comes up close from out of nowhere and plays a musical interlude and then disappears. But Culliford would return.

Little more than an hour later, Captain Hyde said he saw the other ship hovering just out of gunshot range, and he feared it was a pirate since the galleries in the stern over the captain's cabin had been dismantled to accommodate two large brass guns.

Hyde's crew scurried about, frantically trying to ready their ship for battle, preparing powder, ball, rammer, swabber; gathering muskets, pistols, swords; shifting cargo out of the way. Hyde ordered the men to battle stations. "Wee now hoisted our colours," recalled an eyewitness on the *Dorrill*. "The Captain commanded [us] to naile our Ensigne to the staff [i.e., pole] in sight of the enimie, which was immediately done. As they perceived [that] wee hoisted our colours, they hoisted theirs, with the

341

Union Jack, and let fly a broad red Pendant at their maintopmast head."

Captain Hyde, by ordering the flag nailed to the pole, was taunting the pirate that he would *never* strike his flag, that he would *never* surrender. Culliford responded with a bit of deception in his flags, trying to decoy that he was an English merchant ship that outranked the *Dorrill*. The broad red pendant was *not* the bloody red flag meaning no mercy, but, rather, this long narrow streaming red pennant was the symbol of a commodore, i.e., a ranking ship in a fleet of men-of-war or merchantmen. The men aboard the *Dorrill* were not the least bit fooled.

Culliford closed to within "half a Pistoll shott" of the *Dorrill*; the sailors expected to be attacked at any moment. Instead, they saw the pirates all gather together on the quarterdeck, apparently to "consult." Although Captain Hyde could see clearly onto the *Mocha*, he could not *hear* what was going on.

Willock, prisoner aboard the pirate ship, can supply the dialogue.

"Hell was never in a greater Confusion than was then aboard [with] some for hoisting ffrench colours to fight him, some for fighting under no colours, some for not fighting at all, some for running him aboard without fireing a gunn. The Capt.

[Culliford] laid down his charge because of ye Confusion then about ship. They must goo to chuse another Captain."

Pirate democracy had its pitfalls.

The armed angry men yelled themselves hoarse, cursing and debating whether to fight an equal foe. As they ranted, Culliford, who wanted to attack, kept the pirate jogging alongside the Indiaman. But at three in the afternoon the pirates voted to leave the *Dorrill*, and Culliford disgustedly relinquished his command. The *Mocha/ Resolution* backed her sails and veered away, and the *Dorrill* headed as far off in the other direction as it could.

But Culliford didn't let it go. He walked from man to man, trying to convince them to fight. He succeeded, and resumed as captain.

"When the Pirate was about 7 miles distant, [he] tackt and stood after us," observed Solomon Lloyd, East India Company rep, aboard the *Dorrill*. "Att 6 that evening [we] saw the lookt for island [Pulo Barahla], and the pirate came up with us on our starboard side within shott. We see he kept a man at each topmast head, looking out till was darke, then he hailed a little from us but kept us company all night."

The lookout men in the peaks were intended to make the *Dorrill* think that the pirate was awaiting a consort and indeed, Culliford might have been hoping to see the sheets of *Charming Mary*.

"At 8 in the morning he drew near us, but wee [had] had time to mount our other four gunns that were in [the] hold, and now wee were in the best posture of defense could desire." (Solomon Lloyd)

Merchant ships often stow some of the cannon to allow for extra cargo space. Hoisting the 2,000-pound barrels is no easy task at sea. Since it was clear to Captain Hyde that the *Mocha* could sail faster, he decided to confront the bully.

"The Captain resolved to see what the rogue would doo, soo [he] ordered [us] to hand [furl] all our small sailes and furled our mainsaile," wrote Lloyd.

Culliford ordered his men to do likewise and as he drew near, he ordered the musicians to beat the drums and sound the trumpets. The pirates hailed the Indiaman, received no response, and hailed again, and again, and then a fourth time.

"At last it was thought fitt to know what he would say, soo the Boatswaine spoke to him as was ordered, which was that wee came from London. Then he enquired whether peace or war with France. Our answer, there was an universal peace through Europe, att which they paused and then said, 'That's well.' Further he enquired our

Captain's name and whither wee were bound. We answered to Mallacca."

The pirates masquerading as merchants said they were heading to the very same place and kindly invited Captain Hyde to come aboard to drink a glass of wine. Hyde replied that he would prefer to visit them in the harbor at Malacca. Culliford then asked them to lay by for the night, so that he could come aboard them, but Hyde again refused, saying he was already behind schedule. Culliford then queried whether the East Indiaman would be stopping at the nearby Water Islands, and they said, yes.

"After he had asked us all these questions wee desired to know from whence he was. He said, from London, their Captain name Collyford, the ship named the *Resolution*, bound for China."

The Indiaman got under full sail again, and Culliford followed all day Thursday July 8. The next morning around ten-thirty, the pirates came within gunshot of the *Dorrill*, just as the wind died down. "Wee could discerne a fellow on the Quarter Deck, wearing a sword. As [the pirate ship] drew near, this Hellish Imp cried, 'Strike, you doggs!' which [we] perceived was not by general consent for he was called away. Our Boatswaine in a fury run upon the poop, unknown to the Captain, and answered that wee would strike to no such doggs as he, telling him the rogue Every [pirate Captain Avery who took the *Gunsway*] and his accomplices were all hanged. The Captain was angry that he spake without order, then ordered to haile [the *Resolution*] and ask what was his reason to dogg us."

Captain Culliford "stept forward on the forecastle, beckoned with his hand and said, 'Gentlemen, wee want not your ship nor men, but money.' We told [him that we] had none for them but bid them come up alongside and take it as could gett it."

That's how Solomon Lloyd heard the exchange, but Captain Hyde of the *Dorrill* recalled delivering a more stirring riposte to Culliford's demand for money. "If you would have it, it must be out of the muzzles of our guns. Come up fairly alongside and take it."

Captain Willock heard: "It's money we want and money we will have." Reply: "It's well, come and take it."

"Then a parcell of bloodhound rogues clasht their cutlashes and said they would have it or our heart's blood, saying, 'What, do you not know us to be the *Mocha*?' Our answer was, 'Yes, Yes.' Thereon they gave a great shout and so they all went out of sight and wee to our quarters. They were going to hoist colours but ensigne halliards broke, which our people perceiving gave a great shout.

"As soon as they could bring their chase gunns to bear, fired upon us and soo kept on our quarter."

The pirate is ranging up on an angle from behind, which prevents the *Dorrill*'s broadside cannon from returning fire.

"Our gunns would not bear in a small space, but as soon as did hap, [our captain] gave them better than [the pirates] did like. His second shott carried away our spritt saile yard. About ½ an hour after or more, he came up alongside and soo wee powered in upon him and continued, sometime broadsides [volley of all the cannon on one side] and sometimes three or four gunns as opportunity presented and could bring them to doo best service. He was going to lay us athwart the hawse, but by God's providence Captain Hyde frustrated his intent by pouring a broadside into him, which made him give back and go asterne, where he lay and paused without firing."

Culliford was trying to maneuver his ship on an angle across the bow of the *Dorrill*. This would allow him to pump broadsides into the *Dorrill* with minimum risk to himself and also set up for boarding the *Dorrill*. However, to reach that advantage point, the *Mocha* had to pass along the length of the *Dorrill* at great risk.

Willock observing aboard the pirate ship: "I could see the pirates disheartened. Said they, 'We shall get nothinge here but broaken bones, and if we lose a mast, where shall we gett others?' They had received a shott in their foremast, a six-pound ball, which had gone right through the heart of it. Says the Captain, 'We have enough of it [the mast] to fetch to windward of him. Let us goo about ship for he lyes by for us,' and soo he did. Says one, 'You may put her about yourself and you will, for I'll fight no more.' 'Nor I,' says another, 'Nor I, Nor I,' was the cry."

Solomon Lloyd on the *Dorrill*: "About an hour after, he tackt and came up with us againe. Wee made noo saile, but lay by to receive him, but he kept aloof off. The distance at most in all our fireing was never more than two ships length; the time of our engagement was from ½ an hour after 11 till about 3 afternoon."

The lull in the fighting gave the *Dorrill* crew a chance to inspect the extensive damage to both crew and ship. The dejected pirates had wreaked far more havoc than they realized.

"We . . . found our Cheife Mate, Mr. Smith, wounded in the legg, close by the knee, with a splinter or piece of chaine; our Barber had two of his fingers shott off as was spunging one of our gunns, the Gunner's boy had his legg shott off in the waist [of the ship], John Amos, Quartermaster, had his leg shott off [while] at the helme, the Boatswain's boy (a lad of thirteen years old) was shott in the thigh, which went through and splintered his bone, the Armourer Jos. Osbourne in the round house wounded by a splinter just in the temple, the Captain's boy on the Quarter Deck a small shott raised his scull through his cap and was the first person wounded and att the first onsett. Wm. Reynolds boy had the brim of his hatt ½ shott off and his forefinger splintered very sorely. John Blake, the flesh of his legg and calfe a great part shott away."

The boys, scurrying about the ship, carrying messages or gunpowder to the cannon crews, ran great risk, not from the cannonball itself, but rather from the deadly spray of splinters.

The East India ship was also badly mangled: mizzentopmast snapped, rigging shredded with only one running rope intact, five mainshrouds cut in half, an eight-inch-deep half-moon cut out of the mainyard, fore-topmast backstays shot away, cannonball holes in the roundhouse and quarterdeck, and several in steerage and in the forecastle, as well as two cannonballs straight into the bread room just below the waterline. Seawater had poured in before the carpenter could fix it, spoiling the greater part of the ship's biscuit. The deadeye pirates scored direct hits on five cannons, dismounting them off the wooden carriages. "They fired pieces of glass-bottles, glass teapots, chains, stones and what not, which were found on our decks."

The pirate threat was not over.

Culliford, disgusted with his crew, ordered the lights doused that night. The *Dorrill* put out its lights as well and furled its sails. In the pitch blackness, the currents — aided by some lucky ruddering — might drag the ships surprisingly far apart. In the morning the *Dorrill*'s crew could barely see the pirates from the deck, but a man sent aloft could see that Culliford had set his sails to still dog them. The Indiaman's crew quickly knotted ropes, the carpenters repaired gun carriages.

"Our men, seeing the [pirate] stood after us, [we] could perceive [our men's] countinances to be dejected. Wee cheered them what wee could, and, for their encouragement, the Captain and wee of our proper money did give them, to every man and boy, three dollars each, which animated them, and promised to give them as much more if engaged againe." They also promised the "Gentlemen Employers" (i.e., the English East India Company) would give a reward of £5 for each prisoner, and also a "gratuity."

"About 9 o'clock the 10th July wee perceived the rogue made from us, soo we gave the Almighty our most condigne thanks for his mercy that delivered us not to the worst of our enimies, for truly he [the pirate] was very strong, having at least an hundred Europeans on board. Wee lay as near our course as [we] could, and next day saw land on our starboard side which was the Main [i.e., the Malay Peninsula]. Kept on our way."

Then the wounded began to die, mostly boys, unpaid apprentices, killed while defending the treasure of the East India Company partners.

"The 12th of July died the Boatswain's boy, George Mopp, in the morning. Friday the 16th in the evening died the Gunner's boy Thomas Matthews. Sunday the 18th at anchor two leagues from Pillo Sumbelong Islands died the Barber Andrew Miller. The 31st died the Cheife Mate, Mr. John Smith. The other two are yet in a very deplorable condition and wee are ashore here to refresh them."

The pirates, on the other hand, suffered only two men killed and one slightly wounded. Captain Culliford was absolutely right in wanting to pursue the fight; he realized that they had inflicted much more damage, but his bickering crew had refused to follow. Culliford's pirates clearly — and not surprisingly — preferred to bully smaller ships rather than engage in a fair fight against a 30-gun foe.

The turning point in the battle occurred when the *Dorrill* sent that small cannonball sailing through the *Mocha*'s foremast, leaving a clear cylindrical pathway. Any of the pirates could look over and see a disc of sky where solid wood should have been. If an East Indiaman or Royal Navy ship lost a mast, it could head to the nearest port to buy or barter for another. Pirates would have a very hard time finding any shipyard to sell them one. They would have to capture another vessel, an irritating proposition for a crew sailing without a foremast.

The *Dorrill*, crippled, tried to plow eastward but was forced to turn back, do massive repairs, and wait months for the winds to change.

The pirates, free spirits, decided to go get drunk. They doubled back to Achin and bullied some arrack from Dutch ships; they also hoped to steal a ship to act as guard during their upcoming careening of their ship. After that, they would resume living the rogue's life, as unpredictable as the next sail.

The pirates drank their arrack, danced

on deck, and lurked near Achin.

Prisoner William Willock continues the story: "About ye latter end of July [1697] they tooke this [merchant] ship . . . Shee was then very deep laden. Then they concluded they would carry this ship along with them & goo to Negrais and carreen their ship."

Negrais, on the tip of modern-day Myanmar (formerly Burma), is 750 miles north of Achin.

A Chinaman owned the ship. The pirates kept the two Europeans, twenty Malay sailors, and the Chinese cook, which perhaps indicates that Culliford was eating Chinese-style food for a while. The rest of the crew the pirates sent away on a captured Dutch brigantine.

The pirates found plenty of arrack onboard, which they took, and they started drinking and heaving the cargo overboard. They threw so much into the sea that the ship now rode four feet higher in the water, noted the observant Scot.

Captain Culliford then offered a deal to William Willock: if he would navigate them to Negrais, they would give him this captured ship and let him go. He agreed. They gave him eight pirates and a dozen lascars to sail the ship.

Willock reached Negrais in about two weeks in the middle of August and anchored his ship in twelve fathoms outside a diamond-shaped island that guarded the tricky entrance. Once inside, the harbor at Negrais was nicely sheltered, while the countryside had few people and plenty of wild game.

Willock: "Then they brought me onboard of them againe. They told me I must carry them in. I told them that was the place but I had forgot the channell in gooing in, for I had not been there in 10 yeares. Soo in the morning they weighed and stood in for ye harbour."

Culliford navigated the *Mocha* into the harbor but the prize ship failed to swing wide of the island, almost crashing before bearing away to leeward. The pirates struggled for *ten days,* losing two anchors before succeeding in angling their little stolen ship a few hundred yards around the island's pointy tip. They would stay in Negrais for four months.

On September 20, a brigantine was unlucky enough to seek shelter from a storm in that harbor. The pirates fired at him and easily captured the ship and put these new prisoners with Willock on the Chinese prize and took away their longboat. Culliford took his newest toy, the brig, and emptied it on the shore.

The pirates now began the onerous task of careening the 350-ton *Mocha Frigate,* a task made less onerous by forcing the Malay and lascars to do most of the work. These brown-skinned men, treated like slaves, had to hoist all the cargo and cannon out of the ship and tip it over, and scrape the bottom. They sweated in the heat sixteen degrees north of the equator (about ten degrees south of Miami, Florida). While some of the 100 pirates helped, no doubt many acted like drunken jerks.

In early October, the Malays and lascars plotted to overthrow the pirates. They hid the caulking irons and mallets, knives and chisels in a pile near where they slept. They showed butler-like servility bringing the pirates ample tots of liquor. They bedded down on the ground, waiting their chance, while the pirates caroused, and one by one drifted off to sleep. One drunken pirate stumbled over the weapons pile and the plot was discovered.

Willock: "[This] had like to have cost us all our lives but it pleased God to order it otherwise. Only one Coffree [dark-skinned man] they shott to death & two lascars which they punisht soo & burnt their hands & feet wth match that they dyed."

"Match" was not some little wooden stove match, with a combustible tip. Match, sometimes called slow match, was generally a long spool of hempen cord soaked in saltpeter, designed to keep smoldering like a fuse. In the centuries before flintlocks provided the sparks for muskets, a marksman would keep "slow match" burning, and when he was ready to fire, he would touch the tip to the priming powder. The pirate torture was something akin to relentless sadistic burning with cigarettes, on those two very sensitive areas, the palms of the hand and soles of the feet.

The torture and terror achieved the desired goal. No labor unrest whatsoever plagued the duration of the pirates' holiday careen.

Soon, another European-captained ship made the mistake of entering the harbor and the pirates quickly snapped it up. The brig had little the pirates wanted, so they stole only its longboat. Meanwhile, the pirates seemed to be enjoying themselves in stringing Captain Willock along. Culliford had promised him the captured Chinese vessel, but the pirates stripped it of almost all the sails and rigging, and left only one anchor and cable. Culliford, although he clearly liked having a seasoned navigator around, decided not to break his promise outright.

Willock: "Two old sailes they had given me . . . which I was forced to mend and make fitt myself. They would allow nobody to help me, which I did while she lay a-careening."

One month rolled into the next as the Malays and lascars toiled in the heat. Then at the beginning of December an event occurred that the pirates regarded as *extraordinary* good fortune.

A ship from Siam lost its mainmast in a storm and sought the shelter of the harbor. The captain accidentally grounded the yawing ship upon a sandbar, and the outgoing tide stranded it there, leaving it like a buffet treat for the pirates.

The *Mocha* was tipped upon its side but Culliford ordered twenty-four men into one of the captured brigantines to sail out and pretend to offer assistance. As they approached, the vessel shook itself free, but the pirates — brandishing pistols and cutlasses — easily convinced the crippled ship to head toward the shore.

There, the pirates ordered the passengers to go ashore and the crew to unload all the cargo. They announced they were going to burn the boat. The captain begged for the pirates to take the cargo but to let him keep his ship; Culliford refused. When the pirates went below deck to prod the small crew to start unloading, the rogues then discovered huddled among the bales eleven women from Siam (modern-day Thailand). Were they beautiful? Ugly? Tall? Short? Married? Unmarried? Virginal? Experienced? Captain Willock doesn't say, but he does state succinctly that the pirates "made use of their bodyes."

At the time the pirate crew of the *Mocha Frigate* under Captain Culliford totaled forty whites and five "coffrees" allowed to carry arms. We don't know how the eleven women were shared or whether any of them became pregnant. Perhaps there are Thais today with drops of Robert Culliford's blood coursing through their veins. Was there any tenderness? For the next two weeks, these Siamese women clearly made the pirates happy, because Robert Culliford would soon show them an unusual kindness.

Captain Willock, for his part, was preoccupied with trying to make his sorry vessel seaworthy.

Willock: "Out of [the captured ship] they gave me some old rigging with whch I made a shift to fitt her & out of her I gott some Jarrs to put water in for they had taken all ship's casks out of her which would carry 35 tunns of water. They took out of the Siam ship all the best of the goods (the rest they left in her with five horses which dyed before wee sailed for want of water).

"The [pirates] were ready to sail in the morning [of Dec. 22]. . . . I must sail along wth them. They putt aboard with mee 11 Women which they had taken out of the Siam Ship and I must promise to sett them free ashoar because they had made use of their bodyes."

Pirates had learned over the centuries *never* to allow women aboard their ships when at sea, because it invariably led to fights. The few authentic pirate ships' articles stress that prohibition. "No . . . women to be allowed amongst them. If any man were found seducing any of the latter Sex and carried her to Sea, disguised, he was to suffer Death." (Articles of Bartholomew Roberts)

So it is not surprising that Culliford and the pirate crew opted *not* to keep the women aboard the *Mocha* for their voyage, but what is unusual is that directive to Captain Willock: "I must promise to sett them free ashoar because they had made use of their bodyes."

This appears to be some chivalry on the part of Captain Culliford. The pirates certainly did not have to free the women. Were these women originally bound as servants from Siam? The pirates apparently struck some agreement with the women, some deal-with-the-devil, such as "Satisfy us regally, joyfully, willingly, and we will free you." It appears so, and Culliford kept his end of the bargain.

Willock was less interested in the women

than in the future plans of these nautical thieves, plans that might deeply impact trade in the East Indies.

"By what I cold hear amongst them they are now bound for Madagascar to get more men and victuall the ship. Their chiefe place of Randez-vous will be St. Maries, where they expect to gett more men & I believe that severall of those who are now on board will leave them there and take their passage for New England. There at St. Maries lives one Baldridge, an old Pirate who hath sent to him from New England, especially from New Yorke & Road Island, severall Consignments of goods, liquor of all sorts, stores of cordage & sailcloth of all sorts and Ammunition wth Pitch & Tarr wch he sells to the Pirats at great rates. He has built there a great house wch by its situation being on the top of a great hill is as good as a fort. He has some Gunns in it, and all the Country people at his Command for he reigneth there as a King."

Finally, after almost a year, the pirates allowed Captain Willock to sheer off. Perhaps the pirates waved to the eleven women from the rail. Perhaps the women waved back; perhaps the high-cheekboned graceful women spit at them.

Willock: "And now this Evening being the 22nd Dec/br [1697] they sett me clear, blessed be God, for I have been a Prisoner with them 11 months. But what fears, troubles & abuses, nay hunger & thirst I have suffered in this time God alone knowes, for it is beyond my Penn to Expresse it."

The pirate ship *Mocha* sailed for Madagascar, with Captain Culliford and his consort, Jon Swann, aboard and a surgeon named Jon Death and a rogue named Gilliam. They arrived in April on St. Mary's Island and anchored in the harbor, ready to spend some money and have a good time in this outlaw paradise. In a month, a large ship appeared on the horizon heading toward the harbor.

Chapter Eleven

Captain Kidd's *Adventure Galley* stood in ten-fathom-deep water just north of the pistol-shot-wide throat of the harbor at St. Mary's Island. A battery of four cannon perched on a high hill guarded the entrance to the natural harbor, but as far as Kidd could tell, no one was near the guns. A lush and lazy place, it seemed. The sailor in the bow swinging the lead plumb line sang out nine fathoms. Kidd decided to anchor. From the deck, he could see the mast of Culliford's pirate ship. The sailor in the top yards looked out to sea to the north and south for any glimpse of the *Rouparelle/ November* or the *Quedagh Merchant/Adventure Prize* coming up the channel separating the island from mainland Madagascar. Nothing, except some whales, giant flukes pointing skyward before the dive. After manning his two prize ships, Kidd had forty men left in his crew, many of them sick, like

362

his brother-in-law, Sam Bradley, and Darby Mullins, both still troubled by that never-ending "bloody flux" caught in Mohelia a year earlier. Kidd lifted the spyglass and focused the barrel on Culliford's vessel: an Indiaman converted to pirate duty, with gallery carved up for cannon ports and the rail taken down, forechase guns, and more broadside cannon than the *Adventure Galley*. Logic dictated that Culliford had a big pirate crew. That beast didn't just walk into St. Mary's; someone had furled and unfurled all those sails.

Kidd, for his part, knew he could barely scrape together a couple of gun crews; his ship was suffering not only from human disease but from a malady below the waterline. Indian Ocean sea worms were feasting on English plank, riddling the outer sheath of the hull with wormholes.

"The sea was all covered with worms," wrote an earlier traveler to these same waters, "which shine in the night like little candles, and those cursed vermine taking to our ships, they eat their way so far into her everywhere under water . . . that were it not for the pounded glass and cow's hair used in the sheathing, our vessel had sunk."

Kidd was relaying a new shift of eight men — usually alternating lascars with some of his exhausted crew — every two hours below deck to pump her out. If they stopped pumping, the galley — with its £10,000 in gold and jewels — would decorate the bottom of the harbor.

Kidd ached to attack Culliford, but he simply didn't have the manpower. No fool, he also felt very vulnerable to attack. If Culliford's ship was ready, the undermanned, leaky *Adventure Galley* would be easy prey. So Captain Kidd chose prudence over passion, deciding to wait for his two other ships to arrive. Once they and their crews joined his, it would be child's play to take Culliford. But those two other ships might reach the harbor in one day, one week, one month. The winds would shift very soon; it might be that they would *never* arrive. If that happened, he would have to attack alone.

Captain Kidd sent boats ashore and in the meantime, pirogues — tippy canoes sculpted out of tree trunks — came out to him. Kidd quickly learned the *apparent* lay of the land. The massive pirate ship was deserted; Culliford and his crew had scurried ashore into the woods. Were they laying in wait for him? Kidd decided to continue waiting for his two prize ships.

Kidd cautiously began to settle into this outlaw paradise. Being a pirate hunter in a pirate port, he was a tad leery. Kidd first tried to find New Yorker Adam Baldridge, who ran a tavern and trading post for pirates. But, unfortunately for Kidd, Baldridge had decided to decamp the year before, ferrying home his profits to New York City. Kidd later learned that Baldridge had bought a three-quarter share in the brigantine *Swift* from Boston under Captain Andrew Knott (a friend of Kidd's) and had sailed off on one last slaving mission. Before leaving, though, he had invited a few dozen of the loyal Malagasies and their families, who had served him over the years, to come aboard the ship for a farewell party. Baldridge had kidnapped them all to sell as slaves and set sail. Their relatives had risen up and attacked the compound on top of the hill, killing the thirty Europeans — mostly retired pirates — living there.

Kidd found out from the Malagasies that they were now working with another trader, one Edward Welch, originally from New England, who had a fortified compound about four miles from the main harbor. With Baldridge gone, Welch — a short man whom the natives called "Little King" — ran the tavern and trading post.

So, Kidd and Culliford now hovered in strange limbo in this small harbor at St. Mary's Island. Neither knew the other's exact strength. Both men had 30-plus-gun warships, getting creakier by the day. But since the island is thirty-five miles long, they easily could avoid each other, and they did.

Not wanting to lose his prey, Kidd guarded the entrance of the harbor. Culliford could not leave without running the gauntlet of Kidd's guns. And Kidd waited. He daydreamed that despite all the setbacks, he now had the chance to take a pirate, finally. Who knows how much treasure Culliford had on board or on shore? And Kidd knew that Culliford's ship was stolen from the English East India Company. Imagine the boatloads of goodwill he would snare if he sailed up the Thames, delivering the *Mocha*, with his other two prizes in tow.

And Captain Kidd chomped at the bit, preoccupied in paradise. Day followed long day through the entire month of April; Kidd himself climbed to the foretops some afternoons to look for sails. He kept his men aboard working the pumps and keeping the guns clean and the ropes and sails repaired. While Kidd allowed some shore leave especially for the sick, the healthy men no doubt found it nightmarish to have to work so hard while high-cheekboned women with flowers in their hair, wearing thin clingy wraps around their bodies, walked along the shore.

One morning, Kidd took a group of

trusty men and had them carry a chest up to Edward Welch's hilltop home, protected by six cannon. It was very heavy, and the men whispered that this was the 100 pounds of gold Kidd had gotten by trading the opium and silks off the coast of India.

For Robert Culliford, on the other hand, it was peel-me-a-grape time. The rogue was holed up in a Malagasy village, living in a shack on stilts, with a trio of dark-skinned lovelies. Every so often, he tossed a penny to one of the little boys to go fetch him some rum from Welch's shack. He placed his dinner order in the morning and the Malagasies scurried to hunt it or fish it and serve it up. Kidd's presence didn't frighten him.

Kidd waited. With time on his hands, Kidd drew up a secret account ledger of his voyage, down to the penny. On the credit side, i.e., revenues: £10,184 (from the first French fishing vessel prize, to chests of opium sold off India). On the debit (expenses), he tallied £2,587, itemizing costs at London, New York City, Tulear, Johanna, Mohelia, even factoring in interest costs. He subtracted debit from credit to yield £7,597, which he called "Rests due to the Company." And that didn't include the 600 bales in the belly of the *Quedagh Merchant*, worth £40,000, and didn't allow for what he would take from

Culliford. It was a pleasant numbers game to while the time away, stacking future profits.

Then, five long weeks after Kidd arrived, on May 6, 1698 — a fine fall day in the southern hemisphere — someone spotted a sail. Kidd peered through his spyglass. He was relieved that it was *not* a pirate buddy of Culliford, or an East Indiaman. It was the *Rouparelle/November*, finally.

The *Rouparelle* glided toward the *Adventure Galley*, the men on both ships hailed one another. Under Skipper Mitch, the prize ship looked ghastly, with sails frayed and rigging askew. The crew aboard the *Rouparelle* asked whether the Big Prize (i.e., *Quedagh Merchant*) had arrived yet. The answer was no; the *Rouparelle* sailed right past the galley and into the harbor, and the crew ran the ship right toward the shore on a little odd tongue of land in the center of the harbor called "Careen Key." (Today it's "Ile aux Forbans," i.e., "Rogues' Island," and is pockmarked with treasure-hunter holes.)

The troublemakers aboard the *Rouparelle*, such as Joseph Palmer of Westchester, wanted nothing to do with Kidd. The men carelessly tossed the anchors but the ship beached itself in the sand and tipped like a drunken sailor. They knew there was no way that Kidd would pay any shares until all three ships were gathered. So, tired from the long voyage, worried they would never see the other prize ship, they came ashore and scattered among the temptations of the ramshackle village. St. Mary's was a flower-strewn paradisiacal kind of place, where a man might get lucky for a couple of iron nails or some ribbon. They waded ashore to find hump-backed cattle, zebu, on the menu and strange cat-like monkeys, called lemurs, that the locals liked to broil. The sailors, unaccustomed to solid ground, bobbled around with a rolling gait, like some starved lusting herd.

Ashore, the men of the *Rouparelle/November* mingled with some of Captain Culliford's pirate crew, downing imported New York rum and local palm wine. And Kidd, relentless Kidd, waited for *Quedagh Merchant*, carrying almost 600 bales of expensive fabric, worth a small fortune. Kidd had put longtime New York friend Henry Bullen in charge of the prize ship, with a few dozen loyal crewmen aboard. He couldn't avoid those horrible thoughts: Was it lost? Sunk? Captured?

The seasonal winds were shifting: Kidd could see the change in the swaying palm fronds, in the sudden rainy squalls. With each passing day and night, it was becoming less likely that any ship would arrive from the north. Brother-in-law Samuel

Bradley suckled on the breast of a nursing Malagasy mother; a sailor said he had heard mother's milk cured "bloody flux"; it was worth a try.

Then, a week after the *Rouparelle* had touched shore, a new set of sails hove into view. The *Quedagh Merchant* had finally arrived. The men on shore drank another dirty glass of rum, and everyone went out to meet the ship as it came to the anchorage outside the throat of the harbor.

Along with dozens of others, Kidd boarded the *Quedagh Merchant*; Henry Bullen, captain, was dead. The deck was a sea of talk. The delivery of the goods and the reuniting of the crews brought on fiddle and drinks. Men went to Edward Welch's shack to buy severely overpriced rum. Malagasy women worked and played overtime. Kidd stood aloof.

After two days passed, he sent word to the huts and quasi-taverns that he wanted all his men to gather on the deck of the *Quedagh Merchant*. Hungover men stumbled into jolly boats and pirogues, as native women clung to them; one man handed over a comb, another a mirror. About 115 men stood on the deck of the Moorish vessel.

Kidd finally had enough manpower and cannon power to blast Culliford into submission. After the twists and turns of being fired upon by the East India Company convoy and by the Portuguese, after the Royal Navy hassle and the thirst off Arabia, after it all, Kidd could now smell not only victory but the chance for wealth, glory, and even revenge. He would right an old wrong inflicted by Culliford when that brat had helped steal the *Blessed William* a decade earlier. Kidd planned to sail to London: the *Adventure Galley* leading the *Mocha Frigate* (with Robert Culliford below deck in chains) and leading the *Quedagh Merchant* and *Rouparelle* (both legal captures carrying French passports). His little fleet would mark a bold sight on the Thames: the pirate hunter returning with the wickedest pirate ship of the Indian Ocean, and with a pair of prizes worth £50,000.

Kidd, looking down from the forecastle, told his men that now was the time to attack the pirate, to ready their weapons for battle. They outnumbered Culliford and it would take no more than a couple of broadsides to lay him low. It might even be as easy as playing hide-and-seek with Culliford in the woods and simply walking onto the abandoned *Mocha Frigate*. "We have sufficient power and authority to do it," he told them. Kidd wore his sword and two pistols for this occasion. He looked from man to man, from eyes to eyes. The men shuffled on the deck. Silence. The only sound was the wind in the palm trees.

Then someone shouted: "We would rather fire two guns into you than one into Culliford." A gruff cheer went up. Then another man yelled: "Ten guns into you." And: "Where is our money?"

They wanted their shares of the prizes. After almost two years at sea, they wanted some pay.

Kidd, stronger, taller, ornerier, yelled back at them that now was the time to fight Culliford.

Bradinham and Palmer and others called a "parley." They would vote on it. Kidd stood alone; he could see the *Mocha Frigate* in the distance; in his anger, he was ready to attack it alone.

The men voted 100 to 15 to mutiny over to Culliford, to tie their fortunes to the pirate captain. Twice in one lifetime, Culliford had outwitted Kidd. The men said they wanted their shares; Kidd said the shares would be split up at Boston or New York or London, and not sooner.

Kidd cursed at them and he left with his loyal few. Darkness was falling; while the rowdy men began to party, he quietly had himself rowed over to the *Adventure Galley* and from there his little troop walked four miles to stay at Edward Welch's armed compound.

The next morning bright and early, some

of the mutineers scurried ashore to look for Culliford; the rest started to hoist out the 600-plus bales in the *Quedagh Merchant*. This was a huge task but the men were inspired. They were finally going to get some serious wages. Kidd still hadn't shared out any money beyond a few coins here and there. Each bale might be worth as much as £75 in London, but who knows how little here on St. Mary's Island on the black market to the likes of Edward Welch? But they craved some payoff and they littered the beach with bright-colored bales of "Callicoes, Muslins, Silk and white, striped and plain Romalls, Bengals and Laches." Each bale weighed as much as 200 pounds. Bereft of dock or crane at St. Mary's, they had to lower each one into a pinnace and row the burdened boat ashore. They knew the *Adventure Galley*'s commission stated that the cargo must be delivered to Lord Bellomont; they had another rum.

At some point during the days of unloading, Captain Kidd returned. He was accompanied by fourteen heavily armed men and some spear-carrying Malagasies, rented from Edward Welch. His little band was outnumbered four to one; at least Culliford and the pirates hadn't returned. Kidd demanded that the mutineers stop unloading; they refused. He mentioned men in high places whom they were stealing from, who would hang them and gibbet them. They laughed at him. Overmatched, he couldn't fight them, but somehow Captain Kidd convinced them to give him and the owners their full share. We don't know his exact mixture of arguments, threats, and gun-pointing, but in essence, the strength of his personality prevailed. According to Hugh Parrott, "Kidd struck for and received several shares, it might be forty" of 160 shares alloted.

In the divvying up of the plunder on the beach, each man of the 115 received three bales plus about two thirds of a mixed bale. They marked each bale with the man's initials, a process baffling to a mostly illiterate crew. Richard Barleycorn, Kidd's seventeen-year-old cabin boy, was able to mark a nice intertwined RB — probably Kidd taught the boy to write during his six years' apprenticeship, while Abel Owens had to settle for a circle or O. They all couldn't use the same X.

As quickly as possible Kidd had his 150 bales reloaded onto the *Quedagh Merchant*. Over the next few days, the mutineers were shocked to find out how little a bale of silk would buy on Madagascar; they learned a harsh lesson about supply and demand; Theo Turner, who arrived in St. Mary's afterward, said Welch had told him he traded the men bales for liquor. Some of the men even had to "consign" their bales to Edward Welch, who promised to give their share of the sale the next time they returned to this out of the way locale.

The mutineers finally found Robert Culliford; his Malagasy spies had kept him one step ahead of their gang. At first the charismatic Cornish rogue thought it was a trap, but their venom against Kidd sounded too authentic, and he agreed to lead them.

Robert Culliford, after two months of debauchery in up-island huts, returned to the main harbor and climbed aboard the *Mocha Frigate*. He easily convinced his new crew to hurry to clean up the big warship, so as take advantage of the northbound winds and go a-pirating in the Indian Ocean.

Of Kidd's crew, ninety-six deserted over to Culliford.

Kidd was left with a ragtag loyal bunch of fifteen — cabin boys, old men, sick men, a couple of blacks, and a handful of able-bodied New Yorkers. Staying with him, among others, were: deathly ill brother-in-law, Samuel Bradley, faithful cabin boy Barleycorn, and the friend who never wanted to go pirating, John Weir of Carolina.

For the mutineers, it was party time. The ninety-six deserters, along with Culliford's twenty surviving crewmen, voted to go out after ships of all nations. (Culliford, it turns out, had lost half his crew to disease; Kidd alone in the galley — had he known — could have *easily* taken Culliford.)

The pirate orgy began and escalated on board all the ships in the harbor. The men, in a frenzy, grabbed anything portable of value, monkeying up the rigging and down into the hold, rolling biscuit barrels and juggling compasses. They especially wanted to find the captain's gold. They had heard a rumor about the captain having a strongbox full of jewels; they knew Kidd had carried chests to Edward Welch's.

"For the space of 4 or 5 Dayes," Kidd later wrote, "the Deserters, sometimes in great numbers, came on board the [*Adventure*] Gally and *Adventure Prize* and carried away great guns, Powder, Shot, small Armes, Sailes, Anchors, Chirugeons Chest and what else they pleased."

Kidd confronted Dr. Robert Bradinham as he was carrying off the valuable chest of ointments and drugs and surgical tools. Bradinham didn't deign to answer him.

The three ships anchored nearby . . . the men roaring drunk . . . singing . . . pirates . . . Culliford triumphant on the quarterdeck of the *Mocha Frigate/Resolution*.

During the ongoing party, several men swore they would kill Captain Kidd. They worked out a plan to sneak into the captain's cabin and slit his throat, but Kidd had barricaded the door with bales and he laid out forty small arms and two dozen pistols, all charged.

The men desperately wanted to find out where Kidd had stashed his money. They knew from the whispers off the coast of India that Kidd should have about £10,000 in gold somewhere. They banged on the captain's door, and Kidd threatened to kill the first man through and to blow up the ship.

They figured that it was at Welch's house. A motley armed drunken bunch staggered the four miles; the "Little King" stood at the door, no match for all of them; they pushed him aside and grabbed the chest. They pistol-butted off the lock, expecting to be dazzled by jewels and gold bars. Instead they found the captain's shore money to buy provisions: 10 ounces of gold, 40 pounds of silver plate, 370 pieces of eight. To vent their annoyance, they ripped and burned Kidd's journal and a sheaf of other official papers in the trunk.

The mutineers returned and they yelled to Kidd in the cabin to give up the gold.

He told them to come get it. Kidd with Barleycorn at his side feeding him guns should be able to kill a couple dozen, he figured. They well knew that this New Yorker was stubborn enough to blow up the ship. They pounded on the door and pried at it, but no one had the nerve to storm inside. They finally decided to leave him. Against all odds, Kidd had succeeded in keeping the gold and jewels.

As the drunken mutineers were stumbling off, one of them — probably Palmer — spritzed some alcohol and set fire to the boat; a few of Kidd's loyal men raced to put it out.

The mutineers then boarded the *Mocha Frigate/Resolution* and sailed to Careen Key in the center of the harbor. This very small island — a couple of hundred yards across — with a sandy beach around was a good place for the men to clean their ships. The crew of 115 under Robert Culliford cavalierly sunk the 150-ton *Rouparelle* next to the *Mocha Frigate* to serve as a platform to speed up careening.

The lascars, with some drunken pirate help, did the work quickly — two weeks — and Robert Culliford guided the *Mocha* out of St. Mary's on June 15, 1698, a pirate out to take ships of all nations. His luck ran true, or maybe it was his skill. They headed to Johanna, where they spied a French ship sitting in the harbor. The ship weighed one anchor and cut the other, trying to run, but Culliford caught her. The pirates found 10,000 pieces of eight aboard, and ten tons of wine and brandy. They celebrated the destruction of Kidd.

The drunken party that unfolded probably looked similar to the one slaver William Snelgrave witnessed among pirates on the Guinea coast. "They hoisted upon deck a great many half hogsheads of claret and French brandy, knocked their heads out, and dipped cans and bowls into them to drink out of. And in their wantonness threw full buckets of each sort upon one another. As soon as they had emptied what was on the deck, they hoisted up more. And in the evening they washed the decks with what remained in the casks.

"As to bottled liquor of many sorts, they made such havoc of it that in a few days they had not one bottle left, for they would not give themselves the trouble of drawing the cork out, but 'nicked' the bottles (as they called it), that is struck their necks off with a cutlass — by which means one in three was generally broke."

Captain Kidd was stranded in St. Mary's Island, Madagascar, with a skeleton crew and two huge ravaged ships, stuck for at least four months until the October shifting of the winds to the south. Any pirate straying into this outlaw haven could easily take him.

That all said, Captain Kidd still had a treasure in gold and bale goods, sugar and iron, worth perhaps £25,000 . . . if he could get it home.

Future Empire Hanging by a Thread

Chapter Twelve

"The pyrates . . . are unanimously reputed to be English."
— East India Company official

When reports reached the northern coast of India in April 1698 that Captain Kidd, while carrying a bonafide document bearing the Great Seal of the King of England, had captured a Moslem commercial ship, all hell broke loose. Outraged factions threatened to attack Company warehouses; high-ranking officials moved to expel the English traders from India. England's spectacular future in India — the heart of its sun-never-sets British Empire in Victorian days — wobbled in the balance, because if this English Company failed in India, then England failed in India. H. G. Wells in his *Outline of History* deftly explained the odd relationship between company and government.

"These successes [in India] were not gained directly by the forces of the King of England, they were gained by the East India Trading Company, which had been originally, at the time of its incorporation under Queen Elizabeth no more than a company of sea adventurers. Step by step, they had been forced to raise troops and arm their ships. And now this trading company, with its tradition of gain, found itself dealing not merely in spices and dyes and tea and jewels, but in the revenues and territories of princes and the destinies of India. It had come to buy and sell, and it found itself achieving a tremendous piracy. There was no one to challenge its proceedings. Is it any wonder that its captains and commanders and officials, nay, even its clerks and common soldiers, came back to England loaded with spoils? Men under such circumstances, with a great and wealthy land at their mercy, could not determine what they might or might not do. It was a strange land to them with a strange sunlight; its brown people were a different race, outside their range of sympathy; its temples and buildings seemed to sustain fantastic standards of behaviour."

Wells added, in concluding: "The English Parliament found itself ruling over a London trading company, which in turn was dominating an empire far greater and more populous than all the domains of the British crown."

That was what happened later; the day-to-day reality back in 1698 for the English in India was that a mere handful of Company employees, fewer than fifty men scattered among a half-dozen outposts, a gossamer-thin trade link, had to sustain the company's fleet of ships. At Bombay: twenty Englishmen, with Sir John Gayer, knight-general and governor; at Surat: fifteen with Chief Factor (president) Samuel Annesley; Carawar: four under Thomas Pattle; Callicut: five under Thomas Penning; Tellicherry: two; Anjenga: six.

And each of these men had Hindu servants, some as many as a dozen. They found themselves surrounded by cultures and religions that baffled them. "There is another sort [of Hindu] called Yogi's," wrote Captain Alexander Hamilton after visiting Surat. "They contemn worldly Riches, and go naked, except a bit of cloth about their Loyns, and some deny themselves even that, delighting in Nastiness and an holy Obscenity, with a great Shew of Sanctity. They cut nor comb their Hair, and besmear their Bodies and Faces with Ashes, which make them look more like Devils than Men. I have seen a sanctified Rascal of 7 Foot high, and his Limbs well proportioned, with a large Turban of his own Hair, wreathed about his Head, and his Body bedawb'd with Ashes and Water, sitting quite naked under the Shade of a Tree, with a Pudenda like an Ass [i.e., a penis like a donkey], and an Hole bored through his Prepuce, with a large Gold Ring fixed in the Hole. This Fellow was much revered by Numbers of young married Women, who, prostrating themselves before the living Priapus, and taking him devoutly in their Hands, kist him, whilst his bawdy Owner strokt their silly Heads, muttering some filthy Prayers for their Prolification."

Dr. John Fryer of the East India Company could not come close to stretching his mind around Hindu beliefs in reincarnation and sanctity of all animal life. "[Although] Chints, Fleas and Mosquitoes torment them every Minute, [they] dare not presume to scratch where it itches, lest some Relation should be untenanted from its miserable abode."

These outsiders, these Europeans, lived in armed compounds and hired Hindu intermediaries to deal with the local Moslem overlords, who in turn paid varying degrees of allegiance to the faraway Grand Moghul. Aurangzib, aptly nicknamed the "White Snake," was desperately trying to maintain control over his sprawling empire, that ranked among the world's largest, and included the Taj Mahal, a palace built in tribute to his mother.

Although Bombay was nominally the headquarters for the East India Company, Surat to the north still served as the flashpoint for dealings with the Grand Moghul. Surat was a thriving port town situated twelve miles up the deep Tapti River from the coast, with a thick wall, twenty-four feet high, crested with cannonaded towers, protecting the four-mile-square packed heart of the city. "Three or four families [crowd] together into an Hovel," noted Dr. Fryer, "with Goats, Cows, and Calves, all Chamberfellows, that they are almost poisoned with Vermin and Nastiness; but surely they take delight in it, for they will [awaken and] besprinkle themselves with the Stale [urine] of a Cow, as you behold a good Christian with Holy-water, or a Moorman slabber his Beard with Rosewater."

By contrast to the masses, the few Englishmen working for the Company in Surat lived in a state of great pomp and luxury. When the president, Samuel Annesley, ventured outside the compound, he was carried in a gold-brocaded, pillow-strewn litter with forty Moor-men in attendance, led by one carrying the St. George in silk. Rutted roads might have jangled his nerves, but his palanquin, supported by six men, glided along, his arrival announced by trumpets, his passage soothed by flute music. "When they take the Air, they usually frequent the coolest Groves and the pleasant Gardens adjacent to the City, refresht either by the River Tappy, or by water convey'd into their Tanks or Ponds," wrote an eyewitness. "And here the Dancing Wenches, or Quenchenies, entertain you, if you please."

This fine life of profit and pleasure was suddenly threatened in April by news of the capture of the *Quedagh Merchant* by Captain Kidd. The ship carried as much as 400,000 rupees of goods. To make matters worse, the rumor spread that almost half the cargo belonged to Muklis Khan, a nobleman at the court of the Grand Moghul.

The coterie of Englishmen in Surat, a splash of white in a sea of brown, were suddenly besieged. They stayed mostly inside their high-walled compound in the city, waiting to see how the storm would break. They could hear the rhythm of the city change near them, as servants talked excitedly to servants in a gibberish they could not understand.

"We can't sufficiently express the unheard of barbarous usage we have met with from these unreasonable oppressive moors on no real account only bare affirmacions of the rabble." That was what Sam

Annesley had written back in 1696 when the pirate Avery had made his "Gunsway" capture. Now it was happening again.

The Grand Moghul sent a *goozburdarr* (messenger) to the English demanding that the English East India Company agree to recover the *Quedagh Merchant* loot stolen by Kidd and then deliver it to the Grand Moghul. Sam Annesley, the ranking East India official in Surat, refused to sign.

The precise-minded representatives of the East India Company knew that they had not commissioned Captain Kidd and were outraged that his actions might harm them or even destroy them.

At the age of forty-one, Annesley, who had served the Company for literally half his life, was once again facing the prospect of trading in his palanquin for a prison bed of straw, and exchanging silken trousers for leg irons.

Sir John Gayer, lieutenant general of the East India Company — who was safely ensconced in the impregnable island fortress of Bombay — gave orders to Annesley, at the front lines, dealing with the greedy local Moghul governor of Surat, Ahmanat Khan.

The Surat governor, through intermediaries, demanded 50,000 rupees to make the orders of the Grand Moghul disappear. Annesley worried that if the Company paid off the governor for this act of piracy, then it would have to pay bribes every time any rogue waylaid a ship. Annesley stalled, dragging the governor along for a week, not agreeing to anything.

The governor was furious and sent for Annesley to appear before him at the castle. He told him he had worked hard to protect the English from Muklis Khan, one of the most powerful lords of the court, who ran the *vaucaunuvees* (nationwide network of informers). He said if the English didn't reward him, he would abandon them to their ugly fate. "You are strangers some thousands of miles from your Prince and Country to protect you," he said ominously, "and therefore might hope for my greater care and hospitality."

Annesley directed Venwallidas (his local rep) to explain to the governor that the East India Company doesn't commit piracy, that . . . — the governor cut the man off and asked simply, "How much will you give me?" When the rep started another long-winded answer, the governor ordered them all thrown out of the castle.

Sir John Gayer in Bombay didn't want Annesley to make any promises of restitution. "Be as frugal as possible," he chided. Annesley recorded a charge of 111½ rupees (£14) to the governor's menial servants to try to sway their master toward "moderation."

At that moment, word reached Annesley that an outraged group of Armenian merchants were soon to arrive in Surat with a sheriff from the court of the Grand Moghul. The Armenians, he was told, expected a huge payment from the English or else they would demand that all East India Company employees be arrested immediately for piracy. The entourage stopped just outside of town in the late afternoon, providing Annesley with a brief window of time to bargain with the governor.

He hired a new negotiator, who told him encouragingly that this governor can make "what is false appear true and what is true appear false," *for a price*. The negotiator chiseled the governor down to 20,000 rupees (£2,500). Both sides agreed.

When the Moghul's sheriff and the Armenian entourage arrived the following morning, the governor kept them waiting for almost two days. After patiently listening to their complaints, the governor did absolutely nothing to help them. Through a bribe to a household servant, Annesley obtained a copy of the governor's report, explaining the case to the Grand Moghul. The governor laid the blame for the *Quedagh Merchant* capture on . . . Denmark.

The English, though relieved, were a tad

miffed: "We had rather he had lay the blame on all hatmen [Europeans] in general than the Danes, for then the French and Dutch would be engaged to extirpate them as well . . . and bear an equal share [of the expense]."

The angry Armenians remained in Surat harassing the English when, in mid-July, another messenger arrived from the Grand Moghul, this one regarding the claim of Muklis Khan, lord of the spies. The Surat governor once again demanded 50,000 rupees (£6,250) to save the English from this latest mess stemming from Kidd's capture. Annesley started sending harried notes to Sir John Gayer in Bombay, awaiting word whether he could pay another hefty bribe. Sir John kept replying: No!

Everyone was growing impatient. The Grand Moghul sent a note to his own messenger threatening to arrest the man if he didn't return in ten days bringing 200,000 rupees or else the English as prisoners. The Surat governor — needing time to haggle — succeeded in extending the deadline. Finally Annesley got permission to offer a much smaller bribe, which the governor accepted. "We concluded to avoid the greater evils & embrace the lesser one of pishcashing the Governour," Annesley wrote.

Annesley, pleased by the outcome, wrote to Sir John Gayer: "The troublesome business of the Quedah Merchant, God be thanked, we have hopes will be well concluded unless the pirates commit any fresh villainies."

India was safe once again for the English traders. By the standards of the time, the Kidd affair had blown over, relatively painlessly. The Company had paid bribes totaling about £5,000, but had agreed to *no* extreme promises for future indemnity or vast convoy duties. No Englishman had been imprisoned. Annesley for the first time in months risked a palanquin ride to the cool gardens; he lounged by the river.

Five days later, word reached Surat that European pirates had captured an *enormous* Moslem pilgrim ship. (The pirate captains, Annesley would soon learn, were none other than Derrick Shivers and . . . Robert Culliford.) This new problem would dwarf the Kidd affair.

Culliford had sailed the *Mocha Frigate/Resolution* with ninety-six of Captain Kidd's men out of St. Mary's harbor. After the drunken party off Johanna, Culliford had sailed north, hoping to reach the Moslem pilgrim fleet on its return from Jidda to Surat. He headed to the highlands of St. John, off the coast near Daman, and waited for the return of the fleet. Arriving in late August, instead of finding the Moslem treasure ships, he encountered two other pirates lying in wait: Captain Derrick Shivers, an Irish-Dutch pirate from New York, in the leaky *Soldados*, and Captain Wheeler in the *Pelican*. The three ships decided to consort and hover in the same general region. The standard pirate booty rule applied: if any of the three was present within cannon shot at the time of the capture, it would share in the spoils.

They cruised and met and parted and met and drank and watered and cruised and parted through most of September.

That year, Captain Thomas South of the English East India Company's *Chamber Frigate*, along with a Dutch and a French ship, was providing convoy protection to the twenty-six-vessel Moslem fleet, returning from Arabia. Captain South later reported that on September 12, 1698, a brand-new 600-ton ship, *Great Mohammed*, owned by the Turks of Jidda, had separated from the draggled-out convoy, presumably to speed ahead to get water for its 700 passengers.

Almost two weeks later, the captain of the *Great Mohammed* noticed two sails in the distance. Through the spyglass, he noted one flying French, the other English, and a bit further off, he noted a speck that might have been Dutch colors. The captain, still short of water, figured this was the convoy reeling him in, and he veered in that direction.

Culliford and Shivers piled on all sail to meet the confused Turkish captain. At some point, realizing his mistake, the victim tried to escape, but the pirates caught up and fired. The ships exchanged cannon fire. Shivers, who had already sworn to trade in his ship for another at the first opportunity, risked being raked by the Turk's cannon fire to maneuver athwart the hawser for boarding. Culliford cut off any lane of escape.

The men of the *Soldados* flung their grappling hooks and the bulk of the eighty pirates poured barefoot onto the deck of the *Great Mohammed*, screaming unholy oaths, carrying cutlass and pistol. Given the damp powder and the intricacies of reloading on a heaving deck in a hand-to-hand battle, most fired only once, and then used their pistol butts for head-bashing.

The Turks, unlike so many Moslem crews attacked by European pirates, decided to put up a fight. John Brent, for one, a twenty-three-year-old from Livingston, England, was wounded in the leg as he boarded. The hand-to-hand fighting was brief but sharp. The battlefield was so cramped that one wild pirate could wreak havoc.

The Turks later claimed to have killed twenty before being overwhelmed and surrendering. The pirates had an added incentive to be quick. The slow-footed *Pelican* was closing in to share in the capture; it fired shot after shot but none of those balls splashed anywhere near the battle scene. Culliford and Shivers later decided to deny the *Pelican* any share of the treasure.

And it was an immense treasure: 40,000 pieces of Arabian gold, 1,000 ounces of gold dust, 4,000 ounces of silver, and much more in coins of various countries. All told, the merchants pegged their lost loot at 1,850,000 rupees (£231,000), double that of Captain Avery, and fourfold more than Kidd.

The *Great Mohammed* marked the biggest capture in the history of piracy in the East Indies.

The pirates tortured the passengers to find out where every last valuable was hidden; they hung up the *tindall* (lascar overseer) and enjoyed some drunken target shooting, whizzing shots close to his head and groin. They found out what they wanted, then killed the man for making them wait so long. They set 150 men adrift in a boat without oars or sails. Running from one end of the ship to the other, they plundered every nook and cranny, and to celebrate their victory, they raped dozens of women. With no privacy aboard the overcrowded ship, the drunken pirates took the women in broad daylight, bending some over the rail, tying others in the lower rigging. Clothes were ripped, baring breasts, asses, thighs. Foul-breathed rogues gnawed on virginal necks, while fathers and husbands stood helpless below deck, hearing the screams. The pirates "ravished sixty women in ye most beastly barbarous manner," according to a witness. To avoid the shame, four highborn women jumped into the sea; a fifth stabbed herself.

News of this capture reached Surat on October 4 just as Annesley was exulting that he had dodged the calamity of Captain Kidd taking the *Quedagh Merchant*.

The fact that the *Great Mohammed* was a *pilgrim* ship, and not just a merchant ship, unleashed religious fury on top of the usual mercantile outrage. The report of the rape of sixty Moslem wives and daughters, many of them relatives of the men of Surat, raised that fury to new heights.

The port of Surat was immediately closed to English ships — none could leave or enter. No Englishmen could leave or enter the factory compound. Many of the passengers and Turkish merchants who had been aboard the *Great Mohammed* rushed to Surat to press their claims. English spies reported that the victims had been sent money and clothes by their co-religionists, but that outside of Surat they cast away the largess to enter the town in bloody rags, "like fakirs" (Moslem holy men).

As the situation darkened yet again for the English, Sam Annesley recorded events in a kind of diary of desperation. After hard negotiations, he agreed to pay the Surat governor a 30,000 rupee bribe to protect them from the first onslaughts of the Culliford incident.

That Sunday, the Turks and Arabs asked the governor's permission to storm the English compound, take everything, and revenge themselves by killing everyone inside. The Surat governor refused.

The English promptly delivered 15,000 rupees to Governor Ahmanat Khan, who was furious at receiving only *half* of the agreed amount. He said that they should lay the whole sum at his feet and beg him to take it.

"We were forced at last to yield [the other 15,000 rupees]," wrote Annesley, "as a Traveller opprest delivers his purse to a Highwayman. . . . We expect he will come upon a new demand to clear us at [the Moghul's] Court of the Turk's complaints, and the same [demand] he will make on ye next ship taken, so the pirates will be a yearly revenue to him.

"The beastliness of these Moores is so unparalleled as to call in question whether they are human Creatures, did not their form and speech show 'em so. . . .

"The [pirates'] barbarous wicked business will afresh exasperate ye town against us especially ye women's complaints [who] have doubtless been abused, and will represent ye matter ten times worse than 'twas." Sam Annesley, always a businessman, knew that rape would escalate Company expenses.

Annesley now received letters from Sir John Gayer in Bombay adamantly ordering him not to pay any more bribes and not to agree to anything more than convoy duty. Annesley feared the worst. Though he had weathered the recent attacks from the *Great Mohammed* passengers who had arrived in person in Surat to press their claims, he had yet to see what the Grand Moghul, the White Snake, would do about Culliford's capture.

After a tense month in which several English employees were beaten and robbed in the streets, the Grand Moghul's order finally reached Surat on January 4, 1699. The decree was harsh. All three European nations must be held accountable for the pirates' taking the *Great Mohammed*. They must pay back the current losses, agree to reimburse all future pirate losses, and agree to convoy duty. Or else they must leave India immediately.

"A drum was beat in the Towne that no . . . subjects to this [Grand Moghul] sho'd have any comunication with us, or bring us provisions, by which means we were immediately left by all our Serv'ts, Cooks, Washermen, Barbers." The governor sent 250 horsemen to surround the Dutch compound; ominous for all Europeans, he hired 400 more soldiers.

After hearing that the Dutch and French had secretly paid large bribes, Annesley asked Sir John Gayer in Bombay to let him pay, but Gayer refused. Annesley, longtime veteran, warned the company that it would endure shame, financial losses, and a fruitless waste of time before finally agreeing to pay up. "We hourly expect severity from the governor," wrote Annesely.

The governor locked up the English company's three Hindu brokers in a cell, without food or water, only hauling them out for hoisting and beating, not permitting them "to rise for the necessities of nature."

The Surat governor the next day sent officers with 500 men to the English compound, demanding that Annesley sign a document agreeing to the Moghul's demands. "We answered through our gates we could not do it. Your Exc. was Chief and we would write to him . . ."

At seven that night, one of the local brokers delivered a message to Annesley that the governor would beat all the English Company's Hindu brokers with bamboo in the public square so they would never walk again and that his soldiers would then break into the compound to drag the Englishmen out, and that he would not stop torturing them until Annesley signed the document. He said that the French, Dutch, Hindus, Moslems, Turks, and Armenians all swore that English East India Company employees "are the pirates."

Annesley held out for the Company till midnight, but finally concluded that he could avoid it no longer and swore he would sign the document in the morning.

The Dutch signed that night and agreed to be responsible for pirate losses along the pilgrimage sea route to Arabia, but the French persisted in refusing. "The French superior was hauled in the main street and beaten for three hours. [The governor] called for a barber, shaved off his beard and bore holes in his ear and half killed him. The French gave the writing to secure Persia and Ruspora ships."

The governor needed those signed documents guaranteeing European protection of the three main shipping lanes to save himself from the Grand Moghul's rage over his lax handling of the prior Kidd affair.

On January 28, 1699, Sam Annesley signed the document, agreeing to be responsible for any and all losses occurred in the "South Seas" (i.e., the Indian Ocean and out to Sumatra). "Our compliance was necessary," he wrote to Sir John in Bombay.

On February 2, Sir John sent back a note to Annesley, firing him, effective immediately, and replacing the twenty-year veteran with his assistant. Over the next few weeks, Sir John Gayer tried hard to have Annesley's signature rescinded, but without success. Thanks to the agreement, however, trade continued. And over the next few months, reports from Surat to Bombay started to be filled with more mundane matters, such as the high price of coffee and the marketability of myrrh.

But they also started to contain reports of a new headache: ships from a rival English company were arriving in the Indies. Parliament on March 5, 1698, had ended the monopoly of the East India Company and chartered a *New* East India Company — backed by a rival set of wealthy Englishmen, to eventually replace the century-old firm.

The Old Company had lost out in an odd way by ten votes, when many members of Parliament, loyal to them, had skipped the session to see the novelty of a tiger being baited at the Bear Gardens.

The Old Company, however, had no intention of rolling over and playing dead. So it now meant that *two* English ventures would be fighting each other, in addition to fighting everyone else, to gain a foothold in India. This was a battle of greed versus greed, fought by some very wealthy, very tough Englishmen unwilling to share, including some of Captain Kidd's secret backers.

The Grand Moghul, though he was fed up with all the bickering Europeans, nonetheless decided to continue to allow England, France, and Holland to trade in his empire; he especially didn't want to part with the immense five percent customs duties. But the White Snake was not naive, and he was becoming increasingly aware that the three European countries would never reimburse him for every loss due to European pirates, and that rankled him.

The Old English East India Company, to earn goodwill and advantages over its rivals, wanted to show the Grand Moghul that they could be brutally tough on pirates. They needed to hang and gibbet a few pirates; unfortunately for them, English law at the time dictated that they ship all the accused back to England. So the next best thing for them would be to hang some pirates and rush word of their deaths to the Grand Moghul.

In all the various reports to the Moghul,

Culliford and Shivers were almost never singled out for mention. One of the few European or American pirates that the Grand Moghul knew by name was . . . Captain Kidd. Such an easily pronounceable monosyllable: Kidd. Such an appealing target for the vindictive East India Company.

Chapter Thirteen

On St. Mary's Island on June 16, 1698, the day after Culliford had sailed north, Captain Kidd found himself stranded in pirate paradise. After holing up in his cabin for four days with forty small arms primed, he had against all odds saved the treasure of £10,000 of gold dust and bars and pieces of eight and jewels. When the sound of looting had finally died down, he had emerged on the deck.

Kidd discovered that as a parting thievery, Culliford had stolen away Kidd's lascar deckhands, the forced labor gang who had been pumping out the *Adventure Galley*. As Kidd stood on the deck of the ship that he had helped design and had watched roll out of the shipyards at Deptford, he knew it was a matter of hours before the *Adventure* would sink.

Kidd had eleven men and four cabin boys left to him; two of the men, his brother-in-law, Samuel Bradley, and seaman Jan Cornelious, were very ill, several others were in their forties, superannuated for a sailor. It was a race against the water filling the bowels of the *Adventure Galley*.

Kidd rounded up any Malagasies he could bully or bribe into service, and tried to off-load as much as possible to make the ship more manageable. Without much of a capstan crew, he then ordered his men to cut the anchors and mark them with buoys for later retrieval. Every so often the men pumping in the hold would sing out how high the incoming waters had risen.

As the frantic work continued, Kidd could see the shambles aboard the *Quedagh Merchant*, the ship that he would now need. Culliford and the pirates had pillaged it of sails, anchors, gunpowder, and rigging, and anything else that caught their eye. They had taken at least four cannon, a bulky item to shoplift.

Hours later, Kidd ordered the sails unfurled of the *Adventure Galley* so that the breeze would carry the ship ashore in the protected harbor of St. Mary's. As the *Adventure Galley* glided shoreward toward the beach, Kidd had men ready with yardarms or tree limbs. As the ship grounded itself, they propped up whatever side tipped over.

Now Kidd and his skeletal crew could catch their breath. Culliford and the pirates had sailed out heading north in the *Mocha Frigate* in mid-June; Kidd knew that the seasonal winds wouldn't shift until October to allow him to head southwest to round the Cape of Good Hope.

So Captain Kidd was a sitting duck in a pirate port with a treasure to deliver home, and a feeble crew of men, two very sick, four very young, at least four relatively old. If he could bring the ship to New York and show off the French passes, maybe he could salvage the mission. In any case, he could see his young wife, Sarah, and his little daughter again after more than two years apart.

But his ride home was this ransacked 400-ton Moorish ship, so exotic with its Moslem carved curlicues and design, an attention-grabber in the Atlantic. Many, perhaps most men, would have taken the £10,000 in gold, which he had risked his life to save, and hitched a quiet return on another vessel and excused himself with the tale of mutiny. Who would dare to sail a third of the way around the world in *that?* But Kidd knew those remaining 300-plus bales of East India goods were worth ten times more on the other side of the Cape of Good Hope. (Here on St. Mary's, a hard-ass "fence" like Edward Welch paid a pittance per bale — a few quarts of rum — since no one else was offering anything.)

If Kidd could deliver the goods to London or New York, they might easily go for £75 a bale, generating at least another £15,000, plus the value of the ship, and the other trinkets, and the sugar and the iron and the cannon. Maybe he could round up £35,000 for the investors. Then they would at least quadruple their money. Not too shabby. And there was no longer a big crew to split shares with; they had mutinied.

Captain William Kidd, never afraid of hard work or a challenging sail, decided to take the 400-ton *Quedagh Merchant* back to the Atlantic. On the way, severely undermanned, he would have to avoid the Royal Navies of England, France, Holland, and Portugal — and the English East India Company and pirates.

To prepare for the voyage, his small crew had to deal with two ships. First they scavenged the beached *Adventure Galley* of absolutely anything of value. They dismantled the masts, the yardarms, any rigging; they off-loaded all provisions and water casks. They carried the treasure chests to a safe place. Far and away the hardest task was hoisting out the thirty cannon, some of them weighing more than 2,000 pounds.

Gathering the scraps of all sails left, the older sailors sat down to sew enough together to make two sets of sails for the giant *Quedagh Merchant*. When they ran short, they patched triple-thick layers together using material from the bales of striped calicoes. Some of Kidd's sails were exotic quilts.

At some point, Kidd decided the only way to complete the task was to burn the *Adventure Galley* to draw off the last scraps of metalwork aboard. Even a hinge had value in St. Mary's Island. Kidd was a *frugal* man; nothing would be wasted, regardless of the work required to save it.

Kidd's brave privateer ship lay in smoldering ruins. Now he focused on the *Quedagh*. Kidd knew it had to be careened. With the pirates gone, the remaining men sailed it to Careen Key, off-loading everything portable from that vessel and scraping its bottom and retarring the seams. They had to hoist her over and back and then reload her with the 300 bales, provisions, water casks, the treasure, 10 tons of scrap iron ballast, 1,200 bags of sugar, 30 cannon from the *Adventure* to bolster the 20 already set aboard the *QM*.

This was a backbreaking job for the tiny crew. Kidd desperately needed more men. And St. Mary's didn't exactly attract scads of ships.

Kidd, however, was able to land a handful of men who had decided to abandon piracy and not sail with Culliford. Way back when the crew of *Mocha Frigate*, an English East India Company ship, first mutinied and turned pirate, several of the skilled men were forced to join the pirates. Most of them found piracy to their liking; some didn't. John Hales, forty, a gunner's mate on the *Mocha*, chose to leave those "men of desperate fortune" and join Kidd, as did first mate Dudley Raynor. Surprisingly, the hardened rogue James Gilliam, in his forties, chose Kidd over Culliford, and home in Rhode Island over more depredations in the Indian Ocean. More likely, Gilliam quarreled with the crew and was booted off the ship.

Kidd drove the men hard but they were all — except Gilliam — bonded together in the righteous belief that they had refused to turn pirate. The men's hands turned to leather; their bodies became leaner and more tanned. But it's too onerous to work every minute in paradise; Kidd gave them Sundays off. Plenty of zebu to eat, rum to drink, and local women to carouse with. And, St. Mary's Island during the late summer boasted a fascinating natural entertainment. The narrow channel between St. Mary's and the mainland Madagascar was a favorite birthing place for whales. Kidd's men joined the natives in paddling out in pirogues to watch leviathan. They saw fifty-foot mother whales swim alongside fifteen-foot-long newborns; sometimes mama dove, sending her giant flukes skyward, then baby awkwardly tried to copy the move. Some summers, more than a thousand whales gave birth in these secluded waters.

Given the predatory era, Kidd's men also joined in the hunt as well. "The islanders go out in canoes which they row up to the place where those monsters appear," wrote an eyewitness to an earlier St. Mary's hunt, "when near enough, they dart [barbed] irons at them, made fast to ropes of the Mahault-tree [fibers]. . . . The fish being hurt, frets and draws the Line they veer out [and draws] their canoes, which does not daunt those who are in them . . . being all excellent swimmers."

Flanked on either side by the lush greenery of Madagascar and St. Mary's Island, the natives and Kidd's crew took mind-boggling joyrides. The towed canoes bumped and raced over the waves up the narrow channel.

"When the whale is spent with struggling," wrote the eyewitness, Francis Cauche, "they draw her to the shore, cut her in pieces with Hatchets and eat her."

They also were vigilant to boil out as much whale oil as possible; Captain Kidd's voyage home was illuminated by sperm oil from some behemoth beached in Madagascar.

By mid-September, Kidd and crew had succeeded in finishing their preparations for voyage. They were afloat testing out their Moorish ship, waiting for favorable winds.

Someone spotted a sail approaching the harbor. Kidd had only twenty men aboard a 400-ton ship and a pile of treasure and bales. Was it a pirate? Royal Navy? Someone raced up to the battery overlooking the throat of the harbor, and primed the four cannon.

The ship, it turned out, presented little threat; it was a small merchant vessel from London, the *Fidelia*. The captain's name was Tempest Rogers; he came aboard Captain Kidd on the *Quedagh Merchant*. The two men talked awhile, then Rogers sent a boy to tell boatswain Edward Davies to come bring some nails for Kidd. Davies arrived with the nails and he stayed to have a few rums with Kidd. They might have known each other from the Caribbean.

Edward Davies, age forty-nine, boatswain on the *Fidelia*, had survived a long career at sea; he had once narrowly escaped being hanged as a pirate by paying £300 to the colony of Virginia, which used the money in 1692 to help found the College of William & Mary. Several people described Davies as "extraordinary stout," a white rhino of a man, extremely strong.

The trio chatted awhile, then Tempest Rogers said he was ready to return to the *Fidelia*. Edward Davies said he would leave with Tempest, but Rogers told him, "No matter, I'll send the boat back for you."

But Tempest Rogers never sent the boat. Captain Kidd must have been thrilled at the chance of landing this beached whale of a boatswain, a very experienced seaman.

Stout Edward Davies came ashore at St. Mary's and he heard a message a week or so later from trader Edward Welch. (Tempest Rogers, no fool, bought about twenty-five bales of the *Quedagh Merchant* cargo at deep discount from Welch, which by circuitous route would be carried all the way to Boston and sold there to the righteous Puritan merchants.) The Little King told Davies that Captain Rogers had said that if the boatswain wanted to return to the ship, he should go to a place called the "Hill," where white traders used to maintain a battery, and fire off a signal shot to alert the *Fidelia*.

So Edward Davies the next day trudged the four miles off to the Hill, carrying gunpowder, and he fired several shots. No Tempest that day, but the next morning the *Fidelia* appeared teasingly a couple miles off the coast. Davies, sweating, trudged up the Hill again in the heat and fired another shot, but Rogers did not bring the ship closer to shore.

Every day for the next *nineteen* days, Davies lugged his tired immense frame up the Hill in the swelter, and popped off a signal shot, but Tempest never returned.

Edward Davies signed on with Kidd to return to New York.

About two weeks later in late September, the winds finally shifted. Captain Kidd, with a crew of about twenty, set sail south. Kidd insisted on calling the revamped *Quedagh Merchant* the *Adventure Prize*. On their maiden leg, they reached Port Dolphin, 600 miles down the coast of Madagascar.

A Dutch captain, Jan Coin, who stopped there a year later, reported that he had heard that Kidd had arrived "in a rich Arab ship, all burdened with bales of merchandize, in order to re-victual and buy slaves, heading to the West Indies."

The marketplace there at that moment wasn't especially well-stocked with slaves. No one was offering the best able-bodied ones, aged fifteen to thirty, but Kidd did manage to buy a few young slaves there, a handful of boys and a girl. One of them he decided to call Dundee, after his home town in Scotland.

. Port Dolphin was also short on foodstuffs for sale, so Kidd headed around the cape to Tulear on the southwest coast of Madagascar, where he bought live cattle, actually a small herd of mooing hump-backed horned zebu. With that big empty ship, there was more than usual room for a barnyard of pigs, chickens, and ducks. Knowing the mortality of beasts at sea, he brought the animals aboard close to his departure date.

In Tulear, Kidd found a couple more deckhands. Two English sailors, John Dear and John Fishelis, claimed they had been rowing a longboat ashore when they were captured by a French ship and later escaped to Tulear. Kidd would not have asked many questions. Kidd also picked up a paying passenger by the name of Robert Avery.

The captain of an English ship, *Swift*, much later reported spotting Kidd repairing his ship at Tulear. The captain said that Kidd was in a powerful ship with a crew of *200* men. Either this was typical inflation to paint Kidd as the pirate king, or else Kidd was using every trick to appear more manned than he was.

Kidd knew he had made enemies and he was sailing in an exotic ship that *appeared* stolen. Though his documents would back him up, he couldn't take chances: He had to avoid the main shipping lanes and couldn't even consider a stop in the Cape of Good Hope or St. Helena. However, it would be insane to try to sail from Tulear to New York City, so he planned the following route: 2,500 miles at sea to Annobon, an obscure island off central Africa, and then 4,000 miles along the easy trade winds to the Caribbean, and then follow the current (not yet called Gulf Stream) up the American coast to New York.

Kidd now had twenty-two men, five boys, and a handful of young slaves to sail the 400-ton, three-masted Moorish vessel. If attacked, he could man maybe two or three of the thirty-plus cannon on board. From a distance, however, the *Quedagh Merchant* looked like a formidable, if somewhat exotic, ship of war. Kidd took all of the thirty cannon from the *Adventure Galley* and he probably custom-fit a handful of them to add to the *Quedagh*'s weaponry.

From a distance, pirates and Royal Navies couldn't know how shorthanded he was. The art of the bluff always loomed large in naval engagements, especially for pirates and privateers. In colonial America in the 1700s, a slang term evolved for wooden logs carved and painted black to resemble cannon. They were called Quakers, after the pacifist sect, which re-

414

fused to use firearms against their fellow man.

Kidd and his skeletal crew started the long isolated voyage heading south well below the Cape and then north up the inhospitable western coast of Africa. It is a tribute to his seamanship (and probable knowledge of ascorbutic qualities of citrus juice) that he did not lose a single sailor, passenger, or slave on this voyage.

We know absolutely nothing of this three-month trip, which is exactly how Kidd wanted it. He was not spotted by a single ship that reported his whereabouts.

Captain Kidd in the *Adventure Prize* touched at the tiny island of Annobon in the Gulf of Guinea in the armpit of the equatorial African coast. (The Portuguese first discovered this wooded, mountainous island on New Year's Day 1473, hence its name.) The island was a bargain shopper's delight, the natives famed for once selling a roasted pig for a sheet of paper. The harbor on the lee-side made landing a challenge, but the locals, half caste Portuguese-Africans, nominally Catholics, were quite friendly, even lighting signal fires at night for passing ships.

There Kidd loaded fresh wood and water and picked up one more crew member. John Elms said he had been captain of a merchant ship, captured by pirates, and had been set adrift. No résumés required, Kidd signed him on as first mate.

So Kidd had scrambled to land a crew, and among them were clearly some veteran sea dogs. The cabin boys in later testimony mentioned addressing "Captain Elms," "Captain Davies," "Captain Gilliam," and, of course, "Captain Kidd."

Kidd, once out of the Doldrums, followed the trade winds across the Atlantic west to the Caribbean. (Ironically, he came close to crossing paths *again* with Captain Warren, leading a Royal Navy squadron south from England to attack pirates in the East Indies, and specifically to capture Captain Kidd.) We get only the faintest glimmer of daily life aboard Kidd's ship from the later deposition of one of the crewmen. John Dear said that sometimes Samuel Bradley, delirious from his long illness, staggered onto the deck to "condemn and upbraid" the crew for not taking enough pains in caring for the ship. They resented the ranting of the twenty-five-year-old brother-in-law.

In late March 1699, almost ten arduous months after the mutiny, Kidd reached the familiar waters of the Caribbean. Kidd picked the northernmost Leeward Island, Anguilla, near St. Martin. Anguilla, a sixteen-mile-long thin tropical island (fr. *anguille,* "eel"), was scantly populated, often on the verge of a water shortage. It's significant to note that Kidd chose to make his stop in the Caribbean at an *English* colony, fearing nothing.

Captain Kidd must have thought he had pulled off the near impossible, to survive the mutiny, preserve the treasure, and reach an English colony with a shipload of silks.

Kidd, on this huge Moorish vessel, dropped anchor outside the harbor. His men rowed him ashore in the longboat. As they reached the dock after the long pull, they could hear the familiar cadence of the King's English. Actually not this king's. The current William had a heavy Dutch accent. But the cadence of English, the words floating along in the spring heat, the shore beckoning with the promise of fine meals and liquor, of familiar surroundings. The men found the nearest tavern, and tasted their first fresh beer in years, and there some mouth with blackened teeth, some sailor in passing, sputtered out the news that Captain Kidd and all his crew were declared pirates, and that the governors all had orders to arrest them.

How much had Kidd's crew said? Had they revealed themselves? Did that man down the bar know them? The men slinked out of the tavern, trying not to attract attention, and rowed fast away from the sleepy island.

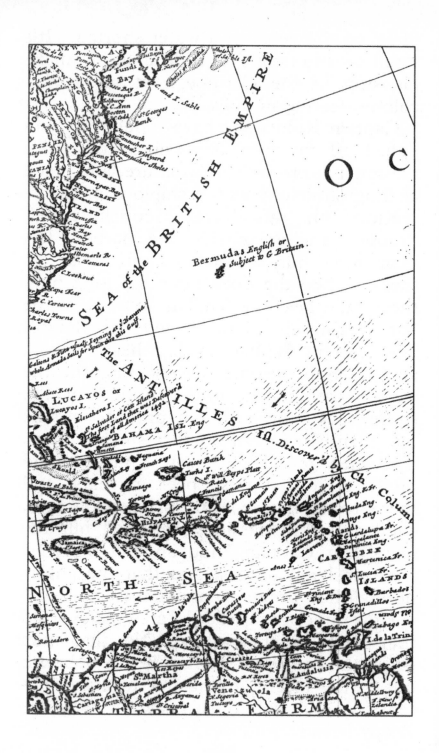

Every colonial governor, it turned out — even Governor George Leonard on tiny Anguilla — had orders to seize Kidd "to the end that he and his accomplices may be prosecuted for the notorious piracies they have committed in the East Indies."

Kidd was flabbergasted, since the captain didn't think he had committed any crime, and his crew took it even worse.

Kidd later wrote: "The news of . . . being proclaimed pirates . . . put the [crew] into such consternation that they [afterward] sought all opportunities to run the ship upon some reef or shoal lest I should carry her into some English port."

No ship in the harbor was strong enough to take him, so he was safe for the moment. Taking no chances, Kidd immediately ordered the tired men to weigh anchor. In four hours, Kidd was adrift again.

Captain William Kidd, of Dundee and New York, was now the most wanted criminal in America.

Kidd was running out of food and water. The *Quedagh* was starting to leak, probably courtesy of those damn worms. The Royal Navy was already looking for him. If Kidd had such powerful backers, he wondered, how did this order get sent to arrest him?

But he had no time to ponder the betrayal of the lords in London who had invested in him and were supposed to protect him. He needed a plan immediately. The Caribbean sun beat down on the worn-out vessel. Where to go?

The men were shouting at him to beach the bitch; they could all slink off in the jolly boat and catch rides on other ships. No one would know anything about piracy, they would just be tars in port looking for work.

Samuel Bradley, haggard, a rich kid ever since his sister's marriage, now a pampered young man wealthy enough to worry about *honor*, wanted to head directly to the nearest English port and surrender. He had seen, held, read the French passes. They exonerated all. They justified all. He pushed Kidd to go to Antigua, where Kidd had been a confidant of Governor Codrington during the war. The crew cursed him out, according to John Dear.

Captain Kidd knew the Caribbean, from a couple dozen privateer missions, from his glory days during the war. He could take his chest of gold and disappear into the netherworld of Caribbean pirate haunts, and then send word to his wife and daughter in New York to come meet him. But if he did that, he would be an outcast for the rest of his life, unwelcome by the English, the French, the Portuguese, the Spanish. He would be double-crossing four powerful lords, one governor, and the king of England himself.

Kidd, never one to waste, wanted to preserve the bales of cargo for himself and the owners . . . but the mission had moved far beyond simple profit and loss. He had enough property in New York . . . he needed his good name and respect to live out his old age.

The decision was maddening. Any more hesitation, half the crew might lower the boat and row to St. Martin. He loaded a dozen pistols. He needed time, hours, minutes, food, water, above all, time.

Captain Kidd, a veteran in these waters, chose to go to the nearby island of St. Thomas, then a Danish West India Company outpost; he hoped to find a temporary safe harbor. It seemed a shrewd choice in lieu of the alternatives. The French and Spanish wouldn't welcome him; venturing too far, pirates might find him. And surrendering to the English required much more finesse than his brother-in-law's plan of merely sailing in with a grin and an excuse.

St. Thomas back then was a smuggler's haven, not exactly a pirate port, but a civilized place with a civilized government that thrived by overlooking the pedigree of much merchandise that passed along its docks. This was Denmark's little beachhead amid giant faltering Spain and burgeoning France, Holland, and England, a kind of tropical Lichtenstein.

On April 6, 1699, Kidd hovered outside the entrance to the main port of St. Thomas, flying an English flag. He positioned his ship just outside the range of the fort's guns. He had his men lower a longboat over the side of the *Quedagh Merchant* and the men rowed ashore to deliver a message from Kidd to the governor.

Kidd's men reached the shore and handed off the message, and then they proceeded to the nearest tavern to get drunk. After that tease on Anguilla and the trouble they were in, they wanted a trough full of liquor. One rum punch followed another and another. St Thomas, the port city, then had one main street that housed the warehouse for the Danish West India Company that specialized in selling slaves to Spanish colonists. Also nearby was a warehouse owned by the Brandenburg Company, a German enterprise. St. Thomas was packed in a couple of side streets with whitewashed brick houses and tile roofs. This commercial port, which didn't niggle over goods, also opened its door to religious refugees, to all manner of Protestants unwelcome elsewhere.

Kidd's note was surprisingly candid and straightforward. He stated that he had just discovered that he was declared a pirate and he requested permission to enter and remain in the harbor under protection of the Danes.

Kidd's drunken sailors rowed back carrying the town's leading merchant, Pieter Smith, and also Lieutenant Claes Hanssen, who delivered the terse *conditional* invitation of Governor Johann Lorentz: "If you are an honest man and can prove to have done nothing unlawful, then you are welcome to enter."

Kidd was wary. He wrote back that he wanted the governor's promise that the Danes would protect him in case an English Royal Navy ship came to take him "without royal orders." While awaiting a response, Kidd approached merchant Smith about buying a sloop from him, but Smith refused. Kidd also wanted to buy £200 worth of provisions, for which he would pay Smith in bales of muslins. Smith again refused.

In a later report to the board of directors of the Danish West India Company, the governor surmised: "From all that, I concluded that his circumstances were not quite straight." So the governor held a council meeting on April 7, during which it was decided that this strange ship and Captain Kidd were not worth a rift with mighty England. "If we do not hand him over, the English royal ships would close this harbor . . . to great damage to our country."

So they sent a message to Kidd that no other promise would be made, beside the original "Enter at your own risk." In the meantime, the governor forbade residents of St. Thomas from selling Kidd any provisions.

Kidd tried yet another gambit. He asked to be protected from English Royal Navy ships for as long as it took for him to send to New York Governor Bellomont, his backer, and receive a passport for a voyage north. Governor Lorentz held firm; the original offer stood, no more.

The leaky *Quedagh* was parked just outside the range of the fort's guns. Half a dozen sloops offered to whisk Kidd and company off to new lives on Aruba or Curacao. Kidd hovered for a total of forty-eight hours, just long enough for the exchange of notes. At night, little boats rowed out to him, and he paid in coin and liquor for information. He found out that his onetime patron, Governor Codrington of Antigua, perhaps his best hope for being welcomed by the English, had died the previous summer.

But he also got wind of a maddeningly enticing but elusive possibility: a *Scottish* settlement on the isthmus in Central

America. Kidd had heard rumors that the people of Scotland — long tired of being bullied by England, their four-times-more-populous neighbor to the south — were trying to set up a colony in the West Indies. Scots would set laws favorable to Scots. Scots might honor a man wronged by the king of England. Scots might welcome his gold.

And now in the harbor at St. Thomas, under the canopy of stars and over the fragrance of rum, a slurring merchant told him that it really existed. A letter from this time describes the kind of report Kidd must have heard.

"The Scotch settlement in the Bay of Darien is . . . on the best harbour and richest country in the world both in gold and all other necessaries for the use of man. I have seen of the ore, which is almost pure of the value of 23 carats. They are kindly received by the Indians, and are building a fortification of 70 guns. . . . They are but two days journey from Panama, have a very good harbour in the South Sea [Pacific Ocean], by which in time they will command the China Trade as well as the East India."

Kidd, drink by drink, knew the motivation for the settlement. The Scots were sick of forty years of England's navigation acts forbidding open trade between Scotland and the American colonies, denying them commerce with the East Indies or Africa. Scots couldn't hold high office in the colonies, and were treated as second-class citizens, a hair above the Irish Catholics but still the butt of English jokes for their kilted Highlanders, their stubbornness, their Presbyterian frugality. English insults were common knowledge.

Ran one London pamphlet: "The Scottish women are, if possible, yet worse than the men and carry no temptation. . . . the skin of their faces looks like vellum; and a good Orientalist might easily spy out the Arabick alphabet between their Eye-brows. Their legs resemble mill-posts, both for shape, bigness, and strength. . . . their voice is like thunder. . . . It is a very common thing for a woman of quality to say to her footman, 'Andrew take a fast grip of my arse, and help me over the stile.'"

The insults typified England's disdain and fear. Scotland's only unofficial presence in the New World was the name Nova Scotia, a holdover from the stillborn Canadian colony granted away by King Charles I to the French.

But the slurring man from St. Thomas also said rumor had it that an English warship was headed there to try to boot the Scottish and help honor *Spanish* claims to the land.

Kidd was so tempted to go seek out the Scottish colony and ask for protection. He agonized over the possibilities: New York, Antigua, Darien. Showing typical privateers' letch for debate, the crew weighed in. Gilliam ranted against surrendering to the English. The clipped pirate had two heavy chests of gold, and he knew customs officials would ask far too many questions. In younger days, Gilliam and Kidd had both sailed into Port Royal, Jamaica, and seen the leathery eyeless corpses of pirates hanging in the harbor.

Feeble Samuel Bradley, however, pressed again and again for Kidd to sail to an English port. Kidd was adamantly opposed to this, as were most of the crew. In the midst of the shouting, the young man, exhausted from two years' illness, a "bloody flux" ever since Mohelia, realizing they wouldn't bend, suddenly got down on his knees and "folded his hands" and begged Kidd to allow him to go ashore. He said he would die if he didn't get to a doctor.

Actually, Captain Kidd — if he were a total heartless rogue — had a huge incentive to let Samuel die; because if he did, Kidd and his wife would inherit the young man's extensive New York properties, including nineteen acres of Manhattan. But Kidd had nurtured Samuel all along, done everything to keep him alive, from tracking down expensive Goa Stone fever remedies to letting him have a cabin.

Now, Kidd, as he stood on the deck with the world closing in on him, could see a glimmer of his wife's features in Samuel's haggard face. He silenced the shouts of the crew. Captain Kidd looked down at thin, wasted Samuel kneeling before him. Another week at sea on rice and brackish water, he *might* die. Kidd agreed to let Samuel go ashore.

The crew, especially boatswain Michael Calloway, was opposed, fearing word of their whereabouts would spread. He shouted that Bradley, who had ragged the men across the Atlantic, should carry nothing ashore. Kidd disregarded Calloway and allowed Bradley to take one chest.

The problem was how to get him ashore. Kidd knew that the men who rowed Bradley to land might not come back. Kidd's skeletal crew would get even more skeletal.

Who should leave? Kidd decided to allow the men who had come along as working passengers and who in no way deserved any of Kidd's pirate problem. Four men would row Bradley: Captain Elms (marooned off Africa by pirates), John Fishelis and John Dear (picked up in Tulear), and Dudley Raynor (reluctant mate from Culliford's *Mocha*), and Raynor's negro boy. Kidd sailed to a spot three miles from the harbor, and let the men lower a boat.

Kidd worried that his brother-in-law was going to be turned over to the English and hanged as a pirate, but he honored the boy's wish. They embraced, Kidd's robust frame enveloping the wasted lad.

Samuel Bradley — in testimony given a couple days later before the governor and council on St. Thomas — defended Captain Kidd, said the Portuguese had fired first and that Kidd had tried to get the men to return the captured Moorish vessels. "You could tell by looking at him that after two years of illness, he arrived still sick on these shores," opined the Danish officials.

Kidd's generosity to Samuel cost him five men, a slave, and a boat.

Now it was April 9, 1699, and Kidd had to decide quickly. He knew that Royal Navy ships were out looking for him. He sailed east away from the English possessions and rounded Puerto Rico and entered the Mona passage.

(The rumor mill in London at this point pegged Kidd's treasure at £500,000, and people began to whisper that four lords and the king had purposely backed a pirate in a kind of "Corporation of Pirates.")

In crisis, Kidd's dominant traits came to

the fore: resoluteness and distrustfulness. It is clear that he couldn't choose anything that might remotely risk him suffering the humiliation of being arrested as a pirate. He couldn't trust the Royal Navy. He couldn't trust anyone; at five years old, he had trusted his father to return, and John Kidd never did. He had to be in control of his fate.

This all led him to make some decisions that look at first glance just like what a pirate might have done, but one enormous difference separated him from them. Kidd still had hopes of fulfilling his original mission, and paying off his investors . . . just doing it his way.

First of all, he needed a new ship quickly — one way or another. The leaky *Quedagh* was too unmaneuverable and stolen-looking.

He found himself in this corridor between Puerto Rico and Hispaniola, which was notorious for tricky winds and storms, a sometime whirlpool, especially in late summer hurricane season.

Kidd reached the area of Mona Island, one of those underpopulated Caribbean islands too isolated, too unimportant for scrutiny by the overextended Spanish *guardacostas*. He was hoping to find some Caribbean skipper to help him. To the southeast of the island, Kidd fell into a calm, and the tide started to wash the ship ashore. Kidd was forced to drop anchor. The most wanted man in the nascent British Empire, a man who considered himself honorable, who regarded his actions fighting the mutineers and bringing home a legitimate treasure as heroic, was becalmed, to fester with his thoughts and vague plans. At least the calm shouldn't bring his enemies any nearer, but there's an old nautical truism that strong winds separate a convoy while a calm brings them together.

For several days, not a breath of wind. Food was running out. And then a sail far off in the distance, a lint speck in a sea of blue. An unknown.

Kidd's men dropped a longboat over the side and rowed toward the sloop. As they neared, they could smell and hear the pigs aboard. A great sound for hungry men.

A voice from the sloop called down to them with the traditional question, asking them from where they hailed. Kidd's men answered, "From Whitehall." (That reply of the name of the royal palace trumps even London, as invoking a ship coming from the epicenter of English power.) "Wee demanded who commanded their shipp," recalled Henry Bolton, the merchant-in-charge aboard the sloop. "They replyed Captain Kidd."

Now commenced the dog-sniff game of appraising the intentions of the other vessel and its commander. The starving men, led by Kidd's quartermaster John Ware, immediately wanted to buy some hogs from the sloop *St. Antonio*. Bolton agreed and he descended into the canoe to be paddled over to the *Quedagh Merchant/Adventure Prize*.

Any man being rowed over to a giant undermanned Moorish ship would probably assume pirate, but very soon after Henry Bolton climbed aboard, Kidd showed him his commission from the King of England to chase pirates. He also showed him his owners' orders. Bolton, the profit motive strong, gave Kidd the benefit of the doubt.

Kidd then decided his wisest move — given the leaky *Quedagh*, Royal Navy, angry crew — would be to buy another ship and sell off some of the bulky cargo. Then at least the wealth would be portable and he would have some options.

Kidd first asked to buy Bolton's sloop, *St. Antonio*, but Bolton said he refused. He instead offered to go to Curacao (Dutch) to look for a ship for Kidd and to try to line up buyers for the 200 or so bales of expensive cloth.

Kidd and crew also gave Bolton a shopping list for provisions. What do near-starving men want after half a year at sea? A barrel full of bottles of ale, a dozen ten-pound wheels of Holland cheese, a barrel of bread, and pounds of sugar candy were among the goods later delivered.

Kidd also sent a note to two English merchants he knew at Curacao, Walter Gribble and William Lamont; this pair hooked the small-time player Bolton up with an open-to-all-deals entrepreneur, Irishman William Burke. The two English merchants facilitated the deal by giving Burke a "Bill of exchange" for 4,200 pieces of eight. (This was probably a short-term loan or quiet investment in buying Kidd's cargo.) In those days before banks and checking accounts, a merchant would generally accept a "bill of exchange" from someone he trusted. That "bill" in turn might be used to buy things or turned into coin by someone else who trusted it.

Kidd in his leaky Moorish ship waited off Mona for Bolton to return. True to the region's freakish weather pattern, the calm was suddenly replaced by hard winds, and within eight days, the *St. Antonio* had completed the 1,000-mile round trip to and from Curacao. That's a brisk pace, especially with a couple days in the Dutch capital of Willemstad. By the time Bolton returned to Mona, other ships had already stumbled on Kidd, or maybe it was no accident; maybe word was spreading from ship to ship about his whereabouts. A

Dutch sloop, Spey — Jan van der Biest, master — and an unnamed French turtle-hunting vessel hovered next to Kidd.

Bolton boarded Kidd and told him that his merchant friends would be sending Irishman William Burke in a brigantine to trade with him. Kidd was forced to wait, and wait some more, for Burke, because no one on either of the two ships already there had any real money. The wind began blowing hard to the south-southwest, the worst possible direction for a man waiting for a ship traveling from Curacao to Mona. The storm winds started whipping harder. Finally, Kidd couldn't take the stuck-in-limbo sensation any longer — maybe it was the waves laying over his vessel or that sitting-duck feeling or perhaps Kidd simply lost his temper. In any case, Kidd cut two of the anchor cables. (He didn't have much of a crew left to turn the capstan in howling winds.) He decided it was better to ride out the storm than to stay fettered like a dog.

The conniving merchant Henry Bolton was aboard Kidd's *Quedagh* at the moment when Kidd cut anchor. As Kidd's ship floated by Bolton's *St. Antonio*, Bolton yelled to his captain, Samuel Wood, to wait three more days for Burke, then to come to the island of Saona, off the south-eastern coast of Hispaniola [modern-day

Dominican Republic].

Saona (or Savona) was a longtime pirate rendezvous. Captain Henry Morgan with his fleet of fifteen ships had selected the island as his meeting place after sacking Porto Bello on the Isthmus. French pirate François L'Ollonais, notorious for killing prisoners by yanking out their tongues, had also used Saona as a rendezvous.

And some ne'er-do-well travelers came there for another reason: The island's guaiacum shrubs provided a rare and much-prized venereal disease remedy, "well known to those who observe not the sixth commandment," wrote a doctor in 1678.

Saona is a desolate sandy island, sixteen miles long, a habitat where hordes of tortoises arrive annually to lay their eggs.

Kidd languished near the eastern tip of Saona, his crew no doubt trying to capture some turtles. Finally, three days later, Burke arrived in the *Marigold*, and then the next day appeared the *St. Antonio*, accompanied again by Dutchman Jan van der Biest in the *Spey*. And then the *Elenora*, John Duncan, master.

This was a feeding frenzy. In those days, much more so than today, it was all barter and bargain. And these merchants knew Captain Kidd was in a bind: time ticking on the arrival of the Royal Navy or maybe a Spanish *guardacosta* that patrolled these nominally Spanish waters. If Kidd wasn't careful, he knew this could turn into a fire sale of his bales of muslins and calicoes. But Kidd, both tight-fisted and tough, tried to bargain as hard as he could.

Realizing that his whereabouts were too well-known, and needing to gain extra time, Kidd headed three leagues to the west to a lagoon on a tiny island of Santa Catalina. With some of his anchors gone, he ordered a crewman to tie the ship to a tree. Santa Catalina was an uninhabited oasis of tropical lushness, with a natural salt lagoon, where sea salt dried in the shallows.

Kidd clearly wanted to wait to try to hold out for a better price, but he lacked leverage, and his men were in even worse shape. Kidd at least controlled the largest quantity. It seems that as a shrewd bargainer, he refused to allow his men to sell anything until he had first struck his deal. Kidd was cornered and it would be a grave risk to the crewmen's health to try to pull a bale out of the hold and exchange it for a quart of rum.

Kidd sold 130 bales for 11,200 pieces of eight, which works out to 86 pieces of eight, or £21½ each. Each bale weighed 120 pounds and might contain 1,000 yards of fabric or more. The price worked out to less than four pennies a yard, which was extraordinarily cheap, about one quarter the going wholesale price. Kidd's men later sold another twenty-eight bales to Burke for an average of a measly twenty-five pieces of eight each. Clearly, Burke could tell the desperate men to take it or leave it.

A surprising side effect of Kidd's huge fabric sale was that Curacao and then later St. Thomas literally became flooded with "the richest Indian silks and muslins," according to a French priest, Père Jean-Baptiste Labat, who wrote home about the bargains he found.

Captain Kidd still needed a new ship, and he used 3,000 pieces of eight to buy the sloop *St. Antonio* from Bolton. (One small catch that Kidd knew nothing about: Bolton didn't own the sloop, and he never repaid the ship's two principal owners, who were less than amused and spent years in court trying to regain their vessel.) While Kidd was forced to sell at deep discount, unfortunately, he was forced to buy at a premium. This ship, once Spanish, long ago stolen, was a fifty-five-ton, beat-up affair, but a fast sailer. Its equipment — from rigging to chains to sails — was very tired, and the longboat for going ashore was a dicey proposition. The *St. Antonio* was later appraised in Boston at £225, or 900 pieces of eight. Kidd had paid more than triple the value.

Kidd first had the sloop *St. Antonio* cleared of any unneeded goods, such as empty casks and some piles of lumber. He filled the hold for ballast with 800 pounds of scrap iron and about 10,000 pounds of sugar in bags.

Kidd's long-suffering crew cleared the decks and with great effort loaded aboard four large cannon, two small cannon, and eight "patereroes" (small mortars). Kidd also loaded ten "small brass bases," which were a kind of mounted musketoon that fired five-ounce balls, and a pile of pistols and ammunition for all of the above. This was one of the best-armed small, ratty ships in Caribbean history.

It needed to be. Kidd, after all his Trader Vic wheeling and dealing, would be carrying 75 pounds of gold and 150 pounds of silver and a pile of jewels: more than 70 rubies and emeralds, sapphires, and diamonds. And, before selling to Burke, Kidd had selected forty of the best bales to carry away with him, including twenty-nine bales of Persian silk. Now Kidd was armed, mobile, treasure-laden.

But he was still a hunted criminal, and although switching to a new ship probably freed him from the immediate threat of Royal Navy capture, he still needed to decide *where* to go. And for Kidd, this next decision would tempt him to take his greatest risk ever, in a life already full of risks, of rock-littered coasts on cloudy nights, of cannon battles, of mutiny.

He told Bolton that he intended to go to New York to be with his family, and also to go find Governor Bellomont in order to clear his name. Very few men would have had the ballocks to peddle their cargo like a pirate, then travel into the heart of the empire. But Kidd, while often foolhardy, was no fool; he planned to proceed to the north with caution, incognito, always keeping his escape route open.

Kidd authorized Henry Bolton to stay and guard the *Quedagh Merchant/Adventure Prize*, optimistically predicting that he would return within three months with sails and rigging to take the ship north. He also assigned Bolton as his agent to sell more of the goods, if the right price could be had. When Kidd returned from New York, he said he would bring documents condemning the *Quedagh* as a lawful prize taken in time of war with France. This paperwork would entitle buyers to resell their bales, openly and legally, and remove any taint of piracy.

Kidd had shown Burke and Bolton all his official documents, especially the French pass for the *Quedagh Merchant*. He had also mentioned that his backers included Governor Bellomont of New York and Lord Orford of the Admiralty. Friends like that could easily make any ship into a fair prize.

Ten members of the *St. Antonio* crew stayed with Bolton on the *Quedagh Merchant*, and a handful from Burke's ship and from Jan van der Biest joined up. Kidd gave Bolton a slave boy and possibly three of Kidd's men stayed as well. That ship, according to Kidd, still held 150 more bales, 20 mounted cannon and 30 more cannon in the hold, tons of sugar and scrap iron.

On May 15, 1699, the ships were ready to leave their secluded lagoon on Santa Catalina. At the very last moment, with no better offer in sight, two of Kidd's men — pals from England, the steward Samuel Aris and cook, Abel Owen — struck a deal with patient Jan van der Biest. The receipt reads: "Received 20 bales of goods with mark SA & SAO, which said [Samuel] Aris consigns to me for sale after payment of six bales for freight of the rest."

The fact that the receipt wound up among Captain Kidd's papers makes it likely that Kidd bought it off the men for real money, and *that he fully intended to return to the Caribbean.*

Six of Kidd's men hitched a ride (for a fee and freight charges) with Burke to Curacao. The tough boatswain Michael

Calloway went, as well as five of the rougher Dutch among the crew. John Weir, master, who started as a passenger from London in 1696, went with Jan van der Beist. These men and their fine goods were warmly welcomed in Curacao.

On May 15, the day of Kidd's departure, unbeknownst to Kidd, the president of council of Nevis dispatched the HMS *Queenborough*, a sixth-rate man of war under Captain Rupert Billingsly to track down and capture Captain Kidd.

As the *Queenborough* departed on its mission, a contagious disease suddenly hit the ship. Each day several men died, and more became ill until the death toll within a week climbed to twenty. All the while, Captain Billingsly, also sick, was heading to Mona to search for Kidd traveling *on a large Moorish ship.*

What Kidd also didn't realize as he fulfilled his decision to head north was that East India Company complaints had prompted a much beloved royal advisor, James Vernon, to alert the king himself. "I believe your Maj.ty may remember the name of this person who was fitted out about two or three years ago and had your Maj.tys Commission to seize the Pirates who infested the Trade to the Red Sea, but he has returnd to his old trade and has Robbd as much as any of them."

Kidd, in high times, had been the king's "trusty and well-beloved captain"; now he was "this person."

At that very moment, the ratty *St. Antonio* carrying its secret passengers and cargo, passed Florida, and approached the Carolinas.

Chapter Fourteen

Finally, after nearly three years of trying to impose his will on 100-plus piratically inclined sailors, Kidd was a passenger. Captain Samuel Wood was piloting the vessel. Also traveling as passengers aboard were the few men and boys who had chosen to come home with him on the *St. Antonio*. From Kidd's original crew of 155 that had sailed out of New York harbor, only ten remained, and four of these were cabin boys. Also accompanying Kidd was pirate-murderer James Gilliam, stout Edward Davies, chatterbox Hugh Parrott, and Ventura Rosair, white-haired cook from Ceylon, as well as Kidd's young slave, Dundee, and a handful of Malagasy slave boys and at least one girl.

The small ship was heavily armed; heavily laden with forty bales and chests for each of the men, plenty of provisions to eat well, including some live oinking pigs.

443

As Captain Rupert Billingsly of the HMS *Queenborough* searched for Kidd off Puerto Rico and the diseased corpses plunked into the sea, Kidd in the *St. Antonio* glided north to New York City. He told Bolton that he intended to contact his patron, the right honorable Governor Bellomont. From day one in the Caribbean, Kidd had acted like a man with friends in *very* high places. Or like a man who *hoped* that he did.

For the next two weeks heading north in the surprisingly fast-moving *St. Antonio*, nothing much happened on the ship, which must have been a blessed relief to Kidd.

(On May 27, again unbeknownst to Kidd, HMS *Queenborough* abandoned its mission, returning to Nevis, reporting twenty-three dead and twenty more very ill; Captain Billingsly requested ten-day shore leave, which was granted.)

By that date, Kidd aboard the *St. Antonio* was nearing the Delaware Bay, that inlet running south of the Jerseys and into Pennsylvania, when the boom-iron of the *St. Antonio* suddenly snapped. Boom-irons are the metal rings that hold in place a boom, i.e., a wooden extension of a yardarm. Unless they fixed it, they would have to carry much less sail.

Transporting all this treasure, finding himself so near to home, Kidd did not want to stop, but the repair needed to be made. Captain Wood on Saturday June 3 eased the ship around the point of what is now Cape Henlopen, Delaware, and up the coast to Lewes, then part of Pennsylvania.

Captain Wood came ashore with four men in a boat, telling the inquisitive locals that he was bound from Antigua to Philadelphia with a cargo of sugar, rum, and molasses. Per orders, he didn't mention Captain Kidd.

However, maybe mentioning the rum was as big a mistake, because a couple of boats flocked out to the *St. Antonio* and one of the men recognized Captain Kidd.

These five men from Lewes who sailed out to Kidd were "old pirates" who had once hit the Indies with Captain Tew but were now trying to settle down as farmers. Three of them spent the night on the *St. Antonio*, reliving old times with Captains Gilliam, Davies, and maybe Kidd. These three and two others, who stayed but an hour, carried £300 of goods ashore.

Although Kidd told them to keep their mouths shut about him, it took only three days for the news of Kidd's appearance to reach Colonel Quarry, the perpetually annoyed Pennsylvania customs collector. Quarry immediately dashed off an urgent message to the governor of Virginia to send the man-of-war north to the Delaware Bay.

While the local Lewes men were aboard,

Kidd learned an astounding bit of news: The mutineers had beaten him home. One week earlier, on the morning of Friday, May 26, several of his former crew, i.e., the mutineers turned pirates, had reached Cape May across the Delaware Bay. To Kidd, who knew how much many of those men hated him, this was crippling news. He could only imagine what stories they must be telling about him.

. The Lewes ex-pirates, awash in rum aboard the *St. Antonio*, also told Kidd of a rumor swirling around that the king had proclaimed a pardon for anyone willing to swear *never* to be a pirate again; they had heard that some of Kidd's former men had come ashore looking for the governor of West Jersey to grant them the pardon.

(William Penn, the founder of the Quaker colony, personally investigated the Kidd incident. The men of Lewes swore to the governor that they had received the goods as a "gift" from Gilliam and Captain Wood, nothing from Kidd. Penn had a certain sympathy for the men. "They are poor and married men and have children," he wrote, "but such men [i.e., former pirates] should not be endured to live near ye sea coasts nor trade lest they become receptacles and broakers for younger pirates." Penn ruled that the men must pay the government half of the £300, and that they must give security — including title to their farmlands — that they would never buy any pirate goods again.)

Kidd had intended to head directly to New York City, but now, in the wake of discovering that his mutinous pirate crew was already there, he decided to be more cautious. The local smithy fixed the boom-iron within twenty-four hours. Kidd then ordered Wood to veer away from the coastal shipping lanes and swing 120 miles to the east around the tip of Long Island and then double back west ninety miles along the Sound to Oyster Bay, twenty-five miles from New York City. Kidd felt safer in the Sound than passing through the high-trafficked narrows between Staten Island and Brooklyn.

The fast little ship, stymied by light winds, took ten days to reach Oyster Bay on June 9, 1699. Wood anchored offshore in the oyster-rich waters. Knowing how dicey his situation, Kidd wanted to contact *in complete secrecy* three people: his lawyer, his wife, and a smuggling sea-captain friend. Ever leery, he was devising a plan that would give him some leverage and some possibility of escape in case the governor wasn't sympathetic. Any moment, a Royal Navy ship might appear on the horizon.

Kidd wanted to send an "express" message to New York City. This wasn't easy since he couldn't send one of his New York men, who might get arrested or simply not return.

But Kidd had chosen this bustling little port of Oyster Bay because he knew two of the town's leading citizens, Justice White and Doctor Cooper. These men would help Kidd send his note and keep silent about Kidd's whereabouts.

So Captain Kidd wrote his note on an oversize piece of paper and then folded it over tightly and the final fold was sealed with wax, in which he made a distinctive impression with his seal ring.

The messenger, sure of a fine reward, rode hard southwest along roads passing very scattered farmhouses in Queens County and Breuckelen. For speed, he switched horses at an inn along the way. As he reached the East River, the Manhattan skyline loomed: a windmill and two church steeples towering over a seaside row of three-story gable roofs. The harbor was crammed with the crosstrees of seventy ships idled by the bad sugar crop in the Caribbean that year.

The messenger stabled his horse and waited for the next barge-like ferry from Brooklyn to Manhattan. Since he could see it on the far side, he took the horn hanging from a low tree limb and hallooed the ferryboat men across the river.

Waiting for the ferry and aboard the boat, the messenger heard the gossip then dominating this sea-faring city. A mysterious ship had recently landed at Red Hook, carrying fifty pirate passengers who were flush with money. The ship was beached, off-loaded, and abandoned before customs officers found it. Now that the men were ashore and drinking, one amazing bit was making the rounds: Gerrard van Horn, a Dutch sailor out of New York, had won 1,300 pieces of eight at one throw of the dice.

The messenger on the ferry glided amid the tall ships toward the New York City dock. He could see the glazed yellow and redbrick buildings that dominated River Road. There was an outhouse far out on the dock, and a ducking stool was being built at the north end of the wharf.

The messenger raced off the boat and bobbed amid the burly cartmen caterwauling for trade in this slow season. He ran amid the very narrow streets to the office of Kidd's lawyer, James Emott. This elderly gentleman ranked among the town's leading lawyers, aggressive, unafraid to battle the Crown. As a founding member of Trinity Church, he had been the one to arrange for his longtime friend and client, Captain Kidd, to buy one of the choicest pews in the new Anglican church. The messenger found Emott and delivered the letter. Examining the seal, Emott confirmed the authenticity. The letter has not survived, but we know certain things happened quickly after its delivery. Lawyer Emott spent less than a day taking care of business for Kidd before leaving New York City with the messenger.

Emott walked over to the Kidd mansion on Pearl Street, and lifted the heavy doorknocker. A servant guided him to Sarah and he told her that her husband had finally returned, and when she calmed down, the lawyer whispered secret plans to her. He next picked his way on the oyster shell–strewn streets to an old family friend of Kidd's, Thomas "Whisking" Clark. Clark was to get a sloop ready, with plenty of cargo room, and once he received instructions, he should pick up Sarah and daughter and sail to a specified location, off the eastern tip of Long Island. Everyone involved was to maintain *absolute* secrecy.

Within a day, word leaked out. Wrote Jonathan De Peyster, a wealthy merchant and one-time mayor, to his brother in Boston on Sunday, June 11: "Yesterday there arrived news that Captain Kidd is in the Sound, which is said to be undisputably true." He couldn't resist mentioning Van Horn's amazing win at dice.

Emott, no youngster, took the ferry to Brooklyn and then, by horseback with the messenger, traced the route back to Oyster Bay. The messenger returned with Emott less than three days after he left. Emott was rowed out to Kidd on June 11, 1699, and the *St. Antonio* set sail east on what is today called Long Island Sound.

Emott quickly told Kidd that his chances for a smooth return home were greatly complicated by the fact that Governor Bellomont had just two weeks earlier gone from New York to Boston. In New York, Kidd was a leading citizen, a "gentleman" on his marriage certificate; Emott ranked high in the legal community; their friends sat on the governor's council and in judges' chairs. Boston, on the other hand, to Emott's way of thinking, was dominated by Bible-quoting, penny-pinching fanatics, especially the father-son ministers Increase and Cotton Mather. He and Kidd had few friends there.

The two men also wanted to reach the governor before Kidd's mutinous crew started flinging about exotic Arabian gold, drunkenly telling pirate stories, getting arrested.

The accused pirate and his lawyer spent a June day together plotting strategy as the *St. Antonio* headed east along the Sound.

At this point, Kidd could still meet up with his wife, Sarah, and daughter, Sarah, and they could all quietly sail off with treasure. Now that there was peace with France, perhaps the French would allow him to live in one of its Caribbean islands, maybe under a new name: Guillaume L'Enfant or some such. Sarah looked very well, he was told.

However, Kidd wasn't slinking anywhere: he decided to risk lingering in the region. He wanted to clear his name, so he had Emott go ahead to Boston to sound out the governor, to seek a guarantee of protection. Would Bellomont believe Kidd's story? Or would he accept the gospel according to the English East India Company that branded Kidd a pirate? Would the gold and silk Kidd had brought back help his cause with the impoverished earl? A Dutchman in New York writing to Colonel De Peyster in Boston summed it up: "Regarding the Cidt [Kidd] affair, I hope that my Lord will act in this with all circumspection, for his enemies are already beginning to brag and say, 'Now it will be soon seen how my Lord will protect the pirates.'"

Nightfall found them short of Rhode Island, so Kidd dropped Emott off in Stonington, Connecticut, and the lawyer started riding the sixty-five miles north to

Boston. For an old man like Emott, this was some hard riding, but he reached Boston the following night, quite late on Tuesday, June 13, 1699.

The old Puritan town was eerily dark, with absolutely no public street lighting provided. Emott on horseback, the sound of hooves clopping on paving stones, glimpsed no more than a fellow walking a lantern here or a dimly lit household there. (The post office hung out a lantern only on nights when a rider was expected; the harbor's lighthouse wasn't built until 1716.) Any horseman entering after curfew was supposed to be stopped by a member of the town's Select Watch, *ten* men hired to walk the *entire* city by night, especially on the lookout for fires.

Emott asked the first man he met in the gloom where the governor was staying, and was given directions to the stately home of one of the town's wealthiest citizens, Peter Sergeant. Emott guided his horse down Marlborough Street and turned between two massive oak trees that framed the entry.

The old man achingly dismounted, then climbed the long flight of red freestone steps. He lifted and dropped the ornate brass knocker; slowly lights appeared within; a servant opened the door. James Emott identified himself and said he had urgent business with the governor.

His gout acting up, and his personal servant unavailable due to a freak accident the day before, the governor was not amused to be disturbed at that hour.

"On the 13th of last Month, Mr. Emot, a Lawyer of New-York, came late at Night to me and told me he came from Captain Kidd, who was on the coast with a sloop but would not tell me where," wrote Bellomont in a letter about a month later. "That Kidd had brought 60 Pound Weight of gold and 100 Weight of Silver and 17 Bales of East India Goods. . . . That Kidd had left behind him a great Ship near the Coast of Hispaniola that nobody but himselfe could find out, on board whereof there were in bale goods, Saltpetre and other things to the value of £30,000: That if I would give him a pardon, he would bring in the Sloop and goods hither and would go and fetch the great Ship and goods afterwards."

The governor also noted that "Mr. Emot delivered me that Night *Two French Passes,* which Kidd took on board the Two Moors Ships which were taken by him in the seas of India (or, as he alleges, by his Men against his Will)."

Bellomont was a hulking, gouty, angry man, with an enormous sense of Protestant righteousness and of aristocratic entitlement. Elegant manners often masked his irritation but clearly his incessant money troubles infuriated him. He was a lord in title, but a man often forced to borrow money from lordly friends or from Scotch merchants or sometimes even from Jewish moneylenders such as Joseph Bueno of Boston.

Bellomont had stunned New York merchants by cracking down on smuggling and piracy. He was described as "condescending and affable," and was able to conceal his contempt for most colonial officials and merchants. His Protestantism had led him to have Jacob Leisler (head sewn back on) reburied in consecrated ground, an act that reopened seven-year-old wounds and split the city like a cleaver. Many of the wealthy in New York had grown to despise Bellomont, and after less than a year, were already murmuring about petitioning for his recall.

Ironically, the old Puritan town of Boston seemed gaga over Bellomont's *noble* rank. The town, en masse, two weeks earlier had given Bellomont and his much younger wife the grandest welcome in the history of the province. "We made a guard from the end of the sound to the south meeting," wrote stone mason John Marshall. "The drums beat, the trumpets did sound, the colours were displayed, the cannons and ordinance from the ships and fortifications did roar, all manner of expressions of joy and to end all, fireworks and good drink at night."

Cotton Mather had unctuously informed this governor of three colonies that Boston was "irradiated with your Excellency's Happy Arrival." The Assembly had immediately voted him a £1,000 gratuity, a gift.

For Bellomont, Boston proved a welcome break from bickering New York. But it didn't last.

That night, Tuesday night, at Peter Sergeant's, bereft of his butler, his gout flaring, late in the blackness of a curfewed town, had come the knock at his door. And now standing there was James Emott, an exhausted old man, and one of Lord Bellomont's least favorite people in New York City. Bellomont was too well-mannered to express his distaste publicly but in his letters, he called Emott "a cunning Jacobite," which in Bellomont's English Protestant worldview was about as low as a man can get. (It was like calling someone a Commie in the United States in the 1950s.) "There was not such a parcel of wild knaves and Jacobites as those that practised the law in the Province of New York, not one of them a barrister, one was a dancing master, another a glover, a third (and he was Col. Fletcher's bosom friend, favourite and land-jobber) condemned to be hanged in Scotland for blasphemy and burning the Bible."

This latter apparently was Bellomont's thumbnail sketch of Emott. Bellomont also knew that Emott handled delivering the "presents," the "tokens of gratitude" from pirates to the previous governor, Ben Fletcher. To top it all, he later referred to Emott as "my avowed enemy." Bellomont was never one to mince personal hatreds. (Kidd, three years at sea, knew none of that.)

Lord Bellomont had, along with the other governors, received the orders from the Lords Justices dated November 23, 1698 to seize Captain Kidd. However, Bellomont, unlike all the others, had not relayed this command to his council or published it. Bellomont, a backer of Kidd's voyage, a man who stood to profit from Kidd's success, had kept it secret.

That night of June 13, the moment he had both dreaded and hoped for, had finally arrived: Kidd had returned. A few days earlier in a letter from New York, Bellomont had learned that some of Kidd's men had returned on a ship of Giles Shelley, and that New York City, with him tucked in Boston, was becoming awash in Arabian gold. But this was Kidd himself. Bellomont was faced with a maddening choice. His "avowed enemy," one of the slipperiest lawyers in New York City, stood before him trying to wrangle a pardon for Captain Kidd, who could still easily flee.

Bellomont sat in an overstuffed chair in Peter Sergeant's house, near hastily relit oil lamps, with his gouty foot propped on a pillow. He expressed joy that Captain Kidd had returned safely with treasure. It was Bellomont who had talked four lords and one king into backing Kidd's voyage for reasons of patriotism and profit. And it was Bellomont who had suffered the past year as stories of Captain Kidd turning pirate had filtered into America. Emott, in Kidd's defense, said his crew had mutinied, and it was they who had committed the crimes.

Bellomont pondered. He showed *great warmth* to James Emott, inviting him to return the following day. Bellomont limped back to the curtained four-poster he shared with his young wife. It's doubtful he slept much that night.

Bellomont the next morning told a servant to call for Duncan Campbell, a thirty-something-year-old *Scot* by birth who had once been described as a "brisk young fellow that dresses à la mode." Campbell was scraping by on the fringes of government as deputy postmaster for Massachusetts Bay. Also acting as something of a spy for Wait Winthrop, governor of Connect-

icut, he wrote him long letters containing the news of the day. (Duncan Campbell's correspondence would evolve into the first newspaper in the American colonies, in 1704, and be overseen by his brother, John, a quarter century before Ben Franklin's efforts in Philadelphia.)

The lordly governor decided to send Campbell along with Emott back to Kidd. Bellomont, a most voluminous letter writer among early governors in America, put *nothing* in writing. Bellomont told *no one* about Emott's arrival and the certain knowledge that Captain Kidd — the most wanted outlaw in the colonies — anchored in the Sound.

On the morning of June 15, Duncan Campbell and James Emott headed south on horseback past the farms and villages to go forty miles to Bristol to catch a boat over to Rhode Island, then by horse to Rhode Island Sound. This time around, Emott had no intention of doing the journey in one single backbreaking day.

The two men carried a simple message from Governor Bellomont to Kidd: Welcome home. I invite you to come to Boston. A pardon is possible.

After Kidd dropped off Emott on June 11, he had several days to kill, days to wonder whether Lord Bellomont would treat him as a criminal or as a partner.

After four days of waiting at the agreed rendezvous spot off Block Island, Kidd's restlessness got the better of him. He decided to sail up Narragansett Bay in Rhode Island along the eastern side of Connonicut Island to Jamestown. Kidd sent a boat ashore to see whether his old friend Captain Paine was at home. The messenger found Paine and rowed him out to the *St. Antonio*.

Captain Thomas Paine was a grizzled veteran of Caribbean privateering; he had been present at a failed pirate attack on St. Augustine in Spanish Florida; he had helped drive the French off Block Island. The captain had hauled numerous captures back to the generous merchants of Rhode Island. And now by 1699, he seems to have semiretired into what could be characterized as the pirate banking and cargo resale business. He had chosen his home address wisely: Rhode Island was the colony in the Northeast that most unequivocally welcomed pirates. In New York, the warmth might depend on the current governor; in Boston, on the amount of profit offered to the God-fearing merchants. But in free-thinking Rhode Island, for decades, pirates were greeted warmly.

We know nothing of the conversation that passed between the men on board the *St. Antonio* but we know that both Captain Kidd and the pirate James Gilliam, alias Kelly, trusted Captain Paine with valuables. Kidd gave Thomas Paine at least three pounds of gold in bars to hold for him; and Gilliam handed him 800 pieces of eight. Witnesses later reported that Gilliam desperately wanted to go ashore and remain there, but that Kidd would not let him. (This again is a measure of Kidd's toughness that he was able to stop murderous Gilliam from leaving his ship without permission.)

Those were the days before Swiss bank accounts — before *any* bank accounts. Back then a man would generally hide his money in his home and/or lock it up in a heavy chest with chains wrapped around it; or he might invest his money.

Pirates (or those embezzling from privateering missions) had more of a challenge. Pirates might park a little bit here and a little bit there with a landlord or a doctor against a rainy day. Part of the reason pirates returning home squandered their wealth was that it was very hard to safeguard it.

Kidd had Paine rowed to shore and then he sailed south to head back to his meeting place off Block Island. Governor of Rhode Island, Sam Cranston, got word that *a strange small armed ship* was in the bay. The governor sent an urgent message to his customs officials. The wind was contrary, but they rowed a boat out with thirty well-armed men ready to confront the *St. Antonio*. The men brandished their weapons, and the customs collector made signals to the *St. Antonio* that he wanted to come aboard. Kidd's response was to fire "two great guns" in the general vicinity of the longboat. The Rhode Island men could see ten cannon, and eight mortars and decided to retreat; they never discovered who was aboard that odd ship.

Kidd sailed back out to his rendezvous point, off Block Island. He stopped briefly close to shore to land two small cannon (weighing 300 pounds each) and ammunition, to be cared for by his friend Edward Sands. Kidd, trying to cover *every possi-*

462

bility, was preparing just in case he needed to make a rushed getaway in some other ship and needed to retrieve extra firepower. His wife might be staying soon on Block Island: he wanted to protect her.

The morning of Saturday, June 17, James Emott and Duncan Campbell hired a sloop in Newport to take them out toward Block Island. The New York lawyer and Boston deputy postmaster, both men in wigs, waistcoats, and buckle shoes, a bit rumpled from their hard two-day ride, stood on the deck of the sloop as it glided out Narragansett Bay toward the Sound. Captain Kidd had asked Emott to pick up a wig for him, and Emott had wisely given the task to younger Duncan Campbell. Perhaps the thought of Mrs. Kidd, now a lovely twenty-eight-year-old, animated his vanity. Or maybe the wig was to garb him in respectability for his entry into Boston.

Duncan Campbell bought a top-of-the-line wig and some other small necessities for Kidd.

The men spied the *St. Antonio* and hailed the ship. Kidd's boat came to take them aboard. The three men descended into the cabin, and the two emissaries from Boston relayed the governor's invitation. Kidd told Campbell a shortened nuanced version of his three-year odyssey. Kidd instantly liked this Scot, Duncan Campbell, all three men conferred. Distrustful as ever, Kidd ultimately decided that the words of welcome were too vague as were the hints of a pardon. Kidd wanted something *in writing,* a letter.

So Kidd decided to dispatch Campbell back to Boston to get a promise in writing. But before he sent off his Scots messenger, he gave him some small exotic tokens of gratitude: two speckled handkerchiefs (a luxury item in those days when nose-blowing was still often done by clamping one nostril shut and venting the other onto the ground) and three quarters of a pound of tea. Kidd overpaid him four pieces of gold for the wig, and gave him a like amount to cover travel expenses.

Campbell, after he got off the Rhode Island ferry, literally raced to Boston, along the twisting rutted roads. He nearly killed his rental horse and reached Boston in little over a day, after sunset on Sunday, June 18. Campbell appeared before the full governor's Council on Monday morning with Lord Bellomont in attendance. Some of the most powerful men in New England attended: Judge Samuel Sewall, Wait Winthrop, Peter Sergeant, John Phillips, Elisha and Eliakin Hutchinson. This local advisory council was supposed to act as a check upon the royal governor. Bellomont only now informed them of his meeting six days earlier with Kidd's lawyer.

Duncan Campbell, fresh from the sloop, said Captain Kidd swore that he was not guilty of *any* crimes, and that his crew had mutinied to go out pirating in the Red Sea with Culliford.

Campbell stood before the august assemblage. "By reason of what his Men had heard in the West-Indies of their being proclaimed Pirates," relayed Campbell from Kidd, "they would not consent to his coming into any Port without some Assurance from your Excellency that they should not be imprisoned or molested."

Lord Bellomont drafted a letter.

Boston, 19 June 1699

Captain Kidd,

Mr. Emott came to me last Tuesday Night late, telling me, He came from you, but was shy of telling me where he parted with you; nor did I press him to it: He told me, You came to Oyster Bay, in Nassaw Island, and sent for him to New York. He proposed to me, That I would grant you a Pardon: I answered, That I had never granted one yet.

And that I had set myself a Rule, not to grant a Pardon to any Body whatever without the King's express Leave or Command: He told me, You declared and protested your Innocence; and that, if your

Men could be persuaded to follow your Example, you would [not hesitate to come] into this Port, or any other within his Majesty's Dominions: That you owned there were Two Ships taken; but that your Men did it violently, against your Will; and had used you barbarously, imprisoning you, treating you ill, most Part of the Voyage, and often attempting to murder you.

Mr. Emott delivered me Two French passes, taken on board the Two Ships which your Men rifled; which Passes I have in my Custody; and I am apt to believe they will be a good Article to justify you. . . . Mr. Emott also told me, You had to about the Value of £10,000 in the Sloop with you; and that you had left a Ship somewhere off the coast of Hispaniola, in which there was to the value of £30,000 more; which you had left in safe Hands, and had promised to go to your People in that Ship, within Three Months, to fetch them with you to a safe Harbour.

These are all the material Particulars I can recollect that passed between Mr. Emott and me: Only this, that he told me, that you shewed a great Sense of honour and Justice, in professing, with many Asseverations, your settled and serious Design, all along, to do Honour to your Commission, and never do the least thing contrary

to your Duty and Allegiance to the King:
and this I have to say in your Defense,
that several Persons at New York, who I
can bring to evidence it, if there be occasion, did tell me, That by several Advices
from Madagascar, and that Part of the
World, they were informed of your Men's
Revolting from you in one Place; which I
am pretty sure they said was at Madagascar; and that others of them compelled
you, much against your Will, to take and
rifle Two Ships.

I have advised, with his Majesty's
Council, and shewed them this letter, this
Afternoon; and they are of the Opinion,
That if your Case be so clear as you (or
Mr. Emott for you) have said, then you
may safely come hither, and be equipped,
and fitted out, to go and fetch the other
Ship; and I make no Manner of Doubt but
to obtain the King's Pardon for you, and
those few Men you have left; who, I understand, have been faithful to you, and refused, as well as you, to dishonour the
Commission you had from England.

I assure you, on my Word and Honour,
I will perform nicely what I have now
promised. . . .

Mr. Campbell will satisfy you, That this
That I have now writ, is the Sense of the
Council, and of

Your humble Servant

Bellomont signed the letter, which was copied by the Council clerk. Bellomont folded the original and affixed his wax seal. Campbell mounted up and headed south to deliver the good news.

Captain Kidd had kept busy after sending Campbell on his way on Saturday, June 17. Kidd had sailed west toward Gardiners Island, a private estate of 3,300 acres, seven miles long, equidistant between the forks of Long Island. Cliffs line the northeast side and the family mansion then stood to the southwest with a view toward the closest point on Long Island. On a spit of land there was the so-called "Fireplace," where people lit signal fires to tell Gardiner to send over a boat.

Lion Gardiner, a Scottish engineer who built forts in Connecticut, had bought the island from the Montauk Indians back in 1638 for "a large black dog, a Gun & ammunition, some rum, and a few Dutch blankets." The Indians had called the place Monchonake but Lion preferred "Isle of Wight." The third-generation owner, John Gardiner, employed Montauk Indians to plant corn and kill whales for him; Gardiner was fluent in the Indian language.

Kidd anchored a ways offshore and had his men row Mr. Emott to the modest dock. Emott, who walked to the manor house, asked Gardiner to provide a boat to take him down the Sound toward New York City, and he didn't bother to mention to Gardiner that Captain Kidd was in that vessel offshore. Emott's next errand was a pleasurable one: he would now go tell Sarah Kidd to come to Block Island to meet her husband. Exit the lawyer.

John Gardiner, using a spyglass from the shore, could see a sloop with six cannon and he noticed as well that two other small ships anchored alongside. Gardiner later said he allowed two days to slip by, but then decided that he would investigate these three vessels hovering so close to his family property. He had himself rowed out in his whaleboat, by his Indians, and discovered the two small craft were New York sloops: one had been carrying a cargo of rum and truckin cloth going to Martha's Vineyard before someone made it worthwhile for the captain to turn around.

Gardiner reported that one New York sloop was commanded by Carsten Luersten and "his mate is a little black man who, it was said, had been formerly Kidd's quartermaster." (The black man had the impressive name of Hendrick van der Heul.)

At this point, it appears, with Duncan Campbell not yet returned, that everyone aboard the *St. Antonio* started to get a little more nervous about their situation, about Bellomont's welcome. Maybe, they decided, it would be wise to off-load some wealth, to hide a little — call it "embezzle" if you like — before the privateer partners started counting pennies and mop handles. Half a dozen of Kidd's crew, the New Yorkers, now took the opportunity to ship their goods — at least four chests and ten bales — eastward *toward* New York and *away* from Governor Bellomont. The hands of the other vessel, an open sloop, also piled the deck high with cargo and delivered a bale each to those leading citizens of Oyster Bay: one to Justice White, one to Dr. Cooper. The rest of the freight was delivered to a warehouse in Stamford but Captain Luersten and mate van der Heul both later testified that they "forgot the name of the person they were to be delivered to."

Gardiner now met Captain Kidd for the first time. Always inclined toward fellow Scots, Kidd, after the first couple of cups of hard cider, decided to trust the man. Kidd told Gardiner he was heading to Boston to see Lord Bellomont; he asked Gardiner to keep three slaves (two boys and a girl) till he came back or sent an order for them. Gardiner agreed, and Gardiner's Indians, in buckskin, paddled the three prepubescent Malagasy kids ashore. None of the child-slaves knew any English; all communication was by hand signals. Pirate Gilliam also sent ashore a small chest with two pounds of gold in it and some jewels. About two hours later, Kidd sent the sloop's boat ashore with two bales of goods and another Negro boy. Kidd's cabin boys stored some bale goods here as well, with simple markings such as RB for "Richard Barleycorn."

Kidd had brought food from Curacao, but he wanted more for an upcoming celebration — the reunion with his wife. "The morning after, Kidd desired me to come onboard," later deposed Gardiner, "and bring six sheep with me for Kidd's voyage to Boston." Kidd implored him to spare a barrel of hard cider, and Gardiner sent two men to fetch it. (A barrel of cider contained 31½ gallons, weighing more than 250 pounds.) Gardiner family tradition has it that Kidd wanted Mrs. Gardiner to roast him a pig, which she did as nicely as she could, and that he gave her a cloth with strands of gold in it and a clay pitcher full of dried fruits. (Family members have been subdividing that bit of cloth for generations and a small square may be seen today on loan at the East Hampton Public Library.)

Gardiner returned ashore; a little later, Kidd saluted him, firing four guns before heading off for Block Island.

Captain Kidd, aboard the ramshackle *St. Antonio*, sailed to wait for Duncan Campbell to return in Hulin's sloop. In a way, he was awaiting a thumbs-up or thumbs-down from the emperor. Bellomont might send a Royal Navy vessel instead.

Campbell had taken Bellomont's letter and departed Boston on Tuesday, June 20, and had once again galloped south. Campbell, the deputy postmaster, carrying this important letter, had ridden hard, his horse sweating, panting in the early summer heat, then suddenly dying underneath him. Campbell had been thrown to the ground but luckily broke no bones. That mishap cost him a day. Duncan Campbell arrived in the Sound on June 23. The Hulin sloop tacked and retacked to the rendezvous area, but failed to find Kidd. Then on Saturday, June 24, Campbell tracked down the *St. Antonio* full of cider-happy men.

Campbell hailed, beaming. His enthusiasm unmistakable, he delivered the governor's letter. Kidd read it quickly, and, buoyed, dashed off a reply.

From Block Island Road, on board the Sloop St. Antonio, June the 24th, 1699

May it please your Excellency,
I am honoured with your Lordship's kind Letter of the 19th current, by Mr. Campbell; which came to my Hands this Day; for which I return my most hearty Thanks.

I cannot but blame myself for not writing to your Lordship before this Time, knowing it was my Duty; but the clamours, and false Stories, that have been reported of me, made me fearful of writing, or coming into any Harbour, till I could hear from your Lordship.

I note the Contents of your Lordship's Letter: As to what Mr. Emott and Mr. Campbell informed your Lordship of my Proceedings, I do affirm to be true; and a great Deal more might be said of the abuses of my Men, and the Hardship I have undergone to preserve the Ship and what Goods my Men had left: Ninety-five Men went away from me in one Day, and went on board the Moca Frigate, Captain Robert Cullifar Commander; who went away to the Red Seas; and committed several Acts of Piracy, as I am informed; and am afraid (the Men formerly belonging to my Gally) that the report is gone Home against me to the East India Company, that I have been the Actor: A Sheet of Paper will not contain what may be said of the Care I took to preserve the Owners Interest, and to come Home to clear my own Innocency. I do further declare and protest, That I never did, in the least, act contrary to the king's Commission, nor to the Reputation of my honourable Owners; and doubt not but I shall be able to make my Innocence ap-

pear; or else I had no need to come to these Parts of the World, if it were not for that and my Owners Interest. There are Five or Six Passengers, that came from Madegasco to assist me in bringing the Ship Home, and about Ten of my own Men, that came with me, would not venture to go into Boston, till Mr. Campbell had engaged, Body for Body, for them, that they should not be molested while I staid at Boston, or till I return with the Ship. I doubt not but your Lordship will write to England in my favour, and for these few Men, that are left. I wish your Lordship would persuade Mr. Campbell to go Home for England, with your Lordship's Letters: Who will be able to give Account of our Affairs, and diligently follow the same, that there may be a speedy Answer from England.

I desire Mr. Campbell to buy 1,000 Weight of Rigging, for fiting of the Ship [Adventure Prize, off Hispaniola] to bring her to Boston, that I may not be delayed when I come there. Upon receiving of your Lordship's letter, I am making the best of my Way for Boston.

This, with my humble duty to your Lordship and Countess, is what offers from, my Lord,

> *Your Excellency's most humble*
> *and dutiful servant,*
> *Wm. Kidd*

He signed the letter with an especial flourish, spiking his W and K. Captain Kidd folded the paper, sealed it with his ring, and handed it to Duncan Campbell. He also gave him 100 pieces of eight to cover his expenses and for Campbell's wife, Susannah, a gold chain and four pieces of fine muslin and speckled calico. Then Kidd rummaged in his chest and pulled out a silver box edged with gilt enamel: in it were four gold lockets each set with a diamond, one loose diamond, and then "a large diamond (almost three carats) sett in a gold ring." He told Campbell to give the jewels to Lady Bellomont.

Lawyer Emott might have suggested this gift-giving strategy before leaving, or Kidd, as a "gentleman," considered this appropriate behavior. This was a finesse around the problem of Bellomont being asked directly whether *he* received anything from Kidd. In any case, in that era, it was commonplace to give "presents" to officials handling your affairs; Samuel Pepys received silver from the victuallers. Bellomont himself searched hard for the proper present to accompany his letters to his patron the Duke of Shrewsbury. Lordly gift-giving is a fine art of subtle shading; of course, when Bellomont did it, there was no vestige of something as crude as a bribe, it was one lord showing appreciation to another. In that letter of recommendation for Kidd a few years earlier, the attorney general of New York had stated to minister Blathwayt, "I do assure yor Honour he will be very grateful." Quid pro quo ruled, but at the highest social levels, the exchange of favors was *discreet*.

Captain Kidd directed Captain Wood to sail closer to Block Island. It was time for the reunion. After three hard years mostly at sea, Captain Kidd would finally see Sarah again. He had taken an enormous risk coming to New England.

This man, who could be violent and remote and distrustful, loved Sarah deeply, and there's absolutely no doubt that it infuriated him to think of her being called a pirate's wife.

Lawyer James Emott had reached New York on June 20 and told Sarah Kidd to sail to Block Island with family friend Thomas Clark, a former New York City coroner, who years earlier had bought property from the Kidds. Clark had a nickname: "Whisking," a fine smuggler's moniker. Nowadays, he kept a secret warehouse in Stamford, Connecticut.

Sarah, as instructed by her husband, packed for more than a brief stay. She brought all the family silver, which included a basin, a tankard, a mug, a porringer, and numerous spoons and forks. It was not that unusual then to travel with your own silver service; it was a sign of wealth, upper-classmanship. (One special point of snobbery was the silver fork, which Sarah had started using over the last few years; most commoners still ate with their hands after hacking off a portion with a knife.) She also carried along 260 pieces of eight, which was a large sum. Sarah and William were apparently thinking about the possibility of needing a getaway, maybe a Caribbean getaway.

Mrs. Kidd traveled to Block Island with her daughter, who was now six years old, also named Sarah. The little girl would have had only the vaguest memories of her father, who had left home when she was three. A maid accompanied them.

Sarah Kidd reached Block Island and stayed at Newshorum at the house of family friends, the Sands, where Captain Kidd had already dropped off two cannon.

This June 25 day, Sarah prepared to see her husband. If she followed the latest fashions, the dress she was wearing skimmed the floor, flounced out by petticoats; her waist was cinched in by a stiff bodice, accentuating her breasts. Derriere, she might have followed *la mode* by sporting a small bustle.

Sarah Kidd wanted company at the reunion, and invited along Mary Sands (whom court records later described as "27 years or upwards") and her husband, Edward, 30. Kidd anchored at the east end of Block Island and the men rowed out Sarah and little Sarah, and Mary and Edward Sands.

The smell of roast lamb, spiced with nutmeg and cloves, floated in the spring breezes; some of the men had actually bathed and put on clean clothes bought from Gardiner and the Rhode Island sloop men. Even rogue Gilliam, ever fond of the ladies, had scrubbed a bit; the deck of the *St. Antonio* was finally cleaned of pig shit and straw.

Kidd himself was resplendent in a waistcoat, which he had pampered in a trunk for most of his voyage. His new wig, parted in the middle, rich brown, hung to his shoulders.

Kidd looked down from the rail and drank in the sight of his wife and daughter approaching the *St. Antonio*. The boat pulled to the side of the small ship. Sarah stood and handed up their daughter. Kidd reached down and scooped up little Sarah. Then his wife was lifted aboard.

Sarah gave her husband a welcome home hug befitting a man who had risked his life to return to her. Three years of stories must have burst from her, three *years* of questions. In a million lifetimes, she never expected her husband to turn pirate. Little Sarah no doubt explored her father's face, touching the contours of this strange man. Most likely, both Sarahs cried. Did tears well in the eyes of the relentless captain? Kidd must have marveled at his daughter. Hours later, after much cider, he and Sarah descended to the scant privacy of the captain's cabin aboard the sloop.

The only eyewitness to the reunion, who left an account, was Mary Sands, and she unfortunately chose to dwell on her meeting with "Cap'n Gilliam," that fifty-ish leather-faced, scarred old pirate. Mary said Gilliam told her that he was very eager to get to Rhode Island, where he had a friend who had promised to protect him.

The next morning, the party long over, Captain Kidd finally allowed Gilliam to leave, and Gilliam hitched a sail ride north to Newport. Duncan Campbell departed as well, with Kidd's gracious letter to the governor and his grateful gift to the countess.

Kidd had written in his letter of Saturday, June 24, that he would now head east around Cape Cod to Boston.

He did the exact opposite.

He headed back west to Gardiners Island.

While Sarah was not literate, she appears to have been very shrewd. Kidd, after talking to his wife, had a change of heart. He scrutinized the wording of Bellomont's letter a bit more carefully, and noticed the conditional nature of Bellomont's promise, that easy-to-overlook little phrase *"if your case be so clear as you have said,* then you may safe come hither. . . ."

Kidd decided to try to give himself more leverage in his upcoming dealings with the governor, maybe even a get-out-of-jail-free card. He would hide the investors' treasure. That way, Bellomont might be forced to free him to let him go retrieve it.

Kidd returned to Gardiners Island, had Thomas Clark rowed ashore, and he came back with John Gardiner; Kidd entrusted Gardiner with a chest containing fifty pounds of gold and fifty pounds of silver. The chest was locked and nailed and corded about. Gardiner's Indian laborers rowed the chest ashore and family tradition holds that John Gardiner buried the Kidd chest full of gold under a spot in Cherry Tree field. (That spot is still marked to this day.)

Kidd left another small chest, also tightly secured shut, that contained what he considered his next most valuable possessions: spices, drugs, and finest cloths. In it were: Goa Stone (an expensive fever medicine made by the Jesuits of Goa), a bushel of cloves and nutmeg, pieces of silk striped with silver and gold, cloth of silver, fine muslin, flowered silk, fine white calicoes.

He also left a bundle of fine India quilts, many silken. Some crew members also decided to leave more goods, such as a handful of bales; and cook Abel Owens and gunner Hugh Parrott deposited two sacks weighing thirty pounds, for which they received a receipt. "And another of Kidd's Men delivered to me," recalled Gardiner, "a small bundle of Gold and Gold Dust, of about a Pound Weight, to keep for him; and did also present me with a Sash and a Pair of Worsted Stockings: And just before the Sloop sailed, Captain Kidd presented me with a Bag of Sugar."

Gardiner later said that he didn't know that Kidd was proclaimed a pirate but that even if he had, he would *not* have acted differently, saying he "had no Force to oppose them."

Kidd was accompanied to Gardiners Island by a sloop from New York, Captain Cornelious Quick, who was taking "Whisking" Clark back. Kidd put several chests and bundles to go with Clark. He marked at least one of the chests with his distinctive symbol: a W, flanked on either side by curvy K's. The chest contained so many odd little items and small piles of beautiful cloth that it almost seems as though Sarah Kidd were allowed to rummage the hold of the *St. Antonio* and make selections: 11 small pearls, a skein of gold thread, a bag with 10 pounds of spice, 3½ yards of silk fringe. Also mixed in were 4 pounds of gold, 40 pounds of silver, and a handful of very important documents that Kidd had guarded halfway around the world, including the *Adventure Galley* account that showed him selling chests of opium and bales of silk in India.

Captain Kidd was once again hedging his bet. Kidd was entrusting his good friend Clark with an amount of goods and bullion that would facilitate a getaway. And, maybe he was embezzling a little bit more. Kidd was no saint; he wanted to clear his name but he also wanted to make sure he reaped some profit from his 1,000 days of misery.

Sarah and William, on a much lightened *St. Antonio*, sailed to Boston. The ship entered Nantucket Shoals and a sailor on deck spotted a sail. It was a Boston-based sloop, under Captain Thomas Way, returning from the Bay of Compeach. They hailed each other and Captain Way came in his ship's canoe over to Kidd. They agreed to sail together round the Cape into Boston.

Yet again, cautious Captain Kidd decided to protect himself against betrayal by Governor Bellomont. He arranged for Captain Way to secretly carry a small cache of goods into Boston harbor for him: three pistols, a pair of stilliards (a balance scale to weigh gold), a turkey carpet, a pendulum navigation clock (bought in the Indian Ocean from Captain Wright of the *Quedagh Merchant*), a bundle of Mrs. Kidd's clothes and a canvas bag weighing six pounds containing 280 pieces of eight, Mrs. Kidd's money.

Clearly, Kidd transshipped these items out of fear that the *St. Antonio* might be seized. He wanted to protect his wife's clothes and pieces of eight from getting muddled up in his own affairs. Also, this money would be handy in case of the need of a quick exit, as would three pistols.

Captain Kidd rounded Cape Cod. There, "his heart misgave him," according to someone who interviewed several of the men aboard. Kidd — with his wife and child at his side in the New England summer sunshine — decided it might be better to double back to grab the treasure on Gardiners Island and then head off to the new Scottish settlement in Central America. Trust in Scots. With each friendly face he encountered, from Emott, from Campbell, he had learned a little more about Scotland's mighty Darien Project.

The Scots a year earlier had outfitted a fleet of three ships with 175 cannon and 1,200 men and women aboard. Wildly optimistic on arrival, the Scots had dubbed their settlement New Edinburgh. Cut off by the Navigation Acts and desperate for goods to trade there, the Scots had been forced to carry along such dubious trade items as 4,000 wigs of Highlander hair to sell to Spanish colonists.

England, Kidd knew, had no intention of allowing the Scots to prosper. The Lords of Trade had decided to honor the Spanish claims in the region over the Scottish ones, and had sent a message to all English governors forbidding them from aiding the Scottish settlers.

At the very moment that Kidd stood rounding the Cape, the most powerful lords in London were deeply worried that this Scottish sea captain, whose treasure was then pegged at an astounding half a million pounds (greater than the Royal Navy's peacetime budget), would sail to Darien and resuscitate the Scots' failing efforts. Kidd's gold might seed this Indies trading emporium that would pry Scotland out from under England's heel.

Kidd stood at the first islands that mark Boston Bay. The day was Saturday, July 1, 1699. It was very hot. Boston loomed in the distance, a town packed onto one single peninsula in the harbor, a two-thirds square mile warren of gray wooden houses intermixed with new ornate brick-and-stone dwellings, a vista anchored in the center by the Old Church steeple.

Kidd ached to join his countrymen in the Caribbean, but he decided to take a huge gamble, to sail into Boston to clear his name. Captain Wood navigated the ship through the tricky entrance to the port of Boston, past the dangerous shore of Spectacle Island and under the guns of the castle, and into the forest of idle masts. The crew of *St. Antonio* heaved anchor close to shore in the late afternoon and word of their arrival was rushed to Governor Bellomont.

If Kidd expected a warm welcome or a brass band, he was sorely disappointed. All was eerily quiet as the town prepared for the Sunday Sabbath, which began at sunset on Saturday.

Bellomont did not appear in person but sent a greeting to Kidd, and he ordered "ample refreshments" be delivered. He also asked Kidd's crew *to be so kind* as to stay aboard until Monday.

Kidd had himself rowed ashore. William, along with his two Sarahs, walked the narrow, mostly unpaved streets to Duncan Campbell's modest house, which they reached before Sabbath curfew, carrying almost nothing from the ship. It was his first night ashore since almost a year earlier on St. Mary's Island, Madagascar; his first night ashore with his wife since New York almost three years earlier in the summer of 1696.

The next morning, an especially hot day, Captain Kidd had the opportunity to attend church, and hear Cotton Mather, famed through the colonies for his impassioned oratory.

"Thou wilt before tomorrow morning be a Companion of the Devils and the Damned," Mather had recently roared at a nineteen-year-old unwed mother, condemned to hang for murdering her bastard child. "The Everlasting Chains of Darkness will hold thee for the Worm that never dies . . . thou wilt fall into the hands of the Living God and become as Glowing Iron, possessed by his Burning Vengeance."

Lord Bellomont did not attend church that morning, blaming his gout, which was no doubt inflamed by Kidd's arrival. The governor was unable to walk without excruciating pain.

In Boston, a summer Sunday afternoon was generally morgue-quiet since authorities forbade "travel, labor, sports and play" on the Lord's Day. Kidd could loll around with his family in the privacy of Campbell's home.

Word of Kidd's arrival spread quickly. New York merchant Abraham DePeyster, in Boston serving as secretary for the governor, rushed out a letter, which reached New York, stunningly, two days later on July 3. The post rider must have raced along dirt roads through unbroken forest, switching horses wherever possible. The recipient, Dr. Samuel Staats, showed the note to Kidd's loony father-in-law, Colonel Samuel Bradley Sr. "This caused him so much joy that he had to kiss Your Honor's letter several times because of the good news; for this simpleton cares for the blowhard [i.e., Kidd]. He sends his very cordial greetings to Your Honor and also to that honest Cidt [Kidd] and his wife."

Robert Livingston, the arch manipulator, also received word in Albany. His most recent double-crossing of Kidd had occurred about a month earlier when Livingston had informed the lieutenant governor of New York that he had heard that Kidd was in the Caribbean carrying half a million pounds sterling, and that the lieutenant governor should alert the royal governors to capture him. Livingston, age forty-five, rode break-neck — greed over safety — through the woods to reach Boston as quickly as possible. (The more pleasant route would have taken more than a week, sailing down the North River, i.e., Hudson, to Throgs Neck and then east on the Sound and up around Cape Cod.)

Livingston had a secret ally in Boston,

fellow Scot Duncan Campbell. A receipt tucked among Livingston's voluminous business notes reveals that he had provided Campbell with more than £20 of milling equipment earlier that year. This would have put the down-at-heels Campbell in his debt, especially since Campbell owed more than £1,000 at the time from various failed business ventures.

The Sabbath finally over, Kidd spent the morning of Monday, July 3, briskly unloading. He ordered the delivery of Mrs. Kidd's bundle of clothes off Captain Way's sloop, but Kidd — still leery — opted to leave the money, firearms, balance scale, clock, and carpet on board.

Kidd, accompanied by his Malagasy slave, walked over to the *St. Antonio*. Apparently in an exuberant mood, he decided to distribute presents, giving one slave boy to Duncan Campbell and another to Robert Livingston. (Almost all wealthy families in Boston then owned at least one slave.) He also gave Campbell an exotic cane for his son, as well as several ten-pound wheels of cheese.

Governor Bellomont put out the word that his gout so indisposed him that the eighteen members of the Council would have to meet at his house, that is, at Peter Sergeant's manse. They arrived there Monday, July 3, and were informed that

Governor Bellomont had summoned Captain Kidd to appear before them at six o'clock that evening.

Sergeant's three-story glazed redbrick house was famous throughout the colony for its dome and its weather vane: a six-foot-tall copper Indian shooting an arrow.

These most powerful men in New England sat around the wood-paneled reception hall, amid the rich tapestries. Lord Bellomont was in an overstuffed armchair with his left foot propped up on a pillow on an ottoman. Kidd arrived promptly. This was his first face-to-face meeting with Lord Bellomont in more than three years, since he had seen him at Dover Street in London.

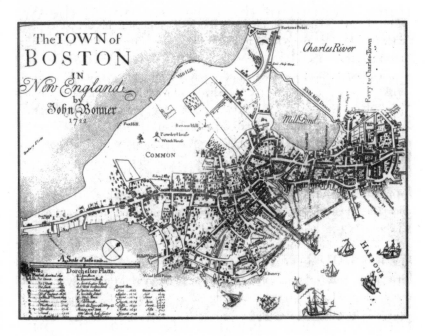

Bellomont — who generally preferred scarlet waistcoats with gold trim and a silver side sword — did not rise to greet Captain Kidd, but his tone toward Kidd was quite gracious and polite. The seaman, who had almost never been in the presence of lords, really didn't know what to expect. Bellomont asked Kidd to give an account of his voyage. Kidd replied that his journal had been destroyed and he "prayed his Lordship to allow him some time" to put his narrative into writing.

Bellomont clearly considered that Kidd's long voyage from the East Indies had already given the captain ample time for the task. The governor, with the Board echoing him, "directed" Kidd to present a summary account of the cargo on board the *St. Antonio* and on the prize ship left off Hispaniola. Kidd — always short-fused — through gritted teeth again requested time to put it in writing, but the governor insisted on a verbal account immediately.

Kidd was awaiting a sign from his backer on how to proceed in this delicate presentation involving large sums of money; instead, he was forced to barrel ahead.

Kidd rattled off statistics. He said he had come north with forty pounds of gold and eighty pounds of silver aboard the *St. Antonio*, forty bales of expensive cloth, five tons of sugar. Kidd added that he purchased all of the above at Madagascar by selling arms, gunpowder, and rigging from the *Adventure Galley*. (This was a significant fudge — perhaps lawyer Emott or shifty Livingston had helped dream it up — because if the profits came from selling a ship that the investors clearly owned, then that fact would wash away any taint of piracy.)

Kidd said the ship in Hispaniola had 150 bales, 70 tons of sugar, 10 tons of iron, 14 anchors, 40 tons of saltpeter, 20 guns in the hold, 30 guns mounted.

"Capt Kid says [he was] forced by his men who have deserted him to do some acts of Piracy but will give a good account to the king and his owners," wrote Council member Wait Winthrop.

The governor politely but firmly ordered Kidd to reappear before the Council at five o'clock the following afternoon to deliver a veritable sheaf of written documents: a narrative of his voyage and invoices of all cargo, signed by himself and principal officers, as well as a list of his 150-man crew and a list of the 100 mutineers. Lord Bellomont ordered that the deputy customs collector Hammond put some "waiters" aboard the *St. Antonio*. (Waiters were low-ranking custom officials, whose duty was to make sure no goods were off-loaded from a vessel.)

Kidd arrived promptly the next day bringing five of his crewmen with him: Abel Owen (cook), Samuel Arris (steward), English Smith and Humphrey Clay (NY sailors), and Hugh Parrott (gunner). The men, as a group, delivered a carefully worded written deposition of the voyage. (Since it bears similar phrases to the one Kidd would later submit, it appears that Kidd helped write it.) Of the captures of other ships, the men said simply: "We took Two vessels, which we carried into the Port of St. Maries."

The Council refused to let the men be so succinct, but questioned them further on the two captures. The sailors described them quite honestly as Moorish ships, one commanded by a Dutchman, the other by an Englishman. Secretary Isaac Addington wrote down their testimony and four of the sailors signed it, while Abel Owens made his mark of an O.

The governor then demanded from Captain Kidd his written account of the voyage, lading, crew lists. Kidd clearly did not appreciate the bevy of commands delivered to a man so recently arrived after hard years at sea. Against all odds, he had made money for this overstuffed gouty lord. Kidd showed his pique. "Kidd did strangely trifle with me and the council," Bellomont wrote much later.

With clipped annoyance, Captain Kidd replied that he had not had sufficient time to write the book requested of him. The governor — more expert at hiding his annoyance — granted an extension, but he attached something of a baffling new deadline. He told Kidd that if he and the countess chose to go for a carriage ride tomorrow, Kidd would have an extra day and should deliver it at 9 A.M. Thursday; otherwise, it would be due at 5 P.M. tomorrow.

Robert Livingston, who had raced there from Albany, called on the governor. Livingston was a wealthy *untitled* American merchant; Bellomont (birth name: Richard Coote) was a *titled* penniless governor. The men sat in complete privacy in Peter Sergeant's drawing room. Livingston began mildly enough but within minutes — greed and fear perhaps addling his brain — he began threatening the highest ranking English official in North America . . . and threatening him in Kidd's name.

The thin, peri-wigged, hook-nosed former accountant, his voice rising, demanded that Bellomont tear up *immediately* Livingston's £10,000 bond guaranteeing Kidd's performance and also tear up the rest of the contracts, or else — and Livingston swore "all the oaths in the world" to back up his threat — Kidd would never bring in the prize ship and would give Livingston his profits privately. "I thought this was such an Impertinence both in Kidd and Livingston," later groused Bellomont in a letter to a fellow lord.

Not a scrap of evidence has ever been found that Kidd wanted Livingston to threaten Governor Bellomont in his name.

Throughout this time, Kidd seemed to have retained the naive belief that if he doubled the investors' money, they would save him.

Governor Bellomont and his lady did in fact decide to take a brief journey on Wednesday, July 5, which gave Kidd an extra day to prepare his narrative.

The morning of Thursday, July 6, Captain Kidd readied another present for Lady Bellomont. Kidd might have blamed his less than warm reception by Bellomont on the fact that he hadn't "rewarded" the governor enough.

Kidd handed Duncan Campbell a green silk bag, containing five pounds of bar gold, worth £250, a sum that would buy a nice piece of Manhattan dock land. Not elegant but so handy in these cash-scarce colonies. Campbell walked to Peter Sergeant's and asked to see Lady Bellomont in private.

Over at the Council chambers, at nine o'clock that morning, Governor Bellomont and the Council waited for Captain Kidd. And waited, and waited. Captain Kidd was sent for at Duncan Campbell's: he came immediately. The governor demanded his paperwork. Kidd said he had been drawing it up before they interrupted him; he fully expected to meet his 5 P.M. deadline. The governor informed him his deadline was 9 A.M.; he dismissed him to complete his writing. As soon as Captain Kidd left the chamber, the governor and Council began to discuss Kidd's edgy behavior.

When Kidd reached Campbell's, he started once again with his influential lawyer, Thomas Newton to work on his narrative. (Kidd had first met Newton in New York during the Leisler treason trial in 1691.) At some point Duncan Campbell returned home and called Kidd aside into another room. Campbell quietly informed Kidd that Lady Bellomont had *refused* to accept Kidd's gift. Duncan Campbell handed the heavy green silk pouch back to Kidd.

The countess's refusal set off alarms in Kidd. He could still take his wife and child and slip onto a boat in the harbor and disappear. He could meet Thomas Way, get his pistols. Maybe the bar gold was too tacky a present, maybe that was all it was.

Almost ready for his appearance at Council, he worked a while longer on his narrative, then his agitation got the best of him. Up until that moment, after five days on shore, Kidd had not yet had a private meeting with Bellomont. This time, both foolhardy and foolish, he decided to go directly to the governor and confront the man. He cast off big and little Sarah at the door; his anger sped him along. Kidd headed along Cornhill Street to Peter Sergeant's house, knowing that was where the earl ate his midday meal. Most privateers caught in an impossible mission would have disappeared. *He came back; he came back. Didn't the lord understand that?*

Back at the council chamber, after Kidd had left in mid-morning, the discussion had moved briskly. Lord Bellomont had observed to several others that he thought Captain Kidd looked very agitated. "He looks as if he were upon the wing and resolved to run away," Bellomont told the others. Bellomont had suggested, and the Council concurred, that it was now time to issue a warrant for Captain Kidd's arrest.

The warrant was issued and Council adjourned. Bellomont was carried back to Sergeant's house and sat at the dining room table awaiting his meal. Baked mackerel was a popular choice for lunch, along with fresh berries.

Captain Kidd, barely controlling his rage, his sword bobbing at his right thigh, came rushing to the door of Sergeant's mansion; two men were following after him, but at that moment they lagged a block or so behind; Kidd flung open the door; he barged inside, stopped, heard Bellomont's voice in the next room, and moved quickly in that direction. The other two men entered the room seconds later, and one of them, the constable, shouted at Kidd to stop: "I have orders to seize you." Kidd put his hand on the hilt of his sword.

Kidd eyed Bellomont. The other man, Thomas Hutchinson, twenty-four-year-old scion of one of Boston's leading families, who had accompanied the constable, calmly walked over and took hold of Kidd's arm. Kidd — a lifelong brawler, a quarterdeck fighter — could have bashed the young man; he could have slashed his way out, or he could have fought his way in toward Bellomont. The gouty lord watched from his chair. The odds would have strongly favored Kidd. Hutchinson politely asked Kidd to submit to arrest "like a gentleman." *It was now the time to fight.* Kidd, for once, controlled his temper. He submitted; the image of the flummoxed scarlet-coated governor was etched in his brain.

The two men escorted Kidd to the dank Puritan jail, a rundown lockup always in disrepair. Other officers raced to the waterfront and out to the *St. Antonio* and found five of Kidd's crew there, arresting gunner Hugh Parrott, foretopman Gabriel Loffe, and three cabin boys: William Jenkins, Richard Barleycorn, and Robert Lamley. Tipped off or just plain lucky, the rest of the crew and passengers had scattered, several heading toward easygoing New York City.

The governor and council dispatched a blue-ribbon panel of Judge Sewall and Nathaniel Byfield of the Council and two rich merchants and the deputy customs collector over to Duncan Campbell's to search for any of Kidd's treasure. They pried open Captain Kidd's chest, and in it found two silver basins, two silver candlesticks, one silver porringer, and several other silver objects, weighing a total of five pounds. In another bag, they uncovered some pieces of eight, nine new English crowns, a couple small bits of silver, a small chain, a small bottle, a coral necklace, one piece of white and one piece of checkered silk — all of which were the life savings of Kidd's servant, Elizabeth.

They were then about to leave when they noticed a couple of sea-beds, basically, the rolled up bedding in which a sailor stored his kit. Tucked inside this pair of everyday sea-beds, they found hidden twenty-two pounds of gold in six bags, including a tied handkerchief containing the five-plus pounds the countess had returned. They also found a bag with twelve pounds of silver.

Captain William Kidd, on his sixth day ashore after a three-year odyssey, found himself in Boston city jail. Thomas Newton, his lawyer, visited him, and the pair finished up the 2,500-word account of his mission.

Hoping that his arrest had been merely for failing to deliver his report on time, Kidd had Newton deliver it to the Council that Thursday afternoon, where it was read aloud. (Hindsight shows that it was accurate . . . *as far as it went;* Kidd skipped the murky Red Sea incident and Portuguese ship *Mary.*) The Council spent the afternoon peppering the other crewmen with questions; at first none of them would go beyond their original statements. Then Hugh Parrott and William Jenkins, an eighteen-year-old apprentice from Bow near London whose master had died, decided they had nothing to hide. The pair described the privateering voyage (denying any piracy), and detailed the off-loading in the Caribbean and the Sound, but neither man revealed the exact whereabouts of the *Quedagh Merchant* or of Kidd's gold that was supposed to be on the *St. Antonio.* (So Kidd still had his ace in the hole on

Gardiners Island.) As the men spoke, Secretary Isaac Addington scratched his quill along page after page until the evening.

Bellomont ordered the Council to reconvene the following morning, Friday, at eight o'clock. Bellomont was racing a deadline of another sort: this Puritan town would shut down like a tomb at sundown Saturday.

Kidd spent Thursday afternoon and evening in jail. He kept demanding to know with what crime he was charged. No one could answer. How much was bail? No one could answer.

Cleanliness next to godliness was not yet a Christian homily so, as darkness fell, Kidd tried to get comfortable on foul straw. The jail was like a hardwood box, with small barred window. Kidd, who had luxuriated the night before next to Sarah, squirmed on the floor, in his clothes.

Bellomont was in no hurry to answer Kidd's questions about bail or charges. He intended to send a message by the next ship to his lordly backers in England, then wait months for orders on how to proceed. Maybe the lords — almost certainly powerful enough to manipulate the colonial legal system to their desires — would want Kidd freed on bail to let him disappear, taking the scandal with him. Or maybe they would want him tried in Boston where the smuggler-merchants on the Council had repeatedly refused to approve the death penalty for piracy. Most likely of all, they'd want Kidd tried in England, where the procession to Execution Dock provided a welcome day of "riot and idleness."

Treasure Hunting: Wife vs. Gouty Lord

Chapter Fifteen

Thursday night. With Kidd in jail, treasure fever now gripped the penniless lord governor. In Peter Sergeant's drawing room, Bellomont's servant stood before him, reporting about his day's activities at the Boston waterfront. Bellomont had sent the man along with a Boston merchant to the taverns to investigate the cost of sending a ship to the Caribbean to seize Kidd's prize vessel. Buying rums around, they discovered what vessels and captains could leave on a moment's notice.

But Bellomont couldn't send the ship until he learned where to send it. Kidd had placed the *Adventure Prize* "somewhere near Mona Island," but he hadn't been more specific. Bellomont needed a treasure map. Tantalizing details galled the lord and added to his confusion: that fifty pounds of gold was nowhere to be found on the *St. Antonio*.

Half listening to his servant drone on about this captain and that, Bellomont caught the man mentioning something about overhearing a conversation in which a rough-looking sailor had negotiated to rent a sloop for £30 to go immediately to Gardiners Island. Bellomont asked for more details, but the servant knew little else. Bellomont was panic-stricken: fifty pounds of gold, and apparently a sloop was headed there in a hurry to pick it up. As he sat there immobile in cushions, his gout suddenly roared up. (A gout attack was once likened to having tiny razor blades inserted *inside* the joints of hand and foot, making the slightest movement agonizing.) It was too late that night to do anything but fret.

Friday morning. The Council's first order of business at eight o'clock was to appoint the five men who had searched Duncan Campbell's to form a committee to oversee and safeguard any treasure. Kidd was brought in for further interrogation.

Bellomont, however much he seethed inwardly, could always appear gracious. Once, some callus-handed farmers were invited to dine with him; the countess was acting a bit haughty, Bellomont chided her: "Dame, we should treat these gentlemen well, they give us our bread." Typical phrase from a talented actor.

He treated Kidd *graciously*. With a smile, he suggested that if Kidd told the truth about the whereabouts of all the treasure, that "he himselfe should be sent for it." Bellomont asked, but Kidd didn't answer. Playing his hunch, the governor then told Kidd he knew that the gold was on Gardiners Island. Kidd hesitated, then replied. "I left [it] in Custody of Mr. Gardiner of Gardiners-Island, near the Eastern End of Long Island, fearing to bring it about by Sea. It is made in a bagg put into a little box, lockt and nailed, corded about, and sealed."

Where is the receipt?

"I took no receipt for it of Mr. Gardiner."

Bellomont asked him where the *Adventure Prize* lay, and Kidd, deciding to trust the lord that he would be allowed to go fetch it, answered: "The ship is left at St. Katharina on the Southeast part of Hispaniola, about 3 Leagues to Leward of the Westerly end of Savano."

After many more questions, Kidd was asked finally: "What about the gold in bedrolls at Duncan Campbell's?" Kidd stared at this nobleman lord who could have welcomed him, and perhaps could still welcome him. "I intended it for presents to some I expected to do me Kindness," said Kidd.

Whatever his faults, Kidd at this moment, was clearly trying to show that honor meant more to him than money. He had slipped into some kind of vision of himself as a gentleman talking to a fellow gentleman. In so doing, he had impetuously squandered his aces in the hole. His reward for his honesty, for revealing exact locations, was to be moved "by mittimus . . . of Justices of the peace" from the town jail over to His Majesty's prison.

Finally understanding how dire his situation was, Kidd requested that the notary public, a Mr. Valentine, file for him and his crew an "Official Protest" of their imprisonment, a detailed document blaming all acts of piracy on the mutineers. The protest was ignored.

Bellomont warned the Crown jailer, Caleb Ray, upon pain of *severe* punishment, not to give Kidd or his men the slightest chance to escape. The previous month, two accused pirates — one-eyed eighteen-year-old Tee Witherly and pock-fretten Joseph Bradish — had escaped with the help of a woman smuggling in a file, and fled into Indian territory. Caleb Ray would now have quite a horde of pirates to guard: more than a dozen of Witherly and Bradish's men were already in custody, and on the Kidd case, the officers had also arrested Edward Davies, the oversized buccaneer, and imprisoned Captain Samuel Wood and his first mate of the sloop *St. Antonio* as well as Thomas Way, who had smuggled a few items into Boston for Kidd.

Bellomont, the instant he could politely escape the council, hobbled into the adjoining room. He called his servant, and fighting the pain in his right hand, he scrawled out a note to Gardiner. (No first name; apparently Kidd had entrusted fifty pounds of gold to a man he knew only as Gardiner.) Bellomont did this all in complete secrecy. The note looks dashed off.

Mr. Gardiner
. . . I have secured Capt. Kid in the gaol of this towne and some of his men, he has been examined by myselfe and the Councill and has Confessed among other things that he left w.th you a prcell of gold made in a box and some other parcells besides all wch I require you in his Majesty's name Immediately to bring hither to me I may secure them for Maj.tys use and I shall recompense your pains in Comeing hither.

I am your friend & servant,
Bellomont

Bellomont signed the letter, folded it and

applied his wax seal, and immediately dispatched a messenger to ride breakneck south to Bristol, to catch a ferry to Rhode Island, to gallop south to Newport, to take a boat to Gardiners Island. Who would get there first, the mysterious stranger who rented the sloop sailing around the crook'd finger of Cape Cod, or Bellomont's man? Both were at the mercy of the winds, only Bellomont's man less so. Fifty pounds of gold awaited the winner.

Bellomont had sent the messenger *in secret*. He also continued to look *in secret* for a ship to send south to the Caribbean. He did not alert the Council to any of his *very first* efforts at treasure hunting.

Sarah Kidd might have sent the mysterious stranger who rented the sloop, or maybe it was Robert Livingston. The race was on.

Saturday, July 8. "I have the Misfortune to be ill of the Gout at a time when I have a great deal of business to exercise both my head and my hand." The Council meeting was canceled. Bellomont had forced a merchant ship heading to England to wait from Thursday (July 6) for a letter he would write, but the captain refused to stay longer than Saturday afternoon before Sabbath shutdown. Clutching the quill in his painful fingers (not daring to dictate to anyone), Bellomont scratched out an extremely long letter to the Board of Trade describing his capture of Kidd. His good breeding tempered his crowing — "it will not be unwelcome news to your Lordships . . ." He justified his various stratagems, such as having his wife accept the first jewels sent so as to lure Kidd into a false sense of trust. He sealed the note and applied the wax seal. Now all Bellomont could do was wait. And, likewise, all Captain Kidd could do, locked up in an overcrowded hot prison, was wait.

Sunday, July 9. The Sabbath. Bellomont was too ill to leave home but a good third of the citizens, the wealthy especially, attended meeting. A day of communing with God. Cotton Mather's diary on this weekend shows a certain preoccupation on the devotion front with new preachers on Brattle Street. "Now I cannot but observe a wonderful thing. Several wretches have arrived among us pretending to preach ye Gospel with a more than ordinary zeal, But ye Flaming Eyes of ye Lord Jesus Christ, who has been affronted by ye Hypocrites, have quickly demonstrated his Holy Preference in his Churches . . . by detecting scandalous plagiarism in their sermons."

Monday, July 10. Lord Bellomont was again too ill to attend Council. This waiting to hear about the gold was tormenting him. Tuesday, July 11. The Council —

eager to do business — came to meet with Lord Bellomont at Peter Sergeant's house. Bellomont was still on tenterhooks about Gardiners Island. Maybe ten chests of gold sat there. The official records of that Council meeting — the ones later sent to England — show that the only major item of business was the discussion of sending a ship to the Caribbean to bring back the booty aboard Kidd's *Adventure Prize.* However, that discussion actually never took place.

The rough minutes of the Council meeting, as preserved in Massachusetts Archives, make no mention of sending a treasure hunter. It appears that Bellomont — later fearing that his secret efforts to get the treasure would look uncouth — had the minutes tailored to paint him as working in public to bring back the goods for king and Admiralty.

What really took place at that meeting? Several taxes, such as one on retail sales of wine and liquor and another on polls and estates, were passed; also improvements to the common jail and to the court system were discussed, then "A bill for applying of one thousand pounds of the tax upon Polls and Estates by this Court to ye use of his Exc.y the Earle of Bellomont, was read a first and second time and passed to be engrossed."

The local merchants were toadying up to Bellomont so he would follow their agenda. (Queen Anne would later forbid these gifts to colonial governors.)

A bill for "Incorporating Harvard Colledge" was read for a first time, as was a bill "for the better keeping of Publick Records." (None of the estimable men discussing the records bill at the time knew that, *ironically*, this very Council entry would be later purged to suit the governor.)

Wait Winthrop, member of the Council, wrote a letter that night to his brother, John Winthrop, governor of Connecticut. After a roundup of family business, he added playfully: "Capt. Kid and his crew are kidnapt here."

To add to Bellomont's misery, his gout attack brought on a fever. His delirium made him fantasize Kidd's gold into a mountain of treasure. Bellomont was at varying times also convinced that Duncan Campbell (his messenger) and Robert Livingston (fellow backer) were trying to "juggle together and Imbezzle some of [Kidd's] cargo."

Wednesday, July 12, 1699. Robert Livingston was officially accused of embezzling and called in to testify to the Council. Livingston denied receiving any treasure but whispered confidentially that Kidd had informed him that he had hidden the gold *somewhere in Long Island Sound*. The Council and Bellomont grilled him until Livingston finally admitted that . . . *Duncan Campbell* had received 100 pieces of eight from Kidd. More pointed questions yielded more denials. The governor dropped his velvet tone. Then Robert Livingston miraculously remembered that Captain Kidd had yesterday told him that the gold was hid upon Gardiners Island. Livingston also suddenly remembered that Kidd had given to him and to Campbell a slave boy each. (Sometime after this interrogation, Robert Livingston fell "into a fit of melancholy" and moved "from Albany to a farm in between that & N. York, resolving to meddle no more with business." He later told Bellomont that he and his family were "frightened out of their wits" that he would have to pay the £10,000 performance bond and be ruined.)

Duncan Campbell, on the other hand, was minutely precise in identifying every item handed out to him, down to speckled handkerchiefs. (Duncan Campbell would keep petitioning the Council for his expenses to be reimbursed; his meager business as a Boston broker for New York City merchants was soon ruined because the New Yorkers were enraged that he had betrayed Kidd.)

Bellomont, in a foul mood over Kidd's disappearing treasure, took his annoyance out on a bill for incorporating Harvard College. The charter of Harvard, the first college in America, had expired. Boston was deeply proud of this highly religious academic institution where scriptures were routinely read aloud to students and preacher Increase Mather was a longtime president of Harvard.

This council of Bostonians, a city famed for haloing itself as the Chosen Place, had inserted a clause in the Harvard bill requiring the Harvard president and vice president and fellows to be either Congregationalist or Presbyterian, no other sects acceptable. Bellomont, an Anglican, demanded that the Council drop the insulting requirement. The Council would weigh his request for five days.

Closer to Bellomont's heart, he made final preparations to hire a ship of 300 tons and 22 guns, with a crew of 60, to sail along with the *St. Antonio* down to the Caribbean to fight Kidd's pirates and reclaim the cargo. The two-month voyage would cost the government £1,700, a huge expenditure that made Bellomont nervous.

That night, a letter reached Lord Bellomont from New York, stating that a sloop had just arrived there from the Caribbean. "They say . . . that the crew Capt.

Kid had left on board his vessel has taken . . . and sold at Curacao most or all of the goods yet on board . . . already three vessels are gone to Holland with those goods."

Was the report true? Bellomont decided to wait for more information before commissioning the big ship, and he was growing more anxious. And still he received no word from Gardiners Island about the chests of gold. Then another report came from New York. On July 10, Stephen van Cortlandt had interrogated four of the sailors on board the little Caribbean sloop, who said they had been drinking a month earlier in Curacao with Kidd's master, named Ware, and that William Whitley had sold ten bales for the bargain price of 1,000 pieces of eight. Bellomont forced himself to continue to wait on authorizing the big ship; meantime, he sent two Council members over to question Kidd in prison.

Bellomont's gout and fever were unrelenting over this week, exacerbated by waiting for Gardiner, and agonizing over sending the ship south. Bellomont knew that one misstep in this scandal and he could lose his governorship and, more importantly, lose his influential friends.

Captain Kidd, at that moment, very quietly, was readying to make an escape, cozying up to jailor Caleb Ray, and trying to round up a sufficient bribe to spring himself free.

And still there was no word from Gardiners Island. For Sarah or for Lord Bellomont.

Monday, July 17, another letter from New York reached Bellomont, this one containing a sworn statement from a Dutch captain, Nicholas Evertse, who had just returned from Curacao. He said he'd seen Kidd's ship burning in a lagoon off St. Helena near Hispaniola, "which was on the 29th of June last, when I saw it on fire."

Bellomont, who was about to seal the contract for hiring the big vessel to go south, instantly changed his mind. " 'Tis said they have burnt that noble ship," wrote Bellomont, "and without doubt it was by Kidd's order that the Ship might not be evidence against him, for he would not own to us that her name was Quidah-Marchand, though his men did."

Captain Kidd, meanwhile, was rotting in His Majesty's prison along with the other accused pirates. No one had been charged with anything, which made some of the judges — several council members were also judges — uncomfortable. Captain Sam Wood and mate Moses Butterworth, hired hands who had piloted the *St. Antonio*, filed a petition that same Monday complaining they had been held for two weeks without being charged or interrogated. They were literally wasting away on the six-pennies-a-day food provided by Massachusetts Bay colony. "I am a stranger and have nothing to relieve myself, [all] being totally taken from me since my arrival in this harbor." These were the days when the prison provided bread and water; the edible entrée selections were strictly à la carte. His petition was shunted aside when a breathless messenger interrupted the Council meeting to bring some very good news to Bellomont.

Sailing in a ridiculously small boat, John Gardiner had just arrived in Boston harbor to deliver Kidd's gold from Gardiners Island. Bellomont later told the story: "My Messenger [had] made great haste, and was with Gardiner before anybody, and Gardiner, who is a very substantial man, brought away the treasure without delay, and by my direction delivered it into the Hands of the Committee. If the Jewels be right, as it is supposed they are, but I never saw them, nor the gold and silver brought by Gardiner, then we guesse that the parcel brought by him (Gold, Silver and Jewels) £4,500. And besides Kidd had left Six bales of Goods with him, one of which was twice as big as any of the rest; and Kidd gave him a particular charge of that bale, and told him it was worth £2,000."

Bellomont ordered a sloop to pick up the rest, and the committee hoped the whole treasure might tally £14,000. Bellomont had won the race to Gardiners Island.

The treasure hunter lord, fresh from this victory, now started a feverish grasping at murky clues. He got wind of Kidd's New York off-loading. "I believe I have directed [my lieutenant governor] where to find a Purchase in a house in New York, which by a hint I have had. . . . I have sent to search elsewhere a certain place, strongly suspected to have received another depositum of gold from Kidd. I am also upon the hunt after Two or Three Arch Pyrates, which I hope to give your Lordships a good Account by next conveyance." One of the pirates in question was: James Gilliam, circumcised captain killer. "If I could have but a good able Judge and Attorney General at York, a man of war there and another here, and the Companies recruited and well paid, I will rout Pirates and Piracy entirely out of all this north part of America, but as I have but too often told your Lordships, it is impossible for me to do all this alone in my single person."

Bellomont was slowly accumulating much of Kidd's booty, but the horrible irony for the penniless lord was that — to avoid scandal and ingratiate himself with his wealthy friends — he must ship every last piece of eight, every speck of gold dust to London. Governor Tantalus.

Captain Kidd lay in the overcrowded prison. He made his first foray toward planning an escape by talking the jailor, Caleb Ray, into letting him out of his cell for a brief bit of leg-stretching and a fine meal. Maybe Kidd planned to overpower the man on this walk or the next, or maybe the captain was angling toward negotiating the proper bribe with Ray.

A messenger burst into the Council chamber late in the day on Tuesday: someone had spotted Captain Kidd in the jailor's house next to the prison. Bellomont — already suspicious of Caleb Ray — had assigned extra guards to stand guard at night but this was mid-afternoon. Bellomont was furious.

The governor, without waiting for advice of Council, scribbled out an order decreeing that Kidd be transferred immediately to Stone Prison, be denied any visitors and be put in irons. "He has without doubt a great deal of gold," explained Bellomont, "which is apt to tempt men that have not principles of honour; I have therefore, to try the power of dull Iron against gold, put him into Irons that weigh 16 Pound. . . . There never was a greater Lyar or Thief in the World than this Kidd."

★ ★ ★

Captain Kidd now lay shackled in solitary in Stone Prison, wearing the same clothes he was arrested in, the humiliating cold iron chafing raw his wrists and ankles. If he had only acted like a pirate and run off with the gold, he would have been fine and free. His confused tiptoeing between legitimate privateering and outright piracy had tripped him up.

Until this point, with access to her spouse, Sarah had followed her husband's lead, assuming as he did that this brief nightmare would end when the governor fulfilled his promise of protection. Now that the governor had personally ordered Kidd shackled and had taken custody of the gold, she knew the score, and she decided it was time for her to try to take charge. Her efforts were made much tougher by the fact that Bellomont was dead wrong about one thing: she and Kidd had almost no ready money whatsoever. The treasure committee on the day of the arrest had snagged the bedrolls of gold and silver at Duncan Campbell's, and had even taken Sarah's own coins and her maid's, and confiscated the family's silverware.

She had a lawyer draw up a petition, which she submitted to Bellomont and the Council the following day, requesting the return of her silver porringer, mug, tankard, forks and other silver items, and her 260 pieces of eight. She said she "had brought [them] with her from New York, whereof she has had the possession for several years . . . , as she can truly make oath; out of which sd Trunck was also took Twenty five English Crowns which belonged to your Pet'rs Maid.

"The . . . most deplorable Condition of your Pet'r [petitioner] considered, she humbly intreats your hon'rs Justice That Returne be made of the said Plate and mony."

On this document, Mrs. Kidd blockprinted an awkward SK, between the words Sarah and Kidd. Twenty-nine-year-old Sarah Bradley Cox Oort Kidd was still unable to write her name.

Relations between the Council and Bellomont had by this time grown strained. The Council had turned down two of Bellomont's candidates for judges and, most recently, had refused to accept Bellomont's proposal on Harvard that a Protestant minister of *any* sect be eligible for the top posts. The Council preferred to continue without a Charter rather than allow such a *godless* person to hold sway at Harvard. Bellomont was not pleased.

It was into this suddenly contentious climate at Council that Mrs. Kidd submitted her petition. The Council "Advised that

Sarah Kidd's July 18, 1699 plea to Gov. Bellomont, asking that he return her money to her. She signed it as best she could, by block-printing her initials.

Mrs. Kidd makeing oath that she brought the Plate and money above mentioned from New York with her, It be restored unto her. As also that Capn. Kidd and Companys wearing Apparel under Seizure be returned to them." (The prisoners in the July heat had been sweating in the same clothes for two weeks.)

While almost all petitions mentioned in Council notes around this time show "Advised and Ordered," this item of restoring Sarah's belongings never received an "Ordered" from Governor Bellomont. He ignored their advice, preferring to hold on to Sarah's money and plate rather than risk letting any potential bribe money near Captain Kidd.

As for the maid, for her to lose 25 English Crowns (£6, 5 shillings) was an incalculable loss. Elizabeth Morris would receive two sets of clothes at the upcoming end of her four-year indenture, but her hard-earned savings would have certainly helped start a new life.

Sarah, since she was rebuffed trying to raise money in legitimate circles, turned to a shadier alternative. She contacted a veteran sea dog by the name of Andrew Knott, the same captain who had sold a 2-gun brigantine to Adam Baldridge off Madagascar. Knott had had a checkered career, first serving king and country by fighting against Canada in 1690, but then sailing as a gunner with pirate Gilliam in the South Seas (i.e., the Pacific Ocean), capturing more than twenty-five Spanish prizes.

Sarah Kidd didn't know how to write so she, with William apparently yelling suggestions through the grate, dictated the letter to Knott who wrote it down.

From Boston Prison,
July the 18 day, 1699

Captain Payen:
  After my humble service to your selfe and all our Good Friends this cometh by a trusty Friend of mine how [who] can declare to you of my great griefe and misery here in prison by how I would desire you to send me Twenty four ounces of Gold, and as for all the rest you have in your custody shall desire you for to keep in your custody for it is all we have to support us in time of want; but I pray you to deliver to the bearer hereof the above mentioned sum, hows name is Andrew Knott. And in so doing you will oblige him how is your . . .
    SARAH SK KEEDE
      ye bare hereof can informe you
      more at large

Once again, Sarah etched her initials, only

522

this time next to a severely misspelled version of her own last name.

Andrew Knott immediately mounted up and took the well-traveled route south sixty miles toward Bristol. He spent the night halfway at a farm. The old sailor saw no point in killing himself to reach Bristol in the dark, when no boats would be leaving. Captain Knott reached Captain Paine on Connonicut Island the next day, delivering the note from the Kidds.

Captain Paine read it, then disappeared into an inner room, his bedroom; he returned carrying seven bars of gold. He weighed them on a "steelyards" (balance scale) and said they came in at exactly 1¾ pounds. Paine, the meticulous pirate banker, wrote the amount on the back of the letter; Knott gave him a receipt.

Captain Knott left soon after. "And upon the Road on my way homeward," Knott lamented later, "the Gold by its weight broke my pocket and I lost one of the bars." Having completed the round trip in five days, he returned on July 23, but waited till after Sunday sunset to enter the town. He didn't want to attract attention to himself on the deserted streets. "The other six [bars] I brought to Boston and Capt Kidd's servant maid . . . came to my house in her master's or mistress's name to aske for the said Gold saying he was in great want of it and I delivered it unto her and Captain Kidd afterward paid me twenty pieces of eight for my journey and pains."

Mrs. Kidd, for her part, weighed the six gold bars and discovered that though the receipt forecast a weight of 1¾ pounds (28 ounces), the gold in fact weighed only 22 ounces. A nice heavy bar had fallen out of Knott's pocket (and no doubt into his other pocket).

Sarah now had some bribe and food money for her husband. Since an ounce of gold sold for more than £3, she had about £66, more than half a year's salary for a merchant captain.

So, on Tuesday, July 25, Sarah Kidd, with money again for lawyers, bribes, and meals, tried to gain permission to see her husband, who remained chained and rotting in solitary.

She (and her lawyer) couched the petition to appeal to a Bible-savvy audience, who knew well the Bible's matrimonial command to "Be fruitful and multiply." Sarah pointed out that her husband — besides being "in want of necessary assistance" — was in need of her "affection." The Council repeated its earlier advice to the governor to restore the woman's silver, and, before it could address the issue of Sarah meeting William in the flesh,

Bellomont announced he was disbanding the Council. Clearly worried that Kidd would escape, Bellomont also ordered keeper Caleb Ray and family banished from the prison, and new guards installed. (Ironically, Ray would later become a trusted supplier of weights and measures throughout the colonies.)

This final Council session on July 25 was long and contentious. Over the past weeks, Bellomont had lobbied hard that the province of Massachussetts adopt the same harsh anti-piracy laws as England. Under current Massachussetts law, pirates were not punished by death, but instead by paying out triple damages for stolen property. Pointing to overcrowded jails, to pirates dining at the Puritans' expense, Bellomont pressed hard for the death penalty. He added pointedly: Massachusetts laws should *conform* to England's. "Three or four councillors stood up at once," Bellomont later recalled, "and one or two asked me with some warmth what the Laws of England had to do with them, and one of 'em said they were too much cramped in their liberties already."

Finally, the frustrated lord, whose gout attack had subsided somewhat, announced that he would be leaving Boston within a day or so to go to his other government in the province of New Hampshire.

That evening between six and seven o'clock, Judge Sewall — skullcapped, fair-minded, and dour — took Lady Bellomont up Cotton Hill to give her a panoramic view of Boston, bringing along several other society ladies, such as lawyer Thomas Newton's wife. Sewall was as giddy as the rest of these affluent Bostonians in the presence of aristocracy. "Mrs. Tuthill's daughters invited my Lady . . . and gave a Glass of good wine. As [we] came down through the Gate, I ask'd my Lady's Leave that I might call it: Bellomont Gate. My Lady laugh'd, and said, 'What a Complement he puts on me! With pleasancy.' "

Lord Bellomont sat late into the night painfully scratching out a long letter to the Lords of Trade, explaining and justifying his actions. "I desire I may have orders what to do with Kidd and all his and Bradish's Crew," he wrote, "for as the law stands in Country, if a pyrate were convict, yet he cannot suffer Death." The implications of his request were clear.

At this time, Lord Bellomont sent to England an enormous packet of more than twenty-five documents pertaining to the Kidd case: Kidd's own narrative, depositions of crew members, of Duncan Campbell, of John Gardiner, Kidd's letter to Bellomont and a "Copy of a French pass

526

taken by Kidd on board the Moorish ship the *Rouparelle*" and a "Copy of a French pass . . . taken by Kidd on board the Moorish ship the Cara Merchant."

Over at Stone Prison, the new guards, thrilled to have the lucrative job, checked Captain Kidd's chains every few hours. Sarah took lodging at an inn, never uttering another word to Duncan Campbell or his wife. Little Sarah must have asked why she couldn't see her father.

The hot summer sun baked the New England town. The new jailor had put her husband where she couldn't even yell in to him. It was as though he was sealed in a trunk, corded about, and chained. Neither Newton nor any other lawyer ever filed a habeas corpus or bail request for Captain Kidd.

The earl pursued his treasure hunting. As his cavalcade was leaving for New Hampshire, after much hesitation, Bellomont gave final approval to Captain Nathaniel Cary to take Kidd's *St. Antonio* down to the Caribbean.

(The choice of Captain Cary was an interesting one: his wife had been accused in 1692 of being a witch at Salem. To that point in his life, Captain Cary had been a prominent law-abiding citizen, but fearing his wife would be hanged if brought to trial, he had helped her escape, first to

Rhode Island, then on to New York and the safety of Governor Fletcher.)

Bellomont, by sending Cary, now hoped to recover booty from merchants Burke or Bolton and from the governors of St. Thomas or Curacao. He also wanted to confirm that the *Quedagh Merchant* was actually burned off Hispaniola.

So, on August 3, 1699, Captain Cary (thanks to a long-ago prison break) was able to hug his wife and children, before setting sail south in search of Kidd's treasure.

Treasure-mad Bellomont continued to send urgent messages to New York, to his lieutenant governor, his cousin, John Nanfan, to be on the lookout for Kidd's pirates and loot. But the good citizens of New York City — with seventy ships idle in the harbor — generally sided with pirates and smugglers over English aristocrats. At least three of the men who sailed with Kidd (Martin Skank, Humphrey Clay, and John Harrison), walked the streets of Manhattan with impunity. Old widow Dorothy Lee, caretaker at Kidd's house, was hauled in for questioning but swore that she knew nothing.

Bellomont blamed the city's pro-outlaw stand on simple economics. The fifty pirates who had come home in June were filling New York taverns, whore houses, and back-alley markets. Bellomont had sent an order to his lieutenant governor to hold one accused pirate *without bail,* but the lieutenant governor took the matter to the Council, which refused. Attorney-General James Graham (the Scot who had written Kidd's letter of recommendation) argued against allowing bail in the morning and in favor of it in the afternoon. (He clearly had lunch with an appreciative pirate.)

Bellomont was convinced that Thomas Clark, Kidd's New York friend, had received the bulk of Kidd's treasure, as much as £10,000. Lieutenant Governor Nanfan sent a letter in August to Governor Winthrop of Connecticut to seize Clark, who had fled there; the request went ignored.

About the only citizen cooperating fully with the government to secure the loot from the pirates was John Gardiner of Gardiners Island. And he was terrified for his life: not afraid of Captain Kidd — who had always been a gentleman in their dealings — but of that circumcised throat-slitting rogue.

Gardiner wrote on August 19: "I now live in [fear] for the man that owned the precious stones, his name is James Gilliam. While I was at Boston he came to my Island and asked my Wife for his precious stones and two pounds of Gold but my Wife told him that she did not care to meddle with anything untill I came home. But the reason she told him so was that she was afeard to tell him that I carried them away."

Gilliam soon found out the truth from one of Gardiner's hired men that Gardiner had delivered Gilliam's booty to Boston. At that moment, Gilliam cursed and muttered that he was only a passenger on Kidd's ship, according to boatman Edward Sands, who was ferrying Gilliam around the Sound. Sands then heard Gilliam vow: "I will be the downfall of Gardiner and his family if it takes twenty years: I will not spare man, woman or child, I will fire all his houses and barns and kill all his cattle and sheep."

Gardiner lived with his wife on that isolated island, alone in that house on the hill but for a handful of farmhands and a few Indians. Every time the wind rustled the trees or the floorboards creaked at night, he imagined Gilliam creeping in, dagger in mouth. Every breeze could bring visitors.

"We shall always live in fear except [Gilliam] should be taken and executed," he complained.

Once again fulfilling his promise to Bellomont, Gardiner in late August returned to Boston to deliver every single remaining item that Kidd or Gilliam or any of the others had stored with him. Gardiner set sail around Cape Cod, carrying the rest of the goods. He arrived in Boston September 1, pulling to a favored position along the town dock.

Bellomont expected great things; he had daydreamed that Kidd's bales and chest were worth thousands of pounds. The treasure committee and Lord Bellomont and the others watched as the locks were broken open. Inside, they found mostly spices and cloth. Bellomont was furious. He had two committee men go to the shackled Captain Kidd in prison on September 4 and find out what was supposed in that o so valuable chest.

Kidd calmly listed "three bags of . . . stone of Goa [fever medicine], several pieces of Silk, stript with silver and gold, cloth of Silver, about a bushel of Cloves and Nutmegs mixed together and strawed up and down, severall books of fine white callicoes, several pieces of fine Muzlins, several pieces more of flowerd silk." He was further questioned about the value of the goods. "Greater value than all else that he left at Gardiners Island except the Gold and Silver." Was there any gold and silver in the chest? "No."

Bellomont seemed awfully annoyed at Kidd — for not having stolen more.

Taking fever medicine? Goa Stone might sell for £10 a ball, but still. . . . Bellomont kept thinking some secret compartment might be found; he peevishly demanded that his five committee men inventory the chest right down to counting out "74 Nutmeggs" and 18 pairs of uppers for slippers, embroidered in silver and gold.

Bellomont now had very little use for Kidd other than keeping him in custody before sending him to England, *if those orders ever arrived.* But what if some smart local lawyer starting pressing for Kidd's rights? Somebody fair-minded like Judge Sewall might actually grant bail.

Bellomont decided to take no chances. On September 7, the lord appointed Kidd's lawyer, Thomas Newton, to the plum job of king's counsel for the Admiralty courts of Massachusetts Bay, Rhode Island, and New Hampshire. After noting that the man was "reputed to be the best [lawyer] in the country," he added that he was also quite pleased that Newton — although it clearly didn't suit his client Captain Kidd — endorsed Bellomont's interpretation that Statute 28 Henry VIII (First Piracy Act) entitled the courts to hold pirates without bail.

Bellomont made another key appointment: notary public John Valentine, who had filed Kidd's "Protest" back in July, became the new register for the Admiralty court for Massachussetts Bay and New Hampshire. Kidd was shorn of counsel.

The leaves in September were lingering green, with autumn hinted in the breeze; mason John Marshall noted in his diary that a "pretty good" Indian harvest was gathered in mid-September. Kidd lay shackled in isolation; Sarah waited. Little Sarah played with dolls.

(Unbeknownst to anyone in North America, in those days of slow communication, the Admiralty on September 12 ordered HMS *Rochester* to sail from London to pick up Kidd.)

The sundial-slow waiting for royal orders to come concerning Kidd so jangled the earl's nerves that he decided to personally join the treasure hunt. Bellomont went to Rhode Island, that hotbed of nonconformists, because he had heard that one of Kidd's pirates was living openly there, one Joseph Palmer. "They cannot be persuaded to keep a pirate there in gaol," he complained of Rhode Islanders. "They love 'em too well."

(To make sure Kidd filed no motions, Bellomont took along Councilor Newton and Register Valentine as paid advisors.)

Although Governor Cranston of Rhode Island failed to deliver Palmer, he did have a present for Bellomont: an unsigned earlier deposition from the pirate. As Bellomont quickly scanned it, he noticed a surprising charge. Palmer "accuses Kidd of *murdering* his gunner which I never heard before."

Palmer in his deposition stated: "Capt. Kid in a passion struck his Gunner, as it was said, with an Iron bound Bucket, w.ch blow he lived not above twenty-four hours after, *but I was not upon ye deck when ye blow was struck.*"

Bellomont was excited at this bit of news — if the French passes somehow saved Kidd, the murder charge might hang him. (Why had Bellomont turned so against Kidd? Bellomont, to clear himself, could either try to exonerate Kidd, a near impossible task that would appear whitewashing, or he could act as an avenging angel crushing Kidd for the good of England. He chose the latter.)

Bellomont needed to find Palmer. Governor Cranston repeatedly refused Bellomont's request to revoke bail for Palmer, making it impossible — even if they found him — to ship the man *as a prisoner* to Boston. Cranston, a salty colonial, finally agreed that if they found Palmer, he would ask the young man to go *voluntarily* to Boston to surrender.

Frustrated in his pirate hunt, Lord Bellomont turned to examining the disorders of Rhode Island, that safe harbor of free-thinkers and religious misfits. With lawyer Thomas Newton at his side, Bellomont documented twenty-five charges against the colony; he was especially outraged that a "brutish, corrupt" man, John Green, served as lieutenant governor. Bellomont's spies discovered that twenty years earlier Green had remarked "that it was no more Sin in the sight of God for one man to lye with another man's wife than for a Bull to leap a Cow upon the Common." (Green was forced to sail to England to defend himself.)

Bellomont concluded his visit, and returned by calash to Boston. When he arrived, he discovered that there were *still* no orders to ship out Kidd, *still* no man-of-war.

Indian summer had rolled into fall and Captain Kidd was still "kidnapt" in Boston. Not a peep emerged from the living grave in which Bellomont had buried the man three months earlier.

The weather in Boston — after a surprising hot spell — turned abruptly cold. "A sore wett stormy daye," wrote mason John Marshall of Monday, October 6. The Council resumed the normal business of governing: repairs to Castle Island, payments to the printer, the granting of "unmarried status" to Abigail Williams, the wife of a sailor, six years absent at sea.

Sarah Kidd, who for at least a decade had been one of the leading wives of New York City, was deeply frustrated up here in frigid Boston. Cold winds were swaying the leaves off the trees, leaving skeletal branches looming against the night sky. On October 12, she put a simple petition before the Council asking it to supply warm clothes to Kidd and his crew in the dank Stone Prison. The Council advised the treasure committee to "provide . . . suitable clothing . . . to prevent there being exposed to suffering or perishing by the cold." The Council advised it but there's no record that Governor Bellomont ordered it. Let the prisoners shiver, especially that "lyar and thief" in the iron chains.

The very next item of Council business, however, was duly "Advised and Consented": "that the treasurer pay unto Thomas Powell, Inn Keeper, the sum of forty pounds eight shillings . . . for the standing and keeping of his Lordship's Coach, calash and horses from May 26 to July 26."

In mid-October, Bellomont received the most *exquisite* good news since the Kidd affair had turned fiasco. Bellomont opened a letter from England and finally learned that Parliament had given orders to the Admiralty to send a ship to bring Kidd and the accused pirates home to London to stand trial. The letter-writer informed him that by the time the governor received the letter, the HMS *Rochester* man-of-war should be well on its way in route to Boston. This welcomed update was accompanied by high praise for Bellomont's capture of Kidd. The lord could exhale: it appeared his reputation would survive Kidd. Maybe he might even profit.

On October 23 Lord Bellomont proposed to Council that a day of public Thanksgiving be declared, to be celebrated a month later on Thursday, November 23, 1699, throughout Massachusetts Bay Colony. Since the 1660s, ministers and governors had been singling out a fall day, sometimes in October, for Thanksgiving, but Bellomont, when he helped seal the choice of a late Thursday in November, wasn't thinking about the first Pilgrims or a good harvest. He was giving thanks that a certain New York pirate would soon be heading to London.

Bellomont's mild euphoria didn't last. The very next day, Captain Cary aboard the *St. Antonio* sailed into Boston harbor, back from his treasure-hunting mission in the Caribbean. "He is newly returned without the least success," complained Bellomont, who was presented with exactly one recovered item: a burnt piece of rope.

The mission went badly from the start. In Antigua, two merchants had shown Cary paperwork proving that they owned the *St. Antonio* (not Bolton, a hired hand). They told Cary that they were outraged that a colonial governor would hijack their ship and they demanded its immediate return. Captain Cary slipped out of Antigua in a hurry, telling the merchants to take their complaints to the courts.

Fighting contrary winds, he then reached Kidd's secret lagoon in Santa Catalina and found tied to a tree . . . a long rope with one end of it burnt and dragging in the water. Cary retrieved this burnt rope, "a bass cable," and carried it back as proof, a cruel keepsake for the lord.

The governor of St. Thomas swore to Cary that no citizen of Denmark had ever traded with Kidd (he conveniently omitted the involvement of the Brandenburg *Germans* who had bought 158 bales from Irish merchant Burke). The governor of Curacao denied any crew members or cargo of Captain Kidd's had ever touched Curacao.

To cap off Cary's failure, when he anchored in Jamaica, the captain of HMS *Falmouth* ordered Cary to strike his King's Colours in the harbor. Cary showed his commission from Governor Bellomont, but the Royal Navy's Captain Mitchell wasn't impressed, and sent over an armed squad to board and haul down the flag.

Bellomont, when he learned of this final slight, was apoplectic with rage, rushing a letter to London demanding that Captain Mitchell be "made an example of for his ignorance and impertinance." Bellomont added: "I am declared Vice-Admiral of these Seas, and if I cannot be allowed to protect a ship I send to sea on HM service in so small a point of honour, 'tis hard." Hard it was for the gouty lord as he sat in his armchair, fingering his burnt rope end.

In Boston, traditionally, late October, early November was especially festive in this Protestant community that refused to celebrate Christmas. Boston, while straitlaced on Sabbath, did have its occasional French dancing master (who would survive a year or two before the Mathers booted him). On October 27, the lieutenant governor hosted an elegant dinner party for the governor and his lady and assorted worthies such as Judge Sewall. Bellomont could enjoy himself somewhat, now that he knew a warship should arrive soon to pick up Kidd and the pirates.

A week later, to celebrate the king's birthday on November 5, Sewall recorded: "The Gov.r treats the Council and sundry other Gentlemen in Mr. Sergeant's best chamber. Guns fired upon account of the

King's Birth-day. At night Governour and Mr. Newton made an illumination." That is to say, the governor and Kidd's former lawyer, Thomas Newton, together commissioned a fireworks display. These Puritan merchants, emboldened by liquor, rushed into the best streets of Boston, and fired salvos into the night sky.

Also enjoying the display, unbeknownst to Bellomont, was the circumcised pirate Gilliam, who had still not been caught, and was rumored to have lots of treasure.

A messenger days later delivered an urgent message to Bellomont from Judge Peleg Sanford down in Newport. The judge had just learned that Gilliam had left Rhode Island to come to Boston, seeking a ship to the Caribbean. Sanford apologized that his information was *two weeks* old but added that the man who carried the message could recognize the mare that Gilliam rode from Rhode Island. "I was in despair of finding the man," wrote Bellomont, who immediately sent for the constable who had captured Captain Kidd. He ordered him to go with the messenger that night to all the inns and taverns in Boston to look for that mare. The men walked quickly down the dark, unpaved streets toward the waterfront, bobbing in the cocoon of light shed by their lanterns. At the very first inn, they found the horse, but the innkeeper said the owner had gone off about a quarter hour earlier without saying anything to anyone.

Bellomont decided pirate hunting prevailed over the Sabbath, even in Boston. The next morning, Sunday, he called an emergency Council session and told them that a "notorious pirate and murderer" was in their town. The Council placed severe penalties for aiding the fugitive, put an embargo on the harbor, and declared an enormous £50 reward for Gilliam. "Whereupon there was the strictest search [that] day and the next, that ever was made in this part of the world," later exulted the earl. Massive Sabbath-breaking was tolerated as hundreds of men fanned out all over the city, ransacking homes, poking swords under beds, stomping on straw in barns, separating the clustered pigs; that night, after Sabbath, the search continued by lantern light. But the men failed to find Gilliam.

During the manhunt, someone tipped Bellomont to go ask Captain Knott if he knew where the pirate might be found. Knott, a shady privateer, denied knowing anything. Bellomont then called for Knott's wife, and walked her past her husband and into another room. Under threat of imprisonment, she admitted that a James Kelley had stayed with them for a few days and might now be somewhere in Charlestown across the River.

Bellomont then called back in "old Pyrate" Knott — and told him his wife had revealed everything. Knott conceded that Gilliam could probably be in Charlestown, and added a detail: "at Francis Dole's house."

Bellomont immediately rushed half a dozen men to row at breakneck speed across the river (no bridge back then); they descended on Dole's house and searched the rundown place, but didn't find Gilliam. Dole, old and ill and poor, said he never heard of the name of Gilliam or Kelley.

The government men fanned out in the dark, carrying lanterns. "Two of the men went through a field behind Dole's house, and passing through a second field they met a man in the dark (for it was ten a clock at night) whom they seized at all adventures, and it happened as oddly as luckily to be Gilliam." Where had the pirate been? "He had been treating young women some few miles off in the Country, and was returning at night to his Landlord Dole's house."

Gilliam was hauled back to Boston and brought to Lord Bellomont. "He is the most impudent hardened villain I ever saw in my whole life," said the earl. That Thursday, November 16, the Jew and the surgeon (as mentioned earlier) scrutinized the prisoner's penis and doomed him.

Gilliam was delivered to Stone Prison, which was overflowing with pirates. A local Indian chief, Essacambuit, had captured and delivered the two escaped pirates, Joseph Bradish ("ordinary stature, well sett, round visage, fresh complexion, darkish, pock-fretten and aged about 25") and Tee Witherly ("short, very small, black, blind of one eye, age 18"). Both these men were chained just like Kidd and Gilliam. To stay warm, they had to move about, rub their hands, stomp their feet, which rattled their chains. Crammed together in another foul stone cell were three of Kidd's cabin boys, three crew men and big Edward Davies. Packed nearby as well were twenty of Bradish's (not yet accused) pirates, ranging in age from eighteen to thirty-five, with the bulk in their twenties, including four Scots and a Dane.

Captain Kidd spent twenty-three and a half hours a day in solitary confinement in a small unheated cell, alone with his thoughts. He firmly believed that he had committed no crime, and clung to the hope that an English jury would acquit him once it saw his French passes, confirming that the two ships he had captured were traveling under French protection and therefore fair game in time of war. His unshakable self-confidence and his anger sustained him, despite the brutal cold descending on Boston.

A huge ice storm suddenly hit town. "The Rain freezes upon the branches of the Trees to that thickness and weight that great havock is . . . made of the Wood and timber," wrote Judge Sewall in his diary. "Many young and strong Trees are broken off in the midst, and multitudes of Boughs rent off."

Bellomont paid out of his own meager pocket for extra armed guards to ensure that no bureaucratic slip-up or Puritan stinginess might give the prisoners any chance to escape.

The prison was so overcrowded that the keeper was allowed — by the tight-fisted Council — to hire someone "to empty ye necessary houses." It's extremely unlikely that the prisoners would be let out of their cells, so the "necessary houses" were probably no more than shit buckets, over which they squatted. The food allowance was an unwholesome sixpence a day per prisoner.

Lord Bellomont waited daily for word of the arrival of the *Rochester* man-of-war, which was battling the wintry Atlantic to make the crossing. Every day's delay increased his anxiety over the prisoners.

Pirate Gilliam, who — unlike Kidd — was not being held in isolation, was able to receive visitors, and one of them smuggled in to him, a two-and-a-half-foot-long crow bar and two files. On the cold night of December 12, Gilliam filed the irons off his legs. He took the crow bar and pried loose one bar from the window, then a second, and was struggling with the third when the jailor, sleeping in the house attached to the prison, heard the clatter of the bars and awoke. He and his assistant wrestled Gilliam into fresh chains. Bellomont the next day ordered Gilliam attached to the wall and to another prisoner.

Kidd yearned for his wife. Little Sarah yearned for her father. The governor yearned for that man-of-war. "Everybody here believes the *Rochester* is blown off the coast and forced to bear away for some of the islands," wrote Bellomont. "The winter storms on this coast are more violent than in any part of the world."

Captain Kidd, still in isolation, his cotton clothes no defense against the chill, decided to try to tempt Bellomont. He sent word through the jailor that he would go to the place where the *Quedagh Merchant* was, and to St. Thomas and Curacao and could bring back £50,000 or £60,000 of treasure. Kidd offered to travel as a prisoner, in irons, to allow Bellomont to rest easy that he did not plan to escape.

Bellomont responded with typical finesse. He replied that Kidd was the king's prisoner and, as a governor, he did not have the authority to accept such an offer. Nonetheless, Bellomont encouraged the jailor to try to discover where Kidd's treasure was hidden. Kidd repeatedly winked that nobody could find it but him and that he would not say any more. (Kidd had learned a hard lesson about squandering aces in the hole, even imaginary ones.)

Though he had already sent Captain Cary south, though he could touch the scorched rope end, Bellomont suspected, as did many powerful people in England and America, that Kidd had much more treasure hidden somewhere. At most, Bellomont had recovered £14,000 and the real number after deducting Gilliam's stash was closer to £10,000. It seemed inconceivable that this notorious pirate, Captain Kidd, scourge of the Indies, had captured so little loot. The rumor mill in London back in August of 1699 had pegged Kidd's treasure at £500,000. By November that figure had dropped to £200,000 but still £10,000 was a pittance for a pirate. Was Kidd holding out?

Christmas came and went, the good Congregationalists of Boston hardly noting the passage of this Papist and pagan holiday. Sam Sewall didn't mention it in his diary; mason John Marshall noted only of December 25: "a very Cold day."

Throughout her family's ordeal, Sarah Kidd remained loyal to her husband. She stayed at a seedy waterfront inn, caring for her daughter, and she was nearly as isolated as her husband. No one invited her to anything. She was disgraced. She would do anything for him, but what could she do?

No one would help her. Robert Livingston, fellow Scot, had disappeared to somewhere near Albany. James Graham, attorney general of New York, did nothing. (Graham later cavalierly wrote to Livingston that he would help him out of this Kidd mess for the fee of . . . "a glass of wine.") Kidd's lawyer Thomas Newton had deserted him for a government appointment, as had Valentine.

Around this time, Captain Kidd (or Sarah) made a decision to try again to raise enough bribe money to buy Kidd's way out of prison. The Kidds sent the family maid, Elizabeth, down to Captain Clark's warehouse in Connecticut to pick up a sack of gold that Kidd had secretly shipped there back in late June. One report claimed that Clark was hiding £8,000 of Kidd's money there, enough to free most any prisoner from most any prison.

The maid made her request, but the longtime family friend refused to give her anything, not even a single coin.

Captain Clark, despite his rough nickname, "Whisking," was apparently afraid of crossing Governor Bellomont, who had already had him arrested once. So, instead of helping Kidd, he agreed to deliver all of Kidd's goods to the governor, but with one caveat. He would only do it *after* it was confirmed that Captain Kidd was in irons on a prison ship to England. Clark was apparently also very afraid of crossing Captain Kidd.

When the family maid was sent away from Clark's without gold, Kidd's latest bribe-escape gambit failed. Kidd was now deeply in need of consolation. On January 21, 1700, Cotton Mather came to the prison to preach to the pirates. He chose the topic of ill-gotten gains, Jeremiah 17:11, as his text. "Hee gets Riches and not by right, leaves them in the midst of his Dayes and in his End shal be a Fool." It's unlikely that Kidd was comforted.

With no ship in sight, Bellomont's gout flared in the joints in his right hand and in his right foot. To add to his anxiety, a group of New York merchants had petitioned the king to remove him because they claimed his high-handed ways were killing trade. Hearing that New Yorkers were laying wagers on how long he would last, Bellomont, to twit them, ordered that 250 gallons of wine and 250 gallons of small beer from Albany be *very publicly* delivered to his home in New York City. He would be staying.

And Kidd would be leaving soon . . . one way or another. At that very moment, Kidd was working on his latest plan to escape (which involved Sarah wheedling the jailor to let him out of his chains).

Unknown to those in Boston, Bellomont's man-of-war *Rochester*, the ship sent to fetch Kidd, had in fact been crippled by winter storms and forced on December 5 to return to London; scandalmongers in England accused the government of trying to make Kidd disappear by letting him die in a Boston prison. The Admiralty instead immediately on December 15 ordered its replacement, HMS *Advice*, to make ready to depart to attempt a foolhardy winter crossing.

Captain Wynn was given special orders to bring home Kidd, *incommunicado*: no one should talk to Kidd, send letters to him, and Kidd couldn't send any letters. Captain Kidd, whose scandal might spiral to the highest ministers, was being treated with care usually reserved for traitors or regicides. As to the treasure (then in England assumed huge), the lords had worded it as politely as possible but directed Bellomont to send an inventory of treasure in triplicate: with one copy in a letter, a second copy given to Captain Wynn, and a third copy to be hand-delivered by a man specially chosen to accompany the treasure from New England to Old England.

The HMS *Advice*, a fourth-rate warship with forty guns, ironically, was the same ship that as part of Commodore Warren's fleet had reeled in Kidd in the South Atlantic three years earlier. (Kidd had dined aboard this ship.)

The journals of the *Advice*'s Captain Robert Wynn and of its newly appointed second Lieutenant, Thomas Langrish, have survived. The HMS *Advice*, it turns out, would run into one of the more unusual calamities to befall a man-of-war . . . and it would happen at the exact moment that Kidd was trying to escape.

After a fast five-week crossing, backed by surprisingly steady winter winds, the HMS *Advice* on February 1, with 197 men aboard, reached Cape Cod.

The *Advice* sailed toward the extensive wharves of Boston just as the weather turned bitter cold. Although Boston's excellent harbor is deep and well-protected, the entrance can be a bit tricky, as a pilot must tiptoe his way among the harbor islands.

Saturday, February 2, was so brutally cold that even the pious Bostonians didn't attend a funeral of a prominent citizen.

Judge Sewall, balding at age forty-seven, had just started wearing a neck-to-brow skullcap in church to keep warm (detesting periwigs), but even he didn't go to church, although the deceased was his own cousin.

On Saturday, February 3, Captain Wynn of the *Advice* was rowed ashore from the ship's anchorage between Bullock's Island and Sheep's Island in Boston harbor. Bellomont was thrilled to receive piles of correspondence and find quite a few more words of praise for his conduct. He quickly wrote to New York: "The [government] Ministers continue to write to me with great kindness and tell me the King is very pleased with my administration in my Governments. If the angry gentlemen of N. York have their Intelligence from better hands than the King's Ministers or of a later Date than the 10th of last December, then I shall believe they are very deep in the secrets of the Cabinet."

From that day of February 3, Bellomont ordered Captain Robert Wynn of the *Advice* to come to Peter Sergeant's house daily so as to be ready for an errand or to take the pirate prisoners at a moment's notice. With undisguised pique, Captain Wynn's expense account stated: "The Earl of Bellomont commanded him to attend his Lordshipp: everie Morning at 7 a clock . . . and was detain'd until Night every day for 32 Days Successive — His Boates crew of 11 men also attending . . . For which Extra Service and to Drink he gave amongst them Each Day 5 s[hillings]: they Rowing him 10 miles out and home Each Day amounts unto £8."

Boston was slowly freezing. Pale Anglo-Saxon cheeks turned red with the bitter cold winds. Exhaled breath hung like a cloud. Lungs ached. Ears, nose, fingertips felt brittle, fragile. The iron chains at wrist and ankle drove a constant chill into the bones. Captain Kidd and Sarah had been priming for this moment for quite a while. Kidd, never one to trust his fate to others such as a jury, was working with Sarah to convince the new jailor to take off his irons.

We don't know whether Sarah slid a soft hand down the man's stubbled cheek, or handed him a pouch of coins. Or was it that Kidd somehow won the friendship of this man, his only visitor for months on end? In any case, the jailor agreed, promising that soon he'd take off the cold iron. Now Sarah had to work on figuring out a way to loosen the bars or get the guards drunk. Knowing the king's ship had arrived, they hurried, aiming for the night of Tuesday, February 13.

Samuel Sewall recorded in his diary: "Feb. 6, 7, 8. were reputed to be the coldest days that have been of many years. Some say Brooks were frozen for carts to pass over them, so has not been seen these Ten years. Ground very dry and dusty by the high wind."

The ten sailors of the *Advice*, awake in the unspeakable dawn chill, rowed Captain Wynn in the longboat the five miles into the harbor from the safe off-shore anchorage, five fathoms deep between Castle and Spectacle islands. Their numb fingers grasped the oars, the rowing keeping their minds off the pain in their frozen faces. No uniform yet existed for the Royal Navy, so these men were bundled in whatever they bought cheap from the Slop Chest. They rowed past bobbing chunks of ice.

On Tuesday, February 6, Lord Bellomont directed the Council to address the issue of speeding the accused pirates on board the *Advice*. Bellomont took his usual high-handed approach; he guided the discussion of the Council and then absented himself for the vote, expecting them to follow his lead, or be rewarded with a veto. "There was something singular and unparliamentary in his form of proceeding in council," observed historian Thomas Hutchinson, the son of the young gentleman who had grabbed Kidd's sword arm.

The governor read aloud to the Council

the orders he had received "signifying his Majesty's pleasure" to deliver the prisoners and the treasure over to Captain Wynn. To peruse the official Council minutes, one would think the Council simply advised the governor to send the prisoners as soon as the ship was readied. But it didn't happen that way.

The debate got a bit thorny. Sewall's diary: "I had ask'd before, What Pirates? . . . Gov. mention'd Kid, Gilliam, Bradish, Witherly to be sent aboard for better security. Council voted to leave it to the Gov.rs Discretion whom to send aboard: only the Gov.r had said to some that enquired, He intended not [to let] them out upon Bail. I think only I, Col. Townsend and Capt. Byfield were in the negative. The grounds I went upon were because I knew of no power I had to send Men out of the Province."

These settlers in New England always had an uneasy relationship with the mother country. Judge Sewall knew that if any man — especially one not even charged with a crime — could be selectively shipped out for trial, then all citizens became vulnerable to a kind of judicial tyranny. Sewall pondered whether he wanted to fight over this precedent using the case of an accused *New York* pirate? He decided that he did not.

The governor ordered Captain Wynn to prepare the HMS *Advice* to receive prisoners. Wynn set his carpenters to work, attaching metal ringbolts in the walls to hold the chains.

February 7, bitterest cold. The entire harbor of Boston is freezing up. "A great deal of Ice drive by us," noted Lieutenant Thomas Langrish in his journal. The men rowed in, as usual, to await orders.

Boston, an island except for the little Neck, became like a fantasy bridal cake kingdom rising off a jagged sheet of ice. The harbor waters became a moonscape.

A frost-bitten messenger arrived from Governor Winthrop in Connecticut with more rumors that the Mohawks were planning to attack. "One Tobie, who murder'd several at Oxford, stirs them up and brings Wampam to our Indians," wrote Sewall. The Council sent a letter to Governor Winthrop asking him to try to surprise Toby's war party.

Bellomont's gout was in full agony; he repeated his anxiety over the prisoners' escaping, and joked bitterly that he'd give £100 to have them magically plunked inside Newgate prison. He wanted them on board very soon.

In this excruciating bitter cold, no one visited Stone Prison. On February 8, the keeper removed the shackles of Captain

Kidd. He later said he did it out of compassion for Kidd's body ache.

He had the shackles off. Sarah could use the guns . . . doubtful . . . Could Sarah get a gun to William? A file? A knife? How much money could she raise? Maybe the keeper could be beguiled to let him and Sarah come to dinner.

Lord Bellomont consulted Captain Byfield over the logistics of delivering the prisoners to HMS *Advice* in this icy weather.

Anchoring a ship in a windy stormy harbor, especially one starting to congeal, makes for a challenge. Captain Wynn couldn't allow the vessel to become frozen in a block of ice because the ice might crush the wooden sides of the ship. He needed to set his anchors and then tighten and loosen various cables to worm a big enough gap in the ice. To make matters worse, huge blocks of drift ice started to hammer the sides of the ship.

The floating ice turned the ship, so that it started to get twisted in its own cables. In the middle of the black night, it got so bad that Captain Wynn ordered his men to re-anchor, working the capstan in the freezing cold. As they were doing so, a block of ice snapped the cable attached to one longboat, sweeping the boat away. The blocks of drift ice were so dangerous —

glowing by in the dark — that the captain ordered the men to throw "fire grapnells" (small but strong anchors with fish-hook sharp barbs) onto the ice ringing Spectacle Island and quickly pull the ship out of harm of the drift ice.

Sunday, February 11, and Monday, February 12: heavy snowfall. Cotton Mather used "white as the snow of Salmon" as his text. The men of the *Advice* worked the anchor lines with little visibility in a blizzard, amid ice floes. Wynn decided the best strategy was to use the thickest cables to work the ship away from the careening drifts and near the protective solid ice near Spectacle Island. The logbook understates: "We making all Security imaginable against ye drift Ice."

Kidd's escape plans in top secret were inching forward, with Tuesday night of February 13 targeted.

On Tuesday morning, Governor Bellomont signed the warrant to put Kidd, Gilliam, Bradish, and Witherly aboard. The guards headed to the prison.

The transporting of the prisoners was to be carried out in great secrecy to prevent any escape attempts, any chance for the accused pirates coordinating with confederates to overpower the escort.

Bellomont expected the usual morning arrival of Captain Wynn to put the plan into action. However, out on the ship, in the predawn darkness, snow — like a ghostly blanket — had covered the deck and rails of the HMS *Advice*, dropped there by a huge storm the night before. The taut anchor cables stretched out fore and aft, pinning the ship like an odd beast, like some trapped butterfly, amid the ice. But in a fluke of Mother Nature, following the night snowstorm, the weather was warming quickly, and at daybreak, a strong sun broke through the clouds, and took the edge off the cold. The wind died down. Captain Wynn debated whether to go get the prisoners; the veteran sailor sensed disaster ahead.

Wrote Lieutenant Langrish: "It thawed a small matter, ye ice parting." The snow turned to slosh on the decks. The men could enjoy the sun as they worked. Wynn decided to wait. Then just before noon Lieutenant Langrish noticed "a very Large Island of ice" moving inexorably on an angle toward the ship's bow.

The freakish warm weather had unleashed a rogue iceberg, which was heading directly for them. Captain Wynn described it as "a fleck of Ice about 1 mile long & ½ broad." The ship was anchored in the gap between Castle Island and Spectacle Island, much closer to Spectacle. They had weathered the storm; now they had to weather the calm. The sun shone; little breezes barely ruffled the men's hair. As they stood on deck, they saw this acreage of ice, with deadly quiet come relentlessly drifting down upon them. Wynn ordered the men to work the anchor cables to pull the ship out of range but there was nowhere to hide. The huge block of ice rammed the *Advice*, driving it hard toward Spectacle Island.

The captain ordered the men to drop the sheet anchor, a kind of short strong emergency brake, over the bow. With a lockpick's feel, the captain let out two and a half turns of cable; the anchor seemed to grab. Then the ice floe won the battle over the spikes of iron. The ship headed straight into Spectacle Island, with a mile of ice propelling it forward. The bow wedged open the ring of shore ice. The HMS *Advice* — sent at such great expense for one accused pirate — crashed hard aground.

The captain ordered the men "to heave off but [they] could make no purchase." Tossing a fire grapnel onto some moving drift ice failed as well to pull them free.

The ship aground could at any moment tip over as the tide went out, and the sea level dropped. If the ship swayed too far, it might sink as the water rushed in the gunports. The captain ordered everything lashed and sealed. Feeling the ship tremble to one side, he screamed at the men to cut the lower yardarms, and haul them into the freezing water to prop up the port side of the ship. Men slip-slided on the ice, trying to wedge yardarms between the ship and ice block. The HMS *Advice* was stranded; the captain sent ten men to row the longboat ashore amid the giant blocks of ice, to get help. (Bellomont at first raged at them, wondering where they had been on this important morning with the sun finally shining, the day set to carry off Kidd.)

Captain Wynn, meanwhile, tried to lighten the ship by having the men empty off several tons of water in casks, needed to meet the daily ration of 200 gallons a day. No luck at floating off.

At four o'clock that afternoon another chunk of drift ice crashed into the ship and some of the thick oak yardarms, strong enough to carry heavy blown canvas, which were now propping the ship, snapped underwater. The ship teetered, and teetered a little further — the men raced to the high side — then it stopped. Heavy cannon were dragged to the high side. Guns were re-lashed and all cargo stowed tautly. The main damage was that the tiller was crushed. At any moment, an ice chunk might send the ship hurtling over.

As night fell, two sloops under sail from Boston dock were able to zigzag amid the ice, and reached the beached *Advice*. Heavy snow began to fall. In the darkness by lantern light, Captain Cyprian Southack of Boston and Captain Wynn tried to figure out a way to offload some of the forty cannon to let the ship float free. But they couldn't manage the offload.

At one in the morning, when the tide rose, the exhausted men were ordered to heave on an anchor rope. The ship trembled; the chanteying got more fervent; they heaved; they pulled the ship free and it bobbed afloat again in five fathoms of water. By lantern, they retrieved their broken yardarms and later gave them — as well as their empty water casks — to the Boston sloops to take ashore.

Finally the men were able to re-anchor the ship in deeper water.

Captain Kidd had been out of his shackles for five days, since Wednesday, February 8, ample time to escape, but Sarah had been unable to put together any jailbreak, with Andrew Knott or anyone else. The captain paced his icy cold cell, he tried to charm his jailor, but he never was able to exit the room.

Lord Bellomont, who had very much wanted to put Kidd on the *Advice* on Tuesday morning, planned to reschedule for the instant the *Advice* was seaworthy. In the meantime, he sent a man over to the prison to check on the pirates, and this is when he first learned that Kidd was unshackled. Bellomont became demented with fury. He rushed orders to reshackle Kidd immediately; he set first light Friday, February 16, as the secret new time for the constables to pick up Kidd, Gilliam, Bradish, and Witherly and carry them in shackles to the *Advice* longboat where they would be rowed the five miles amid the ice chunks out to the *Advice*. Bellomont told only one person — his council secretary Addington — beside the officers physically involved in transporting the prisoners. Bellomont himself would not be present.

In the predawn gloom of Friday, a dozen men arrived at Stone Prison. The keeper used his heavy keys to open door after door; he unshackled the prisoners from the wall-bolts. When they came to Kidd's cell, the ruckus already awaking him, Kidd did not cooperate. He kicked, punched, fought. A half dozen men wrestled him, still in chains, down the steps of Stone Prison. When he realized they were taking him to the man-of-war, he fought harder for a moment and then he let it go.

Kidd was a Scot in the English empire, a man accused of piracy; he knew his chances.

The men pulled at the oars of the *Advice*'s longboat; Kidd watched them feather

The Treasure Committee's inventory of July 25, 1699, lists not only Captain Kidd's haul from the Indies but also the wrongly confiscated personal property of Kidd's wife, Sarah.

amid the ice, he was inhaling deeply his first fresh sea air in seven months. The prisoners were tied and hauled like sacks up into the ship. Once aboard, three of the prisoners were chained together in the gunroom, which had been converted to a jail. Captain Kidd was once again kept in isolation, chained, in a cabin in steerage. After his brief stint in the longboat, he was now in a windowless, low-ceilinged room, chained to the wall. The ship's familiar rocking calmed him. Sarah awoke on shore to find her husband gone.

The HMS *Advice*, however, was not ready to sail. First the yardarms and tiller had to be repaired, and more pirates and treasure loaded. Lord Bellomont had an enormous amount of secret correspondence he wanted to write to his various lordly backers; his gout made it almost impossible for him to hold a quill in his right hand. Bellomont trusted no one enough to take dictation of these letters.

Each morning the numbed dozen crewmen still rowed Captain Wynn to spend their day in excruciating boredom, awaiting the lord's command. Repairs and revictualling were slowed. Of the broken yardarms brought to Boston, some were "tongued," i.e. the broken sections repaired via careful tongue-and-groove carpentry; others were replaced.

Lord Bellomont, extremely cranky and in open hostility with the Council, ordered the Sabbath broken on Sunday, February 18, to bring aboard ten more pirates, who were locked in the gunroom in chains with three "capital prisoners." Over the next week, Captain Wynn loaded 18 tons of beer for the crew and prisoners. (This 4,000 gallons of beer for 200 crewmen and 32 prisoners would last about 5 weeks at half a gallon a man a day.)

On shore, Kidd's former crewman, Joseph Palmer, traveling with friends, *voluntarily* arrived in Boston from Rhode Island and surrendered himself on February 21. Lord Bellomont was impressed by the young pirate's respectable demeanor and the quality of his friends and family from Westchester.

A sloop delivered new and repaired yardarms to the HMS *Advice*, and the navy crew spent two days rigging the masts and yards. While the sailors were at work, another sixteen prisoners were delivered, and chained in the gunroom.

The ship was now ready for the treasure. One niggling matter remained before shipping out the booty. How much would the good Puritans of Boston receive for their role in capturing Kidd, imprisoning him, and storing his booty? The Council decided on the lordly sum of £840, which annoyed Bellomont almost as much as when the five wealthy citizens on the treasure committee demanded to be paid for their work. Lord Bellomont allowed them £90 but complained privately that their demand for salary was "not genteel."

On Wednesday, February 28, when the weather cleared, the treasure chests of gold and silver and jewels were loaded onto the *St. Antonio*, along with six other chests. The *St. Antonio* was also reloaded with the forty bales of East India goods, thirteen hogsheads of sugar, a Negro slave named Dundee, and an East Indian from Ceylon named Ventura Rosair. "I look upon it as a great Mercy of God, that the Store-house has not been broken up, no fire has happened," wrote Sewall.

Weighed again in the storehouse, the gold once again tallied 1,111 ounces or just under 70 pounds. Captain Winn had his clerk cross-checking all the weights and measures and said that they all agreed; however, he wouldn't sign the receipt, until all the goods were loaded upon the *St. Antonio* riding just by the Outward Wharf.

The crew sailed the *St. Antonio* out to HMS *Advice* and the treasure and other goods were carefully hoisted from the sloop into the man-of-war and then stored in the afterhold.

So, now, thirty-two accused pirates and

four slaves were locked aboard. Bellomont, however, wanted to ship off three more prisoners, local *Boston* men who had helped pirate Bradish sell his loot. The Council stood up to the governor in the case of these three *Boston* men, and ruled that their province's charter granted them the right "to try their own people."

Bellomont, fighting his gout, was feverishly writing letters to London. He wanted the lords in London to petition the king for a new grant that would allow them to share Kidd's treasure as a reward for capturing pirates, and would ignore their role in Kidd's original privateering mission. "I hope East India Goods and Treasure that's sent will amount to £20,000, which will reimburse everybody if the King will consent." Bellomont wrote his plan to the Duke of Shrewsbury, then Lord Chamberlain, and sent along with the letter a very rare white beaver skin, as a gift from one aristocrat to another. (Bellomont on the other hand had just turned down a gift of a dozen silver plates from a beholden ship's captain. He wrote privately: "If [the ship's] *owners* had offered me a present, I would have accepted it.") Bribery was so nuanced.

Bellomont was also scheming to have Gilliam's £3,000 in gold and jewels treated separately from Kidd's. "I am told that as

Vice-Admiral of these Seas, I have a right to a 3rd part of them," Bellomont wrote to his London business agent. "If the rest of the Lords come in for snacks I shall be satisfyed." The word "snacks" was a common, though slightly vulgar, word for "shares."

Throughout all this plotting, Bellomont never once mentioned restoring the goods to the original owners or reimbursing the English East India Company for losses.

The governor also detailed a strategy to help in prosecuting Kidd, advising that Joseph Palmer could testify about Kidd committing murder. He wrote to royal advisor James Vernon that Palmer's sister was traveling to London on the *St. Antonio*. "She could easily persuade her brother to tell the whole truth and a *frown* from you will make her endeavour it."

Up almost to the day of departure, Captain Wynn had continued his daily icy commute to Bellomont's anteroom. On one unspecified afternoon, as he was leaving the mansion, a pretty woman succeeded in getting his attention. Sarah Kidd introduced herself. She hadn't seen or talked to her husband for the three weeks he had been chained aboard Captain Wynn's prison ship.

Sarah and William had also long ago decided that it would be best for her and their daughter to stay in America; Captain Kidd hated the thought of her seeing him in irons or on trial.

Sarah asked Captain Wynn if she could send a message of love and farewell to her husband. The Royal Navy officer regretfully informed her that he was ordered to guard Kidd as a "close prisoner," with no visitors or letters.

She reached into a little pouch and pulled out a fine heavy gold ring, and she pressed it into the officer's hand, bidding the reluctant captain to accept it.

I can deliver no message, he said, trying to give her back the ring.

Be kind to my husband, she asked.

He said he could no accept no gifts. She smiled and, walking away, said that he should keep the ring as a "token" until we meet again . . . when you bring my husband back to me.

On March 10, amid ice and snow, the HMS *Advice* set sail from Boston harbor to carry Captain Kidd, the empire's most wanted criminal, back to England to answer for his crimes.

Culliford Leaves Paradise and Flirts with Hell

Chapter Sixteen

Captain Culliford, ready for a vacation, prowled the rowdy deck of the *Mocha Frigate*, which was cluttered with stolen treasure. After Culliford and Shivers had captured the *Great Mohammed* back in October 1698, each man had received £600 in treasure, enough to buy a fine home and a tavern, and never work again . . . if they could get the loot home.

Now every man aboard these two ships — including all ninety-five of Captain Kidd's former crew who had mutinied — was flush with some kind of money: Arabian gold coins, Spanish pieces of eight, Lyon dollars, and German pieces called Rix dollars, chunks of gold, bits of silver, even some English coins.

The men had overwhelmingly voted to head back to America and England, by way of St. Mary's, Madagascar.

So, the captains had bought hundreds of

gallons of wine, and the easy sail south from India had soon turned into a floating womanless party. The men gambled, drank, danced with one another, with songs and tunes mingling in English, French, and Dutch. The pirate fiddler worked overtime.

Around Christmas of 1698, these two ships, propelled by the seasonal monsoon winds, reached the pirate paradise of St. Mary's Island off Madagascar. Captain Culliford, a past master of the region, navigated through the throat of the harbor, seven, to six, to five fathoms deep over a gentle sand. The only dangerous obstacles were the ribs of three wrecked ships, sunk and burned in the harbor: Captain Kidd's *Adventure Galley* and the mutineers' *Rouparelle* and one other. At low tide, the burnt skeletons of these discarded ships protruded above the calm harbor waters like half-eaten carcasses.

As Culliford entered, he saw a midsized ship already anchored there. His rack of forty cannon made him barely hesitate. He quickly learned that vessel was the *Nassau*, funded by the merchants of New York, under Giles Shelley. The pirates were happy to see him.

Captain Shelley, a big pock-marked man, until then stewing in the *empty* harbor, was equally pleased, since he was stocked with just the kind of goods these suddenly rich men would overpay for. Shelley's outward bound bill of lading from New York City listed: 250 gallons of Madeira wine, 28 casks of rum, 2 casks of clay pipes, 8 chests full of pistols, 16 half barrels of gunpowder, and all kinds of European goods, such as combs, scissors, shirts, pants, shoes, hats. The absence of tobacco is easily explained, he had bought it cheap from the Indians on Long Island, and skipped paying export duty.

Culliford and the other pirates couldn't wait to get aboard Shelley to start spending money. To handle the crowds, Shelley ordered his crew of fifteen or so to gather the boards from the wrecked ships and build a little shack on the shore. "Shelley sold liquors out of the said shed," later recalled Dr. Bradinham, "and I often went thither to drink."

Under the arbor of palm trees, in this rain-soaked lush place, the 140 or so pirates crowded in and out of Shelley's shed. Liquored up, some of them wandered down the road to their temporary Malagasy "wives" or to what passed for a whorehouse run by Edward Welch.

St. Mary's was no Port Royal, Jamaica. There were no boulevards of bordellos and taverns. This place was heavy with fruit trees and its streets mere rutted dirt paths.

The natives lived in raised thatched huts and the handful of European traders under Little King Edward Welch lived in a compound on a hill four miles away.

Food was cheap, and the pirates paid as little as two pieces of eight for an entire zebu; the delicacy of this unusual bovine creature was the thirty-pound hunk of fatty meat above the neck, nicely spiced and roasted. Fruit was there for the picking, and rice could be bought for pennies a sack. Pirates could amuse themselves shooting lemurs out of the treetops; one pirate got mauled by a pack of lemurs in an orange grove, his buddies laughing too hard to rescue him.

But Captain Shelley of New York was in a hurry to sell to the pirates, and leave. He knew — and kept it a secret — that a rival ship from New York carrying the same kind of goods was headed straight for St. Mary's. And the rival captain was the ornery Samuel Burgess, working for the unscrupulous Frederick Phillips. Shelley wanted to make his sales, load up his passengers, and exit the harbor. Selling to pirates was always a dicey proposition, especially since he was also selling them weapons.

Captain Shivers bought a silver-plated musket for 40 pieces of eight (£10), and one Peter Varney picked up a pair of matched pistols for £5 and 8 shillings. A group of other pirates pooled together for half a keg of gunpowder.

Shelley also catered to the fashion-conscious outlaw; he sold them flouncy hats and one-size-fits-all shoes. As for the pants and shirts, he sold them needles and colored thread so that they could tailor the stolen silks and madras and calico bought from Edward Welch, receiver of bales from various ships. Many of these men now decked themselves out in colorful — if not always color-coordinated — finery.

While many of the pirates were eager to haul their riches home, Robert Culliford comfortably settled himself along with his great consort, Jon Swann, into Edward Welch's compound. Culliford auditioned some of the island's cinnamon-colored high-cheekboned women for the honor of being Mrs. Culliford. As Captain Johnson reported, "The [pirates] married the most beautiful of the Negro women, not one or two, but as many as they liked, so that every one of them had as great a Seraglio as the Grand Seignior at Constantinople." He also hired on a handful of servants.

Welch's hilltop house was furnished with the riches of fifty pirate captures: silver tea-pots, the carpets of Persia, striped silk hanging in the windows. Culliford from his bedroom could peer out across the thick forest of trees, and see the ocean glimmering turquoise far off. Stone walls guarded the entranceway of the single zigzag path up the mountain, and six cannon were perched menacingly, dragged up there by teams of natives.

Culliford and his entourage feasted on zebu and goat — slaughtered the same day — and drank Caribbean rum. The place was redolent with smells of meat cooking and tobacco smoke. After sunset he lounged in bed with his wives.

Robert Culliford along with Jon Swann decided to stay awhile in pirate paradise.

Captain Shelley had his crew working hard to get the *Nassau* ready for sailing; he had already careened before the pirates arrived. He wanted to leave fast . . . the pirate parties were getting out of hand. Culliford's gunner, after buckets of punch, slurringly threatened: "I have a mind to shoot a [cannonball] through Shelley's ship." Archibald Buchannon (who had replaced the dead William Moore) staggered toward the *Mocha*, but Dr. Bradinham and other inebriates rerouted him back to the shed.

Nonetheless, some of the pirates were clearly not happy to see their comrades agree to speed back to America, after two brief weeks on St. Mary's when the party was just beginning.

Shelley had already lined up about 90 of the 140 pirates to sail back with him at 100 pieces of eight a man. (The pirates couldn't sail their *stolen* ships back; it was much safer to hitch a ride with a semi-respectable merchant.) Then, just what Shelley dreaded occurred on January 11, 1699; the other New York merchant ship, commanded by pugnacious Burgess, sailed into the harbor. The first words out of Burgess's mouth were: "They have built a gallows at New York to hang such people as you." Burgess desperately did not want all his customers to leave; "he wanted to make his voyage [selling to] them," later recalled an eyewitness.

Burgess, like Shelley, was carrying casks of Madeira wine and rum; he even brought a barrel of lime juice (anti-scurvy or cocktail enhancer or maybe both). He too imported guns and gunpowder.

Shelley wasted no time; he offered to drop the nervous passengers at Cape May, south of New York City; he lost maybe a dozen or two to Burgess's gallows lie; he started ferrying men aboard, including quite a few of Kidd's old crew: Dr. Bradinham, Joseph Palmer, Darby Mullins, Edward Buckmaster. (It turned out that Buckmaster wouldn't get home fast enough; his wife had already found a new lover in New York, and had agreed to marry Adam Baldridge, the previous Great White Trader on St. Mary's.)

"Some of the men who were left at St. Mary's did grumble that so many of their crew had left," later recalled Joseph Palmer. He said "somebody fired a shot through Shelley's [ship] as the men were going aboard with some of their things." (The sourest pirates were usually the ones who lost *all* their money at dice.)

Shelley collected fifty pieces of eight from each man, as upfront payment, and explained they would have to pay freight charges on their loot. Shelley would supply a meager daily meal of rice; besides that, it was bring-your-own-food. The crew of fifteen weighed anchor and Shelley promptly announced that the bar was open; Shelley confided in a pirate by the name of Theo Turner, that carrying passengers was more lucrative than slaves, because he expected to rake in heavy profits selling them liquor and extra food and other goods, *for the next five months.*

Captain Culliford also took the opportunity provided by Shelley to send home a dead pirate's share of the loot to the man's wife in New York. Culliford entrusted 3,000 pieces of eight to Edward Buckmaster to deliver to the "Widow Whaley" (probably "William Weily" from Kidd's original crew). While the Admiralty of England at this very moment lagged far behind in paying the sailors returned from war with France, this pirate captain was sending stolen booty around the world to a widow. (The issue of sailors' not receiving their pay in the Royal Navy would spark a riot: "They and their wives and their children have this day fill'd the Admiralty," wrote the acting Secretary of State, James Vernon, "signifying that if they have no better answer from the Navy Board than they had three months ago that it will be hard for them to perish for want of what is their due, that their necessitys will force them upon ill things for a livelyhood." Those "ill things" were clearly piracy.)

Shelley sailed out of St. Mary's harbor, under the curses of Burgess, as a relaxed Culliford waved a bottle.

(When twenty gallows-leery pirates begged off down the coast of Madagascar, Shelley parked twenty slaves aboard in their place; men slept like Siamese twins on the cramped ship. Finally after five months, with forty or so pirates left, Captain Shelley would reach Cape May, in East Jersey, about two weeks ahead of Kidd.)

On St. Mary's, Culliford and Swann and Shivers lived the cushy life, pampered by multiple servants and wives. Culliford could afford the finest of Captain Burgess's wares: rum, wine, guns, pipes, hats, shoes, scissors to trim his hair, a nice mirror in which to admire his handsome, unscarred face.

Burgess tried to tempt Robert Culliford, Swann, and Shivers to buy a ride home on the *Margaret*. The thirty-three-year-old pirate captain pondered to decide whether to sail out with Burgess.

Culliford knew the man well, from their days together almost a decade earlier when they had stolen Captain Kidd's ship *Blessed William* and gone off pirating; they had also sailed together to the Red Sea as privateers-turned-pirates aboard the *Jacob*. And the crew had caught quartermaster Burgess cheating them and, instead of marooning him as he deserved for stealing from his mates, they booted him off at St. Augustine Bay, Madagascar. That was back in September of 1691. Now, on January 11, 1699, this was the first time since that Culliford had seen Burgess face-to-face. He decided that he still hated the scammer.

Since their last meeting, Burgess had caught quite a few lucky breaks, although he probably would not have revealed all to Culliford. The truth was that their ship *Jacob* — after Culliford and pals were waylaid into Moghul prison — had returned to Madagascar where the crew took pity on their old shipmate Burgess, then begging

579

from the blacks. They welcomed him back aboard and the ship set sail for the Red Sea, where they made some fat captures. The *Jacob* returned to New York; several of the pirates bought passes from Governor Fletcher and the ship's secret owners gave the ship itself to the governor.

Burgess, with a nice nest egg from piracy, had set himself up as captain working for New York's richest merchant, Fred Phillips, whose properties included a tract of 240 square miles that would become Sleepy Hollow, New York. Burgess helped oversee construction of an eighty-ton four-cannon brigantine, christened the *Margaret*, and went off on first one, then a second slaving mission to Madagascar.

The Madagascar route was a beauteous thing when it worked: pirates overpaying for booze and weapons, while slaves could be had much cheaper in Madagascar than in West Africa, where the royal companies of the various European powers jacked the prices.

The downside of the Madagascar route was that the ship might run into interference from the English East India Company, which, despite Parliament's opening up the East Indies trade in 1694, still treated the waters like their own private English bathtub. Burgess had already had run-ins. On the *Margaret*'s maiden voyage, he happened near the *Mary*, that same East India Company–commissioned ship that Kidd ran into. Burgess expected the common naval courtesy (of dipped flags or sails or something), but instead *Mary* ignored him. So Burgess maneuvered athwart the hawser of the ship, and then *Mary*'s captain, Thomas Hayes, ordered a shot fired into the water ahead of *Margaret*. Burgess ordered his gunner to fire at *Mary*. "Must I hit her?" asked the gunner. "Yes," Burgess replied. The gunner repeated the question several times, to which Burgess shouted, "Yes, you dog, you son of a whore, why are you so long about it?" Burgess beat the gunner, kicked him, and then stomped on his head over and over until the man's noggin was swollen to "the size of two heads," according to a complaint later filed. As Samuel Burgess returned from *Margaret*'s maiden voyage to New York, he found Governor Bellomont trying to build a piracy/bribery case against the previous Governor Fletcher. Bellomont made a deal with Burgess; if Burgess would testify against Fletcher, Bellomont would lobby the king for a piracy pardon for him; Burgess got his full pardon before sailing out.

Culliford eyed him up and down, and said, No. Swann also said, No. Little King Edward Welch had been seriously wounded in a recent skirmish, and Culliford was now lord of the hilltop chalet.

However, Captain Derrick Shivers, the man who had helped capture the *Great Mohammed*, decided along with eighteen others to travel home with Burgess. Fred Phillips had advised Burgess not to take too many pirates, "lest you won't be able to command them." Also, try to pick those of "civilest and quietest humour." Burgess didn't have much choice.

Phillips also told Burgess to have the pirates each bring aboard a "fat ox and rice." (The deck was always full of zebu shit.) He also directed Burgess to charge the pirates 100 pieces of eight for passage, and to charge them *half the value* of the goods for freight, up from the usual quarter value or less. "Tell them that way you will treat [their goods] as [you would] your own." This was extortion, as was the six-percent-of-value fee he was told to charge for allowing passengers to carry gold and jewels. (Phillips didn't get wealthy by accident: he also counseled Burgess to entertain Edward Welch "especially with liquor" before discussing any deals.)

Sam Burgess, like all merchant ship captains, carried letters, providing a key link in the informal postal service of the world. At least three he brought from New York were addressed to Captain Kidd, unfortunately departed a few months prior to Burgess's arrival. Kidd's would-be correspondents were: Robert Livingston, Lord Bellomont, and his lawyer James Emott. All three, after many polite salutations and health inquiries, hastened to inform Kidd *not* to believe those ugly rumors that everyone at home had turned against him. "Ye shall meet with all ye Incouragements in my power," Bellomont wrote to him. Robert Livingston one-upped the promise: "You may rely . . . that there is no other design than to make you as great and happy as your heart can desire, and this accept as a pledge of ye true Love and affection that yr. Countryman bears you."

Captain Culliford decided to make use of postal carrier Burgess to make sure his good deed went according to plan. Culliford sent a note to Widow Whaley informing her that Edward Buckmaster, aboard Captain Shelley's ship, was to deliver her husband's share.

Mrs. Whaley,

Be it knowen this is concarninge youer husbondes will which so is left wholly to you and yr. children . . . [he] left thirty hundred pieces of eight . . . Edward Buckmaster left in charge to bee delivered the fright [freight] to Bee payed . . . madam, yours to Com[mand]. Rob.t Collov.r

Culliford folded the letter twice and addressed the outside: "ffor Mrs. Whaley Living at Longe Islande or elsewhere." He didn't want Buckmaster to slip away with £750 of someone else's (stolen) money. Robert Culliford and Jon Swann remained with the wounded Little King and their harems on St. Mary's.

Samuel Burgess set sail out of the harbor, the deck of the *Margaret* filled with his motley pirates, dressed in East India silks and striped calicoes, pumps, and hats. Since retail sales had been mediocre and he had only nineteen passengers on a ship that could cram one hundred, Burgess needed to buy slaves to make his voyage profitable; he headed south to St. Augustine's Bay, off Tulear.

Culliford and Swann on St. Mary's pirate paradise settled into a lazy tropical routine. From April, when Burgess left, to August, few, if any, ships came to the outlaw port.

The pirates, to pass the time, joined in on some local Malagasy holidays and attended at least one of the islanders' elaborate after-death parties. For centuries and to this day, Malagasies have believed that death is just the beginning of the more important phase of a soul's journey. They treat funerals joyously, and then, about five years after the person's death (or as soon as the relatives can afford to buy a zebu), they hold a giant village-wide party, called *"famadihana,"* or "turning of the bones." The relatives go to the cemetery and, chanting songs, take the corpse from the tomb, freshen it up with a brisk beating of sticks, then rewrap the bones in a new bright-colored shroud and dance around the grave.

Afterward, a long drum-beating, singing procession down the rutted roads gathers dozens of guests to a party house, where they all drink much palm wine, poured into folded leaves. The pounding drums turn the dancing into an ecstatic free-for-all.

The pirates, one time when they heard the drums, roused themselves to wander down to the party.

For the most part, though, Culliford and Swann lazed about for months.

On August 18, 1699, the routine was suddenly interrupted. A ship sailed into St. Mary's flying the King's Colours. The vessel was a "pink," a style of ship bulging to the middle, pointy at both ends, about forty-five feet long and twenty feet wide. The men on shore, through the spyglass, didn't recognize anyone on board; the captain wasn't one of the usual lot from New York. No honest European ship sailed here, unless it was desperate, half-wrecked in a storm. This "pink," with its meager guns, wasn't strong enough to do much damage. *Who were these people?*

At least four of Captain Kidd's former crew — still living on St. Mary's after their pirating jaunt with Culliford — happened to be in the harbor at that moment. John Walker, Kidd's original quartermaster from New York, had the locals pole him by pirogue to the ship. Walker was hoisted from the tippy little dugout pirogue up onto the deck. By then, Walker would fit the London stage version of a pirate: leathery tan, armed with pistol and cutlass, clothed in colorful rich silk.

Walker, an experienced sailor, talked to the crew and found out that this pink was a slaver. And that its captain, Thomas Warren, had been deputized by his uncle, Commodore Thomas Warren, . . . *to deliver pardons to the English pirates of St. Mary's.*

Walker was flabbergasted. Although the captain showed him the documents, he couldn't read them. About four o'clock that same afternoon, Henry Berkeley, the surgeon of this ship — the *Vine* pink — came ashore to deliver proclamations of pardon from King William III of England. The buckle-shoed surgeon stood on the beach and mustered a "Hear ye, hear ye" and gathered no more than chattering lemurs. No one talked to him.

John Walker rushed the four miles in the heat, up to the mountaintop lair of Little King and Culliford and Swann. He told them the remarkable news. They thought that he was crazy, or drunk, or, if he was telling the truth, maybe it was a trick to lure them to the harbor. The *Vine* would wrap them up and haul them off.

Robert Culliford decided that he alone would go to the ship in the harbor since he alone among the pirates could read. He dressed in his finest silks; he bathed; he combed his hair; he shaved; he wore shoes.

The next morning, pirate captain Culliford was rowed out in the *Mocha*'s leftover longboat. Befitting minor royalty, he brought with him an entourage of Malagasy servants and wives.

He was hoisted into the *Vine* pink. After friendly greetings, he asked to see the captain's instructions and a copy of the proclamation of pardon. On the barely rocking deck, in the bright sunshine, Culliford read the orders addressed to Master Thomas Warren. "We desire you to take with you Twenty proclamations . . . to extend his Royal Grace and mercy to any poor or rich who will accept thereof." Any pirates accepting the offer must swear *never ever* to commit any future piracies. Those reformed criminals helping to locate other pirates, "we shall not only give them pardon but offer rewards." (The Crown's logic was the Royal Navy couldn't patrol the whole Indian Ocean, but a pardon might quickly reduce the ranks of pirates; the East India Company despised the idea.)

The document was signed by Commodore Thomas Warren, and two commissioners, Israel Hayes and Peter Delanoy. (Commodore Warren — indeed the same officer who'd had the run-in with Kidd — was at that moment trying to guide his five-ship squadron to Madagascar.)

Culliford now held up a copy of the pardon: a single large sheet of heavy paper, fifteen inches by twelve inches. At the top was an ornate lion and unicorn insignia, accompanied by the words: "By the King, a PROCLAMATION."

To Culliford, this certainly appeared to be an authentic document, even if it was delivered by an undermanned slaving ship. Because of the heavy Gothic lettering, it took him a little while to puzzle out phrases such as "for the security of the trade . . . by an utter extirpation of the pirates." The proclamation, describing the process for receiving pardon, stated that a majority among the following four men (or their survivors), that is, Commodore Thomas Warren and the three commissioners, Israel Hayes, Peter Delanoy, and

Christopher Pollard may "give assurance of our most Gracious Pardon unto all such Pirates in the East Indies." Culliford read the legalese down the bottom of the page, where he saw, to his surprise, that it noted that two pirates — and only two — were specifically *not* allowed to participate in the pardon. The first rogue's name was "Henry Every"; the second was "William Kid."

Hundreds of men, who had attacked and plundered ships, men who had raped and murdered, were eligible for this pardon, but not Culliford's old shipmate Captain Kidd, the man who called himself an *honorable* privateer. History has failed to record whether Culliford laughed out loud.

The document concluded: "Given at our Court at Kensington, the Eighth Day of December, 1698. In the Tenth Year of Our Reign. GOD SAVE THE KING."

Robert Culliford, a man of enthusiasm, was ecstatic. He asked Thomas Warren to endorse his copy. The two men descended into the captain's cabin, and, over a civil glass of Madeira, Thomas Warren wrote the following on the back of Robert Culliford's proclamation of pardon.

August 19, 1699
By vertue of orders to me Given by Maj.ties Commissioners I hand delivered to Rob.t Collover this Proclamation con-

taining Maj.ties Royall Mercy. he being
willing and desirous to except of ye same by
me. Tho: Warren

At that moment, Robert Culliford began
celebrating. Young Captain Warren, in a
later deposition in London at Old Bailey
Courthouse, recalled that "as soon as I
signed and delivered the said Proclamation,
Robert Collover expressed great satisfaction
and acknowledgements of his Maties Grace
and Favour." Clerks take down depositions
in a kind of drab shorthand. That "great
satisfaction" barely scratches the surface of
Culliford's joy, of his knowing, as Warren's
signature dried, that he — with more than
£1,000 in booty stashed up the hill — was
going to get away with it all, and could return a free man to England, to friends,
family, lovers, to the smugglers' coast of
Cornwall. He "expressed great satisfaction"
indeed.

Robert Culliford folded that proclamation in half three times, and placed it in his
waistcoat pocket. He then gave Warren an
account of the pirates living on St. Mary's
and in the pirate hangouts on mainland
Madagascar, promising the captain that he
would prevail on others to submit to the
king's offer. Within days, Culliford had
convinced seventeen pirates to come
aboard the *Vine* pink. Each received a copy

of the proclamation, endorsed by Thomas Warren.

(Robert Culliford would carry his copy around with him for more than a year; he clearly showed it to many people, because one folded edge on the outside became quite dirty and worn. A slight burn mark indicates that some curious person got it too close to a candle or pipe.)

Emboldened by this *promise* of a pardon, Culliford was now ready to go home. He asked Warren if he and some of his re-formed friends could catch a ride aboard the respectable *Vine* pink. Warren agreed.

But the good captain of the *Vine* still had to fill his tweendeck with slaves before turning homeward; he quickly learned from Culliford that no humans were for sale at that moment on St. Mary's. And Culliford also warned his new friend that the next pirate ship into port might decide to burn the pardons and steal his ship. Warren opted to depart quickly.

At the Little King's compound on top of the hill, it was time for quick farewells. One last feast of zebu, some fresh Madeira from the *Vine*, final lovemaking with a few of his wives. After some soul-searching, Culliford, Swann, and the pirates decided not to take along their servants or wives. Culliford hugged each of his wives and gave each one parting gifts such as ribbons and silks. And some received more of a parting gift than others, when a few months later, a light-skinned baby appeared. (The Malagasies called these mixed-race children "zana-malata," and felt pride, not shame, in the offspring.)

Culliford and the pirates loaded their treasure chests and other goods aboard the *Vine* and within a day it was angling through the throat of the harbor, under the defunct guns, leaving St. Mary's paradise almost bereft of white-skinned rogues.

Captain Thomas Warren doubled the *Vine* pink back south to Fort Dolphin on Madagascar's east coast not only to buy slaves, but also to wait for his uncle's Royal Navy squadron; he wanted the glory of delivering eighteen pardon-seeking pirates. His orders clearly stated that if he succeeded, the commissioners "would recommend him to the King."

But where was Commodore Thomas "Wrong Way" Warren?

His ship, HMS *Harwich*, after leaving England in January of 1699 leading four men-of-war, had straggled south, delayed by his fondness for feasting. (In March, his namesake nephew had decided to go on ahead.)

The Admiralty had given the squadron a twofold mission: to destroy pirates (either by pardon or battle) and to deliver an ambassador from the New East India Company bearing tons of gifts to negotiate a new treaty with the Grand Moghul.

Warren's assignment was an expensive and important mission, as can be seen by the victualing needed just for his ship, HMS *Harwich*: for 197 men: 55,886 pounds of bread (281 days' rations), 6 tons of beer (7 days at a *gallon* a day), 6,539 pieces of beef (32 weeks), 6,494 pieces of pork (32 weeks), 9 bushels of peas (8 weeks), 102 bushels of oatmeal (12 weeks), 96 gallons of oil in lieu of butter and cheese (21 weeks).

Unfortunately for Captain Warren, during his voyage, he never met a single pirate.

Commodore Warren and the commissioners, loaded with firepower, never landed at the pirate haven of St. Mary's; Warren sailed instead up the *west coast* of Madagascar, where he did make a quick wood and water stop at St. Augustine's Bay, dropping off three copies of the proclamation of pardon.

(Even more unfortunately for Warren — the officer who had first spread the pirate rumors about Kidd — the commodore died just as he reached India. His passenger Ambassador Norris, perhaps infected by the "Wrong Way" spirit, took three months to find the Grand Moghul and deliver an *enormous* treasure in gold, brass cannon, silver flutes, clothes, bagpipes, etc., as well as apologies for the heinous actions of Captain Kidd. All of which led to . . . no new treaty.)

In Port Dolphin, Captain Warren's namesake nephew, with Culliford aboard, waited in vain for his uncle on the *east* coast of Madagascar. At some point, very early in their stay, Culliford and the others got a bit antsy over the fine print of the pardon offer. Certainly, they had accepted a copy of the proclamation, but was that enough? Nephew Warren couldn't grant pardons by himself. His uncle's wrong-way squadron was nowhere to be found.

The men decided, with Culliford taking the lead, to draw up another document. It bears the marks of some out-of-work rum-lovin' clerk holed up in Port Dolphin supporting himself by writing slave sale contracts. (The spelling is too fine for Culliford himself.) This document is a run-on sentence tribute to a partially educated man trying to concoct legalese.

To Mr. Thomas Waring Master of ye Vine Pinck of London

Sir /
Wheras by order of his majesties Commissioners you have Published and Dis-

persed amongst us his majisties Royal Proclamation Declaring his most gracious Intention of Extending his Royal Mercy and pardon towards us wee being Humbly Thankfull for ye same and sensably affected with ye vastness of his majistes mercy and clemency, as in Dutty bound to Earnestly Desier with all possible Expedition to Return to his majisties Dominions to Express our Gratittude & Demonstrate ower Thankfullness by Loyally and obediently Surrendering ower selues to his . . .

The document goes on to request "those subscribed hope you will be pleased to carry as passengers to any parte of his majisties dominions . . . Sept ye 8th 1699."

Only six of the pirates could write their own names. Robert Culliford, taking the quill first in line, signed in a bold, confident hand. Next up was Jon Swann, who crafted a very shaky S. Someone else tried to sign his name but made a blotty mess of it. A couple of the illiterate pirates tried to imitate Swann with a single letter of their surname, but most just settled for an X, next to the likes of "Elizzander Malberer's mark."

At least four of Captain Kidd's original crew, who had gone pirating, endorsed the document.

Captain Warren, with Robert Culliford

along to help, went ashore at Port Dolphin to buy slaves, and there they met John Cruger, a New Yorker with an amazing tale of woe.

(Cruger, then a young man, would forty years later become mayor of New York City; his son — not yet conceived — would also serve as mayor and as president of America's first chamber of commerce.)

John Cruger had left New York harbor aboard the *Prophet Daniel*, in mid-July of 1698, heading for Madagascar and the nearby islands to trade for slaves. Cruger was supercargo (i.e., the owners' rep aboard the ship) on the 90-ton ship carrying the usual cargo of pistols, gunpowder, 300 pounds of colored beads, 33 hats, and an especially broad selection of liquor: wine (500 gallons), rum (12 casks), beer (24 barrels), brandy (10 barrels), and aniseed water (125 gallons).

The *Prophet Daniel* headed east around the Cape of Good Hope, touching at Mattatana on the coast of Madagascar, where Cruger bought fifty-five slaves, and then he arrived in Port Dolphin on August 24, 1699. Cruger immediately went to introduce himself to the local king. And this king was quite a piece of work.

Abraham Samuel was a French-speaking, coffee-colored escaped slave, who had fled Martinique in 1696 to join Captain

Hoare's Rhode Island–based pirate ship, *John and Rebecca*. The highlight of their jaunt in the Red Sea was the capture of a 300-ton Moorish ship, which they carried to St. Mary's Madagascar, intending to enjoy pirate paradise. Abraham Samuel's fun was soon interrupted when that native uprising occurred in the summer of 1697, leading to the death of most of the Europeans. Samuel and a dozen or so others had escaped in a leaky ship floundering southward along the coast and making it all the way to a spot a few miles from the harbor of Port Dolphin, where their ship sank. Samuel, naked, was washed ashore, half dead. The queen mother, ruling alone, came to see the shipwreck and, as she eyed his nude body, she recognized by certain marks that he was her long-lost son, a child that she had had with a Frenchman, during colonial occupation.

The near-drowned man was clothed and crowned King Samuel, and he kept a palace guard of pirates. In the ensuing two years, King Samuel earned himself a reputation for brokering deals for slaves and stolen cargo.

John Cruger of New York City had paid his respects to the king, and told him he wanted to buy one hundred slaves. King Samuel told Cruger that, to do the deal, he would need to accompany him twenty-five miles inland to his country residence.

While Cruger was inland, a New York pirate ship under one Evan Jones cozied up to the *Prophet Daniel* in the harbor. He craftily identified himself as a slaver, and said that he had lost his longboat on the passage there. "Could I have a cast ashore?" he asked. (A "cast" was nautical slang for a lift.) The caretakers of the *Prophet Daniel* agreed, and several of the men rowed in for a little drinking. The crews quickly found common ground since some of Captain Jones's men were from Westchester near New York.

Drinking and whoring completed, they rowed back to their ships, and Captain Evan Jones invited them aboard for some fine rum. They drank for a while, then at nine o'clock by the flickering lantern, Jones gave the signal and the pirates overpowered the men of the *Prophet Daniel*. They took the *Prophet*'s longboat and rowed over and captured the ship; the pirates from Westchester ransacked her, taking all the money and rigging and anything else they fancied. (New Yorkers stealing from New Yorkers halfway around the world.)

A messenger, racing from the port, told King Samuel and Cruger the hard news. When Cruger returned to the coast, he found the pirates aboard both vessels. First he hired some of King Samuel's men to shoot at the ships, but two days of whizzing musket balls did little damage. Then Cruger hired two natives to swim out to cut the two ships' anchor cables so that they would drift ashore.

That's when smiling King Abraham Samuel, the mulatto of Martinique, bared his fangs . . . and his pirate sympathies. He ordered his people "not to meddle." (King Samuel commanded 300 warriors and fifteen war canoes.) The pirates had promised Samuel a fine reward/*pourboire* for his protection. They gave him the *Prophet Daniel* and the fifty-five slaves aboard. King Samuel then sold the New York ship to four pirates for 1,400 pieces of eight. He even handed the new owners an ornate bill of sale, signed by "Abraham Samuel, King of Fort Dauphin, Tollannare, Farrawe, Fanquest, Fownzahira."

Cruger protested. His ranting merely succeeded in prompting King Samuel to confiscate Cruger's property on shore: forty-nine small arms, twenty-two casks of powder, and a set of sails. The *Prophet*'s captain, Henry Appel, and two crewmen decided to turn pirate.

So, John Cruger, future mayor, found himself stranded in inhospitable Port Dolphin in early September of 1699 when Thomas Warren in the *Vine* pink, with his pirates aboard, sailed into the harbor.

Cruger negotiated to hitch a ride on the *Vine* to Barbados for the price of sixty-six pieces of eight, and two slaves.

With the winds shifting to the west (and Uncle Wrong Way nowhere in sight), on Saturday, November 18, 1699, the *Vine* pink set sail. For the next uneventful month, Culliford shared the rail and drinks with the future mayor, then a storm hit and worse.

Winds were lashing the waters off the tip of Africa. On Wednesday, December 20, 1699, Captain Warren guided the *Vine* pink out of the squalls and into the shelter of the Cape of Good Hope. Culliford and the other pirates aboard the *Vine* were pleased to spot Samuel Burgess's *Margaret* anchored there, since it was carrying their pirate pals, whom they hadn't seen since April half a year earlier on St. Mary's. Captain Warren, by now friendly with Culliford, obligingly agreed to sail over to the *Margaret*. Culliford and the rest wanted to tell their friends the extraordinary news about the pardons; they expected Warren to distribute a few more copies.

As the *Vine* neared the *Margaret*, Culliford realized something was wrong: No one called out in greeting, and he didn't recognize any of the sailors on deck. Culliford aboard the *Vine* was sailing, unknowingly, into the clutches of

. . . a pirate hunter.

The *Margaret*'s voyage had gone swimmingly well up until three days earlier. Samuel Burgess, the thirty-year-old captain, had bought 114 slaves on the west coast of Madagascar, following orders from his owner, Fred Phillips. "In buying Negroes . . . take care that you receive none (if possible) but such are choice & likely, most young men and boys, not under fifteen years of age, no old men or women nor none defective in any limbs or sight."

Phillips — perhaps thinking more about profit than compassion — also advised: "Buy enough rice so that Negroes always have their full allowance." The owner promised the captain a 2½ percent share of the profits, giving Burgess a huge incentive to deliver as many slaves as possible alive.

During Burgess's stopover in Tulear, his passengers had been thrilled to find those three copies of the proclamation of pardon that Commodore Warren had left there. The pirates had voted, with Captain Shivers in the lead, to stay in Tulear and await the return of Commodore Warren. But Burgess, not wanting to lose his transport money, countered: "Don't wait among the blacks; come to St. Helena and wait there." The pirates agreed.

Phillips had ordered Burgess to avoid other ships and skip most ports such as the

Cape of Good Hope, but Burgess caught that same foul weather off the tip of Africa. The 114 slaves below deck writhed in seasick misery as the ship bounced from whitecap to whitecap.

Burgess was worried. The waves crashing over the ship might have poured down into the ship's hold and soaked his several tons of rice to feed the slaves. And when rice gets wet, it expands; cases have been reported of sodden sacks of rice swelling so much that they damage the ship, even bust it open. Burgess was taking no chances. If he couldn't feed his slaves, he stood to lose his hefty 2½ percent.

Burgess decided to head into the shelter of the Cape of Good Hope and assess the damages. The guns at the Dutch East India Company fort commanded the harbor while the company's taverns were famed for an enormous selection of liquors. The Cape of Good Hope circa 1700 was one place where the English and Dutch generally got along.

Burgess sailed into Cape harbor around noon on Monday, December 18, flying the St. George's cross of an English merchant ship. He passed several ships on his way to good anchorage by the fort. One of the ships he glided by, without saluting, was the *Loyal Merchant*, an East India Company ship under Captain Matthew Lowth.

Captain Lowth's logbook stated: "He took no manner of notice of me notwithstanding I had ye King's Jack and pendant flying but ran under the ye Dutch fort & saluted ym wth 3 Guns wch they returned."

Captain Lowth was not pleased that he had been disrespected by this small English merchant ship. Lowth regarded himself as even more important than your average regally self-important East India captain because he was carrying a privateering commission from the Admiralty to chase pirates, a similar commission to the one bestowed on Kidd.

Captain Lowth wasn't even supposed to be in the African harbor that afternoon. He had planned to leave three days earlier and had already enjoyed his final feast with the governor, but the squally weather had forced him to wait in the shelter of the mountain-ringed harbor. That's when *Margaret* glided by him.

Lowth sent over his boat full of armed

men, and demanded that the ship's captain come visit him aboard the *Loyal Merchant*. Given that the *Loyal Merchant* had thirty-plus guns and 100-plus men, Burgess had little choice but to comply.

Under questioning, Burgess volunteered that he was a New York slaver, with 110 slaves aboard. The gruff seaman didn't exactly apologize for not saluting. The interview was ending when one of the *Loyal Merchant* crewmen, who had rowed Burgess over, informed Captain Lowth that the other ship was "full of white men all clad with ye East India Companies Cloth." (Burgess's pirate passengers were decked out in shirts and pants made from the stolen bales of fine fabrics taken by the likes of Kidd and bartered on St. Mary's.)

Captain Lowth sent his pinnace back to the *Margaret* to pick up the gaudily clad white men for questioning. With Captain Shivers at the fore, they refused to leave. "We have no business aboard your ship," said Shivers. The three dozen armed Company men boarded; the pirates fought, but the ensuing scuffle was more bravado than blood since the pirates' weapons were locked in Burgess's cabin. But in the fracas, eight of the flashy dressers were able to lower a boat, grab their loot, and paddle to shore.

Lowth's pistol-toting men overpowered

the rest, and hauled the snarling lot aboard the *Loyal Merchant*. Lowth sent a force to occupy the *Margaret*.

The instant the pirates climbed aboard the *Loyal Merchant*, they presented their get-out-of-jail-free card to Captain Lowth. "[We] delivered to him three of the King's Proclamations for pardon and a letter under Commodore Warren's hand," said Joseph Wheeler of Boston, "but Capt. Lowth notwithstanding did seize and detain me and the other passengers and the ship Margaret and all their effects aboard."

The East India Company frequently ignored Crown rulings, especially when this far from home. Top man Sir Josiah Child had once chided an employee: "I expect my Orders to be [the man's] Rules and not the Laws of England, which are an Heap of Nonsense, compiled by a few ignorant Country Gentlemen, who hardly knew how to make Laws for the good Government of their own private Families, much less for the Regulating of Companies and foreign Commerce."

In any case, Captain Lowth was looking at a humongous amount of loot. Wheeler, for example, had 3,600 pieces of eight. Twenty-two-year-old Armand Viola — a surgeon's mate from New York who had left Kidd for Culliford — said he was carrying 2,000 pieces of eight, 800 Lyon dollars, 700 pieces of gold, 18 ounces of broken and bar gold, 25 pounds of silver, 2 gold chains, and a locket worth 105 pieces of eight. How did the young man have so much? He explained that two of his friends had died at Madagascar and left him their shares and that "he had won a great deal at play." Lowth ordered all the pirates chained below deck. The next day, Captain Lowth walked from pirate to pirate, taking depositions. Shivers invented a merry career for himself; Burgess cursed at Lowth, got beaten, then gave a surprisingly accurate account of his pirate days.

Then Lowth went ashore to show Governor van der Stel his bonafide royal commission from the king of England to capture pirates. The governor said he was outraged that Lowth would dare to make any capture inside a *Dutch* harbor. Lowth later cattily charged that the governor was mostly upset about lost profits "disgusted yt a Prize of her Value should slip out of his hands."

While Lowth talked to the governor on shore, the fifteen-person crew of the *Margaret* — sailor Nicholas Whore and carpenter Benjamin Herring, even female negro cook, Maramita — tried to mount an attack against the occupying East India Company men. Armed with knives and frypans, their uprising failed.

Still furious, the Dutch governor sent his deputies over to the *Loyal Merchant* with an official protest. Lowth politely saluted their boat coming and going, but he rejected the protest in a few choice words.

On the following afternoon, Wednesday, December 20, the unsuspecting *Vine* pink came hallooing up to *Margaret*; Culliford stood at the rail, with Swann and future mayor Cruger — they were all blithely sailing into a trap. The *Margaret* was half deserted; strange armed men lounged on deck; Culliford could hear the moans of slaves. Not far off stood the imposing *Loyal Merchant*.

Moments later, the *Loyal Merchant*'s boat arrived at the *Vine*; an officer shouted up, requesting that the *Vine*'s captain accompany him aboard his ship.

"I sent for ye Master, whose name was Thomas Warren," recorded Captain Lowth in his log. "Yt *Vine* pink come from St Maries & has aboard 14 Pyrattes, or as he calls them 'Passengers' whereof Captain Culliford that was Commander of ye *Mocoa* was one. I askt [Captain Warren] some Questions about ye Pyrates, what he knew & likewise his own circumstances. He threw down one of his Majesties Proclamations. I told him they were not made for honest men but for Pyratts & if he had any I would examine them, I showing him my Commission."

The East India captain was more than ready to ignore these pardons that didn't suit him. The Old East India Company especially detested the idea of pardons. "We humbly conceive that particular Pardons will rather encourage than be a means of suppressing [pirates]," the Company's governors had written to the Lords of Trade.

Captain Warren refused to allow his passengers to be taken out of the *Vine*. Warren then added indignantly that if Lowth persisted, he would apply to the Dutch for protection.

Upon hearing that answer, Captain Lowth ordered Captain Warren immediately thrown in irons below deck. Lowth set two guards at the door so that Warren couldn't smuggle any notes ashore to the Dutch governor. It had grown pitch dark, so any attack on the *Vine* pink would have to wait for daylight.

So, at this moment, Captain Shivers was in chains on the *Loyal Merchant* with seventeen other accused pirates. Captain Warren, the slaver, the commodore's nephew, was also in chains on the *Loyal Merchant*. Robert Culliford, escape artist extraordinaire, was now in dire peril.

As the hours wore on into late evening and night, Culliford began to wonder why Captain Warren hadn't returned; he couldn't get a straight answer out of the men aboard the *Margaret*.

At daybreak on the morning of Thursday, December 21, Captain Matthew Lowth loaded his pinnace with forty armed men and had himself rowed toward the tiny *Vine* pink, a mere toy bobbing near his heavily armed merchant-warship.

In the dim morning light, he perceived activity aboard the little ship. Were the handful of pirates fool enough to fight him? When the pinnace reached the *Vine*, he saw at the rail a smiling Robert Culliford . . . in the midst of dozens of armed Dutch soldiers. Culliford had apparently gotten word to the Dutch governor, who had sent one hundred men to protect this English ship from the overly aggressive English company.

The East India captain, Matthew Lowth, undaunted down in his longboat, yelled up that he was coming aboard to take the pirates. A Dutch officer replied that was not permissible. Captain Lowth repeated his intention. The Dutch officer calmly informed him that he would be shot. "I called to ym out of my Boat & told ym I did believe ye King of England would not have any Commission of his trampted under their feet."

The Dutch governor kept 100 men aboard the severely overcrowded *Vine* (92 slaves below deck, 14 passengers, 15 crew). Governor van der Stel was not about to let Lowth defy Holland again and capture *another* ship in this Dutch harbor. Captain Lowth, for his part, continued to occupy the *Margaret*, and hoard its £11,000 in "coins of the universe" and 114 slaves aboard and eighteen pirates. It was something of a standoff, with the fate of rogue Culliford and future mayor Cruger hanging in the balance. The Dutch were not eager to open fire on an ally.

When Lowth returned to the *Loyal Merchant*, he had Captain Warren hauled on deck in irons, and he interrogated him again. Apparently, Lowth hadn't asked very many questions before shackling the man.

Now Lowth probed a bit more deeply and discovered that Warren was under direct orders from the commodore to distribute pardons to pirates and to gather information on pirates. It also seems likely that Warren after a night in irons mentioned in passing that the commodore of the English squadron in the East Indies *was his uncle.*

Suddenly, Captain Lowth's tone began to soften. He asked whether Warren had his orders in writing; he replied that he did. Warren signed a note requesting the rest of his papers from the *Vine*. But before a boat could be sent over, a "hard storm" kicked up. The wind from the northwest lashed the ships, and the sheet anchor of the *Loyal Merchant* came loose. The pirate prisoners in windowless gloom, kept not far from the nauseated slaves, rattled their chains and cursed their captors.

Cabo Tormentoso was living up to its name.

Over on the overcrowded *Vine*, conditions were equally miserable, with 200 people crammed on the tossing ship. While the Dutch had saved Culliford and future mayor Cruger from the immediate threat of the East India Company's pirate hunter, all the passengers aboard the *Vine* were now basically at the mercy of the Dutch.

Saturday, December 23, the weather cleared. The Dutch allowed Captain Warren's papers to be ferried from the *Vine*. Captain Lowth read the letter from Commodore Warren to his nephew. Lowth retreated.

"I cleared [his ship] under my hand & so parted good ffreinds," wrote Matthew Lowth in his log. "I spared him four sacks of rice, some tarr and whatever he wanted." Lowth decided that he would not pursue Culliford or any of Warren's pirate passengers.

Captain Lowth had his new good friend rowed back over to the *Vine*, with his parting gifts. Now Captain Warren had to deal with the Dutch governor. He showed him his orders from his uncle, which the governor had a scribe copy into the official records. After having 100 men aboard the little ship, Governor van der Stel clearly knew there was pirate treasure aboard and almost 100 slaves, but he didn't want to offend the nephew of the commodore, if some agreement could be worked out.

Ultimately, money solved the problem.

Captain Lowth of the East India Company, still under the Dutch guns and surrounded by Dutch men-of-war, decided not to be too niggly over the details of disposing of his prize, *Margaret,* and her cargo. Lowth *claimed* an addendum to his pirate-hunting commission allowed him to dispose immediately of any legitimate prize as long as he kept accurate records. So Captain Lowth decided to sell Frederick Phillips's slaves in the Cape of Good Hope.

Lowth needed the governor's permission to bring slaves ashore and sell them. The two sides haggled. Lowth finally agreed — not happily (he claims he was "forced" to do so) — to pay twenty slaves to the Dutch governor, five more to the man's deputy, and five more to the "fiscal," i.e., local chief of police. (The governor also had collected a few thousand English pounds from the eight pirates who had sneaked ashore.)

By Christmas Day, Culliford and the pirates on the *Vine* looked safe under the halo of Captain Warren.

Arrangements were made for a slave auction to take place in four days. Unfortunately for Lowth, he naively expected a fair auction. The Dutch and French Huguenot merchants at the Cape made little effort to outbid one another. Lowth received thirty pieces of eight (£7½) for able-bodied young men, with prices ranging down to twenty pieces of eight for the unhealthy ones and the children. "Indeed, is but giving away," complained Lowth in his log. Lowth also wanted to sell the *Margaret* itself, and he found a couple of local merchants willing to pay a fair price for the ship, but the governor ruled that Lowth could sell the ship only to the Dutch East India Company, which offered him a pittance.

Captain Warren and the pirate passengers decided not to linger. The next day, Thursday, December 28, Warren asked Captain Lowth if he would accept a parting salute from him; Lowth agreed. The gunner aboard the diminutive pink, while passing the towering *Loyal Merchant*, shot off five blasts. The *Loyal Merchant* answered with five.

The *Vine*, carrying Robert Culliford and the future New York City mayor, glided out to sea. Culliford still had his treasure, and his proclamation of pardon.

(Burgess and Shivers and the rest were obviously not so fortunate. Captain Lowth would carry them on a five-month journey in shackles to Bombay, where company officials told them they would have to be hauled back to *England* to stand trial. Captain Shivers, who had helped Robert Culliford pull off the richest capture in the history of East Indies piracy, died in a Bombay prison. So did almost a dozen others before Matthew Lowth returned to ferry the survivors, including Sam Burgess, to London.)

Robert Culliford, meanwhile, aboard the *Vine* began the 1,500-mile run from the Cape to the island of St. Helena.

St. Helena is probably best known today as the final exile of Napoleon, a speck above the waves far from Europe. Back then, the mountainous island was known as the save-the-men-from-scurvy stopping point.

First discovered by the Portuguese in 1502 on St. Helen's Day, the forty-seven-square-mile fruitful island in 1658 was the *first* piece of property claimed by the English East India Company, whose holdings would mushroom into the British Empire in India. The Dutch trading company snatched this strategic water hole a couple of times but the English Company grabbed it back.

St. Helena, dubbed the "Sea Inn," was a hospitable stopover, with plentiful food, especially beef from cattle raised from imported English stock. William Dampier, the privateer, observed that scurvy-wracked seamen, who needed to be toted ashore slung in hammocks, were up and dancing in a week.

The *Vine* pink reached the half-moon shaped harbor of St. Helena on February 2, 1700. They could see a small English town, with stone houses, nestled  in a valley between two small mountains. Captain Warren had fulfilled his promise to set the pirates ashore on English territory. Robert Culliford and three others debarked. "I had no authority to detain him," later deposed Captain Warren. Culliford said good-bye to Jon Swann, who decided he preferred the warm Caribbean to England's harsh winters and would continue on to Barbados.

Robert Culliford stayed in the Sea Inn for a few weeks, looking to book passage to London. William Dampier said that around this time, St. Helena could be a joyous place for a visiting sailor — mostly because the daughters of the English settlers looked upon marrying a sailor as their best hope for leaving this remote island. Dampier described the women, from English parents, as "well-shaped, proper and comely." Quick marriages — or promises of marriage — were not unusual.

No doubt, Robert Culliford partook in one way or another of the charming women who ventured to the punch houses in the harbor.

Culliford discarded his home-sewn suits of East India cloth and bought English garments. He could afford to deck himself out in a fine silver-button waistcoat, pumps, and a new hat.

The East India Company's ship *Sidney*, a merchant man-of-war behemoth with forty guns and a crew of 133, was heading home to England. Robert Culliford and fellow St. Mary's pirate Ralph Patterson — both carrying proclamations of pardon — booked a ride on the Company ship. Paying for their passage, they were treated as passengers. Culliford had the menials carry aboard his locked and corded chest full of gold and silver.

By March 15, 1700, Robert Culliford, traveling in style, with treasure and pardon, was gliding north to England. He could wander the deck of the *Sidney* and share rums with his traveling companions. When they crossed the equator, he could participate in the silly "rites of passage" celebrations. Culliford appeared triumphant on his return voyage.

Captain Kidd, on the other hand, on that same day in March, was also shipboard, heading to England. He was below deck in chains on HMS *Advice*, the ship racing eastward on strong cold North Atlantic winds.

London: Road to English Justice

Chapter Seventeen

"The Earth's my own, I give it as I please,
And to my Vice-Roy, Kidd, I gave the Seas."

— Political Lampoon
skewering Lord Somers

The House of Commons prepared for the arrival of Captain Kidd in the same way Roman lions prepared for a Christian. They had expected him in January, then February, now it was the middle of March. Not since the days of Francis Drake and John Hawkins, or, more recently, Henry Morgan, had a privateer accused of piracy so dominated the English political scene.

"Never has a scandal made more noise," opined the French ambassador Comte de Tallard in a secret report to the French king. Neither hyperbole nor loose diction,

618

that assessment came from a man who had been running a spy network for years.

Kidd ranked as such a huge scandal for the reason that word had leaked out that King William himself and four of the most powerful Whig ministers were secret backers of Kidd's mission. Although printed on Kidd's commission were the names of four little-known investors — William Rowley, a stable groom, a tenant farmer, et al. — the whispers were becoming louder that these men were mere shills for the noblemen: Shrewsbury, Orford, Somers, Romney. The king and these lords were now all accused of hiring a pirate to steal for them. Hiring a privateer to attack the French and pirates was most honorable; hiring a pirate to attack friendly nations was treason. Treason convictions often involved public removal of body parts.

Kidd's captures came at a time when the English monarchy was still surprisingly fragile, half a century from Charles I losing his head, a mere decade from James II being ousted over his Catholic daydreams and absolutist ways. And now factions poked at this imported Dutchman's perch upon the throne, looking to chip away at his power and give it over to Parliament.

These were the early days of political parties in England, and since all of Kidd's backers were Whigs, it made perfect sense that the Tories, the opposition party, ached to interrogate Kidd. They salivated to ask him the one burning question, one that might topple ministers and undermine a king: "Were you, William Kidd, hired to commit piracy?"

The question hung in the air, while the sails of the HMS *Advice* carried the rogue to England. (Everyone assumed he was a rogue; the question was whether the Scot-American captain was a freelancing rogue or a hired one.)

In the meantime, the Tories filled pamphlets and coffeehouses with angry accusations. "Our rulers have laid hold of our lands, our woods, our mines, our money," thundered Jack Howe, Tory, in Commons. "And this is not enough, we cannot send a cargo to the furthest ends of the earth, but they must send a gang of thieves after it."

The Tories grew rabid over Kidd. One harangued with all-world exaggeration: "This [Kidd] grant has beggared Ireland, set Scotland in a flame and ruined England."

Political parties are slippery beasts to define. The Tory platform had opportunistically evolved away from High Church and king after the Whigs gained the ear of King William. So, in Captain Kidd's day, Tory became associated with "Good ol' England," a land where government should be frugal, taxes low, individual rights respected, standing armies avoided.

A platform makes for good copy but the month-to-month reality in the loud scrum of Commons was that each party fought the other for control of the goodies, the dispensing of jobs and estates to their relatives and stalwarts. "There is such a noise," wrote Sir Richard Cocks (Whig) of his first session in Commons, "[that] one can scarce hear or mind what is said, and indeed what is particularly minded is private business, to make parties [alliances], to make court."

After news of Kidd's arrest reached England in late summer of 1699, as the rumors grew louder about the identity of Kidd's backers, the Tories used the opportunity to take especial aim at the arrogant Whig members of the Kit Cat Club.

Much of the real business of government took place then not in Whitehall or St. Stephens, but in a place called the Kit Cat Club, where the Whig elite gathered privately. Never accepting more than forty-eight members (half were usually peers of the realm), the club moved from a literary drinking clique to preeminent power broker. (The name came from Christopher Cat's tavern where early meetings were held.) All of Kidd's backers were members;

summers, they convened at the Flask Inn in Hempstead.

When the Kidd scandal was broached in the House of Commons, the Tories shaped the debate on December 6 to hinge on whether Kidd's original commission was legal. "If the grantees begged only the goods of the pirates themselves, then they begged frivolously and ridiculously," said a Tory acidly. "No doubt their aim was at the merchants Goods taken by pirates."

Could the king grant Kidd the right to bring back stolen goods to share among the investors without the Admiralty or justice involved?

The Whigs defended themselves, pointing out that the king included the phrase *quantum in nobis est* (as much as in our power).

One Tory inquired of Sir Cocks the name of his family estate. Cocks replied, "Dumberton." The Tory then asked: would it be acceptable for the king to grant away Dumberton *quantum in nobis est?*

The debate on December 6 had raged on for nine brutal hours. Candles had to be brought to St. Stephens: the faces in ghastly shadows, framed by mantles of curled, powdered hair, mouths agape with indignation. The unventilated chamber was rank with sweat and perfume and burnt tallow.

"A pirate is an enemy of mankind," said the Whig solicitor general, John Hawles. "By the law of nations, every man, without a commission from any prince, is empowered to take and destroy him, and may hang him at the yard arm."

Throughout the entire debate, no member of Parliament, no Tory or Whig, ever once broached that Kidd might not be a pirate. Both sides assumed Kidd was a pirate: the Tories delighting that he was a pirate and the Whigs claiming that he wasn't *our* pirate.

Finally, the issue came to a vote. Was the grant to the Earl of Bellomont and others, of pirate goods "dishonourable to the king, against the law of nations, contrary to the laws and statutes of the realm, an invasion of property, and destructive of trade and commerce"?

The vote came down: 133 that it was dishonorable and 189 that it was not. The Whigs had survived; the king had avoided the insult . . . for now.

Everyone waited for Captain Kidd to arrive to ask him the one *burning* question. Would he bolster the Tories, and admit he was hired to go a-pirating for the Whig lords and king? Could the Tories get such an admission from Kidd by dangling a pardon? Could the Whigs buy his silence with their own offer of a pardon? What would sway him? Where was truth in all this?

But the House of Commons, nearing the end of its session, could have no way of knowing (in those days before ship-to-shore radio) where on the Atlantic was the HMS *Advice*. On March 16, 1700, the House of Commons proposed to the king that Captain Kidd should *not* be allowed to be tried, discharged, or pardoned until the *next* session of Parliament. (Back then, the king controlled when Parliament met and disbanded.)

The Tories feared Kidd might arrive after their session, then be tried and executed before they could ask *the burning question*. Or the king might pardon and exile him before they asked it.

King William agreed on March 25 to the Commons' request, which meant that Captain Kidd — after eight months in Boston prison uncharged — would now spend close to a year in a London prison, once again uncharged. "How far such an Address could by Law be complied with is not for me to determine," wrote one Whig pamphleteer, "but it seems not very consistent with the Habeas Corpus Act, which ought to be very sacred." (*Habeas Corpus*, dating back to the fourteenth century, was and still is a much-prized English safeguard against prisoners being locked up without due process.)

Kidd's immediate fate was sealed. So were his living arrangements in Newgate Prison.

The HMS *Advice*, at that moment the world's most expensive prisoner transport ship, raced across the frigid North Atlantic. Kidd was shackled in a windowless, unheated cabin in steerage, attended by two Malagasy slave children. (Their names are not recorded but they too would be sent to prison, identified only as "Kidd's boy and girl.")

Every so often a rumble of gruff voices or of rowdy songs came from the thirty-one prisoners locked in the gunroom; each man got a half gallon of beer and a couple ounces of rum a day. The lot included Kidd's loyal crewmen, the apprentices, Edward Davies (stout passenger), James Gilliam (circumcised rogue), Tee Witherly (eye-patched young pirate), and others, all chained together. Also down there were two "blacks": Ventura Rosair, sixtyish cook from Ceylon, and Dundee, Kidd's young man slave.

A calm, the dying of winds, might prolong their lives, postponing their trial, but instead the breezes blew strong and mostly steady. The ship crossed the North Atlantic in a dazzling twenty-two days, with the warship making 264 miles on its best day.

Captain Kidd spent much of his waking hours writing. Under the watchful eye of Bellomont's jailor in Boston, Kidd had been denied quill and paper. Now aboard the HMS *Advice*, he had access to both, maybe thanks to his wife's handing over that gold ring to Captain Wynn.

Writing furiously, Kidd dipped his quill in the chilled ink and scratched out at least twenty-five long letters to various people, to lawyers, to friends in England; most importantly, he wrote a long detailed journal of his voyage, a document that was stitched together into three parcels. Kidd did not waste his time; he began orchestrating his defense. The roll of the ship comforted him after the stagnancy of Boston's prison; however, the steady forward easterly progress he no doubt found disturbing.

The HMS *Advice* did indeed roar across the Atlantic, but, unfortunately, Captain Wynn missed the English Channel. By "dead reckoning" (plotting the course and tossing the log to calculate speed), the captain knew he had reached the vicinity of the tip of Cornwall. Tossing the lead revealed coastal depths of fifty-five fathoms; embedded in the wax tip was brown sand and fine white shells. But the hazy weather denied him the opportunity of a crisp noon reading of north-south latitude. The *Advice* reached the motherland about eighty miles too far north. Strong westerly winds were forcing the ship upon Lundy Island, a sliver of land north of Barnstable Bay. The date was April 1, 1700. Wynn's pleasure at sighting land was spoiled by brisk winds driving the ship upon the lee shore; Captain Wynn thought it safest to anchor until the winds shifted.

On April 3, despairing of sailing right away to loop back south around Cape Cornwall, the captain decided to send an "express" to London to alert the Admiralty of Kidd's arrival.

Captain Wynn ordered the men to swing out the pinnace and row a "young gentleman," John Shorter, over to Lundy Island. His expense account shows him ferried to Clovaly in Barnstable Bay, and from there hiring post horses for the 195-mile journey: to Torrington, to Cholmly, to Exeter, to Hunnington, to Crookhorn, to Sherborn, to Shaston, to Salisbury, to An- dover, to Basingstroke, to Herreforbridge, to Backshot, to Staines, to London.

Saddle-weary, swaddled in road dust, Shorter reached the metropolis late at night on April 5, and went immediately to the Admiralty office. Minutes later, the clerk on duty ordered the message of Kidd's arrival relayed to the secretary of state, James

Vernon. Here was a man who was a commoner, who through sheer competence as Duke of Shrewsbury's assistant, had risen to an exalted position. (James Vernon was the father of Admiral Edward Vernon, for whom Mount Vernon, future home of George Washington, would be named.)

Vernon — who would play a lead role for the king in handling the Kidd affair — combined self-deprecation with immense clear thinking. He was a commoner amidst the wealthy lords but King William III, himself a outsider, seemed to value him. Fifty-four-year-old Vernon had lost all his teeth, and wavered before accepting the exalted position of secretary of state. He complained that he was "without quality, without friends, without an estate, without elocution . . ." Vernon even said he thought he might "fill [his] pockets with stones and leap overboard under the bridge." Vernon took the job, having crisply relayed his message of humility.

The Kidd news reached Vernon, and he immediately wrote to his patron (and Kidd backer), the Duke of Shrewsbury: "[Captain Wynn] says he will go about [i.e., turn the ship] as soon as he can, but I wish he were here now before Parliament rises, that they might take [Kidd's] examination, and determine what should be done with him."

The secret of Kidd's arrival off the west

coast remained a secret till about dawn; within two days it was common knowledge, and then publicly announced. The House of Commons was still in session and Kidd could have been delivered there within a week. Instead the Tory leaders decided to let the Whigs slowly stew in their scandal.

"While the [Kidd case] remained imperfectly examined there was room for Reflections and Surmises," wrote a Whig pamphleteer, "and perhaps 9 or 10 months Imprisonment might prepare a Profligate Man, when he knew his Life depended on it, to say that which he might be Unprepared for on a suddain."

The Admiralty rushed strict orders back to Captain Wynn to keep Kidd *absolutely incommunicado* and to proceed to the Downs, naval anchorage off Kent; duplicate copies of those orders were sent to the Downs, Spithead, Plymouth, and Falmouth to avoid any chance of missing Captain Wynn, perhaps already en route. At the same time, the Admiralty ordered that John Cheeke, marshall, proceed to the Downs in the *Katherine* yacht to carry Kidd back to Greenwich.

He too was ordered to keep Kidd under glass: prevented from sending or receiving letters, or even speaking "with any person whatsoever." (Ironically, the *Katherine* was the same yacht that Kidd had failed to salute almost four years earlier.)

The HMS *Advice* reached the Downs on April 10. Captain Wynn sent Lieutenant Daniel Hunt (whom Lord Bellomont had assigned as caretaker of the treasure) to carry two sealed wooden boxes full of all the Kidd-related documents to the secretary of state, James Vernon. (Lord Bellomont had carefully chosen Vernon over merchant Sir Edmund Harrison, who had volunteered for the job.)

The *Katherine* yacht reached the Downs on April 11, carrying the Admiralty marshall and two files of soldiers. The nascent empire was closing in on Kidd.

William Kidd, shackled below deck, now tried to do what little he could to save himself. He waited till all was quiet and, thanks to a needle stolen by his slave girl, he sewed pages of documents into the lining of his waistcoat.

He also quickly wrote two more letters, in passionate self-defense, to Lord Orford of the Admiralty, who had helped him fight the press gang years ago, and to Lord Romney. "If anything be accounted a crime, 'twas so far contrary to my sentiments that I should have thought myself wanting in my duty, had I not done the same," contended Kidd. "I am in hopes that your Lordship and the rest of the honourable gentlemen my owners will so far vindicate me that I may have no injustice, and I fear not at all upon an equitable and impartial tryal, my innocence will justifie me to your Lordships and the world."

Kidd added — just in case justice wasn't enough of a motivator — that the *Adventure Prize* still contained £90,000, "and I doubt not when I am clear of this trouble to bring the same for England without any diminution."

Captain Kidd entrusted these life-preserving letters to Captain Wynn, who had treated him civilly throughout the voyage. Kidd also handed to Wynn his long journal he had written "contained in three parcels."

The *Katherine* yacht anchored nearby. At noon, Marshall Cheeke and the soldiers boarded the *Advice*. The drummers hammered out a little solemnity. Marshall Cheeke hoisted the chained Captain Kidd over the side and into the pint-sized *Katherine* yacht. Captain Wynn was ordered to accompany the prisoner to London.

The *Katherine* set sail for London. On that day, the House of Commons ended its session, guaranteeing Kidd a long stint in prison.

As the *Katherine* plyed the winds to the Thames, Secretary of State Vernon, over the protests of certain of the lords, decided the best strategy would be to deliver those two wooden boxes of papers to the Admiralty to be opened publicly, even though some of the Lords of the Admiralty were Tories. Vernon's reasoning was that they had absolutely nothing to hide: a patriotic venture had gone bad through the villainy of Captain Kidd. Any attempt to hide information would be perceived as admission of conspiracy and guilt.

The Admiralty clerks, logging in the chests' fifty-plus documents, were stupendously cautious, revealing themselves as one genuinely terrified bunch of bureaucrats. Item twelve on one list states: "a little bit of paper putt between two bundles."

Many of the letters were read aloud at the Admiralty office, giving the Whigs that desired aroma of openness. (What Vernon had failed to consider was the catty writing style of penniless Governor Bellomont.)

Vernon later commented that although he was sure that Bellomont didn't expect his letter to be read aloud, "he might have considered upon what occasion he was writing, and under what circumstances, which made it very improper to show any appetite for those goods."

Bellomont's letter about divvying the pirate treasure and giving "snacks" to all the lords was read aloud, as was his comment that he didn't feel himself "obliged in honour and conscience" to share any of the new profits with Sir Edmund Harrison, because the merchant had given him "a terrible hard Presbyterian grip" when the lord couldn't raise money back in 1695.

The *Katherine* continued for London; on Saturday, April 13, the little ship sailed under the forbidding guns at Deptford, guarding the mouth of the Thames.

Around four in the afternoon the *Katherine* reached Greenwich. Captain Wynn, whom Kidd had asked to deliver those life-or-death letters to Lords Orford and Romney, decided he valued his career over the friendship of the world's most notorious pirate. Wynn sent the two letters by messenger to the Admiralty. He accompanied the little packet with a polite note asking what he should do with Captain Kidd's journal.

Sunday morning at dawn, Marshall Cheeke began preparations to bring Captain Kidd ashore. He searched Captain Kidd, and instead of finding the concealed weapons he was probably looking for, he discovered instead hidden in the lining of Kidd's waistcoat twenty-five pages sewn together. Kidd struggled not to hand them over. And it was then, on that morning, that Captain Kidd, who had remained so strong through the New England winter in Stone Prison as well as through a shackled voyage in the belly of the warship *Advice*, finally broke down. He threw a "fitt"; he ranted, cursed, kicked, acted like a chained bear with a dozen imaginary pit bulls nipping at him. His shackles dented the oak door jambs; he bloodied the guards; he terrified his slave children; and then he passed out in a sweaty clammy heap. A few moments later, Kidd awoke, queasy and feverish.

"After he recovered from the fitt he had," Marshall Cheeke later told the board, "[Captain Kidd] took out a Piece of Gold and gave it to [my] Deputy and desired him to send it to his wife [Sarah], for that he believed he should die, since his Papers were gone."

Kidd's giving away this coin, close to his last money in the world, was a remarkable gesture, an act selfless, demented, lovelorn. One gold coin could support him for a month or more in prison; the deputy — even with this hollow-eyed "pirate" giving him the stare — would never deliver the money.

Kidd released his grip on the deputy, regained his composure, and told him: "If I'm condemned, I hope to be shot and not suffer the shameful death of hanging." Then he asked the man to hand over his knife that he might honorably take his own life. He did not want to be paraded through London to the gallows — with his absolute utter unspeakable shame thrust in his face at every corner by every lout and doxy.

He did not want to entertain them with that five minute or longer gruesome dance of death and the inevitable piss stain.

Captain Kidd, the man once in control, the man who gave orders, was unraveling.

The Admiralty board asked the marshall if Kidd was well enough to come to be interrogated. (No one, especially none of the Tories, wanted Captain Kidd to die . . . yet.)

At two-thirty Sunday afternoon the Admiralty board decided to send its barge to Greenwich to pick up Kidd and Captain Wynn and the marshall and some of the soldiers. At three-thirty, the barge delivered Captain Kidd to the waterside stairs near the Admiralty office by Whitehall. From there, the shackled Kidd was put in an enclosed sedan chair and carried amid a file of soldiers to the ornate Admiralty. He had stepped foot in England for all of three steps.

The Admiralty lords were there to interrogate him: Earl of Bridgewater, Lord Haversham, Sir George Rooke, others. They interrogated him twice over the course of *seven hours*. A clerk wrote down his answers at each session, and afterward, he signed both documents, as did the board. At eleven o'clock, the two depositions by Kidd were folded over and each member of the board applied his seal. Kidd's words were to be held for a year unviewed until the next session of the House of Commons. Much of the city, and the better-informed in the English countryside, wanted to know what Kidd had answered to the burning question about piracy.

The Admiralty board's minutes stated no more than: "Captain Kidd was called in and particularly examined as to the severall Pyracies layd to his charge, which Examination being read to him, he set his Name to it and then the Board signed it."

James Vernon, a day later, cornered Sir George Rooke, an Admiralty lord, and found out what Kidd had said (and quickly relayed it in a letter to the Duke of Shrewsbury). "Kidd tells . . . that he was employed for the *seizing of pirates* . . . ; only as to his own committing piracy he would excuse himself that his seamen forced him to what was done. He gave a plain account who were his owners, and what the fitting out the ship cost; but he said he never saw either my Lord Chancellor [Somers] or your Grace [Shrewsbury]; he had been once with my Lord Romney, but oftener with my Lord Orford, and had been alone with him. . . . He said my Lord Bellomont brought him one day to your Grace's office. His Lordship then had the proposal in his hand, he saw him speak to me, but he could not tell what either of us said. I believe it might be so, for I remember to have seen [Kidd] once, but had no discourse with him." The spy focused almost exclusively on the pirate's *contact with the lords*.

Vernon also mentioned that Kidd was prevented from sending letters to two lords. Not hiding his distaste, Vernon added: "I imagine the fellow would make them believe he was innocent and recommend himself to their protection."

At eleven o'clock on Sunday night, the lords of the Admiralty finished with Kidd. They issued an order stating that since Kidd was accused of piracy, they therefore committed him to Newgate Prison. They further commanded the Newgate keeper to allow Kidd pen, ink, and paper but *only* for writing to the Admiralty board. If Kidd's health declined, the keeper was to alert the Board. "He was particularly advised not to permit any person whatever to converse with him during his imprisonment." Kidd was fated yet again to be put into solitary confinement for months, an unusual prison accommodation in that age of open barracks rooms.

While the Admiralty clerks finished writing up the orders, Captain Wynn of the HMS *Advice* — who had received that touching keepsake ring from Sarah Kidd — came before the board and delivered Captain Kidd's journals, a memoir that would never be seen again.

Just before midnight on Sunday, April 14, Captain Kidd in shackles, surrounded by a file of soldiers, was led by Marshall Cheeke down to the Admiralty Barge. Transportation by water was always preferred, especially downstream, and Kidd, amid the beer-breathed soldiers who had waited nine hours, glided half a mile to Black Friars Stairs. The barge docked and the man in shackles was escorted uphill near Bridewell and St. Bridget's workhouse, their inhabitants, mostly former prostitutes and beggars, allowed idleness only in sleep. By now the lamplighter had done his job, but still the streets of London were vast stretches of darkness with pools of weak light. One such mobile pool of light was the lanterns carried by the marshall and his men as they walked Captain Kidd to Newgate Prison, a black five-story hulking presence on the corner of Newgate and Holborn Street.

Kidd was exhausted, sick, angry. The marshall and his soldiers made an unholy ruckus at the enormous thick wood door, studded and strapped with iron. Hanging above the entrance dangled an enormous pair of shackles, a size suited for Gargantua or Gulliver.

Keeper Fells opened the massive door and Marshall Cheeke and Kidd were immediately hit by the stench. Unwashed humanity and unemptied chamberpots marinated for years to produce an odor that rivaled in vileness the hold of a slave ship. The men at the door fought down the urge to retch; keeper Fells, long inured, invited them in. The long line of soldiers standing behind Kidd instantly alerted Fells that this was no common prisoner.

Cheeke presented orders to Fells, who carried his lantern over to a rack of shackles, from tight small ones, with short chains, to huge heavy ones that could wear out a bull. The time-honored perq for the keeper at Newgate called for him to apply the shackles and then negotiate a payment (or "garnish") from the prisoner for their removal.

Fells, having heard of Kidd's immense treasure, selected a ponderous pair. Cheeke unlocked the Admiralty irons, Fells clamped the Newgate shackles over Kidd's wrists and ankles. The weary captain, almost delirious in the stench and darkness, shuffled forward, his irons rattling on the stone.

Wanting the maximum profit, Fells led him to the Condemned Hold, a horrendous pitch-black inside room, fifteen feet by twenty, stone floor, ringbolts. The only bed was a wooden cot, more of a shelf with no mattress and no linens. The slop bucket was full. Fells rousted the two condemned men out to keep Kidd in isolation. New prisoners paid two shillings, sixpence to exit the room.

Fells led Kidd to the wooden bed. The heavy door moved on its creaking hinges, the key turned in the lock; the bolts slid across. Kidd was alone.

The pitch blackness made the walls and everything else disappear. All that remained was the sound of his own breathing.

Newgate Prison was an especially grim stone hulk, so dark on the inside that the jailor made a minor fortune selling candles. And everything was for sale. Everything. On the common (i.e., petty thief) side, the right to sleep one to a bed, two to a bed could be purchased, as well as a change of bed linens. Basic accommodations ranged from sleeping on the damp stone floor below ground level to a wooden cot on one of the higher floors.

The government had budgeted a grand remodeling after the Great Fire of London, but most of the money was poured into dolling up the outside, with the likes of four life-sized statues whose themes the inmates found ironic: Liberty, Justice, Truth, and Mercy. More fitting? Greed, Cruelty, Sex, and Filth.

The goal of the jailor was to extract as much money as possible from the prisoner before his release or death. Newgate, like most large prisons then, ran a tavern. Male *and female* prisoners, especially those with money, had what was called the "Liberty of Newgate" to wander to the taproom, which on the master felon side was a cellar below ground. The "cellarman" sold rum and brandy for four pennies a quart, while wine cost six times that. "It is an Encouragement to Vice, that the most dissolute of both Sexes, and generally young People too, should live promiscuously in the same Place, and have Access to one another," opined Dr. Bernard Mandeville in his *Enquiry into the Causes of the Frequent Executions at Tyburn* (1725). "The licentiousness of the place is abominable, there are no Jests so filthy, no Maxims so destructive to good manners or Expressions so vile and prophane, but what are uttered there with Applause and repeated with Impunity. They eat and drink what they can purchase, every Body has Admittance to them, and they are debarr'd from nothing but going out. . . . This keeps them up in De-bauchery."

Newgate tavern was, in short, the party hall of the damned.

There, female prisoners sold sexual favors for coins or drinks, and did so with a certain fervor, since a confirmed pregnancy could delay or cancel a trip to the gallows. The prisoner then could "plead the belly."

"Women of every ward of this prison are exceedingly worse than the worst of the men," wrote an anonymous pamphleteer in 1727, "not only in respect to nastiness and indecency of living, but more especially as to their conversation, which is profane and wicked as hell itself."

Veterans of the place also played a little ritualized game with newcomers, charging a fee from those who desired the right to keep their clothes and shoes. "Pay or strip" were the magic words. Perhaps no place in England was lewder, more foul-mouthed, more dangerous, with a more genuine gallows humor than the tavern at Newgate.

Kidd awoke the next morning feverish, wearing the same clothes he would wear night and day for a month until the Admiralty allowed his trunk delivered from the prison ship.

When Kidd's cell door opened that afternoon, he could hear snatches from the taprooms on the master and common side, hoarse voices of men and women, songs, shouts, groans. Kidd could only listen; he was denied the "Liberty of Newgate." His only visitor was grim Fells, or that turn-key's assistant.

And so it went for a week, wretched empty day after wretched empty day. Kidd, not well, in chains, and Fells, visiting daily to deliver food and try to tempt the supposedly wealthy pirate to spend money . . . a roast chicken, sir, a wench, your leg irons removed. The two men haggled for ten days over the chains. Fells was cunning; he had several times dodged charges of helping escapees or selling forbidden privileges. Captain Kidd — stubborn as ever, or beyond caring, or simply broke, or, more likely, all three — refused to pay the standard extortion. He wrote a note to the Admiralty requesting the leg irons be removed.

For their part, the Lords of the Admiralty and their clerks were quite busy, trying to interrogate thirty-seven pirate prisoners, and sorting through the treasure chests and the reams of documents. Joseph Palmer of Westchester was brought in; he told much about Kidd, but, as for his own career, he failed to recall that he had sailed with pirate Captain Culliford and received around £500 for his trouble. The board also examined the circumcised rogue

Gilliam, who as usual denied everything. "I am Sampson Marshall, a respectable merchant." The board sent a messenger to the East India Company informing them that unless the Company had evidence that Gilliam was part of the *Mocha* mutiny or some other piracy, he would have to be allowed to pay bail. (The issue of bail for Kidd was never broached.)

They committed all the pirates (including Kidd's young apprentice boys like Barleycorn) as well as Palmer, Gilliam, and Edward Davies, to Marshalsea Prison in Southwark, the Admiralty's place for pirates.

Fortunately for them, while no picnic in Chelsea, at least doing time in Marshalsea — with mostly debtors and pirates — was easier than logging months at Newgate.

Blessed with a large courtyard, Marshalsea allowed prisoners a chance at exercise, even sometimes skittles or tennis. The indoor accommodations, however, were extremely cramped, with three men to a narrow bed not uncommon. And its taproom, less dangerous than Newgate's, was amply supplied. One summer weekend, the keeper admitted selling 600 pots of beer to 100 prisoners and their guests. "Gaolers . . . not only connive but promote drunkenness and midnight revels," ran one report, "so that most of our gaols are riotous ale-houses and brothels."

After ten days at Newgate, Kidd was still in shackles in his stinking clothes, denied the taproom, visitors, or lawyers or *letters*. The man was marooned, and his man Friday was dour Fells.

On April 23, 1700, some members of the Admiralty board worried that confining an uncharged prisoner in strict solitary was illegal. Ten years earlier, Dutch William, pre-coronation, had signed a "Rights of Man" agreement, preserving Englishmen's liberties, such as bail and habeas corpus. Kidd's incarceration smacked more of a Louis or a Caesar, not England's hard-won compromise between hereditary monarch and elected Parliament. So they called in the nation's attorney general and solicitor general to advise them.

"They were asked whether that Matter [of no lawyers, visitors or correspondence] was agreeable to Law," according to board notes for that session. "They answered that such strict directions had been given in case of Treason and not otherwise [and] then it had been done by the King in Council."

The lords on the board were at first disturbed by the answer, but then the attorney added: "I can't see any harm in it."

That simple phrase from the nation's ranking prosecutor seems to have won the day. After more discussion, they both agreed that if the chief motive in keeping Kidd incommunicado was to prevent his escaping, then it was allowable.

So the Admiralty kept Kidd in isolation. Since almost no one escaped Newgate, their motives were clear: Kidd was locked away from any tampering by Whig or Tory. (The board, perhaps sensing the unjustness of its actions, debated whether to require the attorney general to return to *sign* his opinion.)

Next came the discussion of Kidd's leg irons, and without comment, the board decided to order them removed. Kidd was broke, and Fells lost a payday.

The Admiralty board called in Lieutenant Hunt, who delivered the keys for opening Kidd's chests; papers were inventoried and the treasure was weighed; a goldsmith reported the gold and silver weighed even more than the invoice promised. The board then found time to interrogate Kidd's four black slaves.

Dundee, the young black whom Kidd had bought at Madagascar, had remained imprisoned in the gunroom aboard the HMS *Advice*. The board requested that the East India Company send over translators, but neither the one speaking Portuguese nor the other fluent in the dialects of India could understand Dundee. The other "black" was Ventura Rosair, a sixty-year-old from Ceylon, who claimed that an East India Company ship had abandoned him in Madasgascar and that he had signed on to be Captain Kidd's cook. His English was very shaky.

No one ever specifically accused the young Malagasy, Dundee, or gray-haired Ventura Rosair of committing any piracies. The East India Company knew nothing about them. Nonetheless, those two along with Captain Kidd's child slaves, "a boy and a girl," were remanded to Marshalsea Prison "on suspicion of piracy," until the Admiralty could decide what to do with them.

These four blacks got a glimpse of the extraordinary metropolis of London, of the massive buildings lining the Thames, the Tower, the Bridge, as they were ferried to Marshalsea Prison, where they arrived without a penny.

Without money or friends in that overcrowded place, they got no beds. The "pay or strip" left them in rags. Their food allowance was sixpence a day, moldy bread, rancid beer if they could get it down before it was stolen.

About now, a strange thing happened. Amid all this tight-fisted behavior toward the prisoners, the jailor at Marshalsea (and the Admiralty board later approved his actions) went out of his way to buy clothes for Kidd's two young slaves. The expense account stated: "Bought for the black boy and girl: 2 prs. of shoes (3 shillings, sixpence); 2 prs of stockings (one shilling fourpence); 4 shirts (eight shillings); for mending a pair of shoes (seven pence); for a pr of breeches (four shillings), for two petticoats and a gowne (sixteen shillings); for a pair of stockings and shoes for ye girl (two shillings, sixpence), for mending 2 prs of shoes (seven pence)."

This long list of clothes, which were bought only for the black children and not for the pirate prisoners, at first glance seems amply compassionate. However, it should be pointed out that healthy pirates were worth almost nothing to the jailor, but these slave children were each worth about £15 on London's slave market, an amount equal to a year's wages for many in London.

And maybe the girl, a Malagasy with toffee-colored skin and almond eyes, was worth more. While at Marshalsea Prison, she might have been able to earn a few extra shillings for the jailor. (Over the next few months this slave girl, never identified by a name, drifted from the records, the *only one* of the prisoners related to Captain Kidd whose fate cannot be traced.)

The Admiralty board continued to take

care of business. It ignored the claims of the *St. Antonio*'s owners in the Caribbean, and finished the paperwork for registering the vessel in the Royal Navy fleet. No one who had used the *St. Antonio* had yet been convicted of any crime, and the owners claimed that Burke had sold what didn't belong to him. None of this slowed the government's acquisition of the swift little ship.

Captain Kidd, over in that cold, dank isolation of Newgate, became delirious. He was chilled to the bone and wearing the same stinking clothes for three weeks now. He was not allowed out of his cell at all, not even into the empty Press Yard, a sometimes sunlit courtyard. Kidd swore he was broke, so Fells looked the other way when Kidd handed the clean-up boy two notes to deliver to two distant relatives living in London, asking for help.

On May 7, 1700, a thick-handed older man, with a not so faint odor of fish, stood next to a woman at the Admiralty gate. The man, Blackburn, a fishmonger on Thames Street, "desired that he might have the liberty to Speake with Captain Kidd." The board responded — with maddening precision — that it could not give any order regarding that since Kidd was a prisoner under the care of the keeper of Newgate. (Blackburn, in effect, would have to apply to Fells at Newgate, who would *then* contact the board.)

The woman, Sarah Hawkins, who had been Kidd's landlady in Wapping years earlier and was a relative of his wife, Sarah, delivered a petition to the Admiralty board requesting orders be given for delivering Kidd's "trunk of wearing Clothes & Bedding" to him. The Wapping landlady stood before the powder-wigged lords of the Admiralty and their clerks. "She was told," the board's notes explain, "that if Capt. Kidd found himselfe in want of anything, he had other methods of communicating . . . to the Board." The "Uncle and Kinswoman" were told to leave.

That Kidd was forced to use these two people to plead his case shows the utter bleakness of his situation. Talk about not having friends at court: his advocates were a fishmonger and a landlady. And they weren't even close relatives. (The fishmonger, Blackburn, was Sarah Kidd's first husband's great-uncle; Sarah Hawkins's consanguinity was distant or nonexistent.)

Kidd was left to shiver alone, his cough and ache worsening. No money meant no service from Fells. While Kidd deteriorated, events percolated on the outside.

The Admiralty ordered the *St. Antonio* cleaned and fitted and manned with fifteen men and a master and a mate. It was later sheathed and victualled for an eighteen-month voyage; one of its first missions was to rush-deliver "Letters of Safe Passage" (i.e., passports) to Governor Bellomont so that he could sell them to merchant ships.

The poet John Dryden died. At a massive public funeral, orators sent him on his final journey with eulogies in Latin, Greek, and English.

On a less heralded note, Ventura Rosair, a sixty-year-old from Ceylon who had served meals to Captain Kidd, died on May 13 in Marshalsea prison. His death was succinctly recorded in a later expense account by the Marshalsea jailor. It stated: 10 shillings to the coroner, 3 shillings to the coroner's jury, and 8 shillings, sixpence for "coffin, ground and boardes." A note in the margin from an Admiralty clerk added: "I belive the . . . burial wasn't allowed, which means the jailor will never do it again." The Admiralty had refused to reimburse for the burial; friendless and familyless at death, Rosair was supposed to have been tossed in a ditch.

Captain Kidd was getting sicker. The deputy keeper at Newgate came to the board on May 13 and reported that Captain Kidd had "a great pain in his Head, and shakeing in his Lymbs, and further sayd that he was in great want of his Cloathes."

The board — to avoid *premature* death — resolved that Captain Kidd's trunk of clothes and bedding should be delivered after it was thoroughly searched for papers. The board added that Kidd's relatives Mr. Blackburn, a fishmonger on Thames Street, and Sarah Hawkins, "wife to a butcher in Wapping," be allowed to speak with Kidd in the presence of the keeper or deputy keeper. Most importantly, "they might assist him with money or necessarys." Money talked in Newgate.

The board also decreed that "those two persons said to be his Aunt and Uncle" be allowed to bring a doctor to treat Captain Kidd.

In mid-May, Sarah Hawkins held a vinegar-soaked rag to her nose and walked through the dark stone hallways of Newgate until she was let into Kidd's cell. She found him pale and trembling, this vigorous man laid low. She whispered that a doctor would be coming. His parched lips mumbled a thank-you. She covered him in a blanket she had brought from Wapping. She held Kidd's hand, the first scrap of tenderness he had felt in months.

The doctor probably prescribed bloodletting and a purge, standard remedies for feverish patients. We know that neither Admiralty nor Newgate Prison was willing to pay for treatment for Kidd and that the aunt and uncle footed the physician's bill.

In English prisons, medical care was à la carte. A couple of lines in an expense account at Marshalsea reveal what happens to a keeper who shows compassion.

Nine pirates — not Kidd's men — were quite ill at that moment. The Marshalsea keeper, Christopher Lowman, paid for some treatments, more than a dozen "purges" and "gargles" and "chest plasters," even two "boluses", i.e., pills. Lowman spent a hefty £2 8 shillings on nine accused pirates. The Admiralty refused to pay. "It will seem very hard for [Lowman] to be a loser by the pyrates yet nevertheless," wrote the Admiralty solicitor, "it seems to me to be a new precedent and what was never done before." (The Admiralty apparently found it too ironic to give a gargle to a French pirate about to be hanged.)

For Kidd, the warm blankets, the clean clothes, the money for edible food probably helped him more than the doctor, who visited only once.

As Kidd was just starting to regain his strength, he learned that Dundee, the young Malagasy slave whose words were gibberish to the Admiralty, had died shivering in Marshalsea Prison. The keeper, Christopher Lowman, much kinder than Fells, paid for Dundee to be buried in a coffin. The barefoot teenager, clad in a ratty shirt, would spend eternity far from his home . . . no joyous relatives would snatch up his bones in five years and dance down the roads of his Malagasy village before feasting on zebu.

And the official business of court-ordered death continued: On June 21, 1700, twenty-four pirates including circumcised rogue Gilliam went on trial. Twenty-one were convicted and sentenced to die.

Gilliam (whose clipped manhood opened this book) was approaching his end. His only hope was that the king, always in need of able-bodied sailors, was likely to pardon quite a few of the convicted pirates. Charles Hedges, chief judge of the High Court of the Admiralty, went to Hampton Court to learn the king's pleasure; King William decided to pardon eleven of the twenty-one.

Luckily for *some* of the condemned, Hedges's son, who wrote the note for his father to the Admiralty, listing the names of the men to die, accidentally left off three names. Unluckily for Gilliam, his name was not one of them.

By the end, Gilliam, who had received three pennies a day food allowance, was extremely weak. He was startled out of his lethargy on the parade to the gallows when he heard parts of his life story read aloud, which included redcoat soldiers capturing his pirate ship and biting off the ring fingers of his men. The sham bio had concluded with Gilliam spending the night before his hanging, committing himself "to Devotion for my soul's welfare." At the end, his voice cracked singing his last Psalm. The feeble man died quickly on the crowded scaffold at Execution Dock, his last gasps of air the summer stink of the Thames at low tide. Gilliam was gibbeted below Gravesend at Hope Point.

Around this time, Captain Kidd, who was learning the workings of Newgate, petitioned the board for privileges. Either he was delirious or he dictated it to someone as illiterate as a deputy keeper. (The handwriting is as shaky as the spelling.)

My Lords:
My pressing necessites obligis me to acquiant yowr desiorion your Honors will be plesed allow me a maintines and ye liberty of my friendes to come to me without wich I am likd to perish under my cloices confinment and I deesiore youre lorspps will order me my 2 negro children and the liberty to goo to the chiappell and I shall be ever bound to pray for your Lordships,
                                    Wm Kidd.

The board needed Kidd alive until Parliament met again, so it ordered its solicitor, Charles Whitaker, to give Kidd a generous twenty shillings a week. (That's almost thirty-five pence a day, which was *six* times more than what accused pirates usually received.) Kidd could now start eating well, buy liquor, extra clothes, even books to pass the time.

As for friends, the board added the name of the butcher Matthew Hawkins (husband of Wapping's Sarah Hawkins) to the visitor list. The fishmonger was old and doddery; Matthew, though almost a stranger, was at least closer to him in age.

"The Negro boy Mr. Cheeke is ordered to deliver to Captain Kidd," stated the ruling. Kidd, now in his prison cell, would have someone to handle his plates, wash his clothes, make the fire in winter, groom him a bit.

The board denied Kidd the negro girl.

Kidd's only companion for days on end would now be a Malagasy boy who spoke almost no English.

"And my Lords are willing that he should have liberty from time to time to attend Divine Service in the Chappell provided either you [i.e., keeper Fells] or Deputy be present when he is there at his Devotion."

The severe, plain small chapel at

Newgate was notorious for its Sunday services, in which the condemned men and women sat in the middle next to their coffins, while the Ordinary preached his sermon. Londoners and tourists tipped the guards to let them in to gawk at the soon-to-be-deceased.

Captain Kidd's health, both mental and physical, started to mend . . . though he was still isolated from other prisoners and forbidden any correspondence.

The Old East India Company and the New East India Company continued to bicker. The New Company, claiming the Old had failed to pay the Parliament-mandated five percent fee, seized the Old Company's ship *Neptune*. Both sides gathered with their armies of lawyers in a Crown office to select a jury to arbitrate, "where on a suddain the floor sunk down and let them all into a cellar, where some were bruised but none much hurt," according to a gossip report.

On July 27, the stock price of the Old East India Company stock shot up seven percent in one day on the announcement of the safe arrival off the coast of three of its ships, each carrying as much as £500,000 in cargo.

One of those ships was called the *Sidney*, the same that had had a very minor run-in with Kidd years ago in Johanna harbor. On this current voyage, the captain, by way of making a little extra income, had decided to carry a few passengers from St. Helena. Now, standing at the rail of the East India Company ship, tanned and healthy and free, was thirty-four-year old Robert Culliford. Below deck, his heavily shackled chest was full of gold and silver.

On his way in, Culliford sailed past Gravesend and Hope Point, and there he looked up and saw a bunch of dangling pirate corpses. The harbor pilot pointed out that the newest arrival was a rogue named Gilliam, and Culliford borrowed the spyglass to look at his old pal inside the iron gibbet, swaying in the channel breezes.

Robert Culliford, naively counting on the pardon in his waistcoat pocket, sailed on toward London.

Chapter Eighteen

The towering armed Indiaman *Sidney* hovered at Erith fifteen miles from London stuck in the nautical traffic jam heading upriver on the Thames. Culliford was antsy; he knew how few pirates escape drowning, the noose, tropical disease, the Royal Navy, only . . . to fail to get their treasure home.

It was a toasty July 29; he would be upriver in a couple of days, and his treasure of several thousand pounds would be carried ashore. He clutched his proclamation of pardon. *A couple days seemed an eternity.*

Culliford's traveling companion, the similarly reformed pirate Ralph Patterson, had been sick for weeks. While Culliford had no reason to go ashore immediately, Patterson did. Culliford cooked up a plan; he told Patterson to teeter his way to the captain, cough like a dying man, and beg to be allowed to go ashore to seek a doctor that could save his life.

Patterson, a shell of a rogue, did as his former captain bid; no doubt, he bolstered his argument with a gold coin. Captain Whitwell agreed. The *Sidney*'s boat was lowered, and frail Patterson climbed aboard, and a couple of brawny seamen loaded in after him *the chest of Robert Culliford.*

The sailors rowed Patterson to Coal Stairs in Lower Shadwell, and helped move the sick man and his chest to the Ship With Arms Tavern.

Culliford planned to slip away from the *Sidney* the next day; he and Patterson had set up a meeting place.

Now Culliford, on the deck of the ship, had time to daydream. He had left England more than a decade earlier as a penniless sailor; now he was returning with enough treasure to live like the son of an earl — well, at least the firstborn of a merchant.

He could let his fancy roam. Flaxen hair or brown? Carrot-colored or black? Tankards or quarts? Sherry or rum? He could now marry well. Maybe a goldsmith's daughter? Maybe in his secretest fantasy he allowed himself the thought of splicing with Sir So-and-So's youngest, the impish one. In the meantime, he would enjoy the diversions of London: brothels, casinos, taverns, playhouses, bear-gardens, and soon in late August: the world famous, 600-year-old Bartholomew Fair.

The next morning as the massive ship, with its crew of 100, crawled forward toward the port of London, Captain Whitwell of the *Sidney* promptly betrayed Robert Culliford. He ordered soldiers to surround him and hold him until the message could be relayed to the Lords of the Admirality that the *Sidney* was carrying a notorious East India pirate. The captain's note also advised that another rogue, Ralph Patterson, could be found at the Ship With Arms.

The Lords of the Admiralty dispatched trusty Marshall Cheeke.

By the darkness of the smudges along one folded side of Culliford's copy of the proclamation of pardon, it's clear that Culliford pulled it out of his pocket often — this time, however, to no avail. The Admiralty's pistol-toting minions ignored it.

Cheeke left the *Sidney* and headed in the Admiralty boat over to Lower Shadwell. Ralph Patterson had had a miraculous recovery and was nowhere to be found. Neither was the chest carried in with him.

Marshall Cheeke escorted his one prisoner, Robert Culliford, held on suspicion of piracy, on the hot day of August 1, 1700 to Marshalsea Prison. The Admiralty barge, ferrying Culliford, crossed the Thames to Southwark. Maddening, no doubt, was it to return to England, to see the august sights of the Great Pillar and Thames Bridge but only on the way to prison.

As Culliford was led into Marshalsea, the babel of French spilled over him. During the previous four days, almost one hundred French pirates had been logged in, making the prison obscenely overcrowded. At night unwashed Europeans fought for *floor* space to sleep.

Just as Culliford had expected a pardon, so had these French pirate prisoners. Their captain, Louis Guittar, sailing the ironically named *La Paix* ("Peace") of twenty guns, thought that he had struck a deal with the governor of Virginia, Francis Nicholson. Guittar back in early spring had terrorized shipping off the American coast, capturing five fat merchant vessels, letting his crew hack one surrendered ship to bits just for the fun of it. Sailing away, the thuggish French pirates had taunted: "Why did you break your mast?"

A few weeks later, an English ship, *Shoreham*, carrying the governor of Virginia, tracked down *La Paix* in Lynnhaven Bay. Guittar — whose sartorial signature was a gold toothpick on a gold chain around his neck — made his way upwind so as to sail down and board the *Shoreham*. Guittar flew the bloody red flag, the *"Jolie Rouge,"* meaning no mercy. But at each tack, the English outraced him. During the running battle for the wind, the *Shoreham* pounded the pirate's sails and rigging to shreds, and with direct hits unmounted several of his cannon. Guittar tried a final tack near the shore, but constant small-shot fire sent his men below deck and *La Paix* beached itself. Guittar lowered his red flag. The *Shoreham* stopped shooting.

An English prisoner, purposely freed, swam to the *Shoreham* and told the governor that Captain Guittar was carrying forty English prisoners and that he had set a long trail of gunpowder running to thirty barrels and was ready to blow up the ship.

As if on cue, the French pirates began to sing their final prayers; they showed an amazing eerie drunken harmony in both Latin and French. Governor Nicholson, believing that Guittar *would* blow everything up, agreed that if they would surrender immediately and *quietly*, he would send word under his seal "that they should be all referred to the King's mercy."

On the prison transport from America to England, their hands in irons, their legs tied at night, fifteen Frenchmen had died, leaving ninety-five to find out what exactly "referred to the King's mercy" meant.

Narcissus Luttrell, court gossiper, recorded that since Newgate and Marshalsea were jammed with mostly French pirates that King William "has been pleased to acquaint the French king that he had several of his subjects in prison upon account of pyracy, desireing to know if he would have them sent to France to be tryed there." The French king responded that King William "might try them here by the laws of England, there being no room for favour to be shewn to such *vermin*."

So, Culliford's first tavern in London was the Marshalsea Taproom in Southwark, accompanied by dozens of grim French pirates. Culliford had enough pocket change to pay to have his shackles removed; he got word to the keeper that he could afford a lawyer. He drank English beer while awaiting his legal counsel.

During these same days in early August, over at Newgate, William Kidd in solitary received a visit from one of the three people the Admiralty permitted to see him: in this case, it was the old fishmonger, Blackburn. However, Kidd couldn't even chat with this doddering man without arousing the curiosity of the political parties.

Secretary of State Vernon and the Whigs were so worried about what Kidd might say that they succeeded in spying on even this bit of small talk. Wrote Vernon: "Captain Long, who was a Quaker, and went to the West Indies about the gold mine, came to me, to-day to tell me that he is a near neighbour of a fishmonger towards London Bridge: I think he said his name was Jackson [actually, *Blackburn*], but I am not sure of it: this man's grandson was with Long in his late voyage."

Captain Long was an ideal choice to spy on Kidd. His "late voyage" had been on the ship *Rupert Prize* in 1698 to race to Central America ahead of the Scots and claim the Isthmus of Darien in the name of England. When he arrived too late to foil the Scots directly, Long had used the rest of his voyage to spy on the Scottish expedition. Long was no Scot lover.

Vernon continued in his August 8 note to the Duke of Shrewsbury: "The fishmonger . . . has talked to Long several times about Kidd, that he does not appear much concerned; but what is most remarkable, that Kidd told him he pressed his owners, when the *Adventure Galley* was fitting out, that the seamen might have wages ordered them. But he was answered that they must go upon 'No purchase, no pay'; upon which, he replied, that it could not then be avoided, but they would turn pirates.

"I asked Long whether he mentioned

which of the owners made him that answer? He had not, I perceive, been so nice in his enquiries; but he thought it was my Lord Orford, he often mentioning him as one of the owners.

"I have not heard that Kidd said anything of this nature at his examination, and therefore asked him, whether this fishmonger was capable of putting any such thing in his head? He thought not, since he was an ancient plain man, and a rigid Independent [i.e., not Tory or Whig].

"I bid him take an opportunity to be better informed which of the owners was particularly named upon this occasion; that he should be sure to do it in accidental discourse, and not as if he were employed to ask it. . . . If any thing has been said about no purchase, no pay, I take it for granted it has been Kidd's own proposal."

This level of concern over who proposed "no purchase, no pay" shows just how terrified the Whig ministers were of what Kidd might say. The implication here is that Kidd was saying that his greedy blueblood backers, by demanding a share-the-spoils system for wages, had forced the crew to turn to piracy. It seems like an obscure point, but apparently not to the secretary of state of England.

One item that can be easily missed in Long's spy report is that he said that Kidd "does not appear much concerned." Now that Kidd was healthy again, he was back to showing tough insouciance.

While Kidd was doing mostly solitary time in mid-August, Robert Culliford was at Marshalsea, buying drinks. His new-found lawyer filed a writ of habeas corpus, which made its way to Lord Chief Justice Holt. On August 19, Holt set bail at £200 for Culliford and each of five other pirates. The vaunted English judicial system had functioned efficiently since at that point, there were no eyewitnesses against Culliford or the others. The reformed pirate captain sent a note which somehow found its way to Ralph Patterson, and Culliford was able to promptly pay his £200 bail, as was one Robert Hickman. Culliford bade adieu to the French pirates.

The pirate from Cornwall had stayed a grand total of eighteen days in Marshalsea Prison.

The Admiralty continued to work through its backlog of prisoners to depose. A few days after Culliford departed, on August 24, one John Hales — who had been gunner's mate on the *Mocha Frigate* and who had abandoned piracy to come home with Kidd — mentioned under oath that he had sailed under Robert Culliford when the captain had made some of the biggest pirate captures ever in the Indian

Ocean. Hales applied his mark to his deposition: a straight line with a dash in the middle, a kind of demented H.

A clerk made a hasty scrawl in the margin of the prison accounts, which stated succinctly: "Note that yes.d Hickman and Culliford are since their being bailed, charged upon oath with Severall Piracys and Robberies committed in ye *Mocha Frigate* and a Warrant is out for their apprehension but they cannot be found."

Marshall Cheeke of the High Court of the Admiralty paid five shillings a day to his deputy to search London. He combed the waterfront taverns of Wapping; the man nosed around in the brothels of Ratcliffe Highway, querying prostitute after prostitute; he inspected the bear-gardens. The hunt was especially intense on August 28, 29, and 30, but the Admiralty could not find Robert Culliford.

This pirate from East Looe, with the uncanny knack, had escaped again. He met up with Ralph Patterson, regained a boatload of money, and he fearlessly decided to stay in London and enjoy himself.

His timing was impeccable. The Bartholomew Fair started on August 24. This enormous delta of entertainment, from freak shows to acrobatics, from quack cures to blind tenors, took over Smith

Field, a large diamond-shaped expanse in the heart of London, not too far from Newgate Prison. Barkers enticed passersby into their booths. The main theater companies of London staged ballad operas and Shakespeare revivals. The talent was world class. For instance, not just any tightrope- or wire-walker performed, but that year featured a fat Irishwoman, followed by a pregnant German woman — both operating without a net.

Physical oddities, such as hermaphrodites, were popular as were scantily clad contortionists. Some monkeys were expertly trained . . . to pick pockets.

When Culliford grew overwhelmed with Bartholomew Fair, he could wander just north of Smith Field to the bear-garden Hockley-in-the-Hole, the single most popular outdoor spectator sport at the time. Culliford could easily get lost in a crowd there especially at an event such as: "A MAD BULL to be dress'd up with fire-works, and turned loose in the Game Place. Likewise a dog to be dress'd with fire-works over him, and turned loose with the bull amongst the men in the Ground. Also, a Bear to be turned loose at the same time; and a Cat to be ty'd to the Bull's tail."

However, it was not all fun and games for Culliford. He needed to hide his treasure, and he trusted only sick Patterson. The pair wandered somewhere — we have absolutely no clue where — and hid Culliford's ample loot. A cellar, a bell-tower? Too high. A hole in the ground in the forest? A graveyard? A quick trip to Cornwall? The dunes at East Looe? No one knows. Like most pirates, in those days before banks, Culliford also parked some with friends around town.

The fair finally ended. Culliford returned to his Megs and Pegs in Ratcliffe.

On September 8, the Duke of Bedford died, making his grandson, soon to turn twenty-one, the wealthiest peer in England, with an expected annual income of £30,000, which would increase shortly to £45,000 a year.

On September 16, Marshall Cheeke of the Admiralty stopped paying his deputy to look for Culliford.

Around the same time, Captain Wynn, who had dutifully turned over Kidd's letters and journals, petitioned to have his expenses reimbursed for messengers, post horses, London boats delivering trunks, etc., and was told that he must apply through regular channels. He was advised that it would take the usual year to a year and a half for payment to come through.

Robert Culliford spent the following month enjoying life.

He didn't flee. He bought a new wig and waistcoat. He charmed those near him at the coffee houses.

On October 17, 1700, Robert Culliford, along with Ralph Patterson, was captured. We have no details, other than this time he was committed to Newgate Prison, not Marshalsea, and at this moment Newgate was packed with those same French pirates, who had been shipped there from Marshalsea to await their trial, next door at Old Bailey.

At least forty-four French pirates were at Newgate now, and Captain Guittar, his gold toothpick long gone, welcomed Culliford back into the arms of English justice. Jailor Fells applied the manacles and awaited his bribe. Culliford paid.

So, now Captain Culliford and Captain Kidd were confined within the same prison. Culliford enjoyed the Liberty of Newgate. Kidd remained in isolation. They would meet again.

Chapter Nineteen

The overcrowding at Newgate was easily solved.

Juries at Old Bailey — efficiently hearing the cases of ninety-nine French pirates within four days — found fifty-two, including Captain Guittar, guilty of robbing the tobacco-laden *Nicholson* and the *Indian King* off Virginia. The Crown decided that twenty-four of them would be hanged, in a *simultaneous* mass execution in three places around London's harbor.

Since a general hatred of Catholic France prevailed in England, authorities worried this festive day might be marred by *overly* enthusiastic crowds. The expense account, filed later, noted that money was apportioned for "a rail to go across ye dock to keep out ye mob." To synchronize the exit of so many Frenchmen from this life, the Admiralty rented an extra dozen ladders to supplement its own available equipment. The two dozen died in what was described as a "Spectacle" on November 12. Jeffrey Ellis, the dragger of the Admiralty and his assistants, took four days' labor using a longboat to shuttle twenty bodies from three spots on the Thames and bury them in Limehouse Breach. The Protestant grave-diggers' words probably didn't comfort these Catholic souls on their final journey.

With Newgate less crowded, Robert Culliford could once again choose his table in the tavern, and try to perch a comely coin-clipper on his lap. Captain Kidd was still in solitary confinement, round the clock, with almost no visitors, no chance to exercise, with no ink or paper, a prisoner of his thoughts. (He had in the cell with him his Malagasy slave boy, whom he was teaching English.) This world wanderer could stray fifteen feet.

Captain Kidd remained the only prisoner denied the Liberty of Newgate. And his meager visitor list suddenly shortened by a third when "Uncle" Blackburn, the fishmonger, died.

Kidd, though marooned in Newgate, did try to do a good deed. He wanted the wives of two of his officers, who had died during the voyage, to receive money raised by the traditional auction before the mast of the dead man's goods. He sent Matthew

Hawkins, butcher of Wapping, to find the widows.

Hawkins found them, and as the widows took their first naive steps to press a claim on Kidd's treasure, they found themselves in a crowded knot of hopefuls: the East India Company, Cogi Baba (Armenian merchant), and Greenwich Hospital for retired sailors, a favorite charity of some of Kidd's backers. *And,* penniless Governor Bellomont hadn't given up hope for his one-third share as vice admiral of the seas. (Almost pathetically, he wrote Secretary of State Vernon around this time, requesting at the very least, that he be reimbursed the £71 he had spent capturing the circumcised rogue Gilliam.)

On November 22, 1700, the two widows, with their lawyer, passed the heavy door of Newgate, under the four elegant statues; they gagged at the stench as keeper Fells led them up stone stairs to the Press Yard to Kidd's cell. (The "Press" in the name referred not to journalism, but to "pressing" prisoners with massive weights to make them plead guilty or not guilty, a practice that had recently been abandoned.)

Kidd knew these two women from before the voyage; he had been close friends with their husbands and he told them he was eager to try to help them pry their money out of the Admiralty. To Elizabeth Meade, the news of the inheritance was a godsend because she was on the verge of going to debtors' prison due to an unpaid bill of £10 that her husband, Henry, had racked up in New York before leaving on the voyage with Captain Kidd.

Kidd laid out the story for their case. Henry Meade was ship's master under Kidd; William Berk was quartermaster. Meade died in February 1697 as the *Adventure Galley* bypassed the Cape and long-hauled to Madagascar. Berk died of tropical disease that May, after the careening on Mohelia. Kidd pointed out that they had died well before any of the questionable captures by the *Adventure Galley*.

Their later claim explained: "It is the custome when any officer or Mariner of shipps dies at sea that the captain of the ship should look after the goods of the deceased persons. Captain Kidd took their goods and openly sold them at the Main Mast to officers and Marriners, for which he received 900 pieces of Eight in gold [for Meade]. For the goods of the deceased Berk, he received 450 pieces of Eight in gold." (Values fluctuate, but this equaled about £200 for Meade and £100 for Berk.)

To help with their claim, and the widows would need all the help they could get, Kidd even listed the exact goods each man carried aboard. For Meade, second ranking officer to Kidd, there was "good quantity of brandy," tobacco, sea charts, mathematical books and instruments, and twenty other books, six new suits of clothes, very good linen and bedding, five light-colored wigs, three pair of silver shoe buckles, two sets of silver buttons for sleeves, with stones in them, three hats, and a good quantity of sugar. Berk carried similar cargo.

The ladies petitioned the Admiralty for their dead husbands' money, but were refused. They petitioned directly to the king, but were told that although their request was actually read in the presence of King William, the monarch had replied he had no power to grant them that money and that the widows must apply through the proper courts.

On the verge of debtors' prison, widow Meade looked for a lawyer to press her claim in the High Court of the Admiralty. (She found a lawyer, but eventually lost the case and presumably went to prison.)

These two women were the first women Kidd had been in a room with in over a year. But seeing the widows, so briefly, instead of relieving his loneliness, seems to have increased it. Day followed endless day in the cold stone prison listening to the gibberish of the black boy. "Nothing adds more to my afflictions than being debarred the liberty of the Goale, which all other prisoners enjoy," complained Captain Kidd on December 30 to the Lords of the Admiralty. He dictated the note to a literate under-keeper named Bodenham Rowse, who carried it to the Lords. "Since my confinement I have had a great fit of sickness and am in continual danger of a relapse, which I hope would be prevented, if I might have the liberty of walking up and down, and enjoy the benefit of the air." Kidd's only leverage came from the threat of his dying and embarrassing the Admiralty.

"The Work of the late Parliament about me required only yt I should not be tried, bayled or discharged without [their] knowledge, to all which, with all humility I submit: but I beseech your Lordships, Let me not be destroyed by a close confinement, which is entirely in your powers to remove."

The note concluded, "Your Lordships most humble and obedient Serv:t, Wm Kidd." He signed it himself, still mustering a certain flourish in the oversized W and K.

The board received the request on January 4 and treated it with utmost care, requesting the attorney general and solicitor general to attend its session the following day. When an influential board member,

My Lords.

The great Misfortunes I ly under, will I hope be some Excuse to your Lordships, for this trouble: it is near nine Months since I was sent by your Honours hither, and have been close prisoner ever since; and if it is nothing adds more to my affliction, yn being debarred the liberty of the foale, which all other prisoners enjoy: since my Confinement I have had a great fit of sickness, and am in continual danger of a relaps, which I hope would be prevented if I might have the liberty of walking up and down, and enjoy the benifit of the air: the Vote of the last Parliament about me, required only yt I should not be tried, bayled, or discharged without yr knowledge, to all which, with all humility I submit: but I beseech your Lordships let me not be destroyed, by a close Confinement, which is entirely in your own power to remove: the bearer hereof is one of Keepers, and can more fully inform your Honours about me; so yt I humbly hope you will relive me out of this distress; and My Lords with all submission I remains

Your Lordships
most humble, and obedient
Servt: Wm Kidd

Newgate December
yr 30th 1700.

Captain Kidd's letter from Newgate Prison, dated December 30, 1700, in which he "humbly hopes" that the Lords of the Admiralty will end his eight-month-long stint in solitary confinement.

one Lord Haversham, failed to attend, the two top legal officials left the meeting. (Everyone was being cautious; the bureaucrats believed Kidd might destroy four lords and damage the king.) The board decided nonetheless to tackle the question on its own, deciding that Captain Kidd could walk around Newgate but only accompanied by the keeper or one of his assistants. Kidd during his walks was not allowed "to correspond or discourse with any person or persons whatever."

A bout of cold feet caused the board to run its decision by Lord Haversham's house before sending it over to Fells at Newgate. Haversham approved.

Kidd, Tantalus-like, could now every so often walk the dark stone corridors but if Culliford, or anyone else, so much as hallooed in greeting, Fells was supposed to drag Kidd away. The tavern was out of the question; the empty Press Yard was the likeliest spot.

Now, more than eighteen months after his arrest in Boston, Kidd was slowly moving toward a trial. King William III had agreed to call his Fifth Parliament, in this, his eleventh year on the throne. Elections were now held for the House of Commons.

The English government at the time was an unwieldy mix of king, Lords, and Commons. These were the years when the Commons asserted itself in a major grab for a bigger share of the balance of power. While the monarch was a hereditary post, Parliament could try to redirect the line of succession; Lords was hereditary, with 160 peers of the realm — most fantastically wealthy landowners, entitled to a seat and not always bothering to attend. The House of Commons was filled with anything but commoners. Most members were quite wealthy; they were, in theory, elected to the House, but the elections were degenerating into a strange shadow play of rotten boroughs and seamy political deals. (Old Sarum eventually had a voting population of one, while it boasted two members to the House.) In any case, in 1701, it's estimated that because of property requirements, only 188,000 Englishmen voted out of a total population of five million men and women. (The country was not nearly as democratic or representative as your average pirate ship.)

The elections moved Kidd one step closer to mounting the national stage and revealing all, including the answer *to the burning question* about whether he was hired to be a pirate.

Since Parliament's being called could lead to a trial for Kidd, the Admiralty needed to line up witnesses for the prosecution. Edward Whitaker, solicitor for the Admiralty, approached various prisoners in Marshalsea. On the morning of February 1, 1701, a Saturday, Robert Bradinham, the tipple-fond thirty-year-old surgeon who had decamped to Culliford, was rowed across the Thames from Southwark to the Admiralty. Bradinham was interrogated, then agreed to write up and sign a statement detailing Kidd's numerous acts of piracy. He delivered it to the Admiralty board personally on Tuesday, February 4.

The good doctor, who would clean up nicely for a trial, had come home with Giles Shelley and slipped into Philadelphia. Bradinham had been traveling with his fourteen-year-old Negro slave boy, whom he had unimaginatively named Dick.

Pirate Bradinham had enjoyed himself for about half a year before Colonel Robert Quarry, a zealous customs official, had caught him and locked him in jail. Quarry had confiscated from Bradinham a small fortune in pieces of eight and broken silver, but the doctor somehow succeeded in hiding a roll of gold coins in each of his shoes, which money he later smuggled out of prison via two reputable Philadelphia doctors. Beyond all that loot, Bradinham had entrusted the bulk of his treasure, 624 pieces of gold, to the good Reverend Edward Portlock of Philadelphia's English

Church, but soon *after* Bradinham's arrest, Portlock decided to spread the gospel in the *Carolinas*.

"Bradinham pretends he came honestly by his estate," wrote William Penn after interrogating him, "and that it was his misfortune and not his crime that he ever had to do with Kidd." Penn wasn't fooled.

Bradinham, and his slave, Dick, had been chained together and carried in the back of a horse cart — along with Bradinham's remaining four sacks of treasure — the slow and bumpy way to New York; from there, they were hauled by ship to Boston. Governor Bellomont also interrogated Bradinham. "I got all my treasure by my practice at Madagascar and from legacies from people who dyed," claimed Bradinham. "I know of no ship named the *Mocha Frigate* nor any person called Culliford." The doctor even refused to sign his statement.

Bellomont had written a cover note to accompany the pirates that he sent home on HMS *Gloucester* that summer of 1700 to England. "The pyrates are nine in number, and Robert Bradenham, Kidd's surgeon, is the obstinantest and most harden'd of 'em all."

In England, the Tories barely won the election, which would allow them to call the shots on handling the Kidd affair.

The King called Parliament to session on February 10, and the House of Commons promptly ignored Captain Kidd. War with Catholic France loomed; turf battles with the king beckoned; the Tories decided that the "pirate" who had been waiting a year and a half since his arrest in Boston could wait a little longer.

Europe braced for yet another round of Catholic-Protestant wars, as a French prince had recently assumed the vacant throne of Spain, which might some day soon unite with France to create a Catholic colossus. A giddy King Louis XIV was massing 70,000 soldiers at the Dutch border.

And, the fear of a Catholic ever re-gaining the throne of *England* caused Commons, Lords, and King William to start complicated negotiations that would lead in a decade to bringing over a Protestant German prince, great-grandson of James I, the German-speaking future George I.

Finally, after a month addressing other matters, on March 14, 1701, the House voted to put all the papers relating to Captain Kidd on the table in the center of St. Stephen's Chapel where Commons met. The Commons journal noted with a certain simplicity: "They are in a bag by themselves." Some processes were more informal then; any of four hundred or so members could just stroll up during a break and read what he liked. No clerk guarded them fiercely, and logged the papers in and out. Then the House formed a committee to sort through this stack of papers, and report back. That same day, Christopher Wren, the architect famed for St. Paul's, came to Commons to try to devise some way of ventilating the stuffy place. Inevitably, coffeehouses buzzed with jokes about exhausting "hot air."

Around this time, someone got word to Captain Kidd that Parliament was finally ready to deal with him. It was just at this moment that the Admiralty solicitor stopped delivering Kidd's twenty shillings a week allowance . . . just when the captain would need to eat well, be strong and be mentally clear, and not survive on stale bread and beer. Other expenses could come up now, as well. (If Commons ever gave Kidd permission to send letters, he would need to pay for the quill, ink, paper, and messengers; someone was taking no chances.)

Captain Kidd wrote a note to the Lords of the Admiralty on March 20, complaining that he had not received his subsistence money. "If I should be speedily called to answer [at Parliament], I am wholly unprepared, having never been permitted the least use of pen, ink and paper to help my memory nor the advice of friends to assist me in what so nearly concerns my life . . . I most humbly intreat your Lordships would be pleased . . . [that] I may be permitted to have the use of pen, ink and paper and liberty to discourse my friends without the keepers presence, for which great favour (with all possible Humility) I shall ever remain My Lords/Your Honours most Humble and Obedient servant, Wm Kidd."

The Admiralty decided to pass the request directly on to the House of Commons. Commons resolved that friends and relatives should be admitted to him, in the presence of the keeper, and that Kidd should be allowed pen, ink, and paper. However, with no money, Kidd was hard-pressed to try to take advantage of his new freedoms and he was running out of time: Commons decided that Kidd would appear there in three days on Thursday morning, March 27, along with Henry Bolton, the sleazy Caribbean merchant, and Cogi Baba, the Armenian whose goods were stolen.

Captain Kidd would be the first accused pirate ever to testify before the House of Commons. After 346 days inside Newgate Prison, after talking to perhaps ten human beings during that entire time, Kidd was finally being let outside.

Keeper Fells opened Kidd's cell. With the help of his slave, Kidd had done his best to dress himself well in a clean shirt and waistcoat. Keeper Fells accompanied Kidd down the stone stairs to the entry room. Guards were waiting. Fells opened the heavy door to the street. Kidd walked out into the pale, late-winter sunlight. After so long in Newgate, he squinted trying to adjust his eyes. He breathed deeply. More than a hundred people, curious, gathered outside to see the infamous pirate.

Since the expense records bear no mention of sedan-chairs or coaches or carts, it appears that Captain Kidd with mob and guards walked from Newgate to St. Stephen's Chapel. They headed west on Holborn, then south via Charing Cross.

Several witnesses said that Kidd attracted great crowds, no doubt many were shouting questions at him. *Where did you hide it?* Kidd on the way ordered a few drinks from a coffee-man, at the Court of Wards. A coffee-man in those days also served beer, wine, and hard liquor. Since Kidd eventually racked up a hefty seven-shilling bill, he fortified himself with at least a few pick-me-ups.

The House took care of routine business — Nottingham work house, Norwich debtors' prison, inheritances — before getting to Kidd. Cooling his heels, he slaked his thirst yet again.

Cogi Baba appeared at St. Stephen's; Henry Bolton, Caribbean smuggler, did not. The Tory members were furious when they found that the solicitor of the Admiralty, Charles Whitaker, had bailed Bolton "upon insufficient persons"; they demanded Whitaker appear before them the following day.

St. Stephen's Chapel was a narrow structure, with banks of benches rising on each side and a large table set in the middle. A very stuffy place when filled with 400 orators. (Christopher Wren soon added four ventilator fans to the roof.) Sir Humphrey Mackworth, a Tory, placed on the table two piles of Kidd documents: those relevant, those irrelevant.

Kidd's testimony in front of the Admiralty board from back in April was unsealed and read to the House. The Lords of the Admiralty had asked Kidd that key question, in effect: Did you have secret orders to act as a pirate? His answer had been, in effect: No, I *chased* pirates until my crew mutinied.

Kidd's lordly backers knew they had nothing to fear from those words uttered a year ago. (Their spy, Secretary of State Vernon, had found that out for them.)

But now the lords had to wonder, after

Kidd had tasted months in solitary in Newgate, maybe his answers would be different. Maybe he would lie? Maybe someone had offered him a bribe to say they had hired him to be a pirate? The rumor around London was that if Kidd helped the Tories attack the Whig lords that Kidd might escape the noose.

Captain Kidd was brought before the 400 or so members attending the House that day. He stood alone in the middle of the chamber; the nation's premier criminal was finally on center stage. The speaker recognized members in the bleachers who shouted down questions to him, most of them luring him to harm his backers. There is no transcript of Kidd's appearance, but it's clear that Kidd adamantly denied committing any act of piracy. He said, in effect, that he was not a pirate, had never been a pirate, and was never encouraged by his owners to be a pirate. "Kidd discovered little or nothing," wrote one dismissive eyewitness. Sir Richard Cocks, a Whig member, recorded in his diary: "When [Kidd] was brought to the House, he said the same thing [as he had said to the Admiralty] and no more, to the disappointment of the . . . [Tories] who would feign disgrace those [Whig ministers] they have turned out."

Although no Whig lord had come to help

him in London, Captain Kidd did not tell a lie to save his own life. But he was not defending the lords per se; he was defending himself and his reputation.

The scandal-hungry were dissatisfied; the Tories, who had expected a fresh supply of mud from Kidd, were irate. Kidd was dismissed to the antechamber, where he spent a little more money with the coffee-man. Back inside, the duplicitous letter from Lord Bellomont to Kidd was read, as was Kidd's gracious reply. The House speaker then called Kidd back in to testify. He still stood rock solid by his account that he was no pirate, nor was he ever ordered to be one.

Kidd was already a nuisance and embarrassment for the Whigs; now the American colonial was starting to become one for the Tories, as well.

The House ordered Kidd remanded back to Newgate. By now several hundred people had gathered outside St. Stephen's to catch a glimpse of the man rumored to be the world's richest pirate. After this bewildering day of light and air and loud crowds, Kidd that night found himself locked back in his dark cell at Newgate.

The following morning, the frustrated Tories in the House of Commons unleashed a shard of their anger on the Admiralty solicitor who had allowed Bolton to jump bail; they put Whitaker into the custody of the Commons' Sergeant at arms, pending an investigation.

The House then debated whether Kidd's original privateering commissions and patents had been illegal, and this partisan and highly legalistic scuffle focussed mainly on whether the king could grant away the goods of pirates *before* conviction, since the Bill of Rights signed by King William specifically stated that "Grants and Promises of Fines and Forfeitures of particular Persons before Conviction are illegal and void."

The argument meandered off into such arcane topics as whether *bona piratarum* are the same as *bona felonum,* that is, since pirates are the enemies of mankind, does their booty then fall into a different category from that of other criminals? The verbal fisticuffs even featured a history lesson on Julius Caesar. One Whig debater recited the story of how young Julius, ransomed by pirates, had returned to capture his former captors and was allowed by Roman authorities to keep the pirates' stolen property and to crucify them, all while Julius was still a private citizen. Not surprisingly, Whigs defended the grant; Tories attacked. Calling it "illegal" would be a serious slap at the king.

The candles were pulled out and lit, and

the stuffy hall grew stuffier. Finally, at the end of an almost twelve-hour session, a vote was taken. The speaker ordered the Sergeant at arms to go with his mace to Westminister Hall, Court of Requests, and other places (i.e., taverns) nearby to call all the members for a vote.

The vote came down: 185 judging the grant illegal, and 198 for legal. Therefore, the House of Commons, despite a slight Tory majority, ruled that the grant was within the law. Tories such as Edward Seymour were again furious. (Seymour was an acid-tongued champion of High Church, whose enemies claimed that he had a seven-year stretch when he hadn't even been inside a church.)

Two days later, on Monday, Tory Seymour stood before the House and with great drama, opened a letter, waved it about, and said that Captain Kidd had requested a second appearance before Commons. Finally, here was the moment *when he would confess.* Speaker Harley immediately issued a warrant to keeper Fells to deliver Captain Kidd. Coffee-houses buzzed; crowds gathered again.

Fells told Kidd he was wanted at Commons; Kidd was energized to have another crack at vindicating himself. Kidd arrived at Commons. Mid-debate on some other topic, Sir Edward Seymour slipped out and tried to meet privately with Kidd as he was brought into the building, but two Whig members jostled Seymour, and Kidd was hustled out of that room and into St. Stephen's.

Here, Kidd, with 400 peri-wigged members staring down at him, was asked why he had requested a second appearance. Kidd was flummoxed. He instead asked why he had been called to the House. He said very little, expecting questions. *I will answer your questions. Have you nothing to say?*

The exasperated members ordered Kidd back to Newgate. Sir Edward Seymour was overheard to mutter about Kidd: "The fellow is a Fool as well as a Rogue and I will never credit what he shall say hereafter."

The crowds once again followed the "pirate captain" as he made his way from Commons. Keeper Fells decided to allow Captain Kidd to stop off at a tavern at Charing Cross for a drink. The mistress of the tavern served the privateer and, for years afterward, the establishment enjoyed notoriety as Kidd's watering hole. Meanwhile, the House of Commons, exasperated, voted that Kidd should proceed to trial.

For days, there was something of a mystery about why Kidd had requested a second appearance before Commons and then revealed nothing, and hardly even said anything.

The truth behind it was typical of Kidd's odd luck. On the Sunday, after Kidd's first appearance before Commons, Kidd had been visited by that coffee-man Kistdale, who had come to the prison to collect the seven shillings that Kidd owed him. Kistdale and son and Kidd fell to drinking together in Newgate, and Kistdale told Kidd: "You are a fool to hang for anybody, and you might certainly save your life if you can say anything against Lord Orford or Lord Somers." And Kidd muttered vaguely: "I will hang for nobody, I am resolved to speak all I know."

These were words of an afternoon's drinking. Kistdale, the next morning, without saying a word to Kidd, wrote up a note and had it delivered to Sir Edward Seymour, telling him that Kidd had more to say. When Kidd appeared in Commons, he expected to be questioned; he had no statement prepared. As for Kistdale, the coffee-man, he did brisk business that day, with the huge crowds back.

To make matters worse for Kidd's reputation with the House of Commons, one Colonel Newy, a prisoner in Newgate for bigamy, issued a broadsheet *in Kidd's name* lampooning Commons for its stupidity.

On April 1, the first reading of the Act of Settlement (which would put a German native of Brunswick-Luneburg on the throne of England) once again bumped Kidd out of the limelight.

Captain Kidd was now back in Newgate and he knew that he would be going to trial. Instead of moping after Commons didn't rally to his innocence, he instead put his energies into his defense.

On April 9, he wrote to the Admiralty asking for his allowance money to be restored, and listed other requests. "I . . . beseech your Lordships, yt I may have my papers and commissions or Copys of them, and the use of pen, ink and paper and the liberty of my friends to advise with, and without the keepers presence; these things being so absolutely necessary for my defense, I hope your Honours will not deny me (especially because I know not my accusers) and I can make my application no where else but to your Lordships; I beseech your favour in these things that so nearly concern my life."

The Lords of the Admiralty called in Charles Whitaker's son, who was filling in while his father was in custody. The son said his father told him that he had given Kidd £5 on March 17. (The Admiralty accepted the word of their embattled solicitor over Kidd, who would not receive another penny *until the night before his trial.*)

Colonel Churchill of the Admiralty, who was also a member of Parliament, delivered Kidd's request to the House of Commons. On April 16, the House of Commons agreed that Kidd should have copies of his commission and other papers needed for his defense. Admiralty board notes record: "Captain Kidd is now to be lookt upon . . . as other criminals are in his circumstances." Finally, from April 16th until his trial three weeks later, Captain Kidd had the Liberty of Newgate and the opportunity to meet with any friends without the keeper eavesdropping.

William Kidd went to Newgate Tavern, the party hall of the damned, but not often, because Kidd had no money and the keeper didn't welcome people with empty pockets. Culliford, whose access to cash was dwindling with the jailing of his friend Patterson, now also rarely went there. And the two captains — the one who had enjoyed the life of piracy, and the other who hadn't — did *not* run into each other at Newgate Tavern.

On April 21, the penniless Captain Kidd asked the Admiralty board to allow him to use some of his effects (i.e., the treasure) to prepare for his trial. The board replied that he had petitioned the wrong office, that he must apply to a *judge* of the Admiralty. (He did; a judge denied the request.)

After endless inactivity, Kidd was in a ferment to prepare, to try to save himself and his reputation. Kidd received papers from the Admiralty, but he immediately noticed some stunning gaps. He dashed off a letter requesting the missing items: "Two French passes; . . . Bellomont's letter sent to me from Boston, w:ch was taken out of my pocket, aboard the *Advice* ship, Capt. Winn Commander; Instructions relating to the letter of Mart from the Lords of the Admiralty; a blue-skin'd book in which is mentioned the owners names and yr proportions of money . . . [and] the ship's accounts."

The Admiralty sent over to the House of Commons a request to search for the documents, but no one was able to find Kidd's two French passes. These were the French safe-conducts taken from the merchants aboard the *Quedagh Merchant* and *Rouparelle* that made Kidd's captures of those ships legal under his privateering commission. (Kidd had given the passes to his lawyer Emott, who in turn had given them to Governor Bellomont. The lord had sent them over in the first wave of documents and the passes were read before the House of Commons in December of 1699 and entered into the Commons journal, where they can still be read today in

Volume 13, page 21.)

The heart and soul of Kidd's defense rested on those passes. He searched hard for just the right words to encompass his outrage at the government holding back evidence: he called the act "barbarous" and "dishonourable."

The Admiralty was hardly perturbed. On April 26, Marshall Cheeke posted a notice on one of the pillars of the Royal Exchange, that Kidd's goods were arrested as perqs of the Admiralty and that any interested party should come to Admiralty to lay claim before May 10. This was a preliminary step to auctioning off the treasure, and trumpeted the *presumption* of Kidd's guilt.

Kidd finally around this time had his first opportunity to speak to a lawyer. His trial would be in two weeks and he met with a Dr. Oldish and a Mr. Lemon, both veterans of the court and both Tories. The two lawyers petitioned the court for money for Kidd's defense (including their fees). They were granted £50, but the sum mysteriously was *not* delivered.

Upon his lawyers' advice, Kidd decided to write a letter directly to Robert Harley, Tory, and speaker of the House. (Since Kidd wrote to a Tory, backed by Tory lawyers, it is safe to assume his Whig backers were not rushing to his aid.)

Kidd wrote in very late April or early May to Speaker Harley from Newgate; Kidd knew his trial could not be far off. It is as though the blunt sea captain is becoming aware that there are magic words from him that might free him, but, as in a nightmare, he can't seem to figure out what they are.

May it please Y'r Hon'r:

The long imprisonment I have undergone, or the tryall I am to undergoe, are not so great an affliction to me, as my not being able to give your Hon'ble House of Commons such satisfaction as was Expected from me. I hope I have not offended against the Law, but if I have, It was the fault of others who knew better, and made me the Tool of their Ambition and Avarice, and who now perhaps think it their Interest that I should be removed out of the world.

I did not seek the Commission I undertook, but was partly Cajold, and partly menac'd into it by the Lord Bellomont, and one Robert Livingston of New York, who was the projector, promoter, and Chief Manager of that designe, and who only can give your House a satisfactory account of all the Transactions of my Owners. He was the man admitted into their Closets, and received their private Instructions, which he kept in his own hands, and who

698

encouraged me in their names to doe more than I ever did, and to act without regard to my commission.

I hope Your Hon'ble House will not let an Englishman suffer . . . but will intercede with his Maj'ty to defer my tryall till I can have those passes, and that Livingston may be brought under Your Examination, and Confronted by me.

He apologized for not making a better case on the days he appeared before Commons. "I was in great Consternation when I was before that great Assembly, Your Hon'ble house, which with the disadvantages of a mean Capacity, want of Education and a Spirit Cramped by Long Confinem't, made me Uncapable of representing my Case."

Kidd sent along as well five long handwritten sheets, describing his voyage. It is a self-defense that focuses on the roles played by the lordly Whig backers. Again, Kidd is searching for the magic phrase that will set him free, but because he will not admit to committing any piracy, he never finds it. "I must be sacrificed as a pirate to salve the Hon'r of some men who Employed me and who perhaps if I had been one — and they could have enjoyed the benefit of it — would not have impeached me upon that account."

Of course, Kidd still had not uttered the *special* phrase, which was clearly: "Lord Somers or Lord Orford or Shrewsbury or Romney encouraged me to be a pirate."

The Tory-led House of Commons impeached two of Kidd's backers, Lord Somers (former secretary of state) and Lord Orford (former admiral of the fleet) but used Kidd for only one of a dozen or so charges. Commons would later act as prosecutor in a trial before the House of Lords.

Catholic France was spoiling for a fight. Many commoners in England, regular Protestant folk, felt Parliament was dragging its heels over funding England's entry into the war.

Kidd still had no money; he sat alone in Newgate Prison, or wandered to the tavern where he needed someone to buy him a drink. Very rarely Kidd had a brief conference with his lawyers, who hadn't been paid. The days ticked down to his May 8 trial. Still, he had no money to locate witnesses, documents, evidence. The prosecutors for the Admiralty, on the other hand, interviewed potential witnesses such as Bradinham, and Palmer, as well as Kidd's crewmen Darby Mullins, Robert Lamley, Hugh Parrott, Richard Barleycorn, James Howe, Gabriel Loffe, William Jenkins. They plotted strategy.

Kidd's outrage boiled over into an impassioned speech that he wrote to deliver in court. He accused Bellomont of trickery; he said he could have disappeared in the Caribbean but he came home to clear his name.

My Lord,

If the design I was sent upon, be illegal, or of ill consequences to the trade of the Nation, my Owners who knew the Laws, ought to suffer for It and not I, whom they made the Tool of their Covetousnesse. Some great men would have me die for Salving their Honour, and others to pacify the Mogull for injuryes done by other men, and not my selfe, and to secure their trade; but my Lord! Whatsoever my fate must be I shall not Contribute to my own destruction by pleading to this Indictment, till my passes are restored to me. . . . Let me have my passes, I will plead presently, but without them I will not plead.

I am not afraid to dye, but will not be my own Murderer, and if an English Court of Judicature will take my life for not pleading under my Circumstances, I will think my death will tend very little to the Credit of their Justice.

Just a week earlier, Kidd had written of himself as an "Englishman" seeking help in

Commons; now he was writing of an "English Court" and "my death will tend very little to the Credit of *their* Justice." Kidd was once again becoming a Scot, an outsider, an American colonial; he could see the handwriting even on the stone walls of Newgate Prison. And he would fight it.

The Trial

Chapter Twenty

A dark, narrow passageway, blocked at either end by low, stout barred doors, joined Newgate Prison to Old Bailey Courthouse. Captain Kidd, well-dressed, accompanied by nine fellow prisoners — men and boys with dirty faces, eyes squinting, straggly beards, matted hair, in ragged clothes — were led into the courtroom. They were preceded by their smell.

From the Middle Ages forward, English judges had complained about the particularly vile smell of prisoners delivered from Newgate. The nauseating stench of the prison hung about the men like a cloud, and pervaded the courtroom. (If men of that century, who washed semiannually and rarely used toilet paper, found the smell offensive, then . . . it must have been an odor of Biblical proportions.) One year almost fifty people who worked in Old Bailey died of what was then called "Gaol

Fever." An officer shepherded the accused into the prisoners' dock — resembling a strong wooden animal pen — strewn ankle deep with fresh herbs. But the greenery was insufficient to blot out the stink, and in the 17th century, a tradition developed of judges carrying nosegays into court. At any moment during a trial, if the jurists felt the urge to retch rising, they could nestle the flower near their nostrils and inhale.

On Thursday, May 8, 1701, in the morning, the bedraggled prisoners and neatly attired Captain Kidd entered Old Bailey; they saw the ornate Silver Oar of the Admiralty. Nearby stood the court recorder in lush scarlet robe and full powdered wig, as well as five members of the prosecuting team from the nation's solicitor general, John Hawles, to the Admiralty's brilliant advocate, George Oxenden. These men, in deep contrast to the ratty prisoners, wore scarlet robes and hoods lined with taffeta (if Oxford alumni) or white ermine (if Cambridge).

Curious onlookers whispered in the packed galleries, which rose up on either side of the courtroom, choking off the light. Each person attending had paid an entrance fee, negotiated with various doorkeepers. (These fees to observe justice continued through 1860.)

The floor above held a fine dining room,

and many a judge came back from midday meal with a belly full of meat and head full of wine. Juries routinely expected to be fed, *especially after a guilty verdict.*

The English justice system circa 1700 differed drastically from courtroom practices of today, packed over the ensuing centuries with safeguards for the rights of the accused. Back then, defendants could consult lawyers only *on narrow points of law,* and had to cross-examine witnesses themselves and had to deliver their own opening and closing arguments.

A trial featured a duel of legal unequals: veteran prosecutors against inept self-defenders. That old joke — "A man who represents himself has a fool for a client" — was true for *all* the defendants in Captain Kidd's day.

A peer of the realm, one Lord Ashley, once gave a speech in Parliament advocating that lawyers be allowed to handle *all* courtroom duties for those accused of treason. He lost his train of thought, misspoke a second, then said: "How can I, Sir, produce a stronger argument in favour of this bill than my own failure? My fortune, my character, my life are not at stake . . . and yet from mere nervousness, from mere want of practice in addressing large assemblies, I have lost my recollection. . . . How helpless then must be a poor man, who, never having opened his lips in public, is called upon to reply without a moment's preparation to the ablest and most experienced advocates in the kingdom, and whose faculties are paralyzed by the thought that, if he fails to convince his hearers, he will in a few hours die on the gallows, and leave beggary and infamy to those who are dearest to him?"

Making matters even tougher for the defense, the Crown, in Kidd's day, appointed the judges, who were then beholden for their careers. The king could dismiss them or promote them — based on their track record in delivering verdicts *favorable to the king*. Another old joke: "In Europe, they still used torture to get confessions; in England, they didn't need to."

The judges' main tasks in this era were to orchestrate the trial, and then afterward to interpret the law and recap the evidence for the jury. The most casual glance at any of dozens of State Trials shows that judges usually interpreted in ways quite favorable to Crown prosecutors. Layers of legal nicety neatly led to a noose for the accused.

Punishment was much swifter and harsher back then, often performed within days of the verdict. Also, dozens of offenses called for the death penalty, if not worse (i.e., disembowelment, quartering, etc.). Children as young as seven, both boys and girls, were hanged. Just three years earlier in 1698, Parliament had passed a law that the theft of goods, worth more than five shillings, rated the death penalty. (Five shillings would buy a nice pair of pants.)

The trial itself was usually very brief, an hour or much less, but it was a trial by jury, which was a hallmark of English justice. "It is an extraordinary privilege," stated a French guidebook (1726), "and none but the English are so judged by their fellow citizens."

All in all, however, juries in State Trials rarely acquitted. It was expected of them to convict, to follow the Crown's lead.

In 1670, William Penn, future founder of Pennsylvania, along with another staunch Quaker, Henry Mead, was charged with preaching to an unlawful assembly at Friends Meeting House in Grace Church Street. The judge grew so infuriated at Penn's legal arguments, he threatened to have his tongue cut out. Against all odds, the jury came back with a verdict of not guilty for Mead and found Penn guilty of preaching, but not of the much graver charge of holding unlawful assembly. The lord mayor ordered the jury locked up overnight without meat, drink, fire, or candle. "We will have a positive verdict or you shall starve for it," he threatened. The jury was kept yet an additional day and night but refused to change their verdict; they were ordered locked up in Newgate until they paid each a fine of forty marks (thirteen shillings).

Kidd and the pirate prisoners stood in the dock. Sir Salathiel Lovell, eighty-one years old, was the court recorder. A crotchety man, his nickname in that literate age was "Obliviscor" because he was so forgetful.

The accused pirates in the pen besides Kidd were his loyal six who had refused to go pirating with Culliford: youngsters Richard Barleycorn, Robert Lamley, William Jenkins, and veterans Gabriel Loffe, Abel Owens, and Hugh Parrott. Lumped in with them were Culliford's mutineers: James Howe, Nicholas Churchill, and Darby Mullins.

After almost two years in solitary confinement, Captain Kidd had finally reached the day of his trial, the day to vindicate himself. To him the case was simple: The French passes made his two captures legal. The premature disposal of cargo was forced on him by his crew's mutiny.

As was the custom then, the judges were not yet in the courtroom. Now was the moment for the clerks to handle the legal preliminaries, a mere formality with *most* defendants, but not with Captain Kidd.

CLERK OF ARRAIGNS: "William Kidd, hold up they hand."

Captain Kidd refused to raise his hand.

CAPTAIN KIDD: "May it please your Lordships, I desire you to permit me to have counsel."

Kidd's two lawyers, Dr. Oldish and Proctor Lemon, both Tories, stood in the courtroom wearing long black robes, with hoods lined with fur.

RECORDER (THE ANCIENT SIR SALATHIEL LOVELL): "What would you have counsel for?"

CAPTAIN KIDD: "My lord, I have some matter of law relating to the indictment, and I desire counsel to speak to it."

George Oxenden (1651–1703), Cambridge law professor representing the Admiralty, quickly interjected, and Captain Kidd, a fine sailor, found himself overmatched. (What Kidd lacked in knowledge of the law, though, he made up for in stubbornness.)

OXENDEN FOR THE ADMIRALTY: "What matter of law can you have?"

CLERK OF ARRAIGNS: "How does he know what he is charged with? I have not told him."

SIR SALATHIEL LOVELL: "You must let the Court know what those matters of law are before you can have counsel assigned you."

CAPTAIN KIDD: "They be matters of law, my lord."

SIR SALATHIEL LOVELL: "Do you know what you mean by matters of law?"

CAPTAIN KIDD: "I know what I mean; I desire to put off my trial as long as I can till I can get my evidence ready."

SIR SALATHIEL LOVELL: "You had best mention the matter of law you would insist upon."

OXENDEN: "It cannot be a matter of law to put off your trial, but matter of fact."

CAPTAIN KIDD: "I desire your lordship's favour; I desire that Dr. Oldish and Mr. Lemmon may be heard regarding my case."

CLERK OF ARRAIGNS: "What can he have counsel for before he has pleaded?"

SIR SALATHIEL LOVELL: "William Kidd, the Court tells you that what you have to say shall be heard when you have pleaded to your indictment. If you plead to it, you may, if you will, assign matter of law, if you have any; but then you must let the court know what you would insist on."

CAPTAIN KIDD: "I beg your lordship's patience till I can procure my papers. I had a couple of French passes, which I must make use of in order to my justification."

SIR SALATHIEL LOVELL: "That is not a matter of law. You have had long notice of your trial, and might have prepared for it.

How long have you had notice of your trial?"

CAPTAIN KIDD: "A matter of a fortnight."

SIR SALATHIEL LOVELL: "The court sees no reason to put off your trial, therefore you must plead."

CLERK OF ARRAIGNS: "William Kidd, hold up thy hand."

Kidd again refused to raise his hand.

CAPTAIN KIDD: "I beg your lordships I may have counsel admitted, and that my trial may be put off; I am not really prepared for it."

SIR SALATHIEL LOVELL: "Nor never will, if you can help it."

OXENDEN: "You had reasonable notice, and you knew you must be tried, and therefore you cannot plead you are not ready."

CAPTAIN KIDD: "If your lordships permit those papers to be read, they will be justify me. I desire my counsel may be heard."

MR. CONIERS (CROWN PROSECUTOR): "We admit of no counsel for him."

SIR SALATHIEL LOVELL: "There is no issue joined and therefore there can be no counsel assigned. You must plead."

CAPTAIN KIDD: "I cannot plead until I have those papers that I insisted upon."

MR. LEMMON (LAWYER FOR KIDD): "He ought to have his papers delivered to him, because they are very material for his defense. He has endeavoured to have them, but could not get them."

MR. CONIERS: "You are not to appear for anyone till he pleads, and that the Court assigns you for his counsel."

SIR SALATHIEL LOVELL: "They would only put off the trial."

MR. CONIERS: "He must plead to the indictment."

The gallery murmur grew to a roar.

CLERK OF ARRAIGNS: "Make silence."

CAPTAIN KIDD: "My papers were all seized, and I cannot make my defense without them. I desire my trial may be put off till I can have them."

SIR SALATHIEL LOVELL: "The Court is of the opinion that they ought not to stay for all your evidence; it may be they will never come. You must plead, and, if you can satisfy the Court that there is a reason to put off your trial, you may."

CAPTAIN KIDD: "My lord, I have business in law, and I desire counsel."

SIR SALATHIEL LOVELL: "The course of Courts is that when you have pleaded, the matter of trial is next; if you can then show there is cause to put off your trial, you may; but now the matter is to plead."

CAPTAIN KIDD: "It is a hard case when all those things shall be kept from me, and I be forced to plead."

SIR SALATHIEL LOVELL: "If he will not plead, there must be judgment."

Captain Kidd did not yet quite grasp the old man's mumbled "judgment." He would very soon, and it would bring back a memory of an axeman.

CAPTAIN KIDD: "My lord, would you have me plead, and not to have my vindication by me?"

His naivete was touching.

CLERK OF ARRAIGNS: "Will you plead to the indictment?"

CAPTAIN KIDD: "I would beg that I may have my papers for my vindication."

CLERK OF ARRAIGNS: "William Kidd, art thou guilty or not guilty of the felony whereof thou standest indicted?"

CAPTAIN KIDD: "I cannot plead to this indictment till my French passes are delivered to me."

After two years of being bullied about by under-jailors, now, in the courtroom, he was standing firm.

CLERK OF ARRAIGNS: "Art thou guilty or not guilty?"

CAPTAIN KIDD: "I must insist upon my French papers; pray let me have them."

SIR SALATHIEL LOVELL: "That must not be now, till you have put yourself upon your trial."

CAPTAIN KIDD: "That must justify me."

SIR SALATHIEL LOVELL: "You may

plead it then if the court sees cause."

CAPTAIN KIDD: "My justification depends on them."

SIR SALATHIEL LOVELL: "I must tell you that if you will not plead, you must have a judgement against you, as standing mute."

Captain Kidd, a decade earlier in New York City, had seen what had happened to Jacob Leisler and Samuel Milbourne when they had refused to plead. Their silence equaled a guilty plea; they were hanged and beheaded on Kidd's wedding day. Kidd didn't flinch, despite the robes and the silver oar.

CAPTAIN KIDD: "I cannot plead till I have these papers; and I have not my witnesses here."

SIR SALATHIEL LOVELL: "You do not know your own interest; if you will not plead you must have judgment against you."

CAPTAIN KIDD: "If I plead I shall be accessory to my own death, till I have persons to plead for me."

SIR SALATHIEL LOVELL: "You are accessory to your own death if you do not plead. We cannot enter into evidence unless you plead."

CLERK OF ARRAIGNS: "Are you guilty or not guilty?"

Kidd stood stock-still.

SIR SALATHIEL LOVELL: "He does not understand the law; you must read the statute to him."

CLERK OF ARRAIGNS: "Are you guilty of this piracy or not guilty?"

CAPTAIN KIDD: "If you will give me a little time to find my papers I will plead."

CLERK OF ARRAIGNS: "There is no reason to give you time; will you plead or not?"

Kidd stood still.

MR. CONIERS (CROWN PROSECUTOR): "Be pleased to acquaint him with the danger he stands in by not pleading. Whatever he says, nothing can avail him till he pleads."

SIR SALATHIEL LOVELL: "He has been told so, but does not believe us."

MR. CONIERS: "If there be any reason to put off his trial, it must be made to appear after issue is joined."

SIR SALATHIEL LOVELL: "If you say 'guilty' there is an end to it; but if you say 'not guilty' the court can examine into the fact."

CLERK OF ARRAIGNS: "William Kidd, art thou guilty or not guilty?"

CAPTAIN KIDD: "Not guilty."

CLERK OF ARRAIGNS: "How wilt thou be tried?"

CAPTAIN KIDD: "By God and by my country."

CLERK OF ARRAIGNS: "God send thee a good deliverance."

CAPTAIN KIDD: "My lord, I beg I may have my trial put off for three or four days till I have got my papers."

SIR SALATHIEL LOVELL: "The judges will be here by and by, and you may move the court then; we are only to prepare for your trial. We do not deny your motion but when the court is full they will consider of the reasons you have to offer."

These unusually combative preliminaries were complete. Everyone in the courtroom stood up. The five judges entered in a parade of floor-length scarlet robes. The faces of these elderly gentlemen were framed by a full wig of curls cascading to their shoulders. The garb of Lord Chief Justice Ward was subtly more impressive than his counterparts: his sleeves were trimmed in ermine fur, his stole about his shoulders was ermine, and he wore a long, heavy gold chain around his neck.

The Crown had decided to assign five of its most elite judges to the case. Sir Edward Ward, sixty-three years old, was a former attorney general, raised to the bench as Lord Chief Baron of the Exchequer. (Ward was married to the daughter of one of London's wealthiest merchants, Thomas Papillon, founder of the New East India Company.) Baron Henry Hatsell, sixty years old, had gained notoriety two years earlier, mismanaging the trial of a fellow judge who was acquitted in the murder of a young Quaker girl. Justice Turton was a longtime favorite of King William, who was raised to Baron of the Exchequer after the king's coronation. Justice Gould, who had slowly risen up the legal ladder, was known as strong-willed, because on his first circuit (two years earlier), he had shown the nerve to fine a *baron* for kicking a sheriff and for calling the judge a "liar."

The fifth judge, a veteran Whig, fifty-six-year-old John Powell, bore a very unusual reputation among his colleagues: for kindness and good nature. Jonathan Swift described Powell as "an old fellow with grey hairs, who was the merriest old gentleman I ever saw, spoke pleasing things and chuckled till he cried again." He sat on the bench at the witchcraft trial of Jane Wenham, in which one witness charged that Wenham could fly through the air. The judge leaned down toward the prisoner, and said: "You may, there is no law against flying."

The Crown prosecution team was also loaded with talent, boasting six members, led by the solicitor general, Sir John Hawles, a well-connected Whig who had served in Parliament from no less than four different districts, a clear sign of party favor. Henry Newton and Dr. George

Oxenden represented the interests of the Admiralty. Filling out the team were Mr. Coniers, Mr. Knapp, and Mr. Cowper.

At the time, cases were sometimes handled by a judge and a prosecutor; this was an all-star line-up arrayed against Captain Kidd, and, unfortunately for Kidd's fellow prisoners, arrayed against them as well. (The king — showing his preference in the case — was quoted by the rumor mill as saying that he would like to testify against Kidd, if there weren't a law against monarchs testifying.)

Kidd now finally was inching closer to having his opportunity to ask the judges to postpone his trial. But first, the Clerk of Arraigns had to read the charge against Kidd. The voice droned on, about "King William," sovereign of blah-blah and blah-blah and "William Kidd, mariner" and then instead of piracy, the charge against Kidd was *murder*.

Murder? Murder! This was the first moment that Kidd, after two years, found out that he was charged with the murder of William Moore, and he was accused of premeditated murder, using a bucket as his weapon of choice. He was stunned. He pled, "Not Guilty."

Kidd was now permitted to have his counsel, Dr. Oldish and Mr. Lemon, speak for him on a point of law. Kidd's lawyers argued that because he did not have the passes, the trial should be postponed. "I had no money nor friends to prepare for my trial till last night," Kidd chimed in. Lord Chief Baron Ward responded: "Why did you not signify so much to the King's Officers?"

Either Baron Ward had a refined sense of humor or he was an extremely cruel man, perhaps both. Kidd, furious, started to answer, but the Crown lead, Solicitor General Hawles, cut him off, and suggested that Kidd's trial for *murder* should proceed, since it is no way dependent upon French passes. Baron Ward agreed.

A jury of twelve men was selected. Kidd stared at the panel. "I shall challenge none; I know nothing to the contrary but that they are honest men."

Mr. Knapp made the opening speech for the Crown. He charged that William Kidd on October 30 off the Malabar coast struck gunner William Moore, with a wooden bucket, hooped with iron, on the side of the head near the right ear, and that Moore died the next day from the wound. The solicitor general added that Kidd did this "without provocation."

Sea captains in this time period, by law and by custom, were given enormous latitude in handling their crews. Blows by fist or cane by officers were common to speed up work as were whippings for punishment. Also, a captain could order more creative punishments such as tying a sailor to the mast or denying a sailor water. There were, however, a rare handful of documented cases of charges being brought against captains. Edward Barlow, that East India captain who had tiffed with Kidd off the Red Sea, for one, was accused of killing a sailor because he struck him a few very hard blows with a cane when the man lagged at loading a shipment of canes. The sailor died ten days later, and when Barlow returned to London, the man's widow hired a lawyer to press charges. The lawyer told Barlow it was likely that he might be convicted of manslaughter and get branded an M on the hand unless he settled out of court. Barlow, to avoid the risk, paid her £50 and £5 to the lawyer, and the charges disappeared. Another captain killed a passenger who called the woman who shared the captain's bed a whore. He was acquitted, as was a captain who repeatedly denied water in blistering heat to a young man caught stealing water. The boy fell sick and died.

To make the murder charge stick, the Crown would have to prove "malice aforethought," i.e., that Kidd hadn't hit Moore in a moment of passion, or killed him accidentally.

The Crown called its two prize witnesses, Joseph Palmer and surgeon Robert Bradinham, who would also appear against Kidd in the upcoming five indictments. Both these thirty-plus-year-old men, though prisoners in Marshalsea prison, thanks to some coins handed them by the Crown, looked presentable this morning.

Palmer launched into a detailed telling of the incident, and demonstrated his uncanny gift for remembering dialog. Palmer said that Captain Kidd had walked by William Moore, who was then seated on the *Adventure* deck grinding a chisel. Palmer said that Kidd had confronted Moore, and accused him of trying to dupe the crew into turning pirate. Moore denied the charge; Kidd then called him "A Lousy dog." Moore replied: "If I am a lousy dog, you have made me so; you have brought me to ruin and many more." Palmer then quoted Kidd as saying: "Have I ruined you, you dog?" Palmer said Kidd picked up the bucket and smacked Moore.

The Crown prosecutor quickly jumped in with a question: "Did [Kidd] give him the blow *immediately* after he gave him that answer?" This was an important point because the Crown wanted to prove murder, not manslaughter.

Palmer quickly replied, "No," and testified that Kidd had paced the deck two or three times before delivering the blow. As Moore was being carried below deck, Palmer heard him say: "Farewell, farewell, Captain Kidd has given me my last." To which Kidd replied, "You are a villain." Palmer was also able to describe the wound in great detail because he said that after Moore died, he went to the body and put his fingers into the wound and felt the skull give way. Palmer was a prosecutor's dream.

Now, without lawyer's advice and without documents, it was Captain Kidd's turn to interrogate.

KIDD: "What was the occasion that I struck him?"

PALMER: "The words that I told you before."

KIDD: "Was there no other ship?"

PALMER: "Yes."

KIDD: "What was that ship?"

PALMER: "A Dutch ship."

KIDD: "What were you doing with the ship?"

PALMER: "She was becalmed."

KIDD: "The ship was a League from us, and some of the men would have taken her, and I would not consent to it, and this Moore said I always hindered them making their fortunes; was that not the reason I struck him? Was there not a

Mutiny on board?"

PALMER: "There was no Mutiny, all was quiet."

KIDD: "Was there not a Mutiny because they would go and take the Dutchman?"

PALMER: "No, none at all."

Palmer's perjury stymied Kidd, whose courtroom experience would fill a sailmaker's thimble.

If Kidd had had more time to prepare, he might have been able to gain access to Joseph Palmer's deposition given two years earlier in Rhode Island, in which Palmer stated *"I was not upon ye deck when ye blow was struck"*; he also swore under oath that "Captain Kidd *in a passion* struck his gunner," which would mean manslaughter, not murder.

The Crown proceeded to call Robert Bradinham, but one juryman and kindly Justice Powell were still curious to ask Palmer more questions about the mutiny. They brought out that Moore had been a ringleader two weeks earlier when the English ship *Loyal Captain* was nearby. The Dutch ship posed another potential mutiny. Score one for Kidd.

Bradinham, thirty-year-old surgeon, testified on the medical issue: He stated the wound to the head killed Moore. The prosecution, playing to the non-aristocrat jury, asked Bradinham if he knew Kidd's feelings about the man's death. The good doctor added that about two months after Moore died, Kidd told him: "I do not care so much for the Death of my Gunner . . . for I have good friends in England that will bring me off for that."

Kidd couldn't figure out what question to ask to deflect this outright lie. He made his opening statement in defense, simple and direct. "Some of my men were for making a mutiny about taking [the Dutch ship], and my Gunner told the people he could put the captain in a way to take the ship, and be safe. Says I, 'How will you do that?' The Gunner answered, 'We will get the [Dutch] captain and Men aboard.' 'And what then?' 'We will go aboard the [Dutch] ship and plunder her, and we will have it under their hands [i.e., in writing] that we did not take her.' Says I, 'This is Judas-like, I dare not do such a thing.' Says he, 'We may do it, we are beggars already.' 'Why,' says I, 'may we take this ship because we are poor?' Upon that a mutiny arose, so I took up a bucket and just throwed it at him and said you are a rogue."

Before Kidd could call his witnesses, the Crown's Mr. Cowper shouted a question to Palmer: "Was there any mutiny in the ship when this man was killed?" Palmer:

"There was none."

Judges' discretion back then prevailed over the issue of speaking out. And defense, prosecution, jury, and judges all had the chance to interrupt and try to lob a verbal bomb or defuse one. Baron Hatsell asked Palmer: "Did he throw the bucket?" Palmer: "He held it by the strap."

Before Kidd even began, his two main points — about provocation and accidental injury — were undermined, if not shot down. Without any alternative, Kidd called his loyal but foul-smelling crewmen as witnesses: Abel Owens (Kidd's cook), and Richard Barleycorn (Kidd's young apprentice), and Hugh Parrott, a sailor who had joined up in Madagascar. Unlike the prosecution, which over the past two weeks had interviewed its witnesses, Kidd had no idea what these prisoners, who had been in Marshalsea, would say.

Kidd tried to guide the cook, Owens, to describe the Dutch ship mutiny, but Lord Chief Baron Ward, curls aflutter, sharply informed Owens: "This mutiny occured about a month before Moore's death." Owens was completely confused; the judge was forcing the word "mutiny" to apply only to the physical uprising against Kidd, but not Moore's plotting. Justice Powell, aiding Kidd, asked several times whether or not Moore made a mutiny at the time of

Kidd hitting him. Owens took the word "mutiny" very literally and said, "No." Moments later, Owens said that Kidd stopped Moore's attempt to take the nearby Dutch ship.

On the key issue of premeditation, Kidd, not being an experienced trial lawyer, didn't think to ask Owens whether he'd swung the bucket immediately after the harsh words or whether he'd strolled the deck for a while.

Next defense witness, seventeen-year-old Richard Barleycorn — a fresh-faced colonial servant clearly dedicated to his captain — tried very hard to help, but he got flummoxed quickly by the judges' questions.

First he said there was a mutiny, then he admitted the actual mutiny occurred weeks earlier. A juryman, exasperated by the wrangling, asked simply: "What was the occasion [i.e., motive] for this blow?" Barleycorn responded: "It was thought [Moore] was going to breed a mutiny in the Vessel."

Kidd, to discredit the Crown witnesses, then asked Barleycorn whether the doctor was part of the mutiny. The boy answered, "Yes." But the chief justice interjected to Kidd: "You will not infer that if [the doctor] was a mutineer, it was lawful for you to kill Moore."

In the waters of Old Bailey, Kidd was no

match for these legal men-of-war. Kidd concluded: "I have no more to say but I had all the provocation in the world given me; I had no design to kill him; I had no malice or spleen against him."

A sympathetic juryman wanted to know whether Kidd had done anything to treat Moore's wound. Lord Chief Baron stopped him: "Will you put him to produce more evidence than he can? The court is willing to hear him as long as he has anything to offer for himself."

Kidd added, "It was not designedly done, but in my Passion, for which I am heartily sorry."

Now it was Lord Chief Baron Ward's turn to charge the jury, summarizing and explaining both testimony and law. He fulfilled the prosecution's innermost fantasies.

Kidd's slender reed of hope rested on the mutiny. As to Barleycorn's statement that Moore was breeding mutiny, Baron Ward noted dismissively about "differing stories" and added, with mock sympathy "[Barleycorn] is willing to say what he can for his master."

The judge explained a murder charge, that there must be malice aforethought, "that Law implies malice, when one man without any reasonable cause or provocation, kills another." He pointed out that the passion from a mutiny would have petered in a month's time. "If there be a sudden falling out, and fighting, and one is killed in heat of Blood, then our law calls it Manslaughter: but in such a case as this, that happens on slight words, the prisoner called the deceased a 'lousy dog' and the deceased said 'If I be so, you made me so,' can this be a reasonable cause to kill him?"

Justice was swift indeed back then. The jury left the room to deliberate on the murder; the court didn't wait for a verdict but moved to the next case: piracy charges against Kidd and the nine others. On this day and the following, Kidd would be indicted on one count of murder and five counts of piracy, handled in four separate trials, the latter three involving up to ten defendants. It was dizzying, and potentially fatal.

At this moment, just before the second trial when he would have to make the proper legal motion about his French passes, Kidd's lawyers deserted him.

The clerk announced that Captain Kidd and the nine others in the dock were charged with committing piracy upon the *Quedagh Merchant* on January 30, 1698. They all pleaded, "Not Guilty."

Mr. Moxon, a lawyer for three of the prisoners — men who had mutinied to Culliford, gone pirating, and sailed home with Shelley — requested that his trio be allowed to plead the king's pardon. Men's lives were at stake over interpretation of this pardon. Did the men surrender within the time frame allowed? Did they surrender to the correct authorities? The men mentioned surrendering in America. Lord Chief Baron Ward, from his lofty perch, stated curtly: "The Proclamation does not reach your case." He was ready to move on. Justice Powell, humanely, asked the prisoners whether they could prove they came in under the conditions of the pardon.

The proclamation was read. This was a copy of the same proclamation carried like a talisman by Robert Culliford, now in Newgate. It stated that surrender must be made to one of the four commissioners mentioned. These prisoners had an affidavit stating that they had surrendered to Colonel Basse, governor of West Jersey, in May 1699.

Lord Chief Baron Ward: "If you had brought yourselves within the Case of the Proclamation, we should be very glad . . . but you have . . . surrendered to Colonel Basse and there is no such man mentioned in the Proclamation." Pardon denied.

The prosecution was allowed to proceed. (With no lawyers to help handle it, Captain Kidd failed to jump in at the proper moment to request a postponement because of the missing French passes.)

The murder case was oddly interesting, but the crowds had come for the piracy charges. Although the indictment concerned only taking the *Quedagh*, Dr. Newton, the prosecutor, sailed slowly through Kidd's entire career to paint a portrait of a shipboard devil. "[Kidd] committed many great piracies and robberies, taking the ships and goods of the Indians and others at sea, Moors and Christians, and torturing cruelly their persons to discover if anything had escaped his hands; burning their houses, and killing after a barbarous manner the Natives on the shore; equally cruel, dreaded and hated both on land and at sea. These criminal attempts and actions had rendered his name (to the disgrace and the prejudice of the English nation) too well known, and deservedly detested . . . he was now looked upon as an Arch Pirate and Common Enemy of Mankind."

Kidd had been in solitary confinement for most of the last two years. This marked the first time the New Yorker heard himself described to his face as some kind of monster.

Prosecutor Newton abandoned hyperbole long enough to detail Kidd's taking the *Quedagh*, commanded by Wright, an Englishman for Armenian merchants. He charged that Kidd turned down 30,000 rupees from the merchants aboard and sold the goods on the coast and divvied the plunder, then sailed for Madagascar. He rambled on, somewhat pompously, about the sharing out. At the words "each mariner having about three bales to his share," a sudden loud noise was heard. A door opened.

A court officer looked to the judges and announced that the first jury had reached a verdict. It had taken them an hour, a relatively long time. The first jury entered (in the presence of the second jury.) They were polled as to whether their verdict was unanimous. It was. The Clerk of Arraigns ordered Kidd to raise his right hand. Kidd did. He stared into the faces of the jury.

Clerk of Arraigns (to the jury): "Look upon the prisoner. Is he guilty of the murder whereof he stands indicted, or not guilty?"

Foreman: "Guilty."

That gut-punch two-syllable word put Kidd under a sentence of death, with his only hope of avoiding the noose a pardon . . . from a king who had volunteered to testify against him, or via some kind of intercession by House of Lords or Commons. It had all happened so fast.

With politeness, the chief judge begged the prosecutor to resume his opening remarks in trial number two.

Kidd was dazed. Once again, the pomaded voice of Dr. Newton, advocate for the Admiralty, filled the courtroom. The prosecutor was uttering the name of Robert Culliford, "a notorious pirate now in custody." Dr. Newton said Culliford and his crew at first feared that Captain Kidd had come to take and hang them. "But Captain Kidd assured them . . . [he'd] rather his soul should broil in Hell than do them any harm." Dr. Newton said Kidd gave Culliford many gifts, including money and cannon. Building on the momentum of the guilty verdict, Dr. Newton rose to his conclusion, saying trade would nourish England and that Kidd had harmed trade. "This is the Person that stands indicted at the bar, than whom no one in this age has done more mischief, or has occasioned greater confusion and disorder."

The Crown once again called Tweedledum and Tweedledee, Bradinham and Palmer, as witnesses. With the guilty verdict in hand, despite nine other men's lives at stake, this new legal battle was now turning into more of a show trial, for the prosecutors to demonstrate what English justice does to a man who stole in the name of the king.

Mr. Coniers and Mr. Cowper walked Dr. Bradinham through a step-by-step account of Kidd's entire voyage. Highlights featured Kidd firing on an English ship, kidnapping an English captain, torturing passengers, executing a native tied to a tree, and burning a village.

The prosecutor, layering on details of the capture, tarred the rest of the prisoners with the same brush. For six of these nine tramping the herbs in the dock who had stayed with Kidd and refused to go pirating with Culliford, for them, this trial was a polysyllabic, barely comprehensible nightmare. They too had spent twenty-two months in various prisons waiting to clear their names.

Robert Bradinham looked to each prisoner and said, one by one, yes, so-and-so had been present at the taking of the *Quedagh Merchant* and yes, so-and-so had received a share of the booty. The men, spectators until now, were starting to sense their doom. They makeshifted as lawyers. "Have I not obeyed my captain in all his commands?" blurted out James Howe. "There is no doubt made of that," Lord Chief Baron Ward responded archly. "If any of you will ask him any questions, you may." Jenkins: "I ask him whether or not I was a servant." Abel Owens: "I have nothing to say but I depend upon the King's Proclamation."

Kidd finally rallied with a question. "Did

you not see any French passes aboard the *Quedagh Merchant*?" Bradinham: "You told me you had French passes, I never did see them."

Kidd knew this to be a lie; he had shown the passes to the doctor.

All continued swimmingly for the Crown, until Joseph Palmer made a little slip, letting the truth slide in. By way of background, Mr. Coniers was asking Palmer about the capture of an earlier ship, the *Rouparelle*. Palmer: "[Captain Kidd] took her under French colours, and haled the ship in French. And this Monsieur Le Roy was to pass for captain, and *he shewed his French pass*, and . . ."

At the mention by a Crown witness of a French pass, Mr. Coniers deftly broke in with another question.

Mr. Coniers: "Give an account of his performing the captain. Who ordered him to do so?"

Palmer: "Capt. Kidd ordered him to do so; and they haled him in French and he came aboard, and *he had a French pass*."

Palmer clearly mentioned the French pass twice, but none of the defendants knew enough law to take advantage of the moment. Dark humor for the peri-wigged cognoscenti.

Later, led far afield from the *Quedagh* capture, Joseph Palmer recreated the scene of Captain Kidd meeting the pirate Robert Culliford.

Palmer: "On the quarterdeck, they made some Bomboo, and drank together and Captain Kidd said, Before I would do you any harm, I would have my soul fry in hell-fire; and wished Damnation to himself several times, if he did. And he took the Cup and wished that it might be his last, if he did not do them all the good he could."

Palmer was once again demonstrating his superb knack for recalling dialogue, and this time it was truly superhuman since the Westchester native was not with Kidd when the *Adventure Galley* arrived in St. Mary's and encountered Culliford. (Palmer was on the *Rouparelle*.)

Captain Kidd had both his commissions read into the record. Open-minded Justice Powell, noting that Kidd's commission empowered him to take pirates, asked: "Why did you not take Culliford?"

CAPTAIN KIDD: "A great many of the men were gone a-shore."

JUSTICE POWELL: "But you presented him with great guns, and swore you would not meddle with them."

LORD CHIEF BARON WARD: "When the question was put, 'Are you come to take us, and hang us?' You answered, 'I will fry in hell before I will do you any harm.'"

CAPTAIN KIDD: "That is only what these witnesses say."

LORD CHIEF BARON WARD: "Did you not go aboard Culliford?"

CAPTAIN KIDD: "I was not aboard Culliford."

LORD CHIEF BARON WARD: "These things press very hard upon you. We ought to let you know what is observed, that you make your defense as well as you can."

Such sympathy. The man wanted a full gladiator show — with the preordained victim fighting for his life. It would be no fun if Kidd didn't awkwardly lunge and parry.

Although Edward Davies was next door in Newgate, it took the Crown several hours to deliver him. Davies, the stout buccaneer, was sworn in. He testified that yes, he had seen Kidd's French passes. However, Lord Chief Baron Ward ascertained that Davies couldn't read *French or English*. "Then you cannot say they have any relation to the *Quedagh Merchant*," he noted drily. Davies fumbled about a Captain Ellms telling him they were French passes.

Kidd's three young servants, novices at the law, tried to demonstrate that they were servants acting under orders. Richard Barleycorn stepped forward. "Here is a

Certificate from the Parish where I was born," he said, proud of his English heritage.

"That will signify nothing," Lord Chief Baron Ward stiffly replied. "We cannot read certificates, they must speak Viva Voce." (It must have seemed baffling to Barleycorn, who knew no Latin, to hear that the judges *could not read*.) Intimidated, the boy did not ask to have the document dictated into the record.

Some of Kidd's character witnesses, such as Capt. Humphrys, were starting to arrive in Old Bailey. His lawyers, before they disappeared, had sent for them. (All this should have been done over the preceding two weeks.) Kidd at this point could at least defend himself to the gallery, to the rumormongers.

CAPTAIN KIDD: "What do you know of me?"

CAPTAIN HUMPHRYS: "I knew you, Sir, in the West-Indies in the beginning of the late war, and I know you had the Applause of the General, as I can shew by the General's letter. I know nothing further of you."

KIDD: "Do know any thing that I was guilty of any Piracies?"

HUMPHRYS: "No, but you had the general's applause for what you had done from time to time."

LORD CHIEF BARON WARD: "How long was this ago?"

HUMPHRYS: "Twelve years ago."

WARD: "That was before he was turned Pirate."

KIDD: "There is nothing in the world can make it appear I was guilty of piracy. I kept company with Captain Warren for six days."

MR. CONIERS: "I believe you kept Company more with Captain Culliford than with Captain Warren."

KIDD: "I never designed to do any such thing."

The prosecution rested its case.

KIDD: "I have many Papers for my Defense, if I could have had them."

WARD: "What papers are they?"

KIDD: "My French passes."

WARD: "Where are they?"

KIDD: "My Lord Bellomont had them."

WARD: "If you had the French passes, you should have condemned ships."

KIDD: "I could not because of the Mutiny in my ship."

WARD: "If you had anything of disability upon you, to make your defense, you should have objected it at the *beginning* of your trial; what you mean by it now, I cannot tell. If you have any thing more to say, you may say it, the Court is ready to hear you."

Kidd stood there silent, flabbergasted that this judge — wigged, gowned, hovering over him — had the audacity to claim that Kidd hadn't complained about his passes earlier. What *could* Kidd say to such a man?

Lord Chief Baron Ward gave his charge to the jury. He retraced the string of atrocities laid to Kidd, and included the *Quedagh Merchant*. He then simplified the case down to whether the *Quedagh Merchant* was a "ship and goods [that] belong to the King of France or his subjects, or . . . sailed under a French pass." If it traveled under a French pass, that will "excuse him from being a pirate." But Ward quickly added: "As to the French passes, there is nothing of that appears by any proof, and for ought I can see, none saw them but himself, if there were ever any."

Ward was playing out a charade for a select audience who knew the truth about the passes. The lawyers at the Admiralty knew, as did members of the House of Commons. It is very *unlikely* that the judges who socialized at the highest levels of English society had never heard about the French passes.

Within half an hour, the jury returned with a verdict. Each juryman was identified by name and polled whether the verdict was unanimous.

Clerk of Arraigns: "William Kidd, hold up thy hand."

Kidd held up his hand, the very same hand that had repeatedly grasped those French passes.

Kidd stood there, hand in air.

Clerk to jury: "How say you, is he guilty of the piracy whereof he stands indicted, or not guilty?"

Foreman: "Guilty."

The question was asked regarding each of the other nine prisoners. The three young servants were found not guilty, since they had no choice but to obey their masters; the rest were guilty.

Now Kidd stood under two death sentences.

It was late afternoon. The court, with efficiency, indicted Captain Kidd and the other nine prisoners on four more counts of piracy: taking the *Mary*, the *Rouparelle*, and two Moorish ships. The court was adjourned until the following morning, eight o'clock Friday, May 9.

Kidd and the rest walked down the narrow corridor back to Newgate.

Throughout that Thursday night, Kidd's anger mounted. The man who had been held two years without a trial lost his final last speck of respect for English justice.

Now he was cast adrift, likely to die soon . . . all he could do in court the next day was try to save his family name, his reputation, his honor. *If he did well, maybe the name William Kidd would go down in history as a martyr, a Scottish man of New York City betrayed by English lords.*

At dawn, the keeper roused the prisoners, and just before eight o'clock, he marched them down the foul corridor to Old Bailey. Lord Chief Baron Ward was gone, as was kindly Justice Powell. Captain Kidd was feisty from the outset; his lifelong sharp tongue was back. Kidd could not stop this judicial theater, but with barb after barb he would show the packed gallery who he thought the real rogues were.

Kidd stood in court as damning testimony by Bradinham and Palmer washed over him again. Lies intermixed with truth, all jumbled until Kidd couldn't keep quiet another second.

He pointed at Bradinham, and exploded to Judge Turton: "He knows no more of these things than you do. This fellow used to sleep 5 or 6 months together in the hold."

The gallery tittered.

Justice Turton: "I assure you he gives a very good Account of the matter."

Kidd, the picture of a sea captain, stood there defiant in wig and waistcoat, a big man gone a bit gaunt but still a hostile glow in his eyes.

The Crown then "set up" Joseph Palmer to testify. The Westchester native, with the ear for dialogue, described how Captain Kidd planned to attack one of the Moslem pilgrim ships off the Red Sea.

Palmer: "And some of our men said, 'We will go among them tonight.' 'No', says Capt. Kidd, 'we will go in the morning, and then we will take our choice.' "

Kidd jumped in: "Did you hear me say so?"

"I heard you say so," said Palmer, holding his ground.

"I am sure you never heard me say such a word to such a *loggerhead* as you," said Kidd. Laughs from the crowd. With death hanging over him, Kidd is the freest man in the courtroom.

Baron Hatsell offered to let Kidd have his commissions read aloud. "It availed nothing then. Here is all these men saw the French pass."

Palmer: "Indeed, Captain, I never saw it."

Kidd: "You left my ship, with 95 more men, and went a-roguing afterwards."

More character witnesses finally arrived for Kidd. Colonel Hewetson and Kidd had remained friends; Hewetson had been the one to take Kidd to visit Admiral Russel,

and there in the company of Hewetson —
as opposed to Livingston or Bellomont —
Kidd had been treated with respect, invited
upstairs. Hewetson testified to Kidd's valor
in the war. "He fought as well as any man
I ever saw . . . we had six French men[-of-
war] to deal with and only mine and his
ship."

Kidd: "Do you think I was a pirate?"

Colonel Hewetson: "I know his men
would a gone a-pirateering and he refused
it, and his men seized upon his ship."

The court's business turned briefly to the
others on trial for their lives. The nine accused made feeble attempts at self-defense
— three calling themselves servants, three
saying they relied on the proclamation of
pardon, three that they merely obeyed their
captain. Throughout the moments of these
men's statements and questions in this
third trial, Captain Kidd, throughout, un-
relentingly, stared at his ship's surgeon.
Kidd never took his eyes off the man.
Then Kidd, interrupting the proceedings,
blurted out: "Mr. Bradinham, are you not
promised your life, to take away mine?"

Justice Turton: "He is not bound to answer that question. He is very fit to be
made an Evidence for the King. Perhaps
there can be no other than such as are in
his circumstances."

Justice Turton eloquently summed up

this third trial for the jury. "Pirates are *Hostes humani generis,* the Enemies of all Mankind, but they are especially so to those that depend upon Trade. And these Things that they stand charged with are the most mischievous and prejudicial to Trade that can happen."

Justice Turton outlined the crimes, stressed the *lack* of French passes, explained about servants. It took this jury half an hour to bring back guilty verdicts against Kidd and six of his men, while once again finding the three young servants not guilty.

The final jury for Captain Kidd was now impanelled. Apparently, the Crown was low on jurymen and had intermingled several who had brought in the guilty verdict in Kidd's murder trial.

Each prisoner was asked how he would plead. This time, three of them (Howe, Owens, Churchill) pled guilty and submitted themselves to the king's proclamation. Those three were set aside.

Mr. Knapp was even briefer this time in his opening statement. He race-walked Bradinham through the fourth retelling of the incidents.

When Kidd got his chance, he asked: "How came you to keep this account, when for five or six months together you were under deck?"

Solicitor general: "Go on, Mr. Bradinham, and give an account of your further proceedings."

Kidd: "I hope the King's Council will not put him in the way. It is hard that a couple of rascals should take away the king's subjects' lives. They are a couple of Rogues and Rascals."

Bradinham, in the course of other testimony, strayed to Kidd's exposed nerve: The subject of Culliford. Kidd's fuse shortened.

Mr. Knapp: "What presents did Captain Kidd make Culliford?"

Bradinham: "He gave him some shirting stuff."

Kidd: "What! Did I give him shirting stuff?"

Then Palmer later poked the same sensitive spot. "There were four guns in the ship, and [Kidd] presented these guns to Culliford."

"Did I present him with my guns?" shouted Kidd. "Because I would not turn Pirate, you Rogues, you would make me one."

With that, for Kidd, the gladiator contest was over; he and the rest now refused to play along, or play to the crowd.

Solicitor general: "Will you ask him any questions?"

Kidd: "No."

The solicitor general repeated to each of the six prisoners, "Will you ask him any questions?" And each said, "No." It was time for the prisoners to make their defense. Said Kidd: "I will not trouble the court any more, for it is a Folly."

Justice Turton fell to the summation. For brevity's sake, he said he wouldn't recount Bradinham and Palmer separately, "because they agree in all things." The jury exited and returned a few minutes later. The foreman said he would speak for them. The clerk instructed Kidd to hold up his hand. He did.

Foreman: "Guilty."

Mercifully, once again, Kidd's three boys were found not guilty. After surviving three trials, they now would be eligible for release, pending payment of their prison fees.

Everyone remained in place. The court had other immediate business.

The barred door leading to Newgate opened, and in walked Robert Culliford, along with a couple of other accused pirates. Kidd might enjoy the spectacle of watching his lifelong nemesis convicted of piracy.

Culliford and Kidd had not seen each other since St. Mary's harbor in Madagascar three years earlier in June of 1698, when Culliford had sailed off with Kidd's crew.

For two days this courtroom had been filled with wrangling over the relationship between Kidd and Culliford, and now here was Robert Culliford and yet no one asked him what really happened. Kidd was convicted. Culliford's version was unimportant now; it was beside the point.

The court moved on to these other accused pirates. A grand jury came back with fresh indictments. Robert Culliford, Nicholas Churchill, Darby Mullins, James Howe, and John Eldridge were indicted for the capturing the *Great Mohammed*, a first-class heist with £60,000 taken, and sixty Moslem women kept aboard as playthings.

Culliford pled, "Not Guilty," as did the others. Kidd watched intently.

Culliford was thirty-five years old; he had spent six months in Newgate. He still looked stylish, though a bit frayed, wearing the clothes he had bought during his two months free in London. More indictments poured out. Culliford and several others were called for taking the *Satisfaction* (that ship whose captain, William Willock, had kept a diary). Culliford and one Hickman were indicted for yet another capture.

Culliford (and the others) pled not guilty to all charges.

The court was just about to begin these new pirate trials when Robert Culliford's lawyer suddenly arrived in Old Bailey. He whispered something to Culliford, who looked alarmed. The whispering intensified. Kidd and the gallery watched.

Culliford's lawyer sang out that his client wanted to change his plea.

The judges conferred, then agreed to accept the retraction. Following his lawyer's instructions, Culliford stated: "I plead Guilty, and I argue that I came in under the Proclamation of Pardon."

Culliford, in one breath, was taking an extraordinary risk.

His lawyer had explained to him that to take advantage of the pardon, he must plead guilty and admit to being a pirate. Obviously, a man who claimed to be not guilty had no need of a pardon.

But if the judges rejected his bid for pardon, his guilty plea would stand, along with a mandatory death sentence. So, if this panel of stern-faced older men looming over him cited some bit of legal fine print and decided to deny his pardon, he would die, probably within two weeks.

Robert Culliford's lawyer explained to the court that his client had surrendered to Thomas Warren, who had been deputized by his uncle, the commodore. A clerk read aloud a deposition from the commodore's nephew. The judges said nothing, one way or another.

The other accused men, following Culliford's lead, switched their pleas to guilty, and pled the pardon, all except one John Eldridge, who swore his innocence, and demanded a trial. Bradinham and Palmer quickly placed Eldridge aboard Culliford's ship and he was convicted within half an hour. During the trial, everyone waited for the judges' ruling on the pardons.

Now was the time. Silence was ordered; the gallery hushed. The prisoners shifted uneasily. Kidd watched Culliford, the pirate who had eluded him so often.

Judge Turton, with no fanfare, announced: "The judgment against Robert Culliford is . . . respited." Culliford looked to his lawyer; the man smiled, nodding his head approvingly. "Respited" meant an indefinite reprieve, not yet a pardon, but a *very very* good sign. The Crown had basically agreed to wash away a decade of crime. Judge Turton ordered an officer to move Culliford to one side, away from the convicted pirate prisoners. All the other pardon requests were denied; the men's guilty pleas stood.

Culliford, suddenly spared, now had a front-row seat to see Captain Kidd and the others sentenced.

The convicted men were walked to the bar.

Clerk of Arraigns: "William Kidd, Hold up thy hand."

Kidd raised his hand.

"What canst thou say for thyself? Thou hast been indicted for several Piracies and Robberies, and Murder, and hereupon hast been convicted; What hast thou to say for thy self, why thou shouldest not die according to law?"

Kidd: "I have nothing to say, but that I have been sworn against by perjured and wicked People."

Clerk: "Nicholas Churchill, hold up thy hand, what has thou to say . . . ?"

Churchill: "I came in upon His Majesty's Proclamation."

And Howe, and Loffe, and Parrott and Mullins, and Hickman all were asked the same question, and all responded that they came in according to the king's proclamation.

The demand for silence was made, for the pronouncing of the sentence.

Dr. Oxenden (advocate for the Admiralty): "You the prisoners at the Bar . . . you have been tried by the Law of the Land, and convicted; and nothing now remains, but that Sentence be passed according to the Law. And the sentence of the Law is this: You shall be taken from the place where you are, and be carried to the Place from whence you came, and from thence to the Place of Execution, and there be severally hanged by your Necks until you be dead. And the Lord have Mercy on your Souls."

William Kidd: "My Lord, it is a very hard Sentence. For my part, I am the innocentest Person of them all, only I have been sworn against by Perjured Persons."

The Newgate keeper came up behind Captain Kidd and he jerked the captain's hands behind his back. He took a narrow strip of whipcord, which had been fashioned into a small noose, and slipped Captain Kidd's thumbs into it and pulled it tight. He did the same to each of the eight men. This was an English tradition dating to the Middle Ages for prisoners under sentence of death. The men were marched single file back to Newgate.

Moments later, Culliford was led to Newgate as well, *with no whipcord around his thumbs,* no choking sensation at his throat. The former pirate captain would no doubt soon head to Newgate Tavern for a celebratory rum.

The crowded courtroom slowly emptied except for about two dozen jurymen who remained into the night to eat the "dinners" that they had been promised.

Chapter Twenty-One

Now that Captain Kidd and the others lay under sentence of death, they found that they had a new best friend, a constant companion: Paul Lorrain, the so-called Ordinary of Newgate, the priest assigned to comfort the condemned.

Paul Lorrain was a French Huguenot who had become a presbyter of the Church of England. At first glance, his appointment at Newgate might seem like a lowly assignment, tending to the dregs of the dregs, but quite the contrary, the post was much sought after, because it was so . . . lucrative.

No other priests heard the dying words of the most notorious criminals in England. No other priests could peddle those words to a curious public. Paul Lorrain routinely sold a broadsheet on the day after an execution. It was reported that that he accumulated a staggering £5,000 fortune over his twenty-year career.

Lorrain visited the condemned men on Saturday, May 10, the day after the trials. "I did . . . pray with them," he later noted, "and admonish them to self-examination, and Repentance." He promised them that he would visit them once in the morning and once in the afternoon every day except Sunday until the scheduled execution. On Sundays, he would preach to them *twice* in a more public setting.

The heart of Lorrain's mission — for the sake of their immortal souls — was to wrest a confession of criminal guilt and worldly sin from the prisoners. If the prisoner did that deeply and sincerely, he might receive the mercy of Jesus Christ and avoid the fiery pit. Miraculously — and this no doubt reflected well on his job performance — almost every one of the condemned, *as recorded by Lorrain,* was ultimately penitent. One doubting playwright nicknamed the condemned at Newgate: "Lorrain's Saints."

The next day, Sunday, the men attended chapel and sat in the Condemned Pew in the center, next to a coffin. As usual, crowds packed the spartan paint-peeling place of worship. At least this week the convicted pirates knew that the coffin was not for them, but rather for one John Shears, slated to dangle the upcoming

Friday at Tyburn.

Paul Lorrain preached twice that day, taking first for his topic, Matthew 25:46. "And they shall go away into everlasting punishment; but the righteous into life eternal." The "they," of course, were the unrepentant criminals. The "righteous" gallery could sit there smugly and watch *them*, invigorated by the mere fact of *not* being them.

Under the shadow of the noose, Captain Kidd decided to try one last gambit to save his life. On Monday, May 12, he sent a letter to Robert Harley, Tory speaker of the House. His anguish was clear.

> *Sir. The sence of my present condition (being under Condemnation) — and the thoughts of haveing been imposed on by such as seek't my destruction therby to fulfill their ambitious desieres — makes me uncapable of Expressing my selfe in those terms as I ought. Therefore I doe most humbly pray that you will be pleased to represent to the Hon'bl. House of Commons that in my late proceedings in the Indies I have lodged goods and Tresure to the value of <u>one hundred thousand pounds</u> which I desiere the Government may have the benefitt of. In order thereto I shall desiere no manner of liberty but to be kept prisonner on board such shipp as*

may be appointed for that purpose, and only give the necessary directions, and in case I faile therein I desiere no favour but to be forthwith Executed acording to my Sentence. . . .

> *Sir Y'r Unfortunate*
> *humble servant,*
> *Wm Kidd*

Kidd figured £100,000 had a better shot than £30,000; he awaited a reply.

During the coming week, Lorrain pursued the ten men for confession, and every single one of them, *except Captain Kidd,* opened his heart to the persistent preacher. But Kidd repeatedly rebuffed Lorrain, admitting absolutely no guilt; he was hard to the priest. He said over and over that he expected a pardon. Kidd might have been saying this just to shoo the black-garbed Bible-spouter away. In any case, he told Lorrain, if he didn't receive a pardon, he'd confess at "The Tree," meaning the gallows.

Unfortunately for Kidd, he couldn't go drown his sorrows at Newgate Tavern or go settle old scores with Culliford; he and the condemned men were sequestered in Condemned Hold away from the rest of the prisoners. The law's logic was that a man with nothing left to lose might find it amusing to gouge out another man's eyes or turn an annoying fellow's scrotum into a tobacco pouch. The dozen convicted pirates, on the other hand, could have drinks brought into Condemned Hold and women, as well, if they could pay.

Monday turned into Tuesday, then Wednesday. Kidd's reprieve to go treasure hunting was a gossamer lifeline, he knew. Then on Thursday, May 15, 1701, he was informed that visitors were coming up to see him. Maybe the Tories saw the light; maybe the Whigs were rewarding his silence. Maybe his wife had disobeyed him — he hadn't want her to see his shame — and had come over to England.

Instead, standing in front of him was Cogi Baba, the Armenian merchant of the *Quedagh Merchant*. He showed up in the dark barracks room of Condemned Hold with two interpreters, Mr. Persia and Mr. Anglois, wanting to know where Kidd hid his ship in the Caribbean.

Kidd, in a black mood, didn't hand them any treasure map — it was his only hope for a reprieve. But before getting rid of them, he did mutter that he wished he could have returned the *Quedagh Merchant* goods to the rightful owners.

The morrow, Friday, May 16, 1701, was a hard day. Not only because he heard the crowds roaring for John Shears to appear so they could accompany him to the gallows — no, he was used to those crowd roars — no, it was that this date marked the tenth wedding anniversary of William, now forty-seven years old, to Sarah, now thirty-one years old. He hadn't seen or held his wife for a year and a half. He knew — unless a miracle occurred — he would *never* see her again and would *never* see his daughter grow up in New York. Lorrain wrote over and over of Kidd's flintiness, coldness; clearly, the laconic Scot chose not to share thoughts about his wife and child with the priest. Little Sarah would lose her father at about the same age that he had lost his.

Everyone reacts differently to a knowledge of his or her own imminent death. Legend has it that the highwaymen in Newgate responded with a reckless "Carpe Diem," downing as much booze, enjoying as much sex, as their budget allowed before their final kick out into eternity. They treated death, like life, as one vast joke.

A newspaper, the *London Post-Angel*, found it noteworthy to state: "Tis reported, whilst Captain Kidd was in jail, no Woman came near him but his wife's Aunt." It was assumed that men under sentence of death would be tempted; it was *news* when a man didn't partake. Kidd in Newgate thought about his wife and his daughter in New York and he waited for the pardon that probably would never come.

That afternoon, while in the large prison cell with the other condemned men, he heard the shouts of the crowd as John Shears was hauled away in a cart to Tyburn. Faraway snippets of drunken songs, laughter tumbled over the top of the stone edifice. And he waited. The hours passed far too *quickly*.

William Kidd's letter to the House of Commons achieved a result far different from the one Kidd desired. Word of this £100,000 treasure leaked out; rumors started flying about the secret hoard of Captain Kidd, rumors that would remain alive to this day, three centuries later, and would prompt treasure hunters to dig holes all over New England, the Caribbean, and Madagascar.

Robert Harley and the House of Commons ignored Captain Kidd's offer, which he had the misfortune to send at a moment of political crisis for the Tories. The day that Kidd's note arrived at Commons so did an astounding defiant letter, anonymously written by Daniel Defoe (decades before *Robinson Crusoe*), who claimed to represent the will of 200,000 Englishmen, wanting to stand up to Catholic France.

The note, written in a tilted script, concluded: "Englishmen are no more to be slaves to Parliament than to a King, Our name is LEGION and we are many. Post-script. If you require to have this Memorial signed with our Names, it shall be done on your first Order, and Personally Presented." The French ambassador who had written about the Tory majority's reluctance to go to war, said that a sea-change in attitude had occurred in two days, "which would be surprising in any other country except England."

The issue of Kidd's life — however important to him — was shoved from the national stage.

Captain Kidd couldn't get the attention of any high-ranking politicians — Tory or Whig. Execution date was set for Friday, May 23, in late afternoon. The king (or his advisors) further decided that the corpse of Captain Kidd would hang in chains on the Thames.

On Sunday, May 18, the chapel at Newgate was packed. Guards that morning pocketed higher fees than usual from the faithful wanting to observe the final Sunday on Earth of the notorious pirates.

They let the people into the chapel; female prisoners whispered in the upstairs gallery, a ragged curtain half screening them from the men below. On the other side, a high bank of barred windows let out onto a courtyard, where prisoners gathered who preferred exercise over God. (A visitor in 1760 complained that the prisoners out-side disrupted the divine service.)

Onlookers could barely read the ten commandments etched upon the wall. The black paint on the condemned men's pew looked leprously patchy, as anxious condemned fingers had scratched away swatches and strips.

Captain Kidd sat in the condemned pew with ten other men — three of his loyal men, five of Culliford's men, and two Frenchmen. And there were a couple of coffins at Kidd's side, but none of them was his. He would not be buried, would not rest in peace; he faced the bitter prospect of picturing his own lifeless body suspended in chains, a human scarecrow to deter anyone from piracy.

Kidd could not resist the bitter thoughts: He had tried hard not to turn pirate; he had tried to play by the privateer code, perhaps a shade fast and loose, but just a shade, and now he would be a symbol of *piracy* for years to come. His name would be "pirate." Lorrain said the thoughts galled Kidd.

The fellow worshipers, the paying crowd, watched the Dead Men Praying.

Paul Lorrain at the teetering pulpit chose Ecclesiates 12:13 for his topic: "Let us hear the Conclusion of the whole Matter, Fear God, and keep his Commandments, for this is the whole Duty of Man." Lorrain hammered home that fear of God makes men wise, leading them to act in a way that will obtain both a present and eternal reward. In the afternoon, Lorrain chose a New Testament theme, from 2 Corinthians 5:10: "For we must all appear before the Judgment Seat of Christ, that every one may receive in his body, according to that he has done, whether it be good or bad."

"I concluded the Whole," Lorraine later wrote, "with an earnest Exhortation (principally directed to the Condemn'd Persons) that they would return to God with their whole Heart; and so obtain their great Pardon sealed before they were called to the great Bar of God's Justice. The pressing necessity and indispensable Obligation they were under, of doing this, I lay'd close to them constantly, even to the hour of their Execution; representing to them the severe Wrath and terrible Judgment of God which will certainly fall upon Sinners, unless they speedily and sincerely forsake their evil Ways and repent, and, in order to this, *patiently and submissively,* take that temporal Shame and Punishment . . . ingenuously acknowledging their faults and . . . making all Satisfaction and Reparation to the World."

Lorrain's industry paid off, with all other

condemned men *except Kidd*. He said the other prisoners to varying degrees confessed their sins, especially feeble Darby Mullins. The men waited, most drank, some had sex. That entire second week after the trial, Kidd continued to avoid the ministrations of Paul Lorrain, saying he still expected a pardon. One broadsheet account stated that Kidd did not seem "to be in any way terrified or afraid at the approaches of Death."

Both French prisoners, Jean du Bois and Pierre Mingueneau, denied any piracy, but they did tell Lorrain that they had committed many other sins and they implored God's forgiveness. Despite Lorrain's best efforts, the Frenchmen were steadfast in wanting to die as Roman Catholics.

Forty year old David "Darby" Mullins represented Lorrain's biggest success, filling the Ordinary's ears with confession after confession. Mullins was a sadsack Irishman who'd lost his wife, his job, was living in a tiny boat in New York harbor hauling firewood when he had signed up with Kidd; then in the East Indies he became deathly ill with the bloody flux and still was feeble. He told Lorrain that he didn't know that it was unlawful to plunder the ships of Moslems. He admitted to much swearing and profaning the Sabbath, which he sincerely believed caused his downfall. "He was a poor unlearned Person, not very much acquainted with any Principles of Religion," wrote Lorrain. "Yet he was willing to be directed; and expressed great Hopes, that through the Merits of Christ, he should find Mercy, and obtain Salvation."

On Thursday night, May 22, the night before the scheduled execution, Captain Kidd was led into a small room that was nine feet by six feet, with a vaulted ceiling. The walls were lined with oak planks, studded with broad-headed nails. A bench with a Bible on it stood at the far end. A high, narrow, double-barred window let in the spring air and the sound of rain. A single candle in an iron holder shed a pool of feeble light. "I was told by those who attended them that criminals who had affected an air of boldness during their trial and appeared quite unconcerned at the pronouncing sentence, were struck with horror and shed tears, when brought to these darksome abodes," wrote John Howard who visited Newgate in the 1770s.

Perhaps other prisoners but not Captain Kidd. Solitary confinement was nothing new to him. He remained strong, unrepentant.

On execution morning Paul Lorrain woke up early. He rounded Captain Kidd and the other men up into the chapel. "Having given them further admonitions to Repentence and Faith, they seem'd to me very desirous and earnestly striving to die in God's Favour; only I was afraid of the hardness of Capt. Kidd's heart."

Dr. Bernard Mandeville observed execution morning first hand in Newgate in the early 1700s, and he wrote that the men enjoyed a "substantial breakfast" with "seas of beer" swilled, and that Bedlam prevailed with prisoners shouting to one another, drinking and joking while the guards looked on, harried and tense. The men blustered more oaths than usual and blackened hands passed drinks around. They still retained hopes for pardons, which — with utmost cruelty and high drama — were usually delivered at the gallows.

The procession was scheduled to leave Newgate at two o'clock in the afternoon. Marshall Cheeke of the Admiralty, already far along in his arrangements, had booked three carts to haul the ten prisoners from Newgate to Execution Dock in Wapping. He had also rented horses and saddles for himself and his few men, even agreeing to a surcharge to have them dropped off at Newgate and picked up at Execution Dock. The marshal had paid for a temporary gallows to be built on the shore at Wapping, one that would hold half a dozen men on a temporary platform that could be yanked away. He had lined up the executioner who would receive £1 for each man killed and the traditional extra shilling sixpence for each noose made. He had also agreed to tip the sheriffs of London and the high constables of Middlesex to provide an armed guard. All was set.

Paul Lorrain decided there was time for one last session in the chapel after midday meal, and he brought the men there. Then Lorrain departed to go ahead to Execution Dock, to meet the other clergymen and make his way through the swelling crowds.

As soon as Lorrain was gone, William Kidd on this day scheduled to be his last, began drinking rum, lots of rum. Every account says Kidd was drunk on the way to the gallows. He gave a shilling to the two Frenchmen, which should have bought them about a dozen drinks. He gave his young black Malagasy slave to the keeper at Newgate.

William Kidd, who considered himself a respectable man wronged, got good and drunk on this final afternoon.

An enormous crowd, with war fever everywhere, followed the convicted pirates to the gallows. Dr. Mandeville described a similar procession as "one continued Fair for Whores and Rogues of the meaner sort." He observed that apprentices and journeymen especially flock to it like a holiday. "The days being known before hand, they are summons to all Thieves and Pickpockets, of both sexes to meet." All along the route, every sort of tradesperson, from old ladies with a couple of bottles in a basket to tavern owners, sold drinks.

One of the favorite pastimes of hooligans was to fling a dead dog or cat covered in human excrement, high into the air over the thickest part of the crowd. "Whilst these ill-boding meteors are shooting through the air, the joy and satisfaction of the beholders is visible . . . To see a good suit of clothes spoiled by this Piece of Gallantry is the tip-top of their Diversion."

Marshall Cheeke, on horseback, was the standard-bearer of the silver oar of the Admiralty, and he led the procession away from Newgate. The sheriffs and their deputies, most on horseback, preceded and followed the three carts carrying the prisoners.

Captain Kidd was roaring drunk. The procession rumbled along broad Cheapside flanked by tall buildings and past Royal Exchange and East India Company headquarters on Leadenhall and finally along Minories toward Tower Hill, where the huge stone fortress stood by the Thames, symbol of England's power. Off in the distance, over the treeless hillside, Kidd saw the pleasure boats jockeying close to the shore to watch him die. Kidd raged at times, muttering that "my money hanged me," and he shouted that no one would let him return the goods to the owners; he ranted about not being allowed to keep his own money.

The three-mile procession from Newgate to Wapping took more than two raucous hours. "Tho' before setting out, the Prisoners took care to swallow what they could," wrote Dr. Mandeville, "to be drunk and stifle their Fear, yet the Courage that strong Liquors can give, wears off, and the Way they have to go being considerable, they are in Danger of recovering. . . . For this reason they must drink as they go; and the Cart stops for that Purpose three or four, and sometimes half a dozen Times, or more, before they come to their Journey's End. These halts always increase the Numbers about the Criminals; and more prodigiously, when they are notorious Rogues. The whole March . . . seems to be contrived on Purpose, to take off and divert the Thoughts of the Condemned from the only Thing that should employ them. Thousands are pressing to mind the Looks of them. Their Companions . . . break through all Obstacles to take Leave: And here you may see young Villains . . . tear the Cloaths off their Backs, by squeezing and creeping thro' the Legs of Men and Horses, to shake hands with him."

Many people fought their way close to Kidd to yell at him, "Where did ye hide the treasure?" He didn't answer any of them. Someone also struggled through the throng to shout at Kidd that Lord Bellomont had died in New York. (The two-month-old news was just reaching London.)

Kidd stopped to drink a dram to the governor's sudden death.

As the onlookers drank more and more, the execution procession turned into a swaying mob that had to be beaten back by ragged deputies on scruffy horses. The din mounted.

The cavalcade surrounding Kidd finally rumbled down through Wapping, the seamen's neighborhood, toward Execution Dock. The prostitutes and barkeeps of Ratcliffe Highway had but a short walk to enjoy the festivities. Kidd, bound in the cart, reached the Thames at Wapping, which at low tide features a nice wide shore, like a rocky beach. (At high tide the spot becomes completely submerged.)

Kidd from the cart, through bleary eyes, saw the gallows, his last podium. Pardons had been known to arrive as the prisoner was cinched in the noose and even after. The enormous crowd that had squeezed through the narrow streets of Wapping further contracted through the choke point of Wapping Stairs and out onto the temporary shore.

There the simple gallows stood: one wooden beam held up by two vertical beams, and a raised platform, with some steps leading up to it. Short stout posts, that could be yanked, supported the platform, which had to be sturdy enough to hold the doomed men, the executioner, and a couple of priests.

Beyond the gallows, Kidd, a man who had spent his life at sea, saw ships of all sizes. He could smell the river and the damp shore through his alcoholic haze.

The pardons finally arrived. Marshall Cheeke walked to the cluster of prisoners and hauled out six men, the ones who would be spared: two of Kidd's loyal men and four of Culliford's. The crowd watched the men's faces intently, to observe the joy of each saved man, tears, clenched fists, smiles, their trembling.

The remaining four men would be hanged: Captain William Kidd, Darby Mullins, Jean DuBois, and Pierre Mingueneau. The gallows' guests were set: a Scottish-American, an Irishman, and two Frenchmen.

Executions in 17th century England were supposed to be civics lessons. The criminal was to admit the error of his ways, concede the justness of his punishment, and beg forgiveness of God. Many executions didn't go according to script, with the highwaymen especially hamming it up with last minute bravado.

The *London Post-Angel* reported: "Capt. Kidd was such a hardened wretch as this: for he not only drank to excess that Day. . . . but at the gallows he was unwilling to own the justice of his condemnation."

Paul Lorrain, a man with an agenda, provided the most detailed account of the execution. "Having left [Kidd], to go a little before him to the Place of Execution, I found (to my unspeakable grief) when he was brought thither, that he was inflam'd with Drink; which had so discomposed his Mind, that it was now in a very ill frame, and very unfit for the great Work, now or never to be perform'd by him. I prayed for him, and so did other worthy Divines that were present, to whom (as well as to myself) the Capt. appear'd to be much out of order, and not so concern'd and affected as he ought to have been."

Kidd was the life of the party.

The marshall intoned the order of execution. Each of the prisoners was allowed his final say. The huge crowd, that sea of faces, miraculously hushed itself, because dying words ranked high on the event's entertainment. It was six o'clock, with the sun starting the bathe Southwark across the Thames in a reddish glow. Far-off church bells chimed.

The executioner stood the four men under the nooses. He snugged one around the neck of each man. He trussed a rope up under their arms in the back, pinning their elbows together. The setting sun incarnadined the furled masts tilting above the water.

Darby Mullins, a shell of a man, and the two young Frenchmen, all in ragged Newgate clothes, had little to say. It was Captain Kidd's turn. He was dressed well, in waistcoat and breeches. He stood out from the drab preachers and deputies.

Kidd shouted out in slurring syllables that his conviction was not just, that he had done nothing wrong. He blamed his mutinous crew and others for his troubles, singling out Robert Livingston and Lord Bellomont as villains. Paul Lorrain whispered to Kidd to admit to the multitude that God had righteously brought him to the gallows. Kidd scoffed at him but he did toss the preacher a bone, saying that he had "confidence in God's Mercy through Christ," and that he died "in charity with the World."

Lorrain led the four men in a short prayer, joined by the other divines on the platform. When it was done, Captain Kidd had more to say. He bellowed that all captains should beware of false promises made by greedy men.

The Newgate priest led the four prisoners in singing a penitential psalm. This psalm-singing had become quite a crowd favorite. An eyewitness called the performance "frightful and impertinent."

The psalm-singing by the Irish, the Scot-American, and the French pair was done; Lorrain said a brief prayer recommending them to God. He descended from the platform as did the hangman. During that brief pause, Darby Mullins called out: "Lord have mercy upon me! Father have mercy upon me!" And the Frenchmen uttered prayers in French.

Captain Kidd said nothing.

The hangman and his assistant yanked the blocks from under the platform and the four men dropped about six inches and started kicking out their legs. And then Captain Kidd fell to the ground.

The crowd shouted and surged.

While overhead three dying men kicked their legs in that spastic dance upon air, Kidd lay below on the ground, dazed. Kidd saw Death close up. He watched the faces of three men go purple, their trussed arms waggling as their feet jigged until they died. Pee covered their crotches. The crowd roared throughout.

The sheriff's deputies roughly grabbed Kidd. Sometimes, in parts of England, in that rare case when a rope broke, it was viewed as an act of God and the man was reprieved. Not Captain Kidd. It took a few minutes for the hangman to clear away the broken-down platform; someone had to go fetch a ladder.

Paul Lorrain said that the fall sobered Kidd, and that the startled captain lost his angry passion and became calm. The accident granted Kidd at least ten extra minutes of life; to Lorrain, it presented an opportunity for Kidd not to die in bitterness or boozy delusion.

The hangman climbed up the ladder and slung a fresh noose over the bar. He propped the ladder against the post and prodded Kidd to mount, guiding him toward the top step. Paul Lorrain received permission to talk to Kidd. The priest climbed awkwardly a few steps up, until his head was near Kidd's waist. He later said his station was "incommodious and improper." But from that vantage point, the priest claimed he heard Kidd "declaring openly that he died in Christian love and charity with all the world." (Chalk up another victory for pious Lorrain, who climbed down.)

But another account, written for a broadsheet, stated that at that moment, in his breathing *after*life, Kidd told those around him to send his love to his wife and daughter back in New York City. And he said his greatest regret "was the thought of his wife's sorrow at his shameful death."

The executioner kicked out the ladder. Kidd dangled, tried hard *not* to struggle, and died, as the sun set over London. Captain Kidd's mission on the *Adventure*, conceived for profit and patriotism, had led instead to the end of a rope; his restless urge, against his young wife's wishes, to once again command more than a merchant ship, had brought him here to Execution Dock.

Lorrain rushed off to the printer. After the crowds dispersed, the deputies cut down the bodies, and they were each tied to a post so that three tides would wash over them, the traditional execution by the Admiralty.

Marshall Cheeke of the Admiralty and his assistants had worked up quite a thirst and Cheeke's expense account showed that they spent nineteen shillings "at a Taverne in Wapping and at the Horne Tavern." That amount bought them more than a hundred drinks.

The king, that evening, in a sign of support for the Whig lords, dined at the house of the Earl of Romney, one of Kidd's backers.

The next morning, the Admiralty sent an express letter to India via HMS *Royal Bliss* alerting the Grand Moghul that England had executed the dread pirate Captain Kidd.

Thomas Sherman, a deputy, buried the two French Catholic pirates in Limehouse Breach. As for poor Darby Mullins, the records are silent; maybe some Protestant charity buried him or some anatomy school borrowed him.

The dank Thames water washed over Captain Kidd three times, his corpse now bloated and pasty. The deputies untied Kidd's body and lifted it into a small Admiralty boat and carried it twenty-five miles downriver to Tilbury Point.

The Crown and the board of the Admiralty had shrewdly chosen Tilbury for displaying Kidd's corpse because this was where the Thames flowed out into the sea, and was unavoidable for all London ship traffic. Daniel Defoe in his tour of England called Tilbury Fort "the key of the River of Thames, and consequently of the City of London." An enormous fortress stood there. Back on August 8, 1588, Queen

Elizabeth had made her famous speech there to rally the troops to fight the Spanish armada. "I know I have the body of a weak and feeble woman, but I have the heart and stomach of a king, and a king of England too; and think foul scorn that Parma or Spain, or any prince of Europe should dare to invade the borders of my realm."

The assistants loaded Kidd's slimy, wet body out of the boat, and a burly blacksmith, James Smith, carried the lifeless captain up the long flights of stone stairs. At the top, he dropped the corpse inside a custom-fit iron cage that lay open on the ground. He squeezed Kidd in and hammered the cage shut.

Tilbury stood on a spit of land surrounded at back by the marshes of Essex. In Captain Kidd's day, the pentagon-shaped fortress had a platform facing out toward the Thames, with 106 cannon ranged there, some of them capable of shooting forty-six-pound balls. Admiralty orders required that Kidd's body be placed "so that he may be most plainly seen."

William Kidd, born in Dundee, married in New York, hanged in London, was then hoisted in chains onto the oak gibbet at Tilbury. For years afterward, men and women aboard all ships going to and coming from the trading metropolis of

London could see him there swaying in the breezes, the Admiralty's stark warning to anyone contemplating the merry life of piracy.

Robert Culliford

Chapter Twenty-Two

On Friday, May 23, 1701, Robert Culliford along with other prisoners in Newgate heard the immense tumult that accompanied hauling Captain Kidd to Execution Dock.

Over the coming weeks, Culliford, who had pled guilty and seen his sentence "respited," fell into a kind of legal limbo. He no longer had access to funds to pay a lawyer to pursue his pardon. And the Admiralty, with war looming, lost interest in his case. So Culliford cadged drinks in Newgate Tavern. He was a stunningly vigorous thirty-five-year-old to have survived in *that* prison since November.

The five-story stone building got hotter and smellier as summer arrived. Clerks, compelled to visit on official business, drenched handkerchiefs in vinegar. The seven men convicted on the same day as Captain Kidd received pardons, and as soon as friends or relatives scraped together the prison fees, they left. Also, Dr. Bradinham and Joseph Palmer received their promised pardons and departed.

Without any outside money, Culliford subsisted mainly on six pennies a day allowance, with no end in sight, no up, no down, no champions, no lawyer.

Then Robert Culliford, with his uncanny knack for wriggling out of disaster, caught a break.

In late July, Captain Matthew Lowth of the East India Company, delivered to Marshalsea Prison a very important prisoner: Samuel Burgess. Lowth had captured Burgess and the treasure-laden *Margaret* twenty months earlier off the Cape of Good Hope, and held him on suspicion of trafficking with pirates.

This confiscation case wouldn't have mattered all that much except that the *Margaret*'s owner, Frederick Phillips, happened to be the richest man in New York City and was hellbent on recovering his money. He sent his son, Adolph, over to London to argue that Lowth's capture was illegal, that *Margaret* was traveling under a safe-conduct pass from Governor Bellomont and that Captain Burgess shouldn't be held responsible for his pirate passengers' prior actions.

Phillips pegged the value of *Margaret*'s cargo, slaves, and monies at an eye-catching £20,000. Since Captain Lowth had made the seizure under an Admiralty commission while working for the East India Company, some very powerful people might have to reach into some tightly sewn pockets to reimburse the Dutch New Yorker.

The simplest way to defeat Phillips's claim (and make a potential lawsuit witness disappear) would be to convict Samuel Burgess of piracy and hang him alongside Kidd. Burgess's skeleton would also send a message to those upstart American colonials about selling supplies to pirates or ferrying the rogues home. At first the Admiralty couldn't find a witness against Burgess, but then someone remembered Robert Culliford.

The pirate captain from Cornwall could testify about Samuel Burgess's criminal career from first stealing Captain Kidd's ship in 1690 to his pirate voyages in the East Indies. Culliford was more than willing to screw his old cheating quartermaster, and save his own life.

One pesky hurdle, however, prevented the Admiralty from using this star witness. In his current legal limbo — neither pardoned nor sentenced — the prevailing legal code forbade Culliford from testifying. Admiralty officials set about remedying the situation.

In reading the sheaf of documents by various officials requesting a pardon for Culliford, one gets a sense of a genuine enthusiasm for saving this guy. (His pardon requests do *not* read like rote clerkly performance of duty.) The rogue once again apparently showed a roguish charm.

"I verilly believe that if Culliford hath not voluntarilly prevailed on the rest of the pyrates to accept of the said Proclamation," deposed Thomas Warren for Culliford, "the said pirates would not have submitted."

Thomas Lechmer, an Admiralty lawyer, wrote on November 8, 1701, that Culliford's sentence was respited because "he made so strong and plain a proof to ye judges."

Thomas Bale, solicitor to the Admiralty, requesting a pardon, wrote of Culliford on December 9, 1701: "There is so little proof against Burgess that there is no probability of convicting him without [Culliford]."

Fall flowed into winter. A chill descended on stone Newgate. In February, the Admiralty convinced Queen Anne to extend her grace and mercy to Robert Culliford "to be inserted in Our next Generall Pardon that shall come out for the Poor Convicts of Newgate."

The Admiralty had been holding up the Burgess trial, awaiting Culliford's pardon.

Now, Thomas Bale walked to the various offices to see about finalizing the queen's mercy, but he was disturbed to discover that Culliford's document would require the Great Seal, and cost quite a bit in fees. Every bureaucrat, dealing with this death row man, held out his palm. "I have been with Collover to know whether he can raise money for it," wrote Bale. "He, having sent to his friends to try what they would do for him, says they will do nothing as long as he continues in prison."

Culliford, during his two months free in London the previous year, had stashed money with various friends. He now sent messages to them, but they all figured the pardon was a pipe-dream, a dodge to get him drink money; they expected their pal to die in prison; they all refused him. As for bags of gold, if Culliford had any hidden under floorboards or buried near Cornwall oak trees, he decided to take a huge gamble, a life-and-death roll of the dice, and not tell anyone on the outside where to find them.

Culliford, instead, calmly asked Bale to let him out and he swore that he would return with the money.

Bale tried to get him a furlough from Newgate but, when that failed, he did the next best thing — he asked the government to pay Culliford's fees.

The Crown granted Culliford an unusual "special pardon," which Bale carried past coin-hungry hands by late June, just in time for Burgess's trial.

Robert Culliford entered Old Bailey Courtroom, neat and coifed, the picture of a ship's captain, and he testified against Burgess. He apparently cleaned up quite nicely and showed himself articulate and convincing. A jury convicted thirty-two-year-old Burgess of piracy, and he was sentenced to hang at Execution Dock. (The Phillips family would later wrangle a pardon for their captain.)

Robert Culliford, after he heard the jury's verdict at Burgess's trial, was now free to go, to walk out of Old Bailey. His almost two-year dance with the legal system was finally at an end. The proclamation he had received off St. Mary's Island, Madagascar, and carried folded in eighths had *barely* saved his life.

This pirate captain, who once had more than £2,000, departed Old Bailey without a shilling in his pocket; he passed by Newgate's statues of Justice and Liberty, carrying little more than the hope that he might recover some of his gold from his former friends, or from secret hiding places.

That summer afternoon in 1702, Robert Culliford disappeared into the streets of

London, blending in among the footmen and the lords, the sailors and the fruit-sellers. He never appeared again in official records, and for three centuries he escaped the notoriety that he so richly deserved.

Epilogue

Captain Kidd's treasure was gathering dust in the warehouse of the Admiralty. Now that the captain was parked in his lifeless perch at Tilbury, the Admiralty deemed it time to auction off the goods. On November 13, 1701, at the Marine Coffee House on Birchen Lane, "gold and silver and some Diamonds, Rubies and other Things seized as the goods of pirates" were offered for sale, with Admiralty Marshall John Cheeke, presiding. Rules stated that all items were sold "as is" and had to be paid for, within a week.

The catalog of the auction has survived with the names of the winning bidders scrawled in the margins and the prices paid. Listed there, among other items, was Captain Kidd's gift to Lady Bellomont of a gilt enameled box containing gold diamond rings and loose diamonds. Lord Bellomont had assumed the largest diamond must be

785

"Bristol Stone," i.e., paste, but the good governor was wrong, and the diamond fetched £25. Auction lots ranged from five gold bars weighing almost ten pounds each down to a "little hank of silver thread," worth four pennies.

Captain Kidd's treasure, which in rumors had been first pegged at half a million pounds sterling, generated about £5,500, which was collected by Marshall Cheeke of the Admiralty.

However, neither king nor Admiralty, nor any of the lords of London could touch the money because a lawsuit hung over it. English courts would now have a chance to restore the stolen goods to their rightful owners.

Cogi Baba, the Armenian merchant, filed a claim in Admiralty court, stating that he and fellow merchants lost £60,000 due to Captain Kidd's capture of the *Quedagh Merchant*. His detailed filing recounted step-by-step their trading voyage to Bengal and back, carrying muslins, silks, calicoes, opium, sugar, saltpeter, iron. He claimed that Captain Kidd's jewels originally belonged to the merchants and that Kidd's gold and silver flowed directly from Kidd peddling their cargo off the coast of India.

The Admiralty court sent out fact-finding missions to Ispahan, Bengal, and Surat. For two years, the case languished in a dead calm until the fact-finders returned; then the court found that information they delivered was too vague to use.

On November 21, 1704, more than three years after Kidd's trial, the judge made a final ruling. He restored *a certain portion* of the goods to the turbanned merchants and granted the rest "to the Lord High Admiral as perquisites of the Admiralty of England."

The judge ruled that Cogi Baba had failed to prove that Kidd's gold had come from the sale of *Quedagh Merchant* cargo; he did concede that some of the forty bales found on the *St. Antonio* belonged to Cogi Baba and colleagues. The court, however, found itself unable to find a reputable translator of Persian; the judge therefore decided that he couldn't grant those bales with Persian receipts to Cogi Baba. He added, *with a deep show of sympathy:* "And the [Persian markings] were found in the Bayles of the Greatest value and it is not to be doubted but if they could be translated there will likewise appear like reason to restore them as well as the others to the claimants."

The judge granted Cogi Baba the eleven bales carrying Armenian receipts, worth £891; the court subtracted £305 for "charges" and "import duties" for bringing the goods into England, which left Cogi to collect £585 and 7 shillings, i.e., about 1/100th the value of the cargo.

The balance of £6,472 went to the Admiralty.

A handful of noblemen lighted on an unusual way to clean this tainted money.

The minutes of Greenwich Hospital for November 23, 1704, recorded: "A clerk informs the board that it should petition her Majesty for . . . the effects of the Pyrate Kid . . . which her Majesty has signified she will give to said Hospital."

For decades, the Royal Navy had docked a pittance of sailors' pay to fund the retirement of broken-down old tars but, despite the tithe, England had few places to shelter the peglegs who had served the nation.

Greenwich Hospital was supposed to rectify that. William and Mary had commissioned Christopher Wren to design the hospital, with one stipulation — it shouldn't block the queen's view of the Thames from the so-called Queen's House up the hill. Wren designed two spectacular symmetrical domed wings to stand like elegant sentinels.

Four months later, on February 8, 1705, the board reminded itself again to apply for Kidd's money. In April, the board decided to designate part of Kidd's money, about £4,000, to buy Queen's House from Colonel Sidney, nephew of the Earl of Romney, one of Kidd's backers. On June 6, 1706, the board finally received Kidd's money.

Over the next decades, Wren's plans were followed. A handful of extremely lucky codgers from the high seas lived in this spectacular but vastly impractical residence. The expensive buildings, gorgeous to see from the Thames, could hold only a few hundred patients. "They do amiss who say this decoration is ill employed," wrote William Maitland in his *History of London* (1760). "For the honour to the government is the greater, the meaner the objects for whom it provides."

Robert Livingston, New York merchant, relentlessly pressed for a share of Kidd's treasure right up to the day that Greenwich Hospital received the money. Livingston in early *1706* visited several of the lordly backers and argued that Kidd's treasure actually came from the sale of their *Adventure Galley*, and not from any pirate captures. The Lords lamented that he must be able to prove it.

Livingston was preparing to leave England in May of 1706 when he found himself suddenly arrested. Sir Richard Blackham, the shady merchant who had secretly bought part of Kidd's and Livingston's shares in the *Adventure Galley* back in

1696, wanted his money back. Livingston's incarceration was hardly Newgate; he was allowed to stay at the Sign of the Saracen's Head at Gravesend at his own expense. "Although the misfortune is great," he wrote to his wife, "I have faith that God who brings forth light out of darkness will arrange everything so as to redound to his Glory."

Perhaps God did help in the negotiations. Blackham, who had paid £396 to the wily Albany merchant, demanded £500, counting interest, now a decade later. Livingston, under house arrest, offered £100. Livingston's lawyer maneuvered to move his client to a more *sympathetic* jurisdiction; at that point, he and Blackham settled on £170 and Livingston's promise not to sue Blackham for false arrest. He boarded ship for America.

Over the years, Robert Livingston filed claim after claim to the Crown for reimbursement of huge sums he allegedly spent feeding and clothing the troops in New York, *plus interest*. His letters and account books to justify these claims fill mind-numbing volumes. His feud with the next governor led him to accuse Lord Cornbury of dressing up in woman's clothing. At one point, Livingston was charged with embezzling £19,000, but the charge didn't stick. Ultimately, tight-fisted

Robert Livingston prevailed, and when he died in 1728, he left a huge estate to his heirs, including a tract of 160,000 acres of prime New York land. His descendants have included the first governor of New Jersey, a mayor of New York City, and several senators. One of his grandsons signed the Declaration of Independence.

Lord Bellomont had died penniless in New York on March 5, 1701, two and a half months before Captain Kidd's hanging. The Earl was sixty-five years old, his cause of death listed as "gout in the stomach."

At Boston, the upwardly mobile orchestrated a 46-gun salute to be fired from the castle at sunset on April 7. Also, a day of fasting was declared in his honor.

At New York, after a funeral at public expense, Bellomont was buried in the chapel at Fort William Henry on the southern tip of Manhattan. The Council — under pressure from Bellomont's cousin, Lieutenant Governor Nanfan — commissioned the stone-cutter William Mumford to carve Bellomont's family arms onto the facade of the new City Hall but the following year, the opposition party took control and voted to have the tablets torn down.

Bellomont had racked up huge personal

and public debts, including not paying the soldiers' salaries; local authorities refused to allow Lady Bellomont to leave the city. His corpse was barely cold in the ground when Robert Livingston wrote to the Lords of Trade complaining that Lady Bellomont had failed to turn over £800 that the Lords had sent to buy a gift for the Indians. Livingston patriotically hoped that the £800 would someday have "its proper effect with our Indians," and he volunteered himself, as Indian agent, to distribute the largesse.

When the next governor, Lord Cornbury, arrived, he continued the order preventing Lady Bellomont from leaving the colony. She, however, cajoled the Royal Navy captain of HMS *Advice* (the ship that had taken Kidd to England in chains) to carry her across the Atlantic. Before leaving, she also convinced two men to stand bond for the £10,000 that she, in the name of the late governor, was accused of owing to the troops. The new governor stated in a later letter to the queen that the two men who stood bond for her, were "not worth £10 apiece."

Lady Bellomont succeeded in returning to the family seat in County Sligo, Ireland, a second generation of English Protestant landlords among the Irish Catholics. (Her husband's English-born grandfather and his sons had been rewarded with huge tracts of land for their victories over the Irish Catholics.)

No record exists that the New York troops were ever paid their £10,000 in back wages.

In 1790, when New York City appeared likely to become the capital of the United States, a house for President Washington was built. During construction, workmen wanting to use stones from the old fort, stumbled upon the tomb of Lord Bellomont. Authorities transferred his bones in a lead coffin to St. Paul's Churchyard, placing them there unceremoniously without a grave marker. The tomb also contained many silver plates bearing the Bellomont family crest. With Revolutionary fervor, patriots melted these down and turned them into spoons.

After receiving his pardon, **Dr. Robert Bradinham**, the Crown witness against Kidd, tried to pay off his prison fees, by making a claim at the Admiralty to have his pirate booty restored to him. Dr. George Oxenden, advocate for the Admiralty, opined there had never been a case where "evidences" for the king were granted stolen loot. "They being Goods of Pirates, he has no property in them." Dr. Oxenden advised against giving "a fixed proportion," because that could set a precedent that would be harmful to the king when greater amounts were involved. Nonetheless, he recommended giving Bradinham 1,058 Lyon dollars and 7 pounds of broken sterling and 3½ ounces of broken gold, about half his treasure.

The Admiralty decided even such a precedent was too dangerous, and Bradinham received nothing. The surgeon then sued William Penn for £40 that he claimed had disappeared when he was first arrested in Pennsylvania. Penn dashed off a furious note in May 1702 to the Lords of Trade, complaining of being dogged by that "pyrate."

The **four lords**, who backed Captain Kidd's *Adventure Galley*, all survived the scandal, with slight bruises, mostly to their reputations. (The merchant Sir Edmund Harrison seems to have lost the most money.) Lord Orford, war hero, former first lord of the Admiralty, was impeached by the House of Commons on May 8 (the first day of Captain Kidd's trial) on ten counts, including two that involved Kidd. The procedure then called for him to stand trial in the House of Lords, judged by his peers, with Commons acting as prosecutor. Lord Orford, on May 16, denied any wrongdoing, and as for Kidd, he said Kidd (then alive) was answerable for his own actions, and denied ever promising him protection for any illegal acts.

That same day, Lord Somers, former chancellor of England, was impeached on fourteen counts, including one involving Captain Kidd. He harrumphed that the public would have received great benefit if Captain Kidd had fulfilled his mission.

War fever distracted the Tories from their hounding of these Whig lords. The House of Commons and the House of Lords fell into a squabble over procedures for the upcoming trials. The tiff escalated. The Somers trial began in Lords on June 17; the articles of impeachment were read against him; Lord Rochester announced that Commons might begin its opening remarks and in the 513 seats reserved for Commons, not a single member was there. The entire House of Lords burst out laughing, according to a report by the French ambassador. After seven minutes of waiting, Lord Rochester declared Lord Somers acquitted. The same farce was reenacted a week later in Lords, clearing Lord Orford.

The **Old East India Company** and the **New East India Company** continued to squabble over trade to India, but both suffered a huge setback. The expensive mission (£70,000) of Ambassador Norris to the Grand Moghul, with all its cannon and warships, failed miserably. The issue of English pirates — personified by Captain Kidd — proved the deal-breaker as Norris refused to guarantee that the Company would reimburse the Moors for any losses due to English pirates.

On November 16, 1701, the Grand Moghul, despite learning of Captain Kidd's execution, issued an order to lock up all Englishmen, seize their goods, and stop their trade. Sir John Gayer, who had relayed some of the most damning reports on Kidd, was put under house arrest in Surat and remained so for the next ten years until his death.

Although this turmoil helped encourage the two companies to merge, each side still held claims against the other for stolen ships and cargo, as did various independent companies, who had ventured into their Indian Ocean bathtub. In August of 1705, Queen Anne cleared the way for merger by granting a pardon to both of the East India Companies for all crimes "from the beginning of the world" through July 1702.

The united English company fought its archrival, the French, for dominance of India, and it won, creating, arguably, the most successful company in the history of the world. (It eventually handed over the subcontinent to the British government in 1858.)

In the early 1770s, Parliament granted advantages to the East India Company, for importing tea into America. On December 16, 1773, a band of Boston men disguised as Indians threw forty-five tons of East India Company tea into the harbor. The following year, New Yorkers, not wearing any disguises, also hurled that Company's tea overboard. Sharp business practices helped spur Revolution.

For two centuries, some British historians doubted the existence of **Kidd's French passes.** In 1910, Ralph Paine, an American doing treasure-hunting research in London, found Captain Kidd's two passes, misfiled at the Board of Trade.

Sarah Kidd waited in vain for her husband to return from London. The news of his hanging arrived instead, followed by a warrant issued in August of 1701 for the confiscation of Captain Kidd's estate. Authorities forced Sarah and her daughter to move out of the family mansion on Pearl Street; their other properties were seized, as well as household furniture and other goods. The new attorney general, Sampson Broughton, assigned to New York, wrote to the Crown asking permission to live in one of Captain Kidd's houses. "I have eight in family and know not yet where to fix them, houses are so scarce and dear and lodgings worse in this place." (Manhattan's tight real estate market had already begun.)

Sarah Kidd, however, did not curtsey and hand over the properties; she hired a lawyer and fought, arguing that these lands were hers from her first husband, and weren't the property of Captain Kidd. The case dragged through the courts.

In the meantime, her ailing brother, **Samuel Bradley,** came home to New York. Although Captain Kidd had helped save the young man's life in St. Thomas, Samuel, at only twenty-five years old, was already broken down. He died in 1703 and the inventory of his estate listed: two old swords, worth eleven shillings. His prime Manhattan properties were still embroiled in the Captain Kidd fiasco.

That same year, 1703, the thrice-widowed Sarah married her fourth husband, an East Jersey merchant, Christopher Rousby. Together, they fought to regain her property and on May 2, 1704, Queen Anne granted back to them the title to the mansion on Pearl Street, and to Samuel's house on Wall Street and to 38½ acres on Saw Mill Creek.

Despite the piracy charge against Captain Kidd, Trinity Church honored the family's purchase of a pew, and church records show Sarah and kin in the 1700s occupying Pew Number 4, right at the front. (Kidd's block and tackle had helped hoist the stones.)

The former Sarah Kidd had four children with Christopher Rousby, and, tellingly, she named her last one William, still harboring a certain fondness for the man who died upon the gallows. Sarah moved to New Jersey and outlived her fourth husband. She attended the wedding of her daughter by Captain Kidd, also named **Sarah,** who married Joseph Latham, a shipbuilder. (Any DNA descendants of Captain Kidd would trace their lineage through Sarah Kidd Latham and Joseph Latham.)

Sarah Bradley Cox Oort Kidd Rousby outlived her daughter, as well. When she signed her will in 1732, at age sixty-two, she was finally able to write her own name. She died a very wealthy widow in 1744, and left part of her fortune to Captain Kidd's grandchildren.

Acknowledgments,
Sources and Index

Acknowledgments

I spent two weeks on Ile Ste. Marie in Madagascar, exploring the site of the Kidd mutiny and the pirates' cemetery. I hereby officially apologize to my travel companion, Eppie, for constantly rushing his lemur photography.

Early on, I made the inexcusable mistake of going to London during the one week of the year when the Public Record Office closes for cataloging; Paul Carter was insanely kind enough to ship me copies of dozens of documents, a supply that tided me over until I was able to return the following year. To Jeff Kaye and Alexandra Frein, thanks for the room and the toddler wake-up service in Tooting Bec.

Farther north on the same island, I want to thank Scottish historian David Dobson for his stellar job in unearthing Captain Kidd's childhood in Dundee, and in pinning down the captain's elusive birthdate, reported wrongly in *Britannica* and elsewhere. David, you're always welcome to come visit again in Pelham, NY, explaining Conventicle intricacies and delivering bottles of rare whiskey.

I probably owe my greatest debt to Bill Prochnau, that rare double threat, a novelist *and* nonfiction writer, who tried to rescue me from drowning in a sea of anecdotes. He gave me two weeks of his life, for which I am truly grateful. Yes, I promised to wash your car.

I also want to thank Bob Miller and Leigh Haber at Hyperion, and Esther Newberg at ICM. I met tattooed pirate-lover Pat Croce when he was buying Captain Tew's chest at a Christie's auction; those four 76er club box tickets helped put wind back in my topgallant sails.

In addition, I must thank two dead people: Dunbar Hinrichs, an insurance executive/amateur historian, who left a hand-typed bibliography at Cornell, a kind of treasure map leading to rare Kidd documents, and Harold T. Wilkins, who wrote a nutty book quoting more primary source documents than most researchers find in a lifetime.

Also, thanks to Hank Schlesinger, Patrick Montgomery, Jerilyn Tabor, Dr. Walter Straus, Betsy Lerner, Peter Guzzardi, Robert Ritchie (for his book), Catherine

Clinton, Susan Squire, Craig Rhodes, Jim Traub, Brenda Newman, librarians everywhere, Georgia, Ziggy, and Kris.

Sources

MANUSCRIPTS

Public Record Office (London)
COLONIAL OFFICE PAPERS:

Massachusetts Bay Council Minutes (CO5:787)

Massachusetts governor's documents sent to the board of trade (CO5:860; CO5:861). Includes Palmer's original deposition.

Government reports from the Leeward Islands (CO152:37). Kidd's Caribbean days.

Plantations General (CO323:2). Contains Madagascar eye-witnesses and Capt. Willock's prisoner memoir aboard Culliford.

Admiralty Papers:
Captain's Letters (ADM 1/2004) Kidd's letters; (ADM 1/2636) Thomas Warren's letters; (ADM 1/2638) Robert Wynn's letters.

Admiralty reports (ADM 1/3666) many legal and expense documents, relating to Captain Kidd.

Admiralty board minutes (ADM 3/15, 3/16)

Ships' Logs (ADM 51 series). Best: 4105 HMS *Advice* Iceberg log.

Greenwich Hospital (ADM 67/3)

High Court of Admiralty:
Pretrial Depositions (HCA 1/15, 1/16, 1/29, 1/53). A cache of detailed accounts by men under the noose.

Papers confiscated from the *Margaret.* (HCA 1/98). Includes Culliford's note to the widow (171), and devious letters to lure Kidd (114, 123). Pirate's note to dad (183).

Kidd's sworn testimony, revealing his correct birth place and year (HCA 13/81, p. 313). Found by David Dobson.

Lawsuits (HCA 24/127) #57 Kidd's officers' widows; #107 Cogi Baba; #110 prosecution witness Bradinham.

Cogi Baba's claim (SP 42/117)

The British Library (London)
ORIENTAL AND INDIA OFFICE
COLLECTIONS:

Reports from East India Company factors are in IOR E/3/52, E/3/53, E/3/54. Best: 6439 Kidd's note; 6444 Monks describe Kidd encounter.

East India ship's logs: L/MAR/A/CV–CVIII, CXXXII

Letters from Bombay G/36/113

Letters to Bombay G/36/96, G/36/97 Surat reports on pirates and consequences.

Manuscript Division:

Duke of Portland MSS/Harley Papers (Add Misc 70036) Vol. 36, pp. 35–135. Key set.

U.S. Library of Congress (Washington, D.C.)
Immense collection of America-related

documents photocopied from London originals. However, scattershot for Kidd. Consult: Griffin, Grace "A Guide to Manuscripts relating to American History in British Depositories Reproduced for the Div. of MSS" (Library of Congress, 1946).

Morgan Library (New York, NY)
Livingston Papers including: "Journal of Robert Livingston during his Voyage to England, 1694-1695" tr. A. J. van Laer and several Kidd-related letters.

Yale University (New Haven, CT)
Dunbar Hinrichs donated microfilm of many key Kidd documents found in the PRO as well as photocopies of Max Lekus's translations from Royal Danish Archive material.

New York Historical Society (New York, NY)
De Peyster and Graham letters about Kidd.

NY State Archives (Albany, NY)
The fire of 1911 gutted the collection of Kidd era documents. However, some Kidd real estate records remain. (Deeds A0453. Books 9, 10, 14; British Historical Mss A1894)

Massachusetts State Archives (Boston, MA)

Two versions of Council Minutes are here; and yet another (CO5:787) is in London. The rough notes differ in interesting ways. Sarah Kidd's requests, with her awkward S.K. (Vol. 61, pp. 316–317).

Massachusetts Historical Society (Boston, MA)

Winthrop papers

Cotton Mather diary

John Marshall working class diary

Private Collection: Pat Croce, Co-owner of Philadelphia 76ers

Journal of Lt. Thomas Langrish, of HMS *Advice,* Kidd's prison transport.

PRINTED MANUSCRIPT MATERIAL

Some key Kidd documents have been transcribed and published in:

"Privateering and Piracy in the Colonial Period: Illustrative Documents," J. Franklin Jameson, editor (New York, 1923)

"Calendar of State Papers, Colonial Series, America and West Indies" Vols.

13–21 (London, 1910) Some paraphrasing.

"Journals of the House of Commons" Vol. 13, (London, 1547–)

"Documents Relative to the Colonial History of the State of New York" (Albany, 1856)

SEVENTEENTH CENTURY AND OTHER EARLY PUBLISHED ACCOUNTS

Anon. *A New Guide to London, or Directions to Strangers* (London, 1726).

Anon. *Memoirs of the Life of John, Lord Somers* (1716). Kidd deal from lord perspective.

Anon. *Piracy Destroy'd* (London, 1701). Conditions in Royal Navy.

Barlow, Edward. *Barlow's Journal . . . 1659 to 1703*, ed. Basil Lubbock (London, 1934). Illustrated account of long life aboard ship; tangled with Kidd near the Red Sea.

Calef, Robert. *More Wonders of the Invisible World* (London, 1700).

Cocks, Sir Richard. *The Parliamentary Diary of . . . 1698–1702* (Oxford, 1996).

Cruger, John. *Account of a Voyage to Madagascar*, 1700, printed in "Valentine's Manuals" (NY, 1853).

Dampier, William. *A New Voyage Around*

the World (London, 1697).

Dankers, Jaspar, and Peter Sluyters. *Journal of a Voyage to New York, 1679–1680* (Brooklyn, 1867).

Defoe, Daniel. *A Tour thro' the whole island of Great Britain* (London, 1724, reprint).

Dellon, Dr. Charles. A *Voyage to the East Indies* (London, 1698), tr. from French. Rare account.

Evelyn, John. *Diary of . . .* (Oxford, 1955).

Fryer, John. *A New Account of East India and Persia, Being Nine Years' Travel, 1672–1681* (London, 1698).

Gay, John. *The Beggar's Opera* (London, 1728).

Grandidier, Alfred, ed. *Collections des Ouvrages anciens concernant Madagascar* (Paris, 1907).

Hamilton, Alexander. *A New Account of the East Indies* (Edinburgh, 1727). Scottish sea-captain; stubborn, high-strung like Kidd.

Howard, John. *The State of the Prisons in England and Wales* (Warrington, 1780).

Hutchinson, Thomas. *The History of the Province of Massachusetts-Bay . . . 1691–1750* (London, 1768).

Labat, Pere. *Voyages aux Isles de l'Amerique, 1693–1705* (Paris, 1931).

Lediard, Thomas. *Naval History of En-*

gland (London, 1735).

Lussan, Raveneau de. *Journal d'un voyage* . . . (Paris, 1695, reprint 1992 in French *Les Flibustiers de la mer du sud*; also tr. English, 1930). Undeservedly overlooked privateer account.

Luttrell, Narcissus. *A Brief Relation of State Affairs . . . from September 1678 to April 1714* (Oxford, 1857).

Maitland, William. *History of London* (London, 1760).

Mandeville, Dr. Bernard. *An Enquiry into the Causes of the Frequent Executions at Tyburn* (London, 1725).

Mather, Cotton. *Pillars of Salt: An History of some Criminals Executed in this Land* . . . (Boston, 1699). Gallows speeches Matherized.

Miller, Rev. John. *New York Considered and Improved, 1695* (reprint Cleveland, 1903).

Moyle, John. *Sea-Chirgueon* (London, 1702).

Ovington, Rev. John. *A Voyage to Surat in the Year 1689* (London, 1696, reprint Oxford, 1929). Mixes eyewitness with scholarly armchair reporting.

Pepys, Samuel. *The Diary of* . . . (London, 1976). Ed. Robert Latham and William Matthews.

Sewall, Samuel. *The Diary of* . . . *1674–1729* (reprint NY, 1973).

Sloane, Dr. Hans. *A Voyage to the Islands, Madeira, etc.* (London, 1707–1725).

Swift, Jonathan. *A Discourse of the Contests and Dissentions Between the Nobles and Commons in Athens and Rome* (1702, reprint: London, 1967).

Teonge, Henry. *Diary of . . . 1675 to 1679* (London, 1825). Chaplain's life at sea.

Vernon, James. *Letters Illustrative of the Reign of William III . . .* (London, 1841). G. P. James Ed.

Ward, Ned. *A Trip to New England* (London, 1698). Wicked satire about God's chosen merchants.

———. *The London Spy* (London, 1698). Observant, satirical.

———. *The Wooden World* (London, 1760). Salty, merciless, very funny guide to Royal Navy life.

SELECT SCHOLARLY ARTICLES

Andrews, Wayne, ed. "A Glance at New York in 1697: The Travel Diary of Dr. Benjamin Bullivant" (*New York Historical Society Quarterly* [60] 1956, pp. 55–73).

Anon. "New York's Land-Holding Sea Rover" (NY, 1901). Real estate research by Title Guarantee & Trust.

Hill, S. Charles, in "Indian Antiquary." Episodes of Piracy in the Eastern Seas

(Sept. 1919–Jan. 1920; April 1924; April 1925; May, July, Sept., Nov. 1926; Jan.–March 1927) Primary source gold mine.

Hinrichs, Dunbar. "Captain Kidd and the St. Thomas Incident" in *New York History* (37) 1956, pp. 266–280.

Judd, Jacob. "Frederick Philipse and the Madagascar Trade" in *New York Historical Society Quarterly* (1963), pp. 354–374.

Leder, Lawrence. "Records of the Trials of Jacob Leisler and his Associates" in *New York Historical Society Quarterly* (1952) pp. 431–457.

Leder, Lawrence. "Robert Livingston's Voyage to England, 1695" in *New York History*, pp. 16–38.

Leder, Lawrence. "Captain Kidd and the Leisler Rebellion" in *New York Historical Society Quarterly* (38) 1954, pp. 48–54.

Rediker, Marcus. "Under the Banner of King Death: The Social World of Anglo-American Pirates, 1716 to 1726" in *William and Mary Quarterly* (38) 1983, pp. 203–227.

Ritchie, Robert. "Samuel Burgess, Pirate" in collection *Authority and Resistance in Early New York* (New York, 1988). Ed. William Pencak, pp. 114–137.

Anonymous. *Full Account of the Actions of the Late Famous Pyrate Capt. Kidd* (Dublin, 1701). First published contemporary account, was written by a relative of Governor Bellomont.

Bonner, William. *Pirate Laureate: Life & Legends of Captain Kidd* (New Brunswick, NJ, 1947). Folklore and literary trails.

Brooks, Graham, ed. *Trial of Captain Kidd* (London, 1930). Court transcript; British establishment view.

Hinrichs, Dunbar. *The Fateful Voyage of Captain Kidd* (NY, 1955). Annotated timeline for obsessives.

Paine, Ralph D. *The Book of Buried Treasure* (NY, 1926). 102 pages on Kidd, especially his treasure, by the man who rediscovered Kidd's French passes.

Ritchie, Robert. *Captain Kidd and the War against the Pirates* (Cambridge, 1986). Scholarly investigation bolstered by fifty-six pages of footnotes.

Seitz, Don, ed. *The Tryal of Captain William Kidd* (NY, 1936). Excellent court transcript; bizarre bibliography.

Wilkins, Harold. *Captain Kidd and his Skeleton Island* (New York, 1937). Treasure trove of great documents, followed by inane treasure-hunting theories.

Besson, Maurice. *Freres de la Coste* (Paris, 1928).

Biddulph, John. *Pirates of Malabar* (London, 1907).

Cordingly, David. *Pirates* (London, 1998). Best *illustrated* overview of pirates. All-star contributors.

Cordingly, David. *Under the Black Flag* (NY, 1995). Excellent general interest book on pirates.

Deschamps, Hubert. *Les Pirates à Madagascar* (Paris, 1972).

——. *Pirates et Flibustiers* (Paris, 1952).

Dow, G. F. and J. H. Edmonds. *Pirates of the New England Coast* (Salem, 1923, reprint).

Exquemelin, Alexander. *The Buccaneers of America* (Amsterdam, 1678, numerous reprints). Great eyewitness account of Henry Morgan's brutal privateering against New Spain.

Gosse, Philip. *The History of Piracy* (London, 1932). Gullible.

——. *The Pirate's Who's Who* (Boston, 1924). Quaint.

Grey, Charles. *Pirates of the Eastern Seas* (London, 1933).

Johnson, Charles. *A General History of the Robberies and Murders of the Most Notorious Pirates* (London, 1724, reprinted in dozens of editions). Irresistible pirate bios, blending eyewitness accounts with some yarning.

Lydon, James. *The Role of New York in Privateering Down to 1763* (Ann Arbor Microfilm, 1956). Illegal business history.

MacIntyre, Donald. *The Privateers* (London, 1975).

Rediker, Marcus. *Between the Devil and the Deep Blue Sea: Merchant Seamen, Pirates and the Anglo-American Martitime World, 1700–1750* (NY, 1987). Brilliant, well-researched.

REFERENCE BOOKS, BIOGRAPHIES, ETC.

Andrews, Charles. *Guide to the Manuscript Materials for the History of the United States to 1783, in the British Museum . . .* (Washington, 1908).

——. *Guide to the Materials for American History, to 1783, in the Public Record Office of Great Britain* (Washington, 1912).

Birdwood, George. *Report on the Old Records of the India Office* (London, 1891).

Bridenbaugh, Charles. *Cities in the Wilderness: The First Century of Urban Life in America 1625–1742* (NY, 1938).

Burns, Alan. *History of the British West Indies* (London, 1965).

Burrows, Edwin, and Mike Wallace. *Gotham: A History of New York City to 1898* (NY, 1998).

Cotton, Sir Evan. *East Indiamen: The East India Company's Maritime Service* (London, 1949).

Crowhurst, Patrick. *Defense of British Trade, 1689–1815* (Folkstone, 1977).

Danvers, Frederick. *The Portuguese in India* (reprint: NY, 1966).

DePeyster, Frederick. *Life and Administration of Richard, Earl of Bellomont* (NY, 1879).

Dickens, Charles. *Sketches by Boz, 1833–1839* (London). "The Old Bailey." "A Visit to Newgate."

Earle, Alice. *Colonial Days in Old New York* (NY, 1896).

Ehrman, John. *The Navy in the War of William III, 1689–1697* (Cambridge, 1953).

Elliot, H. M. *History of India as told by its own Historians* (London, 1877).

Friedelbaum, Stanley. *Lord Bellomont: Imperial Administrator* (NY, 1956).

Furnas, J. C. *The Americans: A Social History of the United States, 1587–1914* (NY, 1969).

Grandidier, Alfred. *Histoire . . . de Madagascar* (Paris, 1908).

Grose, Captain. *Dictionary of the Vulgar Tongue* (London, 1788, Chicago reprint 1971).

Hooper, W. E. *History of Newgate and Old Bailey* (London, 1935).

Hrodej, Philippe. *L'amiral du Casse* (Paris, 1999).

Innes, J. H. *New Amsterdam and its People* (NY, 1902).

Keay, John. *The Honourable Company: A History of the English East India Company* (New York, 1991).

Kemp, Peter. *The British Sailor: A social history of the lower deck* (London, 1970).

Leder, Lawrence. *Robert Livingston 1654–1728 and the Politics of Colonial New York* (Chapel Hill, 1961).

Manucci, Niccolao. *Storio do Mogor (Mogul India, 1653–1708)* tr. William Irvine (New Delhi, 1966).

Marsden, Reginald, ed. *Documents Relating to the Law and Custom of the Sea* (London, 1916).

Milton, Giles. *Nathaniel's Nutmeg* (NY, 1999).

Morris, Richard. *Fair Trial: Fourteen Who Stood Accused from Anne Hutchinson to Alger Hiss* (NY, 1952). Thirty-five pages on Kidd.

Murphy, Theresa. *Old Bailey: Eight Centuries of Crime, Cruelty and Corruption* (Edinburgh, 1999).

Nanda, Meer. *European Travel Accounts during the Reigns of Shajahan and Aurangzeb* (Kurukshetra, 1994).

Perrin, W. *British Flags* (Cambridge, 1922).

Phelps-Stokes, Isaac. *The Iconography of Manhattan Island* (New York, 1916–1928).

Reich, Jerome. *Leisler's Rebellion: A Study of Democracy in New York, 1664–1720* (Chicago, 1949).

Sachse, William. *Lord Somers: A Political Portrait* (Oxford, 1975).

Sarkar, Jadunath. *History of Aurangzib: based on original sources* (Bombay, 1973).

Smyth, W. H. *Sailor's Word Book: A Dictionary of Nautical Terms* (London, 1867, reprint 1996).

Sobel, Dava. *Longitude* (NY, 1995).

Somerville, Dorothy. *The King of Hearts: Charles Talbot, Duke of Shrewsbury* (London, 1962).

Stock, Leo, ed. *Proceedings and Debates of the British Parliament respecting North America* (Washington, 1927).

Valentine, David. *Manual of the Corporation of the City of New York* (NY, 1841–1867). An uneven fascinating multivolume collection on the history of New York City, compiled by Valentine.

Yule, Henry, and A. C. Burnell. *Hobson-Jobson: The Anglo-Indian Dictionary* (London, 1886, reprint 1996).

Wells H. G. *The Outline of History* (Garden City, 1920).